Way of BLESSING
Way of LIFE

Way of BLESSING
Way of LIFE

A CHRISTIAN THEOLOGY

Clark M. Williamson

Chalice Press
St. Louis, Missouri

All scripture quotations, unless otherwise indicated, are from the *New Revised Standard Version Bible*, copyright 1989, Division of Christian Education of the National Council of Churches of Christ in the USA. Used by permission. All rights reserved.

Cover Art: Marc Chagall, "Yellow Crucifixion." Collections du Centre Georges Pompidou/Musée national d'art moderne, Paris.
Photo: Philippe Migeat © Photothéque des Collections du Centre Georges Pompidou/Musée national d'art moderne, Paris.

Cover Design: Grady Gunter
Interior Design: Wynn Younker
Art Direction: Elizabeth Wright

This book is printed on acid-free, recycled paper.

Visit Chalice Press on the World Wide Web at
www.chalicepress.com

10 9 8 7 6 5 4 3 2 1   99 00 01 02 03

Library of Congress Cataloging–in–Publication Data

Williamson, Clark M.
    Way of blessing, way of life : a Christian theology / by Clark M. Williamson.
        p.   cm.
    Includes bibliographical references.
    ISBN 0–8272–4243–3
    .1. Theology, Doctrinal. I. Title.
BT75.2W547   1999
230–cd21   99–42495
                                                                CIP

Printed in the United States of America

Contents

Acknowledgments

I would like to express my gratitude to friends who have talked theology with me over the years. Sadly, several of my post-Shoah theological friends and friendly critics, A. Roy Eckardt, Paul M. van Buren, and Father Edward Flannery, died as this volume was nearing completion. All responsible theologians will miss them deeply. Ed Towne and Joe Jones, with whom I have engaged in the team-teaching of systematics, have contributed to the development of this theology in more ways than are evident. Gerry Janzen and I have had a more than three-decade discussion that has opened up the scriptures for me in ways I could not have previously imagined. It is difficult to say whether it is our various agreements or disagreements over the years that have been more fruitful. The members of the Christian Scholars Group on Judaism and the Jewish People have given their critical attention to my work on several occasions, and it is better for it. My rabbis, the late Sidney Steiman, Murray Saltzman, Jon Stein, and Dennis and Sandy Sasso have been remarkable conversation partners and teachers from whom I have discovered the warmth, vitality, and intelligence of the synagogue. My colleagues at Christian Theological Seminary in our faculty colloquia and ongoing conversations have made my work better than it would have been.

This book is dedicated to Barbara, the companion of my life.

Introduction

Any theologian bold or reckless enough to offer for publication yet another systematic theology ought, at the minimum, to offer some justification for doing so. What is there about this book that is sufficiently distinctive to hold out some promise that it might be worth reading? The answer is that this is the only one-volume systematic theology that is written from a post-Holocaust (or post-Shoah) perspective that is in the tradition of correlational or conversational theology, that tries to be in conversation with the Jewish tradition at the same time that it strives to be appropriately Christian, that is a relational and neo-process theology, that seeks to engage in a new and postcritical (not uncritical or precritical) reading of the enchanted story that is the biblical narrative and, in doing so, that addresses several major forms of structural sin or systemic evil.

A Church Theology

The church ought to be a safe place in which Christians can talk with each other about matters of ultimate importance. It can be, and sometimes is, a sane asylum where we can trust one another enough to engage in conversation about what it means to be Christian in the only time and place that we will ever have a chance to do this—our own context. The purpose of this introduction to theology is to encourage Christians to regain the capacity to speak with one another about God and life and the intersection between the two. Its further purpose is to encourage the church to bear witness in word and deed to the gospel of Jesus Christ.

This is a theology more for the church than for the academy. It is written to be understood. That does not mean that no technicalities ever enter into the picture. It does mean that I try to make things clear enough that readers committed to understanding the Christian faith can participate in the ongoing conversation. Some theologians write as though they would be offended should anyone understand them. This theology tries to make clear what Christian teachings mean by showing what questions they answer, how they answer those questions, and what practical difference it makes to affirm those teachings. For example, until we are clear what practical difference it makes to think of the world as created by God, it makes no difference to us and is an "idle" belief. Once we see, however, that it makes "all the difference in the world" as to how we treat the world, how we behave in relation to it, then we get the point.

A Conversational Theology

Christian faith is a way of life. It is a way of life that involves words and deeds, words acted out in deeds, and deeds interpreted by words. To paraphrase the eighteenth-century philosopher Immanuel Kant, words without deeds are empty; deeds without words are blind. It might be easy, if it were remotely possible, to dispense with trying to understand our faith and get busy doing what we ought to do. But it is just at that juncture, of knowing what we ought to do and ought not to do, that disagreement looms and conversation becomes imperative.

The deepest issues that face the contemporary church and threaten in new ways to divide congregations and denominations turn on questions of what we ought to do and why. Should we engage in an interfaith dialogue with Jews, as some churches claim, or launch a new evangelistic effort to convert them, as others claim? Can women be ordained or should they be silent in church? Are gay men and lesbians welcome in the church and, if so, in the ranks of the clergy? Or are they, at best, to be tolerated but not welcomed or, at worst, to be vilified? Do we really believe in the gospel for the poor and in being the church for the poor? Or are we happier in our middle- and upper-middle class congregations where we never meet the scruffy and the smelly? Has the church a word to say about the environmental crisis, and what should that word be? Are we willing to let our high-energy-consumption lifestyles be more than minimally affected by this crisis?

Christian faith is a way of life. Christians are a community of people who walk the way of life through ever-changing historical contexts. Each new context presents to us new questions and challenges, challenges to which the church must respond with answers that are appropriate to the Christian faith and adequate to the situation. A tradition remains a vital source of living faith when the community pauses along the way to talk about the issues that it faces. It is in our conversations with one another and with those who have walked this way before and dealt with other crises that we discover ever anew how the word of God is a "lamp unto our feet and a light unto our path."

This theology tries to strike up a conversation between the Christian scriptures and tradition on the one hand and the context in which we live on the other. Throughout history the community of faith has always faced new challenges. It has always wanted to know, in relation to these challenges, the answer to a set of basic questions: Who is God? Who is Jesus Christ? Who are we? What are we supposed to do?

For such a theology, conversation becomes the controlling metaphor, the way of approach to all other matters. Scripture, for example, becomes a conversation partner with whom or with which we have a conversation. Members of other faith traditions, such as Jews, are no longer objects ("its") about which Christians talk, but subjects with whom we have conversation. The context in which we live, analyzable as it is in a myriad of ways, is another conversation partner.

A genuine conversation has its ethic. Conversation is not a verbal form of warfare, in which winning (at all costs) is the goal. In authentic conversation, no party to the conversation dominates either the conversation or the other parties. The topic dominates the conversation. For example, in conversation with the scriptures, the topic or question dominates. Fundamentalists and authoritarians want the text to dominate. Those who absolutize their own experience want it to dominate. Neither wants conversation because each refuses to be questioned or challenged. The fundamentalist will not let the text be questioned, and those enamored of their own experience will not allow it to be questioned. For a conversationalist, anything and anyone can be questioned. In scripture the God of Israel not only can be questioned, but approves of being questioned. That leads us to this definition of idolatry: An idol is anything or anyone that claims, explicitly or implicitly, to be above question.

Conversational theology differs from "dialectical" approaches to theology as much in tone as anything else. Associated with polemics, dialectical theology emphasizes difference and disagreement, sharpening contrasts. For it, conversation tends to become debate. Conversational theology is more concerned about listening to those to whom the church has never before listened, such as Jews and women, than to sustain sharp disagreement with them. After all, we have tried sharp disagreement for 1,900 years, and what it has produced has been the destruction of most Jews and the loss of whatever claim to authenticity the church might ever have had. Perhaps it is time to try listening, to value understanding at least as highly as we do being right. To put it better, no position that is right could ever conflict with love of the neighbor.

For most of Christian history, Christians did not find it necessary to engage anyone else in conversation. As long as Christianity was the one true religion, established and enforced by the state, no point of view differing from the received dogma had any political, moral, or civil right to be expressed. Heresy was a capital crime. No other religion was tolerated except Judaism, which lived at the not-so-tender mercies of Christians. In our pluralistic world, Christians can no longer put everyone else in their place. The great benefit of this changed circumstance is that it gives Christians the opportunity to be true to our own deepest insights and revelations, to know what it means to love the stranger as we love ourselves. Conversation gives us a way to do just that.

This does not mean that a conversational theology never disagrees with another viewpoint. It means, rather, that the grounds for disagreement can only be reached after we can fairly be said to understand those with whom we disagree. To know what we reject is part of knowing what we mean by what we affirm. To reject nothing is to affirm nothing. A conversational theology, for example, rejects anti-conversational, authoritarian ways of doing theology.

In other words, conversation-stoppers are out of bounds. One convenient conversation-stopper is the appeal to inerrancy, in any of its forms. One such form appeals to scripture or tradition or the authority of the pope as infallible. Experience is frequently used as a conversation-stopper, as in "Who are you to question my experience?" Scripture, tradition, the authority of the pope or anyone else, and experience are all always interpreted. Scripture is scripture-as-interpreted, tradition is tradition-as-interpreted, my experience is my-experience-as-I-understand-it (which may not be too well). Interpretation is never inerrant and always open to question.

Questioning keeps us intellectually and theologically alive. Questioning the "obvious" arrangements of the present is one way that God opens us up to God's inbreaking future. When some of us were growing up in the church, the questions that have dominated theological discussion during our adulthood had not yet been raised. The dropping of atomic bombs on Hiroshima and Nagasaki had not happened. We were not yet aware of the Holocaust going on in Europe against eleven million people, six million of whom were Jews. The discovery of the church's long tradition of preaching and teaching contempt for Jews and Judaism lay in our future, although some alert scholars were trying to get it on our agenda. The civil rights movement had yet to take place, and the debate about racism in society and the church was still a distant reality. The women's movement for freedom and equality had not happened, nor had questions been raised about whether they were to be fully equal Christians in the church. The issue of the relation of the church to the religions of the world still awaited rethinking.

On these questions and others, a vigorous discussion is going on in today's church. The purpose of this theology is to enter into conversation with such questions, to reinterpret the Christian faith in relation to the context in which we live, and to interpret that context in the light of the Christian faith, so that we can at least have a conversation among ourselves about what God gives and calls us to be and do in this time and place. Christianity in any of the many forms it takes helps us to interpret the world in which we live in light of our understanding of God and Christ so that we might understand how to live in the world. As the world is always changing, so must our understanding of it and of how to live in it.

This is a conversational theology in another sense. It is in no sense under the illusion that the answers here put into play in the conversation will either be widely accepted or hold good for all time. It is simply an attempt to contribute to the conversation and, in so doing, to help keep it going.

Conversation Partners

A good idea is a good idea, no matter its source. A good idea is one that is helpful, useful because it makes a practical difference in how we understand the world we live in or understand how we should live in the world. Ludwig Wittgenstein once said that to understand is to know what to do next. William James said it earlier when he remarked that the best ideas are those that help us "get from next to next" in our experience and in our living.

Useful ideas, ideas that enable us to make progress in the ongoing conversation, are found in all sorts of places. Those thinkers and movements who have been the source of most of the ideas I have found useful are important conversation partners in this theology. Calling them conversation partners means that they are respected, as conversation partners should be. It also means that there is room for disagreement and a need for conversation with these same thinkers.

Process Thinkers

The process thinkers have been major conversation partners of mine for a long time. From them I long ago picked up ways of talking about reality that some people today call "postmodern" (anyone who has bothered to read Alfred North Whitehead's criticism of the modern philosophers would not call him a "modernist"). I think of this handful of ideas as a "modest metaphysics," which is to say that I think they are true and have yet to be disabused of them. When and if I am, I shall repent. These ideas stipulate that whatever is actual is involved in becoming, that the world is evolutionary, that it is both a creation and a creating, and that human beings are both creatures and participants in this ongoing creativity. Everything exists in relation to everything else. Nothing exists in and of itself; everything has a context and is part of the context of other things or persons. In the beginning and in the end and in between there is communion. Experience has to it depths not completely open to observation or description. At the heart of reality is mystery on which we have only a marginal grasp. There is no purely objective knowing because the knower and the known participate in and affect one another. Knowledge and meaning are less discovered than created, although they are not created "out of nothing."[1] Faith is not reducible to a human construct.

Two qualifiers should be stated. First, these ideas are now the common property of all kinds of thinkers, and few find vigorous

---

[1]Some readers will rightly detect here the influence of Bernard E. Meland in such books as *Faith and Culture* (New York: Oxford University Press, 1953) and *The Realities of Faith* (New York: Oxford University Press, 1962).

opposition. One hardly needs to be a process thinker to find them useful. Second, at some points in the text disagreements with some characteristic emphases of process theology will come to light. These have to do with the doctrine of creation out of nothing and the doctrine of the Trinity and will be obvious when they appear. Nonetheless, these disagreements are sufficiently strong that this theology is probably best referred to as a "neo-process" theology.

Paul Tillich

It was from Paul Tillich, whom I had the privilege to know during the last years of his life, that I first learned that theological statements are answers to questions, and that we understand their meaning when we understand the questions they answer. Tillich called these questions and answers "existential," meaning that they are questions of how we understand ourselves in relation to God, Christ, the kingdom of God, and so forth. He did not mean that they are existential in the sense of being reducible to statements about human beings and their self-understanding.

From this we learn several important lessons. First, questions are just as important as answers, perhaps more important. A good answer is good, in part, because it is useful in putting us onto the next question. Second, Christian faith and theology can be questioned. Only by questioning inadequate formulations of our faith do we open the way to more adequate formulations. Third, to not understand the question is to not understand the answer. Bumpersticker theology proclaiming that "Christ is the answer" neglects to tell us what the question is; hence, it fails to make clear what the answer means. An answer to an unasked question is meaningless and irrelevant.

Further, the questions change over time. Tillich said that the deepest questions faced by the early church were those of death, sin, and ignorance (idolatry) which it answered with its christology of Christ as the Life and Light and Redeemer of the world. The major issues for the Reformation period were, as expressed in Luther's anguished cry "How can I find a gracious God?" those of guilt and condemnation to which the Reformers responded with the doctrine of justification by grace through faith. The things that motivate reflection in our time, argued Tillich, were the anxieties of emptiness and meaninglessness, despair, and estrangement.[2]

---

[2]The interested reader can find an introductory discussion in Tillich's *The Courage To Be* (New Haven: Yale University Press, 1952).

While no fundamental human question ever disappears, new issues push themselves to the forefront of conversation. We listed some typical contemporary issues above. Responsible theology engages the questions of its time and place. Responsible theology recognizes that it can be questioned.

Post-Shoah Theology

The post-Shoah theologians contribute to the understandings articulated in this systematic. "Post-Shoah theology" is a vibrant but still minority movement in contemporary theology. *Shoah* is a Hebrew word for whirlwind, destruction. It is used today to refer to what the historian Lucy Dawidowicz terms "the war against the Jews."[3] Karl Barth, a giant of twentieth-century theology, said disapprovingly in a July 1944 lecture in Zürich, Switzerland: "We do not like the Jews as a rule; it is therefore not easy for us to apply to them as well the general love for humankind."[4] John Chrysostom, archbishop of Constantinople in the late fourth century, said of Jews: "Where Christ-killers gather, the cross is ridiculed, God blasphemed, the Father unacknowledged, the Son insulted, the grace of the Spirit rejected. If the Jewish rites are holy and venerable, our way of life must be false. But if our way is true, as indeed it is, theirs is fraudulent."[5] Jews are "fit," said Chrysostom, "for slaughter."[6]

Barth was right, but made his point quite gently. Jews have hardly ever been regarded by Christians as neighbors whom God has given us to love. They have been those on whom we feel free to make demands, but not among those whom God demands that we love as we love ourselves. But that is too light a way to put the point. Notice: Chrysostom said that if Judaism is true, Christianity is false, but that because Christianity is true, Judaism is false. On this view, being Jewish is based at best on a mistake, at worst on a sin, the sin of rejecting Jesus as messiah, killing Christ, and in their daily worship

---

[3] Lucy S. Dawidowicz, *The War Against the Jews 1933–1945* (New York: Holt, Rinehart and Winston, 1975).

[4] Quoted in Daniel Jonah Goldhagen, *Hitler's Willing Executioners* (New York: Alfred A. Knopf, 1996), 25.

[5] John Chrysostom, *Discourses Against Judaizing Christians*, trans. Paul W. Harkins (Washington, D.C.: The Catholic University of America Press, 1979), 10–11.

[6] Ibid., 8.

ridiculing, blaspheming, insulting, and rejecting everything for which the church stands.

The logic of this view is that there should be no Jews. While that logic never became the official position of the church, neither could it be successfully repressed. Christians would find ways to act out the story that they had so long been told. Through enacting church laws regulating all aspects of Jewish life and relations between Jews and Christians, through making these church laws into state law in Christendom with its established church, through the outbreaks of mass murder from the eleventh century through the pogroms in early twentieth-century Russia, to the Shoah there runs a clear line of Christian teaching and practice of contempt against Jews and Judaism.[7]

This is not just a matter of bad behavior. Bad ideas precede bad behavior. The first sin is against language. Anti-Judaism is a systematic way of interpreting or, rather, misinterpreting, the Christian faith. It is found not only in the numerous tracts "against the Jews" written by the church fathers but in discussions of Jesus, Paul, the doctrines of the church, the sacraments, christology, scripture, in short at every point of Christian teaching.[8] God is the God who made with the Jews a provisional, temporary covenant and now punishes them for being faithful to it. Jesus Christ is the mediator through whom God established a new covenant that displaces the old covenant and the people of the covenant. Jesus lived his life in conflict with Jews and Judaism, taught against Jews and Judaism, was crucified at the hands of Jews and Judaism, and was raised by God in victory over Jews and Judaism. The meaning of their scriptures is entirely "emptied" into ours. The church is the replacement people, not Jewish, anti-Jewish, and better than Jewish. We Christians are the beneficiaries of all this.

Post-Shoah theologians see all this as not only "pre-Shoah" theology, the kind that helped make the destruction of Jews possible,

---

[7] A few of the many histories documenting this story are: Leon Poliakov, *The History of Anti-Semitism* (New York: Schocken Books, 1974); Edward H. Flannery, *The Anguish of the Jews* (New York: Paulist Press, 1985); and Robert S. Wistrich, *Antisemitism: The Longest Hatred* (New York: Pantheon Books, 1991).

[8] This point is amply demonstrated in Williamson, *A Guest in the House of Israel* (Louisville: Westminster/John Knox Press, 1993).

but as theologically incoherent.[9] At every point it denies the good news of God's unfathomable love of the ungodly, news that cannot be true for us if it is not true for Jews. Consequently, the entire panopoly of Christian doctrine needs to be radically rethought in light of the good news of God's justifying grace. Mere denunciations of anti-Semitism (the modern, racist, and secularized version of traditional anti-Judaism), racism, and bias do not name the evil of anti-Judaism that Christian theology must reject as contradictory of the gospel.

Narrative Theology

Narrative theology is a significant new movement in contemporary theology, both Jewish and Christian.[10] Narrative theology makes the point that when we wish to describe someone's character we tell that person's story. The principle of process in process philosophy—to say what an actuality is is to describe how it became what it is—is a narrative principle. For this reason, some early narrative theologians were process theologians (e.g., Will Beardslee[11]). If we want to say who a person is, we tell a story that exhibits that person's character. The biblical narrative enables us to do this with God. We come to know who God is as a character in the persistent patterns of whose storied behavior over time there is no inconstancy. Many Christian narrative theologies concentrate on what they call the gospel narrative to yield the character of Jesus and God-acting-in-Jesus.[12]

---

[9] Some post-Shoah theologians are: Paul M. van Buren, *A Theology of the Jewish-Christian Reality*, 3 vols. (New York: The Seabury Press, 1980, 1983, San Francisco: Harper & Row, 1988, vol. 3); A. Roy Eckardt, *Elder and Younger Brothers* (New York: Schocken, 1973); *Your People, My People* (New York: Quadrangle, 1974); Darrell J. Fasching, *Narrative Theology After Auschwitz* (Minneapolis: Fortress Press, 1992); R. Kendall Soulen, *The God of Israel and Christian Theology* (Minneapolis: Fortress Press, 1996); Marvin R. Wilson, *Our Father Abraham* (Eerdmans: Grand Rapids, 1989); Rosemary R. Ruether, *Faith and Fratricide* (New York: The Seabury Press, 1974); John T. Pawlikowski, *Christ in the Light of the Christian-Jewish Dialogue* (New York: Paulist Press, 1982); and Michael E. Lodahl, *Shekhinah Spirit* (New York: Paulist Press, 1992).

[10] The works of William Placher are fine representatives of narrative theology. See, e.g., *Narratives of A Vulnerable God* (Louisville: Westminster John Knox Press, 1994).

[11] William A. Beardslee, *A House for Hope* (Philadelphia: The Westminster Press, 1975).

[12] See Ronald F. Thiemann, *Revelation and Theology: The Gospel as Narrated Promise* (Notre Dame: University of Notre Dame Press, 1985).

But if narrative theology is to live up to its promise, it has to pay attention to the larger biblical story. On its own terms, to know who God is is to pay attention to those behavior patterns that, over time, exhibit no inconstancy. Hence, the narrative theologians whose influence is most evident in this systematic are those who seek to do precisely this.[13]

Throughout this systematic, for this and other reasons, there is an insistence on reading the Christian story in the light of the whole of scripture. Furthermore, there is an insistence on the theological claim at the heart of narrative theology: that God's character consists in those stories that over time exhibit constancy. Another word for this is God's faithfulness, God's *hesed*, that faithfulness on which we may utterly rely when all other faithfulness, including ours, is open to question.

Feminist Theology

For some time, feminist theologians have been important to the theological conversation that comes to expression in this book. When I started the course on women and theology at Christian Theological Seminary in the 1970s, Marjorie Suchocki graciously helped in the effort to think it through. Lori Krafte-Jacobs was a student in the course and later wrote a Ph.D. dissertation on methodology in Jewish feminist theology. Rosemary Ruether's book on anti-Judaism and Christian theology, *Faith and Fratricide*, aided in integrating two different interests and commitments.[14] Further, I have benefitted from team-teaching systematic theology with Rebecca Prichard.

Historically, the church has been, at best, ambivalent toward women. As Elizabeth Clark puts it, they were both "God's creation, his good gift to men—and the curse of the world."[15] In whatever way we reconstruct the relationship of Jesus to women and their roles in the Pauline churches, the unhappy reality is that women were increasingly defined as less than fully human. Aristotle's view of women as "defective males" was adopted by Thomas Aquinas who argued

---

[13] The Jewish narrative theologian Michael Goldberg makes this point well in his *Jews and Christians: Getting Our Stories Straight* (Philadelphia: Trinity Press International, 1991); see also the works of R. Kendall Soulen and Darrell J. Fasching cited above.

[14] Rosemary Ruether, *Faith and Fratricide* (New York: The Seabury Press, 1974).

[15] Elizabeth A. Clark, *Women in the Early Church* (Collegeville: The Liturgical Press, 1990), 15.

that women do not participate as fully in the image of God as do men. His reasoning was that women are less rational and spiritual than men but are useful for propagating the species. They are not useful as conversation partners and should not be ordained.[16]

Such views impact all theological doctrines, particularly those of God, humanity, creation (nature), and the church. In discussions of these topics, the contributions of feminist theology will be taken into account.

---

[16] See the selections from Thomas' *Summa Theologica* in Elizabeth A. Clark and Herbert Richardson, eds., *Women and Religion* (New York: Harper & Row, 1977), 78–101.

Chapter 1

Blessing, Life, and Conversation: Thinking Theologically

The Way of Blessing and Life

Christian faith is a way of life and blessing. The earliest Christians described themselves as those "who belonged to the Way" (Acts 9:2); and they instructed one another in "the Way of God" (Acts 18:26). They followed Jesus Christ, the "pioneer" of their faith, who went ahead of them, pointing out the path for them to follow (Heb. 2:10; 12:2). They did not think that they were the first followers to step out onto the way of life that God gives and calls us to walk. Convinced that Rahab, Moses, Abraham and Sarah, Isaac, Abel, Enoch, and David had preceded them in this way, they said: "God is not ashamed to be called their God; indeed, he has prepared a city for them" (Heb. 11:16).

They were pilgrims, "strangers and foreigners...seeking a homeland" (Heb. 11:13–14). In walking the path of faith, they set out onto the way that God had long ago revealed at Sinai to the people Israel: "Today I have set before you life and death, blessings and curses.

Choose life so that you and your descendants may live..." (Deut.
30:19). Abram and Sarai were the first whom God called into God's
future for and with us. God promised: "In you all the families of the
earth [read: all the Gentiles] shall be blessed" (Gen. 12:3). Jesus Christ
is God's "Yes!" to this promise: "For in him every one of God's
promises is a 'yes.'" (2 Cor. 1:20). When Mary and Joseph presented
Jesus in the temple at Jerusalem, Simeon sang to God: "My eyes
have seen your salvation, which you have prepared in the presence
of all peoples, a light for revelation to the Gentiles and for glory to
your people Israel" (Lk. 2:30–32). Those who told such stories of
Jesus had long ago responded to his call to join in the way of faith
when he bid them "Follow me."

Christian faith, when loyal to its biblical origins, is both a way
and a way of life. It is a way walked by a community, not just by
isolated individuals. As a way of life it is an alternative to the death-
dealing ways of the world. Its followers do not engage in the death-
dealing practices of the world. A route walked through history, into
the future, it is a strange kind of way. Ordinarily, if we want to know
how to get from one place to another, we read a map. Once we
have found it, we know how to get from where we are to where we
want to go. But the way of faith is a way in both time and space; it
leads into the future, it follows a pioneer, and its God calls us forward. We respond anxiously because, unlike geography, the future
has not been mapped. We have been given a sense of the goal and
the basic direction. But there are forks in the road into the future
and decisions to make.

A Way of Life and Blessing

The way of life that the God of Israel disclosed to the Israel of
God is a way of blessing and shalom. After giving the Torah to Israel, God said: "I have set before you life and death, blessings and
curses. Choose life so that you and your descendants may live" (Deut.
30:19). When God called Abraham and Sarah forward into the way
of faith, God promised them: "In you all the families of the earth
shall be blessed" (Gen. 12:3). The way of life is shown to the people
of God as a way of blessing, of well-being. Life and blessing belong
together. To choose against them is to bring curse and death upon
ourselves. Curse is what we get when we sinfully reject God's gracious blessing. Blessing is freely offered as a gift, but we have to
decide to accept it and allow ourselves to be transformed by it.

God likes life, lots of it, and in great vari⟨
ning, scripture makes this abundantly clear. A
and sea from each other, God said: "Let the ear
tion: plants yielding seed, and fruit trees of every
bear fruit with the seed in it" (Gen. 1:11). God calle⟨
After creating the sun, moon, and stars, and wi
night, God said: "Let the waters bring forth swarr.
tures, and let birds fly above the earth across the ⟨   ⟨ny
(Gen. 1:20). God found them good, too, blessed the⟨⟨ and said: "Be
fruitful and multiply and fill the waters in the seas, and let birds
multiply on the earth" (Gen. 1:22). Then God said: "Let the earth
bring forth living creatures of every kind: cattle and creeping things
and wild animals of the earth of every kind" (Gen. 1:24). God found
them good as well.

Then God decided to "let be" human beings and to let them be
in God's image. So God created us in God's image, male and female, blessed us as well, and said: "Be fruitful and multiply, and fill
the earth and subdue it; and have dominion over the fish of the sea
and over the birds of the air and over every living thing that moves
upon the earth" (Gen. 1:28). This "dominion" is one of service; the
other creatures have also been found good, been blessed, and been
allowed to be fruitful and multiply. Human dominion does not cancel the right of other species to their home on the earth.

This is made clear when God decides what the human beings
may eat: "every plant yielding seed…, and every tree with seed in
its fruit; you shall have them for food" (Gen. 1:29). God does not
say that we may eat birds, fish, animals, or even the roots of plants.
In Eden, only plants yielding seed and trees with seed in their fruit
may be eaten by human beings. To make it plain, human beings
may not kill to eat. This is a considerable limit to our "dominion."
Life is the gift of God, who breathes it into human beings; it is maintained by God (Ps. 66:9; 27:1), and a long life is God's satisfying gift
(1 Chr. 29:15). One of the ten words (what Christians often call the
Ten Commandments) says simply: "You shall not murder" (Ex.
20:13).

"I came," said Jesus, "that they may have life, and have it abundantly" (Jn. 10:10). As Paul says, Jesus "confirms" (Rom. 15:8) the
gift and promise of God to the Israel of God, and in Jesus God makes
good on, redeems the gift of life and blessing from the assaults of sin
and its death-dealing ways. The ministry of Jesus was greatly occupied

...aling lives maimed by hunger, illness, and the economic and *...itual* oppression brought about by Roman occupation. Jesus discloses to us the God who is the ground and end of life and its nurturer and redeemer; in him was life and in him we are dead to sin and alive to God (Rom. 6:11).

Notice the language of faith: Life is a gracious gift to be gratefully received, not a possession to be grasped and controlled. Life is given to be shared with others, with other human beings, with all the living things in the water, on the earth, and in the air; it is not to be exercised at the expense of their lives. To live, to live well, to live so that others live well is a blessing. As Julian of Norwich wrote, our faith is "That all shall be well, and all shall be well, and all manner of things shall be well."

In his commentary on Genesis, J. Gerald Janzen says that "the divinely intended governing principle is the power of blessing."[1] Genesis 1 and 2 display the world and human beings within it "as a place of blessing and fruitfulness" and describe a garden "as a picture of the total blessedness of creation." The purpose of salvation history, of God's acting salvifically in history, "is to counteract the workings of evil in the world and to restore the world to its divinely intended blessedness."[2] The biblical story of redemption, from its beginning in Abraham, "is a journey in blessing from a single person to all the families of the earth."[3] Blessing is well-being, and "Abram and his descendants are called to serve the well-being of all human communities, by becoming the kind of community they would all like to become (cf. Deut. 4:5–8)."[4]

Blessing is well-being, *shalom* (peace) with oneself and, because we are related to all else that is, with God, and with all our neighbors, with all the living things in the environment that are also to be fruitful and multiply. As the Hebrew people in their nomadic stage, Jews today greet one another with the word "shalom." "Seek peace, and pursue it" (Ps. 34:14) is both gift and command from God. Although often violated by the kings of Israel and the princes of the church, the normative witness of the Bible is a story of peace. The very name of Jerusalem, a city of strife, contains the word "peace"

---

[1] J. Gerald Janzen, *Abraham and All the Families of the Earth: Genesis 12–50* (Grand Rapids: Eerdmans, 1993), 4.

[2] Ibid., 5.

[3] Ibid., 15.

[4] Ibid., 17.

(*Yerushalayim* related to *shalom*). Shalom was the heart of Israel's hope for the days of the Messiah, the reign of God: "In his days may righteousness flourish and peace abound, until the moon is no more" (Ps. 72:7); "they shall beat their swords into plowshares, and their spears into pruning hooks; nation shall not lift up sword against nation, neither shall they learn war any more" (Isa. 2:4). The sages of Judaism remarked: "Hillel says: 'Be disciples of Aaron, loving peace and pursuing grace, loving people and drawing them near to the Torah.'"[5] The way of life and blessing says No to the death-dealing ways of war.

Shalom finds its confirmation and redemption in Jesus Christ, understood as the "Prince of Peace" longed for by the prophets of Israel (Isa. 9:6). His birth announced by choruses of "peace on earth" (Lk. 2:14), he taught that peacemakers are blessed (Mt. 5:9). His departing words to his disciples were: "Peace I leave with you; my peace I give to you" (Jn. 14:27). The whole of the biblical witness testifies to the interdependence of peace and justice upon each other; without one, the other is never stable. "Steadfast love and faithfulness will meet; righteousness and peace will kiss each other" (Ps. 85:10).

Marjorie Suchocki develops the concept of "inclusive well-being" as the norm for what human life essentially is and ought to be and as the standard against which sin is assessed.[6] Inclusive well-being implies that all things within the world are interdependent upon one another, that God genuinely interacts with all others, and that God is always God with the world, as the world is always God's world.[7] Our moral, spiritual, psychological, emotional, intellectual, and physical lives find their basis in interdependence. "Infants and children are nourished," says Suchocki, "not only by food, but also by caring attention, by arms that hold, voices that sing, and faces that smile."[8] Apart from such warm interdependence, the human spirit withers.

We are loved into loving precisely by such a gracious affirmation that engenders our becoming genuinely human.

---

[5] *Torah from Our Sages: Pirke Avot*, trans. Jacob Neusner (Dallas: Rossell Books, 1984), 1:12, 31.

[6] Marjorie Suchocki, *The Fall to Violence: Original Sin in Relational Theology* (New York: Continuum, 1995), 66.

[7] Ibid., 67.

[8] Ibid., 69.

Yet the "raw fact" is "that in an interdependent world, the well-being of one depends in some sense on the well-being of all."[9] The health of the community is affected by the health of its natural environment and vice-versa. Destruction of fragile soils by impoverished people leads to famine; excessive burning of fossil fuels produces global warming that results in more frequent and violent storms that yield floods, tornadoes, and hurricanes with their destructive consequences. God is both the One (indeed, the only One) who interacts with all others and the One whose intent is for the well-being of all. God suffers with God's creatures the ill effects of sin and ill-being and struggles with us to transform ill-being into well-being, to bring good out of evil.

The Way of Faith: A Long Walk

Christian faith is a way of life, walked in time, through a long series of cultural shifts and the unpredictable ups and downs of history. It is a way of life and blessing, which we are given and called to walk. It has turned out to be a long way, although some of our forebears thought it would be accomplished within their lifetimes (see Mk. 13:30, for example). Theology is the practical wisdom, the result and process of thinking about matters of faith, that seeks to help us walk the way of faith without straying from the path of life and blessing or that tries to help find the path again after we have lost it for a while.

Although the way is long and the Christian life is both task and gift, we are not without help as we try to follow Jesus Christ, the pioneer of our faith. Whether we seek a way out of our own bondage (as the Hebrews did from Egypt) or a way out of the illusory comforts of middle-class America, there is God, who provides the way and calls us into it. There is God's self-revelation illuminating the way in the history of the people Israel, through the Torah and the prophets, and in Jesus Christ. There is the book that we carry on the way. It is a book that, if we study it diligently, we will find to be a lamp to our feet and a light to our path (Ps. 119:105). There are all those, Christians and Jews, who have thought hard about how to walk the way of life on whose resources we may draw. There is the church, a community of fellow-walkers, companions on the way. There is the goal of the way: the redemption of God's creation in the new heaven and the new earth, the new Jerusalem, when the

---

[9]Ibid., 72.

way of death will have finally been overcome, when "death will be no more" (Rev. 21:4), and we will all have been made new. Maybe we will even learn to love one another.

Anti-Judaism: A Death-Dealing Way

A hallmark of contemporary theology is the awareness that we are compelled to name sin and evil. The first evil that we name in this chapter is anti-Judaism. Others, that we call "structural sins," will be named at the end of this chapter. This awareness puts us on notice that we speak not only to those outside the church, but to the church itself, calling it to reconstruct its practices, including its use of its own language.

Theological matters would be neat and clean if we could juxtapose the "good" church and the "bad" world to one another for the purpose of contrasting them. Things are not that simple. In its zeal for asserting the truth of the way that God gave to the church and called it to follow, church leaders have too often felt the need to deny the truth of any and all other ways of faith and the faithfulness of those who followed them. Of all other ways, that of Judaism and the Jewish people have suffered the most from the church's obsessive commitment to the proposition that only we are right, only we are among the blessed. So we manage to turn God's gift of blessing and life, given to us by the Jew, Jesus of Nazareth, into curse and death for the people from whom we received it.

A visitor to any number of European cathedrals encounters at the entrance statues representing two women. These allegorical women represent the synagogue and the church; their medieval Latin names are *Synagoga* and *Ecclesia*. They also appear in Christian art in stained glass and illuminated manuscripts. It is at the approach to the sanctuary that they make their most effective, if silent, witness to how the church has brought cursing and death upon the Israel of God. From them Christians receive voiceless confirmation of their understanding of the victorious church and the defeated synagogue.

My wife and I were recently confronted with Synagoga and Ecclesia at Notre Dame in Paris. They face each other across the front, central door to the church. Ecclesia stands upright, a crown triumphantly placed on her head. In one hand she holds a staff topped by the cross and in the other, in some versions, a chalice. Sometimes both stand under a crucifix, with blood flowing from Jesus' wounded side directly into Ecclesia's chalice. Ecclesia's posture is vertical and strong, her stride purposeful, and she stares dominatingly across the door at Synagoga.

Synagoga, on the other hand, sways backward, sagging in her defeat by Ecclesia. In one hand she holds a spear that is broken and does not support her weight. She has used the spear to pierce the side of Jesus. Her other hand holds the five books of Torah (unless, as in some versions, she has dropped them). Her eyes are blind-folded, reflecting the church's contention that the Jews are "blind" to the meaning of their own scriptures. Ecclesia is strong, having conquered Synagoga. Synagoga is weak and defeated, full of hate and obduracy, has killed Jesus, and now awaits exile. An important thirteenth-century theologian and teacher of Thomas Aquinas, Albertus Magnus, described the pair this way:

> To the right of the Crucified, a maiden is portrayed with a joyful expression and beautiful face and crown. It is Ecclesia, who reverently received the blood of Christ in the chalice ...whereas on the left stands a figure with eyes blindfolded, a sad expression and bowed head from which the crown falls; it is Synagoga who has spilled this same blood and still despises it.[10]

These two women express the power relation between the syna-gogue and the church in Christendom, reflecting and reinforcing for generations of worshipers the church-sanctioned realities of Jew-ish life in European countries. Not to be missed in the artistic depic-tions of these two figures is the fact that Synagoga is blindfolded. Were the Jews not willfully blind to the truth of what they missed in rejecting Christ, so the ideology went, they would convert and cease being Jews. The church reassured itself: To be a Jew is to make a mistake.

The implication, ultimately genocidal, is that there should be no Jews. Raul Hilberg, a historian of the Holocaust, maintained that since the fourth century there had been three anti-Jewish policies: "conversion, expulsion, and annihilation."[11] This was the logical and historical sequence: "The missionaries of Christianity had said in effect: You have no right to live among us as Jews. The secular rulers

---

[10]Albertus Magnus, cited in Wolfgang S. Seiferth, *Synagogue and Church in the Middle Ages: Two Symbols in Art and Literature*, trans. L. Chadeayne and P. Gottwald (New York: Frederic Ungar, 1970), 102. Numerous examples of the pair are shown in Gertrude Schiller, *Iconography of Christian Art*, vol. 2, trans. Janet Seligman (Green-wich, Conn.: New York Graphic Society, 1972).

[11]Raul Hilberg, *The Destruction of the European Jews* (New York: Harper & Row, 1979), 3.

who followed had proclaimed: You have no right to live among us. The German Nazis at last decreed: You have no right to live."[12] And so about six million Jews were slaughtered, one quarter of them children.

Killing Jews had always been denounced in the official policy of the church, and the Nazis were not authentic Christians in disguise. Nor is it the case that the rise of the modern world made life safer for Jews; the Holocaust did not happen in the Middle Ages. But that the church had to denounce the killing of Jews by Christians, as in the Crusades and pogroms too numerous to count, reveals much that might otherwise go unnoticed.[13]

What it discloses is that the church took the way of life and blessing that it received as a gift from the God of Israel and the Israel of God and turned it into something with which to bring death and curse upon the people Israel.

Anti-Judaism (or, in its more virulent form, anti-Semitism, a modern, racist rejection of Jews), is a disease in its own right and not simply another form of racism. Although preceded in the ancient world by Egyptian, Greek, and Roman expression of bias against Jews, largely because Jews did not participate in the "civil religion" of those times, Christian anti-Judaism is a new development, newly virulent.[14] Anti-Judaism is the church's gift to the catalogue of the world's evils, a contagious gift that has spread beyond its origins and now distributes its malaise in various quarters of the world. A view and practice inherited from the church fathers, it contends that Jews have been abandoned by God, displaced in the covenant with God by Gentile Christians, and that they should see the light and convert. Its premise is genocidal: There should be no Jews. When legal mistreatment and persuasion failed to convince Jews of the truth of these propositions, Christians turned to population expulsions and pogroms, although without ecclesial sanction.[15]

---

[12]Ibid., 3–4.

[13]For the fate of Jews in the Crusades, both in Europe and Jerusalem, see Steven Runciman, *A History of the Crusades*, vol. 1 (Cambridge: Cambridge University Press, 1951), 134–41, 287.

[14]See Robert L. Wilken, "*Insignissima Religio, Certe Licita?* Christianity and Judaism in the Fourth and Fifth Centuries," in *The Impact of the Church Upon Its Culture*, ed. Jerald C. Brauer (Chicago: The University of Chicago Press, 1968), 39–66.

[15]This long, sad story has often enough been told. See Clark M. Williamson, *Has God Rejected His People?* (Nashville: Abingdon Press, 1982), 89–122; *When Jews and Christians Meet* (St. Louis: CBP Press, 1989), 55–70; and *The Church and the Jewish People* (St. Louis: Christian Board of Publication, 1994), 25–33.

Anti-Judaism is an ideology, a distortion of truth in the interest of the power and benefit of the institutional church and, particularly, its leaders.[16]

It lives on in the churches, including the mainline churches, and particularly in the ways in which preachers and teachers misuse the language of faith. Usually this misuse of language is unconscious and unintentional; like the glasses we wear and of which we are equally unaware, it is simply the way we have always "heard" the Christian faith discussed. We appropriate anti-Judaism without recognizing or examining it. It goes widely unchallenged because, unlike women and African Americans, there are no Jews in the churches. So, for example, some feminists who would not tolerate sexist language in the church can manage not to notice anti-Jewish language and the practices that it both reflects and reinforces.[17] We Gentile Christians long ago forgot what Paul (or his student) urged us to remember:

> that you were at that time without Christ, being aliens from the commonwealth of Israel, and strangers to the covenants of promise, having no hope and without God in the world. But now in Christ Jesus you who once were far off have been brought near by the blood of Christ. For he is our peace. (Eph. 2:12–14a).

Theology: What Is It?

Theology is the conversation that the community, the church, has with itself and its neighbors as it walks the way of faith through history into the future. That is the first meaning of the term "theology," simply all the conversations that we have with each other as we seek to walk faithfully along God's way through history. Sometimes it is what we say to those who see us, the witness we bear by walking the way and by explaining why we do this and who it is that we are following. We talk with each other in the community for

---

[16]For a study of how anti-Judaism and the stern insistence on separation between Jews and Christians followed lines of power and authority in the church, see John Gager, *The Origins of Anti-Semitism* (New York: Oxford University Press, 1983).

[17]For feminists who are self-critical about anti-Judaism in feminist theology and scholarship, see Katharina von Kellenbach, *Anti-Judaism in Feminist Religious Writings* (Atlanta: Scholars Press, 1994); Susannah Heschel, "The Denigration of Judaism as a Form of Christian Mission," in Clark M. Williamson, ed., *A Mutual Witness* (St. Louis: Chalice Press, 1992), 33–47; "Anti-Judaism in Christian Feminist Theology;" *Tikkun* 5/3, 25–28; and Judith Plaskow, "Christian Feminism and Anti-Judaism," *Cross Currents* 28: (Fall 1978) 306–9.

many reasons. Sometimes we do it to offer praise to God and Christ through the Holy Spirit for giving and calling us to the way of life, because we are elated by God's exuberant gifts to us. Sometimes we do it to let others know that they can share the love of God and neighbor, that this love is not held close to the vest, but generously spread about by the God who, we are confident, is not only "our" God, but the God of each and all. We do not possess or control God, but are called and claimed by God. We find God's loving grace so exciting that we cannot keep it to ourselves. Sometimes we talk with each other to help keep up our spirits. The way, as we noted, is long, and we become disheartened that the walk of faith turns out to be more difficult than we had first imagined. So Paul says: "Encourage one another and build up each other, as indeed you are doing" (1 Thess. 5:11).

There is another reason why we talk with each other, and the kind of talk it involves is what we customarily call "theology." As we walk the path of faith from the past through the present into the uncertain future, we face difficulties and opportunities and come to many crossroads. Sometimes the difficulties are of our own making or are inherited from our past. We find we have to rethink what had seemed to be settled. We have to decide how to deal with complications and opportunities, which fork of the road to take. Our conversation together has always been eminently practical. Often it is critically so. We have to decide in which direction lies the future to which God calls us, how to deal with the new events and developments with which history confronts us as we walk through it and contribute to making it. We talk together to come to an understanding of how scripture and tradition, the recorded conversations of those who went before us in this way, intersect with the situation in which we find ourselves so as to illuminate the path.

In short, theology is an ongoing conversation with ourselves, with others (for example, with Jews who also follow Abraham and Sarah in the way of faith), with our contemporary context, and with our tradition. It is not the absolute Truth (capital T) worked out in solitude from the point of view of someone perched on a mountaintop looking down on all the human beings struggling through the valley below. It is generated on the way by a community committed to walk the way of life and blessing faithfully through the terrors of history.

When we have come to some provisional understanding of the Christian faith, and all our understandings are provisional, we know what to do next. "Ideas," said William James, "are...helpful in life's practical struggles." The best ideas are those that do the best job "in the way of leading us…"[18]Let me qualify that a bit. Theology thinks about practice and issues in new practice. It is a practical wisdom. As such it involves both ontology (how we understand the world in which we live in its ultimate dimensions) and ethics (how we live in the world that we so understand). We are not finished with any theological point until we can talk about the difference it makes to how we see things and to what we intend to do.

Witness and Theology: A Distinction

The community, in walking the path of faith, witnesses to the God in whom it believes. It makes this witness with the whole of its life, in what it does, what it refuses to do: in its hymns, creeds, prayers, in what it says to itself and others about what all this means. Our witness is, in part, what we and others hear us say and not say, and equally in what others see us do or fail to do: "Let your light shine before others, so that they may see your good works and give glory to your Father in heaven" (Mt. 5:16). Our task in the church is to make the Christian witness, in both word and deed, words acted out in deeds and deeds articulated in words. Our task when "doing" theology is to think critically about whether and how well we are doing so.

Since the task of theology is defined as thinking about the church and its task of making the Christian witness, we need to have in mind some understanding of the task of the church. Here is the definition that I offer to our ongoing conversation:

> The church is that community of human beings called into existence by God, through the Holy Spirit, to live from and by the gospel of God, witnessing to the grace and command of the gospel as the call and claim of the God of Israel offered to all the world and hence to the church in Jesus Christ, and doing so both to remind itself of what it is about, and, on behalf of the world, that it might, one day, reflect the glory of God.[19]

---

[18]William James, *Pragmatism* (Cleveland: World Publishing, 1955), 59, 61.
[19]Clark M. Williamson, *A Guest in the House of Israel: Post-Holocaust Church Theology* (Louisville: Westminster/John Knox Press, 1993), 248.

We do theology in the context of and on behalf of the church and the world. Why we do it and how we do it will make no sense unless we make clear what the church is given and called to be. The task of the church is to *make* the Christian witness to the gospel of Jesus Christ; the task of the theologian in the church is to *think critically* about the way in which the church makes its witness. All Christians are and ought to be theologians in the church. Theology is "faith seeking understanding." One cannot be a Christian without some understanding, however adequate or inadequate, of the Christian faith. To do theology intentionally is to work at the task of improving one's understanding of the Christian faith, both as to how we understand what we are to believe and what we are supposed to do as a result of so believing. Often, of course, we learn what we are to believe from doing what we ought to do. Theologians serve the church not by doing whatever the church asks them to do, but by serving the purpose that the church is given and called to serve. The purpose of critical thinking is constructive: to test how the church makes and interprets its witness and so to help the church make its witness in ways that are appropriate to the gospel of Jesus Christ, illuminating the situation in which we find ourselves, and morally plausible in proposing at least relatively adequate understandings of what we ought to do next.

The distinction between making the Christian witness and thinking critically about it is not a separation.[20] We cannot make the Christian witness without thinking about what we are doing, and we cannot think about it without also making it. This distinction is mainly a matter of emphasis. The church puts more stress on making the Christian witness than on thinking critically about it; theologians place the accent more on thinking critically about how the witness is made than on making it. Usually the same person does these two things. In preparing to preach a sermon, the preacher thinks about how to interpret the scriptures so that the congregation can hear an illuminating, transforming word; in the act of preaching, she concentrates more on making that witness than thinking about it. Later, when she thinks about using the sermon again, she may scratch her head, ask "How did I ever say that!?" and decide to write a new one.

---

[20]See Schubert M. Ogden, *On Theology* (San Francisco: Harper & Row, 1986), 1–21.

Having the Audacity to Criticize

"Different models of faith," argues Darrell J. Fasching, "have different ethical consequences."[21] An authentically biblical understanding of faith places it in the context of the covenant between God and God's people. Covenantal faith involves a conversation between faithful people and God, in which we are expected "not only to trust and obey God but...also [to be] allowed to question (and even to call into question) the behavior of God..."[22] Radical trust in God's gracious love not only permits, but requires, questioning; it evokes an audacious faith. Abraham is a model of faith who epitomizes both trust in God and *chutzpah,* the audacity to question even God. Abraham both obeyed God in the matter of the binding of Isaac and confronted God over the fate of Sodom and Gomorrah in defense of the stranger (Gen. 22 and 18:16–33). Jacob wrestles with the stranger (Gen. 32:22–32) and is named "Israel." Faith is a dialectic of trust and chutzpah. Unlike his orthodox friends, Job continually grills God, who says to Job's orthodox friends: "You have not spoken of me what is right, as my servant Job has" (Job 42:7).

Rabbi Irving Greenberg develops this into a norm for contemporary theology in the midst of the death-dealing ways of the twentieth century: "Nothing dare evoke our absolute, unquestioning loyalty, not even our God, for this leads to the possibilities of SS loyalties."[23] In the context of the covenant with the living God of Israel (to whom Jesus prayed), faith is a dialectical relation between trust and chutzpah, obedience and questioning. Unquestioning obedience is not morally desirable; it is not asked of us and should not be given. Biblically, only an idol cannot stand up to questioning. Only idols refuse to be questioned. God invites questioning. By the same token, a questioning unaccompanied by actively living out the way of life is also inauthentic. Covenantal faith is not merely an attitude of the mind, a matter of believing or assenting to a proposition. A Hebrew term for faith, *emunah* (from which we get "amen"), connotes faithfulness, trust. It suggests the ability to remain steadfast amid unsettling circumstances. Those who know God "walk

---

[21]Darrell J. Fasching, *Narrative Theology After Auschwitz* (Minneapolis: Fortress Press, 1992), 50.

[22]Ibid.

[23]Irving Greenberg, "Cloud of Smoke, Pillar of Fire: Judaism, Christianity, and Modernity after the Holocaust," in *Auschwitz: Beginning of a New Era?* ed. Eva Fleischner (New York: KTAV, 1977), 38; cited in Fasching, *Narrative Theology After Auschwitz,* 15.

faithfully" (1 Kings 2:4; Isa. 38:3). Abraham and Sarah had faith and stepped out into the future to which God called them, confident that they would encounter God in the future. Abraham Heschel summarized it: Biblical faith requires "a *leap of action* rather than a *leap of thought.*"[24]

When we learn to read the gospels with minds educated about the Jewish context in which the story is set (an important educational project to undertake), we begin to notice stories about chutzpah. Jesus tells a parable about how to pray by describing a man who not only had the chutzpah to go to a neighbor at midnight and ask for three loaves of bread, but persevered in rapping on the door until the neighbor gave him the bread. The request was met "because of his persistence" (Lk. 11:5–13). That is the attitude we should take into prayer to God! Jesus makes the same point in the parable about the unjust judge and the nagging widow whose continued pestering wore him down until he did the right thing (Lk. 18:1–6).

The gospels testify to the fact that Jesus both asked questions and was willing to be questioned. To the man who addressed him as "Good Teacher," he responded: "Why do you call me good? No one is good but God alone" (Mk. 10:18). To the "lawyer" who asked him, "And who is my neighbor?" Jesus told the parable of the good Samaritan and asked: "Which of these three, do you think, was a neighbor to the man who fell into the hands of the robbers?" (Lk. 10:36). To those who asked, "By what authority are you doing these things?" (Mk. 11:28), he retorted: "I will ask you a question; answer me, and I will tell you by what authority I do these things. Did the baptism of John come from heaven, or was it of human origin? Answer me" (Mk. 11:29–30). A story is told about the rabbi whose students asked him: "Why does a rabbi always answer a question with a question?" Responded the rabbi: "So, what's wrong with a question?"

Ways of Doing Theology

Because theology is "faith seeking understanding," it is properly the concern of every Christian. Every Christian already has some understanding of her faith. The question is whether that understanding is thoughtful, whether it is worked out in conversation with those

---

[24]Abraham J. Heschel, *God in Search of Man* (New York: Farrar, Straus & Giroux, 1955), 238; quoted in Marvin Wilson, *Our Father Abraham* (Grand Rapids: Eerdmans, 1989), 185.

who have pondered these matters at length, and whether or to what extent it takes into account the "signs of the times." One important task of every local congregation is to provide occasions for study and reflection that will help people mature in the Christian faith.

While theology should hardly be confined to the clergy, it is acutely important in the preparation of ministers for the service of the church. A major task of ministers is to be teachers of the Christian faith.[25] Ministers "do" theology every time they preach a sermon, teach a Sunday school class, discuss with the congregation or board how its mission should be focused, talk about the meaning of life and death at a funeral, counsel those in distress, or try to help people figure out how to effect the intersections between the faith they hold and the work they do in the world.

We do theology in many and varied ways, not only in the mode of "systematic" theology. Most theology in the history of the church has not been done systematically. Paul the apostle, Dietrich Bonhoeffer, and Martin Luther King, Jr., did theology by writing letters from prison. Martin Luther did theology by writing commentaries on books of the Bible. Most clergy do their theologizing in sermons, in the teaching of classes in the meaning of the Christian faith, or in writing the weekly column for the congregational newsletter. Gerard Manley Hopkins did theology by writing complex and beautiful poetry. Most of us do it when we think seriously about a moral issue we face, or when we have been dealt a heavy blow of grief over the death of a loved one. All Christians need to take seriously their theological responsibilities every time they talk, think, or write about life or the Christian faith. When we ordain pastors, we place into their hands the care of the churches. Being a competent theologian is essential to being a good caregiver.

In a seminary or divinity school faculty, everybody does (or everybody should do) theology. Some, located in the fields of Bible and history, do historical theology. Historical theology is the disciplined study of the Christian and biblical past in order to understand what is understood to be the witness of faith and how that witness responded to its own historical context and the questions posed by that context. We do not study the Christian, Jewish, or biblical past out of a merely antiquarian interest. Study of the Bible

---

[25]See Clark M. Williamson and Ronald J. Allen, *The Teaching Minister* (Louisville: Westminster/John Knox Press, 1991).

and Christian history is intended to serve the present and the future, to engage in conversation with the past in order to serve the "way of life" in the present.

Others do practical theology. Practical theology has often suffered from being limited primarily to the clergy and from being regarded as doing little more than providing an assortment of clerical techniques. Yet God calls the whole people of God to walk the way of life, the way of faith. By baptism into this people we all become ministers of Jesus Christ. The purpose of ordained ministers is to represent to the people of God their *own* ministry; theirs is a representative ministry (we will say more on this later). Hence, practical theology has as its audience the entire people of God. Anything it specifically addresses to the clergy is on behalf of the whole people of God. Practical theology seeks to ask and answer the question, What ought to be the shape of the Christian witness in the time and place in which we are given and called to make it?

Some of us do systematic theology. Systematic theology usually focuses on such critical questions as the appropriateness, credibility, coherence, relevance, and moral plausibility of the Christian witness. We are concerned to ask and answer such questions as: What kind of sense do the witness and language of the Christian faith make? In what way is our talk credible? How is our witness appropriate to that to which we claim to bear witness? Is our witness morally plausible; does it cohere with our obligation to love our neighbors as ourselves?

Finally, while these three disciplines are obviously distinct from one another, they are also intertwined. None of us could do our business without the rest of us. Nor is there a hierarchy of value or importance among these disciplines, with one being on top (take your pick) and the others ranked below it. Each one is a specific way of engaging in the critical and constructive thinking on behalf of the church that theologians are given and called to do.

Critical Thinking and Criteria

To speak of "critical thinking" is redundant; thinking *is* critical. Free associating may be fun, but it is not thinking. Often we use the expression "on second thought," when what we ought to say is "on thinking." When we ask simple questions, such as, "Is this true?" or "How does that work?" we are thinking. To think critically is to do one's thinking in the light of certain defined and defended criteria (also called norms, standards, or rules). Historically, the church referred to its symbols (creeds) as the *regula fidei*, the rule of faith, or the *regula veritatis*, the rule of truth. They served to set out the limits within which Christian talk was orthodox or appropriate to the gospel. For example, talk that denied the humanity of Jesus Christ (the docetic heresy) or that denied that the God incarnate in Jesus Christ was the God of Israel (the Marcionite heresy) was declared out of bounds. A contemporary heresy, for example, would be a doctrine of humanity that denies that women are fully human.

The importance of the concept of heresy is that it reminds us that there are ideas and practices to which Christians ought to say no. Indeed, if we do not know what the Christian faith denies, we are altogether unclear about what it affirms, if anything. To affirm that all people are made in the image of God requires us to deny sexism and racism. Alternatively, affirming sexism or racism, whether explicitly or implicitly, denies the claim that all people are made in the image of God. A church without a concept of heresy is a church that denies nothing and, consequently, affirms nothing. What should be affirmed and denied, however, always needs to be worked out anew. It is more important today to deny militarism than Nestorianism.

Many norms, values, and standards, often referred to as "universals," have come under sharp attack from contemporary thinkers who call themselves "postmodern." People are wary of standards or criteria, so often having been offered a bill of goods that included false claims to universality or objectivity, particularly claims that served to reinforce the power or domination of some groups over others. The strength of postmodernism lies in its critique of precisely such abuses of power. But those who have suffered oppression are not well served by the argument that all norms or criteria are nothing more than the politics of the powerful. Protest against oppression implies that oppression is wrong, and that conclusion further implies that it is wrong in the light of some standard.[26]

Some criteria that are helpful in thinking about and reinterpreting the Christian faith are suggested by James A. Sanders' description of the hermeneutical axioms that biblical writers used in the

---

[26]See, e.g., Michel Foucault, *The Archaeology of Knowledge*, trans. A. M. Sheridan Smith (London: Tavistock, 1972); and Luce Irigaray, *Sexes and Genealogies*, trans. Gillian C. Gill (New York: Columbia University Press, 1933).

process of reinterpreting and contemporizing the biblical tradition in new and puzzling circumstances.[27] Essentially, the biblical writers worked with five axioms or principles: First, they always struggled to monotheize whatever ideas or wisdom they borrowed from other traditions; second, they used a "constitutive" or priestly axiom that bespeaks God's love for Israel or the church, that is, for this particular community or person; third, they used a "prophetic" or critical principle that stressed God's love for all people and, indeed, all creatures; fourth, they understood God to "betray a divine bias for the weak and dispossessed"; and fifth, they understood that God works in and through human sin and error (*errore hominum providentia divina*).

The monotheizing axiom (1) reminds us always to ask the critical question, whether we have made our witness or done our theology "to the greater glory of God" (*ad maiorem gloriam Dei*, as the grand old formula has it). The church, being a community of sinners as well as saints, is prone in its rhetoric and theology to formulate its witness in ways that benefit and glorify itself. Instead, our witness should glorify God and Christ. The constitutive axiom (2) reminds us always to ask how a particular piece of witness testifies to the empowering and reassuring good news of God's gracious love for this person or this community. Taken by itself, the constitutive axiom becomes exclusivist—God loves or saves only this community. The prophetic axiom (3) prompts us to recall that the gospel also declares God's love for all people everywhere and, indeed, for all God's creation and requires that we pay attention to issues of social, structural sin and questions of justice. Our faith must be both demystified and deprivatized; salvation is deeply personal, but never merely private. It involves the solidarity of all God's creatures. The prophetic axiom is inclusive, universalist.

Within this we are particularly commanded by God throughout the biblical witness, and decisively in Jesus Christ, to be concerned with (4) "the least of these," those in need of food, water, clothing, companionship, housing, work. "Truly I tell you, just as you did it to one of the least of these who are members of my family, you did it to me" (Mt. 25:40). The idea that God accomplishes God's purposes through human sin and error (5) will enable us to be more tolerant toward the sins and foibles of others who have toiled in the

---

[27]James A. Sanders, *Canon and Community* (Philadelphia: Fortress Press, 1984), 51.

way, critically appreciative of the tradition that precedes and makes us possible, and more accepting of ourselves as the forgiven sinners with whom God has to work. In the ministry of Jesus of Nazareth and the letters of Paul, we find all these motifs clearly at work.

It is worth noting that the axioms or criteria that Sanders sets forth are drawn from scripture, not imposed on it.

Theology relates to the witness of faith, whether in scripture, tradition, or contemporary experience, not as the "judge" as to whether this testimony is true, appropriate, or morally credible. Theology listens to the witness of faith, responds, seeks to enter into conversation, sometimes is transformed, sometimes questions. My friend Mike Vogel, unbeknownst to him, has taught me a lot about doing theology. Mike was a young teenager when the Nazis took him to Auschwitz and put him to work emptying trains and sorting clothing and valuables. The rest of Mike's family were killed there. Every time Mike tells his story, and he has told it thousands of times, bearing witness *against* death and curse and *for* life and well-being, he tells it with the emotional pain and freshness of the first time.

What is theology to do with this witness to life and blessing, this witness against death and curse? First, listen to it and attend to the moral claim that it makes on us. Second, set about reinventing our moral imagination. Historically, the universe of Christian moral discourse has not included Jews among those neighbors whom we are given and called to love. They have been a people with obligations, of course, chiefly to convert to Christianity. But the long, sad record indicates that Christians have seldom felt and officially denied obligations to them. So theology seeks to reinvent our moral imagination in relation to Jews, women, the environment, and all the "alienated others" of our ambiguous history. Third, theology is about not only transforming the world so that it might reflect the glory of God and bring well-being to all its inhabitants, but evoking openness among Christians to being creatively and redemptively transformed by God's grace.

"Are your wonders known in the darkness, or your saving help in the land of forgetfulness?" (Ps. 88:12)

One day Charlotte's eighty-year-old mother walked into the kitchen, looked at her daughter, and asked, "Who are you? What are you doing in my house?" Charlotte recognized that her mother was suffering from the ravages of memory loss because of Alzheimer's disease. Those of us whose loved ones have been so afflicted know what it does to its victims. Increasingly they do not know the loved ones to whom they have been long related. Because who we are is deeply involved with those to whom we are related, they progressively lose their sense of identity. Unless the church cultivates its awareness of its tradition, its communal memory, it too can lose all sense of what its identity is and who these neighbors are.

Hence, one of the conversations we engage in as we walk the path of faith is with those who walked it before us. By "the Christian tradition" we mean simply all those Christian communities in all those particular places who faithfully bore witness to Jesus Christ and made it possible for us who came along later to take our place among the walkers of the way. They are our parents, grandparents, great-grandparents in the Christian community. They were neither all-wise nor all-powerful, nor lacking in ambiguity. They were not all-wise in what they said and did in the name of Jesus Christ; sometimes they were horribly mistaken, as in what was said about and done to Jews, women, and members of other religions, and in the ignoring of nature as the world of God's creation and the theater of God's grace.

But it would be sophomoric, having learned the failings of our parents, to deny them the regard we owe them for having been the source of the only life we have. To have any life at all is to have some particular parents, with all their faults. To have any spiritual life is to stand in some tradition. We should neither genuflect to the tradition nor patronize it. It was never perfect, but in no generation did it fail to bear witness to the gospel of Jesus Christ. For all its sexism, for example, significant women played consequential roles in it, such as Macrina, the teacher of the great Cappadocian theologians.[28]

"Remembering an enchanted past," says Edward Farley, "is one way a people endures through time. Because of this remembering, a people is not forced to reinvent all truth, all wisdom, all life solutions

---

[28]See Gregory of Nyssa, *Life of St. Macrina,* in Elizabeth A. Clark, *Women in the Early Church* (Collegeville: The Liturgical Press, 1983), 235–43. For other excellent collections of writings by and about women in the history of the church, see Patricia Wilson-Kastner, et al., eds., *A Lost Tradition* (Lanham, Md.: University Press of America, 1981); and Elizabeth Clark and Herbert Richardson, eds., *Women and Religion* (New York: Harper & Row, 1977).

every generation."[29] The Christian tradition, indeed the very concept of tradition, has had heavy sledding since the eighteenth century. The modern tradition has been the tradition of the rejection of all tradition. The absolutizing ways in which the church historically appealed to and used (or misused) tradition have also come under proper criticism from feminists and African Americans. How can a feminist accord authority to a tradition that has supported patriarchy, sexism, and oppression? How can an African American recognize the authority of a tradition that scorned and derided his community? How can the tradition help them sing the Lord's song? Such thinkers represent all who recognize that the authors of ancient texts had their agendas, agendas that were often at odds with the very gospel they were concerned to articulate. And for Christians who are not deeply versed in the modern and postmodern critics of tradition, "television, the rock concert, the corporation, and the shopping mall may do" what the critics do not: "bring about a traditionless society."[30]

So, tradition brings with it its problematic status in our time. Yet simply to repeat the modern tradition of the rejection of all tradition is no solution. This solution subjects us to the ravages of memory-loss: ignorance of who we and our neighbors are, ignorance of who the God of Israel and of the church is, ignorance of what we are given and called to do. Instead of either the rejection of tradition or its uncritical repetition, let us consider another possibility: tradition as a dynamic, self-correcting, transformative force.

Let us think of "tradition" not as a noun, standing for a static thing, but as a verb, deriving from the Latin *traditio*, "to pass on." To pass the Christian faith on to the next generation is to engage in the work of the Christian tradition. For all our sins and failures, and we are all *simul iustus et peccator* (forgiven and a sinner at the same time), nonetheless others can learn the love of God and neighbor from us and be transformed by knowing that they are given the gift of love and are thereby enabled to give it to others. The Christian faith is available to us only through particular witnesses, as life itself is available to each of us only through a particular set of parents.[31]

---

[29]Edward Farley, *Deep Symbols: Their Postmodern Effacement and Reclamation* (Valley Forge: Trinity Press International, 1996), 29.

[30]Ibid., 36–37.

[31]For a particularly helpful discussion of tradition, which the argument of these paragraphs follows, see Jaroslav Pelikan, *The Vindication of Tradition* (New Haven: Yale University Press, 1984), 54–58.

Tradition as Self-Critical, Creative Transformation

The noun *traditio* suggests that when we pass on a tradition, as members of a family do when they tell stories from the family history, we incorporate people into it and give them a sense of identity and belonging, knowing who and whose they are. "Church history," said Gerhard Ebeling, "is that which lies between us and the revelation of God in Jesus Christ...Through it alone has the witness of Jesus Christ come down to us."[32] Not to know the story of those who have walked the way of faith throughout history is not to know who we are, to whom we are related, where we have come from, or where we are going. With regard to the Christian tradition, we have few choices. We can either understand it or let it shape us in ways of which we are unaware; we can be conscious participants in it or unconscious victims of it. If the latter, we will reenact the worst parts of it, those that are genuinely destructive, and will deprive ourselves of benefiting from its more authentic parts.

At whatever point we look back upon the community of faith throughout its history, we always find it in this situation: It has a tradition (or a set of traditions not easily reconcilable with each other) that it inherits. At the same time, it encounters unanticipated events in its different historical context. The new context sets new problems for the community. In the wild swings of history, with its precipitous ups and downs and monumental cultural shifts, these problems can be massive. The community of faith has to reinterpret its tradition radically in order to make sense of its new context. The biblical people, across five major cultural epochs and in the tumultuous history of the Middle East, had frequently to rethink their interpretation of the tradition in order to answer anew the questions: Who in this situation is God? Who are we? What ought we to do?

Tradition is a sense-making enterprise. The community walking its way through history has to make sense of its faith in relation to the situation in which it finds itself and to make sense of the situation in relation to its faith. It has to revise its understanding of the tradition in order to include this new situation in it, and it has to understand this situation in the light of its faith in order to know what to do in that situation. It engages in a two-way conversation between its context and its inherited tradition, with the aim of being

---

[32]Gerhard Ebeling, *The Word of God and Tradition* (Philadelphia: Fortress Press, 1968), 29.

able to answer the question: What are we, as the people of the Way, to do in this situation?

The Christian tradition is not passed on, like a stone, from generation to generation. Rather, it is a sociohistorical process that is creative, self-critical, and revisionary. It finds ways to address the word of salvation to situations that prior generations could not have imagined. Our task, and this is one reason we do theology, is to take up this responsibility for our generation and try to carry it out faithfully. Theology is, as Delwin Brown calls it, a "caregiving" activity.[33] As caregiving, theology is charged with unpacking the meanings of Christian symbols and doctrines, with examining how these meanings "might be related to actual and possible modes of life," and with evaluating, thinking critically about these meanings.[34] We do not have to answer all theological questions perfectly and for all time to come, as though we did theology in a way that would be eternally adequate. We are called to quite enough of a task without that, the duty of grappling with the daunting issues of our time. Conversation with those who went before and had to do the same is helpful.

In the prevailing culture of our day we have what Gregory Baum calls "the pluralism of the shopping mall."[35] By this he means the relativism characterized by arbitrary options, lazy thinking, and an unwillingness to be challenged intellectually. In this situation, "an unrooted person, a person not identified with a religious or secular wisdom tradition, is a prisoner of public opinion and hence unfree."[36] Such a person is also morally and intellectually confused, and from such confusion arise many of the problems that move people to seek counseling. The church is strong in its capacity to provide counseling, at ministering to those who suffer from the church's own inability to help them make sense of who God is, who they are, and what they are given and called to do. But the teaching of the Christian faith, and the theological reflection necessary to do that teaching, is the more primary form of caregiving.

---

[33]Delwin Brown, *Boundaries of Our Habitations: Tradition and Theological Construction* (Albany: State University & New York Press, 1994), 138, 147.

[34]Ibid., 138–39.

[35]Gregory Baum, *Essays in Critical Theology* (Kansas City: Sheed & Ward, 1994), 38.

[36]Ibid., 39.

Churches and Christians that take their identity from the surrounding culture are unfree to be Christian. Like Robert Lifton's "protean people," named for the mythical sea god Proteus noted for his ability to assume different forms, protean people lack fixity or boundaries and are marked by fluidity.[37] In the mythology of *Star Trek*, Proteus has been replaced by the figure of the shape-shifter, Odo, in *Deep Space Nine*. So-called "mainline" churches manifest strong tendencies to be protean, boundaryless shape shifters. Open to all influence from everywhere, citing "diversity" as their norm when confronted with any issue whatsoever, they lack identity and centeredness. They fail to recognize that some things might be incompatible with the gospel of Jesus Christ and are, consequently, averse to critical theological reflection. They waver in proclaiming a sure and certain word to their congregants or to the world. Nor do enough pastors respond warmly to the possibility of being authoritative (note: not authoritarian!) teachers of the Christian faith. Yet this is the one thing that we need them to do.

Mainline churches need to learn how to be open without loss of identity, how to be centered without being closed off to the great issues and questions and human suffering of this present death-dealing age. We can find this by rediscovering what is at the heart, the center, of its tradition. As Tillich might have put it, the church needs to rediscover "the courage to be itself."[38] For the church to find its heart (its "coeur" in French, its courage)[39] is the major theological task of our time. The church must find the courage and grace to proclaim and teach what is at its heart and what it is given and required to announce, what will build up, as nothing else can, the community of those who would walk the way of life.

The Ways of Death: The Contemporary Situation

"The thief," said Jesus, "comes only to steal and kill and destroy. I came that they may have life, and have it abundantly" (Jn. 10:10). In our time, the thief rules. The death-dealing ways of the twentieth

---

[37] Robert Lifton, *Boundaries: Psychological Man in Revolution* (New York: Vintage Books, 1970), 37–38, 43–44, 51.

[38] Paul Tillich, *The Courage to Be* (New Haven: Yale University Press, 1952), esp. 113–54.

[39] Rita Nakashima Brock develops this metaphor nicely in *Journeys By Heart* (New York: Crossroad, 1988): "To take heart is to gain courage," xiv.

century, its orientation toward death, are reflected in the realities of world hunger and starvation, ecological disaster, the still-ominous threat of nuclear destruction, the new international economic "order," classism, racism, sexism, and the continuing bias against the "other," as reflected in the church's anti-Judaism. Sin is not merely personal, but is related to structural causes, to the powerful impact of economic and political institutions that can be named, an impact that can be resisted, but usually is not. Here, perhaps the greatest personal sin is the refusal to resist the powerful. The name for this kind of sin is not "pride," but "sloth," the laziness that puts us to sleep in the face of systemic injustice.

A premise of all theologies that stand in the tradition of the social gospel, of the contemporary liberation theologies and of recent Roman Catholic social teaching, is that existing forms of government, economy, and society "are neither divinely ordained nor naturally given but are historical products of the decisions of men and women in times past as to how their lives should be governed."[40] What human beings have created, human beings can change. With that ability comes responsibility. Contends Schubert Ogden:

> Because the scope of human power and responsibility includes, in principle, the whole social and cultural order, the love for our neighbors as ourselves entailed by faith in the gospel lays upon every Christian the responsibility for fundamental change in society and culture themselves—for such structural or systemic change as may be necessary to overcome the inequality and injustice of the existing order.[41]

As long as we understand sin in ways that privatize it, hold to a view of salvation that reduces it to an individualistic and otherworldly matter (ultimate or "otherworldly" salvation should undergird and empower Christians in their this-worldly tasks), and regard social transformation as occurring in some miraculous manner, thinking that if only individuals change, the social context will take care of itself, the church will fail to address "the weightier matters of the law" (Mt. 23:23) in our time.

---

[40]Schubert M. Ogden, *Faith and Freedom* (Nashville: Abingdon Press, 1989), 21.

[41]Ibid., 22.

Five Death-Dealing Ways of the Twentieth Century

Let us call these other ways "systemic injustices" or "structural sins."[42] A systemic injustice affects an entire system, somewhat as cancer affects the entire bodily system of a human being. Structural sin attacks the body politic. A systemic injustice affects all members of a system and the system as a whole. All systemic evils are interrelated with one another, and each affects every human being and the earth itself. Let us briefly describe some structural sins of our age. This list of death-dealing ways is not exhaustive. Several concerns not explicitly mentioned here, such as homophobia, are addressed in the chapters that follow.

One is the unjust exploitation of nature in its biological, zoological, physical, and chemical dimensions. The whole ecosystem, in which human beings participate and on which we depend, is under threat. We will call this ecological threat "homocentrism," the view that only human beings are of value, and only they are to be saved. The realities are stark: Huge tracts of the Brazilian rain forest, source of much of the world's oxygen, have been destroyed since the sixteenth century. A swath of rain forest as large as the state of Indiana can disappear within one year. Air pollution, water pollution, the destruction of ecosystems such as forests and their replacement (if they are replaced) with monocropping tree farms, the destruction of species by eliminating their habitats—these are some of the major forms of the ecological crisis. Is this what an ethic of creation calls for? Is it an example of the way of death or the way of life made clear in the covenant between God and all the living things (Gen. 9:8–15)? Theology and the church today cannot be silent on this issue.[43]

Another is the unjust distribution of goods and services favoring a wealthy minority and exploiting the labor and lives of the majority of people on the planet. This is "classism," so called because it is the exploitation of one socioeconomic class by another. The powerful economic actors today are giant transnational corporations that require national governments to offer them favorable conditions and,

---

[42]The latter term is from Gregory Baum, *Essays in Critical Theology*, 189–204.

[43]Some helpful resources for dealing with the ecological crisis are: Richard C. Austin, *Hope for the Land: Nature in the Bible* (Atlanta: John Knox Press, 1988); John B. Cobb, Jr., *Sustainability* (Maryknoll: Orbis Books, 1992); Jay B. McDaniel, *Of God and Pelicans* (Louisville: Westminster/John Knox Press, 1989), *Earth, Sky, God & Mortals* (Mystic, Conn.: Twenty-Third Publications, 1990); and Charles Birch and John B. Cobb, Jr., *The Liberation of Life* (Cambridge: Cambridge University Press, 1981).

if these conditions are not met, relocate their factories in countries where labor is cheap, workers have no protection, taxes are low, and few laws protect the environment. The globalization of the economy, coupled with an ever more sophisticated technology, produces a new and growing kind of un- and underemployment. We now see less the traditionally unemployed and more of the employed but underpaid, more who are in constant danger of losing their employment, and more part-time employees without health benefits. The idea of a "living wage" progressively disappears.

In urban and rural environs we experience increasing social disintegration. Poorer countries are forced by "free" trade agreements to produce goods that are desired in more well-to-do countries, rather than those needed for the well-being of their own people. Immigration, both legal and illegal, of people from poorer to richer countries increases (as from Mexico to the United States), as does resentment toward immigrants, minorities, and women because of the belief that they take away jobs from those who used to have them. Witness the current attempts to decrease immigration and to repeal affirmative action laws that have benefited women and minorities.[44]

The result for many people is a decline in the quality of employment and a surge in the sense of insecurity. In Third World countries and the destitute parts of other countries, the grinding effects of poverty are incredibly destructive. About 30 children a minute, 1,800 an hour, over 43,000 per day die because they do not have simple nutrition or access to elementary vaccines.[45] Meanwhile, we spend more than a million dollars per minute for military purposes.[46] We "trample the head of the poor into the dust of the earth, and push the afflicted out of the way..." (Am. 2:7).

Sexism is the third structural sin, the deep and prevalent oppression of women and of all those dependent on women, mainly children and the elderly. The novelist D. H. Lawrence remarked that men are willing to accept a woman as "an angel, a devil, a baby-face, a machine, an instrument, a bosom, a womb, a pair of legs, a servant, an encyclopaedia, an ideal or an obscenity; the one

---

[44]See the discussion of these points in Baum, *Essays in Critical Theology*, 30–31, 50–51.

[45]Dr. James Grant, executive director of the United Nations Childrens Fund, as reported in the *Manchester Guardian*, 139/7 (August 14, 1988), 6.

[46]Matthew L. Lamb, "Liberation Theology and Social Justice," *Process Studies*, vol. 14 (1985): 103.

thing he won't accept her as is a human being."[47] The Christian tradition largely bought into the system of sexual status of the Greco-Roman world, with the result that it justified the oppression and subjugation of women: "Woman is naturally subject to man," said Thomas Aquinas, "because in man the discretion of reason predominates."[48] For this reason, women can be of help to men in reproduction, but not in conversation, and women cannot be ordained because they are "in the state of subjection."[49] The relation of sexism to classism and racism is shown in that the majority of the poor are women and those dependent on women–children and the elderly, and that African American women face the triple jeopardy of being black and women and among the poorest of the poor.[50] How does the church today answer Jesus' question: "Ought not this woman, a daughter of Abraham..., be set free from this bondage on the sabbath day" (Lk. 13:16)?

Racism is a fourth structural sin, the repression of millions of people who, in particular places, belong to ethnic groups that are dominated by other ethnic groups in those places. In America the chief victims of racism are African Americans, Native Americans, and Hispanic Americans, but every ethnic group, at some time, has been marginalized. The sociologist Gunnar Myrdal long ago pointed out the vicious cycle of racial prejudice and economic discrimination. With still too few exceptions, African Americans are forced into the lowest economic status that results in their having poor housing, high crime rates, high disease and infant mortality rates, and little ambition. These are then taken by prejudiced people as "evidence" of racial inferiority.[51]

How federal money is spent illustrates the relationship between militarism and other structural sins. From 1960 to 1967, for example, the United States spent $348 billion on war, $27 billion on space, and $2 billion on housing and community development.[52] The chief

---

[47]Cited in Letty Russell, *Human Liberation in a Feminist Perspective* (Philadelphia: Westminster Press, 1974), 148.

[48]See Thomas Aquinas, "On the Production of Woman," in *Women and Religion*, ed. Elizabeth Clark and Herbert Richardson (New York: Harper & Row, 1977), 88.

[49]Ibid., 96.

[50]Anne Carr, *Transforming Grace* (San Francisco: Harper & Row, 1988), 103.

[51]Gunnar Myrdal, *An American Dilemma* (New York: Harper & Row, 1964), 75ff.

[52]Louis L. Knowles and Kenneth Prewitt, eds., *Institutional Racism in America* (Englewood Cliffs, N.J.: Prentice-Hall, Inc., 1969), 119.

recipients of the service benefits of American society are the middle and upper classes. Wealthy school districts can provide excellent educational opportunities to their children, while the ghettoized underclass receives the worst of everything: "the worst housing, the worst and most ineffectual schools, the worst jobs. The only thing they received a disproportionately high share of is unemployment and disease."[53] African Americans constitute about 12 percent of the American population, but have only 7.2 percent of total U.S. income and control only 2.3 percent of its total wealth. Meanwhile, since the "War on Poverty" began in 1964, the "dollar gap" between the median incomes for African American families and white families multiplied about four times.[54] How shall the church take seriously the commandment to "love the alien as yourself, for you were aliens in the land of Egypt" (Lev. 19:34)? Do we hear the voice of Jesus: "I was a stranger and you did not welcome me, naked and you did not give me clothing, sick and in prison and you did not visit me" (Mt. 25:43)?

Militarism, the violent use of force to defend a system of unjust relationships, is the fifth structural sin and related to all the others. There is internal militarism, whereby injustice within a nation is defended by the military or the police, and external militarism, the violent expropriation of power outside a given nation resulting in oppression. Sometimes two evils collide, as when a corrupt internal militarism is taken over by an external corrupt militarism. The ultimate form of militarism is the nuclear threat, which is also the ultimate form of homocentrism or ecocide, the threat to the environment, which coincidence demonstrates the interrelatedness of the systemic injustices.

Altogether apart from potential threat, however, well over 100 million people have already been killed in wars in this century. Yet the nuclear threat is real enough. On a television talk show, Elie Wiesel, who has written poignantly of his experiences in Auschwitz, commented that during the Holocaust every Jew was targeted for death, because the aim of the Nazis was to make the earth "Judenrein," "cleaned-up of Jews." "Now," he said of the nuclear threat, "we are all Jews." The complex problem presented by

---

[53]Harold M. Baron, "The Web of Urban Racism," in ibid., 165.
[54]Theodore Cross, *The Black Power Imperative* (New York: Faulkner Books, 1984), 208.

militarism is partly that, since the beginnings of the Cold War in the 1950s, many modern countries and a good number of Third World countries have moved to a permanent war economy. We produce incredible quantities of weapons, weapons that make us less rather than more secure. We have tried to solve the problem of absolute peace, presented by nuclear weapons, by concentrating on instruments of genocide. Effective use of such weapons in a "first-strike" designed to prevent nuclear war would be suicidal for the attacking country.[55] Yet we trustingly hope that such a conflict will not happen by "accident," putting out of mind the awareness that we are protected by "software." Jesus no doubt says of us what he once said of Jerusalem, "if you, even you, had only recognized on this day the things that make for peace" (Lk. 19:42).[56]

"What contemporary ideology criticism has uncovered," says Sandra Schneiders, "is the intrinsic connection among all forms of systemic domination."[57] In plain English that means that an African American, ghetto-dwelling, single mother suffers not only from racism, but also classism and sexism. Also, she lives in the most polluted part of town, downwind from the incineration facility and closest to inground toxic pollutants. In short, we can distinguish the structural sins from each other, but we cannot separate them from each other.

Choose Well-Being! Theology for a Church on the Way

It will not be possible to deal in depth with these (and other) "signs of the times" as we make our way through the theological topics that lie ahead of us. But we will seek to relate each topic we discuss to one of them, in order to illustrate the scope of the covenant that God graciously gives us and by which God calls us to live, to indicate something of the character of Christian discipleship, and to show how theological ideas can be "helpful in life's practical struggles," as William James so nicely put it.

---

[55]Paul R. Erlich, Carl Sagan, et al., *The Cold and the Dark* (New York: W. W. Norton & Co., 1984), xxiii.

[56]Paul Tillich's *Theology of Peace*, ed. Ronald H. Stone (Louisville: Westminster/ John Knox Press, 1990) is a collection of Tillich's essays on peace that relates many of the themes of his theology to questions of war and peace.

[57]Sandra M. Schneiders, "Does the Bible Have a Postmodern Message?" in *Postmodern Theology*, ed. Frederic B. Burnham (San Francisco: Harper & Row, 1989), 67.

Throughout we will be doing theology in a way that locates the Christian faith and the New Testament within the larger orbit of the whole of scripture, so taking seriously the witness of the people Israel and recognizing that that is how the writers of the New Testament intended themselves to be understood. Those writers did not enter upon their tasks with full hearts and empty heads. They used the scriptures (i.e., what we call the "Old Testament") heavily in describing and interpreting Jesus Christ and did not assume that they always had to tell us they were doing so. They made clear not only that the things concerning Jesus Christ happened "in accordance with the scriptures" (1 Cor. 15:3), but thereby that the home field of Christian talk is the scriptures that we share with the people Israel. Christians who want to learn how to talk the language of faith must learn how to "play at home," on their home field, before they try to "play away."[58]

---

[58]Ian Crombie first spoke of words as playing on their "home ground" or "playing away." See his comments on language and analytic philosophy in *New Essays in Philosophical Theology*, ed. Antony Flew and Alasdair MacIntyre (London: SCM Press, 1955), 109–30; Crombie's use of the terms occurs on p. 111. Paul M. van Buren develops Crombie's insight in his *The Edges of Language* (London: SCM, 1972), 84.

Chapter 2

The Direction of the Way: Revelation

God and the People on the Way

Revelation, as the biblical witness testifies, is a bipolar affair. It has what Paul Tillich calls "the giving side" and "the receiving side."[1] God does the giving, and the community does the receiving. We can also call these two sides of the revelatory event (and revelation occurs in events, not "in general") the objective and subjective poles of revelation. Unless God gives it, there is no revelation; unless someone receives it, there is no revelation. Biblically, those to whom revelation is given, and who receive it, are either already walking the way of faith or are started upon the way by the revelatory event.[2] Revelation is not an "inert" thing; it gets you moving.

---

[1]Paul Tillich, *Systematic Theology*, vol. 1 (Chicago: University of Chicago Press, 1951), 111.
[2]This last comment paraphrases Paul M. van Buren in *Discerning The Way* (New York: Seabury Press, 1980), 167.

Revelation happens throughout the history of the community of faith and still occurs in the present, as it will in the future. Let us use Tillich's distinctions and refer to revelation that starts a people on the way as "original," or better, "originating" revelation. Then there is the revelation that occurs when, say, Susanna has an "aha!" experience, "sees" what she had not seen before, and enters upon the way or comes into a deeper understanding of her faith. We will call that "dependent" revelation, because while it strikes Susanna with originating force, it hinges on the original revelation.[3]

God reveals God's self freely and to whom God pleases. This is what is usually meant when theologians affirm a doctrine of "general revelation." God does this by whatever means or instrumentalities God pleases. God's doing so is a matter of what the psalmist calls God's "good pleasure" (Ps. 51:18). It is not our right to instruct God as to whom God is free to disclose Godself. To say that revelation is always an event is not to say that it cannot occur wherever and whenever God pleases. It is merely to say that it does not occur "in general." Revelation is always particular. Whether members of other religions know God by God's self-disclosure to them is a question much asked. We will take up this question later, after discussing some other matters.

The term "reveal" means to unveil, to remove the covering by which some object is hidden and so to expose it to view. The Bible hardly ever uses the term in this general sense. "Reveal" and "revelation" almost exclusively refer to God and divine things and are technical-theological terms. They are fundamentally important for understanding the Bible, which consists of testimony to or confession of the revelation of God.

God is the proper subject of revelation, God's self in God's being and works. In revelation, God reveals God's self and we are dependent on God's revelation of God's self for our knowledge of God. All human efforts to gain knowledge of God by independent inquiry are fruitless (1 Cor. 1:21: "The world did not know God through wisdom"); such pretended knowledge of God is to God's own self-disclosure as chaff to the wheat (Jer. 23:28). God is not an object accessible to our observation in the world. God is not an in-the-world being, who exists alongside other beings and is perceptibly distinguishable from them as they are from one another. God is

---

[3]For these distinctions in Tillich, see *Systematic Theology*, vol. 1, 126–28.

the One in whom the world has its being, the One from whom all things come and to whom all things return, the Alpha and the Omega. The knowledge of God must be granted us by God.

Ideas of revelation are found among most religions, with the possible exception of Buddhism. God is nowhere conceived as directly accessible in the same way as objects of sense-perception. But the Bible asserts revelation in a strict sense, according to which God is both the subject and the object of revelation. Revelation does not consist, primarily, in the disclosure of supernatural knowledge or the disclosure of the future, although it has much to do with God's promise and our hope. Neither is revelation cognitively empty. The main theme is God's revelation of Godself. Nor do we acquire revelation from God by some technique; we receive it only by waiting upon God (Ps. 123). It is a living encounter with God's person.

The Identity of God

God is the giver of revelation. What God gives in revelation is knowledge of God's own self; God is the gift of revelation. God works upon our hearts to open us to receive God's gift; God is therefore also the giving of revelation. God is the giver, the gift, and the giving. What God graciously gives is God's love; God is the lover, the love, the loving. Alternatively, God is the revealer, the revealed, and the revealing. The concept of revelation, therefore, has an implicit trinitarian structure to it; God plays three roles here. The content of revelation is the living God; this is the decisive, originating revelation to Israel (Jer. 10:10). God reveals Godself as the living and personal God whose revelation is therefore laden with mystery; for God reveals God's self as the Lord (a non-patriarchal Lord, by the way) whose ways are higher than our ways and whose thoughts are higher than our thoughts. Even in the divine self-disclosure, God remains hidden ("Truly, you are a God who hides himself, O God of Israel, the Savior," Isa. 45:15).

The personal character of God's revelation is expressed in the language of the Hebrew Bible by the name of God. The name bears a fuller connotation than we associate with it today and comes nearer to our idea of person or personality. Personal beings make ourselves known to one another by communicating our names. When God makes known God's name to Moses, God makes Godself personally known to Moses. Something like a formal introduction is recorded in Exodus 3:11–15, where the divine name is communicated to Moses. Knowledge of God's name means for those to whom it is given that they have access to God's presence in prayer. God says of the temple: "My name shall be there" (1 Kings 8:29). To know the name of God is to have a sure refuge (Ps. 9:9f.). Refuge is a metaphor for salvation; to know who God is, is part of what it means to be saved.

Let us pause a bit over this matter of God's "name."

But Moses said to God, "If I come to the Israelites and say to them, 'The God of your ancestors has sent me to you,' and they ask me, 'What is his name?' what shall I say to them?" God said to Moses, "I AM WHO I AM." (Ex. 3:13–14a)

At the conclusion of this passage, the *New Revised Standard Version Bible* has a footnote indicating that the name of God can also be translated as "I WILL BE WHAT I WILL BE." The reason for this is that in biblical Hebrew there are no tenses as such. In English we have the simple past, present, and future tenses and can say such things as: "I was speaking to her yesterday, I am speaking to her now, I shall speak to her later." In Hebrew the verbs would be the same in each case, because each states an action as going on or not completed.

In Exodus 3:13–14 God discloses God's name to Moses as *Ehyeh asher ehyeh*. This name is notoriously difficult to translate. The classical Latin (Vulgate) and English translations have it: "I am who I am," in spite of the fact that Hebrew has no simple present tense. "I will be what/who [or whatever/whoever] I will be" is much closer, but odd enough to give translators cause to put it in a footnote. What does it mean that God names God's self as "I will be who I will be"? That, if we want to know who God is, we have to pay attention to what follows in the story, to what happens, to find out who and what God is.[4]

So, God is the God who creates the world, liberates the people Israel from bondage in Egypt, is with them and leads them through the wilderness, leads them to a land of promise where they are to live by the *Torah* (a word meaning "way" or "instruction") that God gave them at Sinai, whose Torah is a light to their path, who as the *shekhinah* (literally "dwelling"–God's dwelling with God's people) suffers the pain of going into exile with the Israel of God. God is the

---

[4]For a significant discussion of the name of God, see Bernard Lee, "Sacrament," in *The Becoming of the Church*, ed. Bernard Lee (New York: Paulist Press, 1974), 209.

God whose dwelling with God's people is so radical as to be made incarnate in the Jew *Yeshua ha Notsri* (Jesus of Nazareth), in whom God took upon Godself the negativity of the sin of the world in crucifixion, yet whose presence with Jesus' community was no more annulled by that suffering than by all the suffering and death in the history of the Israel of God. The shekhinah is a rabbinic "name" for God, not another being alongside God; it is God as always with us, radically identified with us, no matter what.

The Jewish theologian Michael Wyschogrod helps immensely in understanding the revelation of God as witnessed to by the scriptures of Israel. Central to his theology is God's gracious and irreversible election of Israel as the people of God.[5] The people Israel is a corporeal reality, a physical, earthly human family, the children of Sarah and Abraham. God freely and unfathomably chose the earthly people Israel as a blessing and to be a blessing. In the people Israel, God sank a carnal anchor in the world. Had God chosen a people for more "spiritual" reasons such as their piety or conduct, argues Wyschogrod, God could terminate the choice in the event that their belief or conduct proved inadequate. Such a covenant would be what Christians have called "works righteous," a covenant made with a people based on their merits. Instead God graciously made an eternal covenant with an embodied people.

There is a rabbinic *midrash* (interpretation) of Psalm 119:124 that helps us. The psalmist says: "Deal with your servant according to your steadfast love." The rabbis commented:

> Perhaps you have pleasure in our good works? Merit and good works we have not; act towards us in *chesed* [steadfast love, grace]. The people of old whom you did redeem, you did not redeem through their works, but you did act towards them in *chesed.* So do thou with us.[6]

How, then, does Wyschogrod understand the Christian confession that God has revealed Godself to us decisively in Jesus Christ? First, he is not greatly exercised by Christian claims that Jesus is the messiah of Israel. In the history of Israel there have been numerous people whom some Jews have thought to be the messiah. Rabbi

---

[5]See Michael Wyschogrod, *The Body of Faith: God in the People Israel* (San Francisco: Harper and Row, 1989).

[6]Anthologized in C. G. Montefiore and H. Loewe, eds., *A Rabbinic Anthology* (New York: Schocken Books, 1974), 91.

Akiba thought that Simon bar Cochba was the messiah (bar Cochba led the uprising against the Romans in 132–135). Yet Rabbi Akiba remains authoritative, often cited in the Mishnah and Talmud. Whether a given person is or is not the messiah is a point on which Jews may be in error and yet continue to be good Jews.

What about the church's claim that God was incarnate in Jesus? Wyschogrod argues that Jews cannot simply disavow this claim, without denying God's freedom to be who God will be. Israel can reject this claim if it is understood to mean that in Christ God turned God's back on God's promises to Israel. But setting aside this ideological interpretation, God's incarnation in Jesus can be interpreted as an escalation or intensification of God's covenantal relation with Israel. God's covenant with Israel has always involved "a certain indwelling of God in the people of Israel whose status as a holy people may be said to derive from this indwelling. Understood in this sense, the divinity of Jesus is not radically different—though perhaps more concentrated—than the holiness of the Jewish people."[7] God had always been a God whose "dwelling" (shekhinah) had been with the people Israel; the function of the ark and the temple had been to provide God with a place to dwell, and in the exile the Shekhinah went with Israel. The language of incarnation in the Gospel according to John is that of shekhinah: that of God's tabernacling, "dwelling among us" (Jn. 1:14).

Ehyeh asher ehyeh is still ahead of us, beckoning us onward, as Jesus (whose name was "Yahweh is salvation") always was and is ahead of his disciples. Our earliest gospel ends with the young man at the tomb saying to the women: "Go, tell his disciples and Peter that he is going ahead of you to Galilee..." (Mk. 16:7). Yet the God who is always ahead of us is also always with us. "As Rabbi Hanina ben Teradion said: 'If two sit together, and words of Torah are between them, the Shekhinah rests between them.'"[8] Similarly: "Where two or three are gathered in my name, I am there among them" (Mt. 18:20). Christ is God's shekhinah incarnate among us, *"emmanuel"* (God with us: Mt. 1:23).

This is who God is.

---

[7]Michael Wyschogrod, "Christology, the Immovable Object," *Religion and Intellectual Life* 3 (1986): 79.

[8]*Pirke Aboth,* 3:2, in *The Mishnah,* trans. Herbert Danby (London: Oxford University Press, 1933), 450.

Media of Revelation

God may reveal Godself in, through, or by way of whatever means or media God pleases. God reveals God's self in history. The fundamental fact of Jewish faith is the liberation of Israel from the house of bondage and the giving of the Torah on Sinai; by these acts God makes Godself known to Israel and gives Israel to understand who Israel is, and what Israel is to do. The exodus, the wilderness, living in the land of Israel, exile, return, rebuilding, Jesus of Nazareth, and the creation of the church—all are historical events interpreted by the community of faith as revelatory of God.

God makes use of ordinary means to disclose God's self. But because God is the God who will be who God will be, ordinary means do not make use of God. Nor can God be identified or equated with any object, including the Bible, and thus turned into a thing subject to our manipulation.

God raises up prophets to speak for God and to interpret God's revelation in history and in Torah. These, by God's grace, became the great agents of God's revelation of Godself by God's word. "Word" is not the intellectual communication of abstract truth. Word means also: thing, act, event. Frequently a prophet will act out in life the word that God gives the prophet to speak. The prophet "enacts" or "embodies" the word. God's word and work are one: The word of God is the signifying aspect of God's work. The revelation of God by God's word is an essentially personal transaction, because intelligible address is the proper means of communication between persons. The Bible has theophanies as rare occurrences. Revelation is like a dialogue in which God addresses God's word to human understanding and elicits an understanding response (Isa. 6). God graciously decides to reveal Godself to the people of God not as the "wholly other" but by "one of your brothers, like unto me [Moses]" (Deut. 18:15). God comes to meet us where we are. Compare Deuteronomy 30:14 and Romans 10:8: "The word is very near to you; it is in your mouth and in your heart for you to observe." There is no need to climb to the mountaintop to find it.

Law (Torah) as a Medium of Revelation

The idea of "law" leaves a bad taste in the mouths of many Christians. The reasons for this state of affairs are numerous and to some extent understandable. Many Christians grew up in religious environments that were unnecessarily restrictive and inhibiting and react against that early experience by simply rejecting law. It is easy to point out ways in which law has been used to oppress the powerless and buttress the powerful. Those of us who participated in the civil rights movement remember how laws could be used in the attempt to suppress protest against injustice. Women, minorities, and African Americans know well how law can be both fallible and idolatrous. Is law anything more than the codification of a given society's way of organizing power and practicing violence to keep things that way?

Law can also be rejected because of the anti-Judaism that runs so deeply in Christian culture. After all, does not Christianity uproot the law from any important place in the light of faith? Is not ours a religion of faith and grace instead of legalism and works-righteousness? Did not the law fail as a means of salvation, and did not Paul say so? (That this is a caricature of Paul should be obvious.)[9] Who can be justified by keeping the law?

As Edward Farley discerningly points out, law is more complex than these objections allow. There is present in the law, he says, another voice:

> This is the voice of the other human being whose vulnerability and need are part of our face-to-face relations. Recall the recurrent themes of Israelite law: the adjudication of personal injuries, the protection of the family structure, the treatment of the stranger, the plight of orphans and widows, the oppression of the poor by the rich, the cruel and unjust behavior of kings and rulers.[10]

What Farley calls the "vulnerable other" is the one whose voice "speaks through the law." The most vulnerable other is God, the One who not only affects all others, but who is affected by all others, and God's voice also comes to expression in the law. God's relation to the law is dialectical, a matter of yes and no. On the one hand, the purpose of the law is to protect the vulnerable others, to be the social form of love of neighbor. On the other hand, laws tend to be static, and no law can be equated with God who will be who God will be.[11] Neither can any understanding of the gospel.

---

[9]For an excellent study of Paul on the question of the gospel and the law see, e.g., E. P. Sanders, *Paul, The Law, and The Jewish People* (Philadelphia: Fortress Press, 1983).

[10]Edward Farley, *Deep Symbols,* 80–81.

[11]Ibid., 82.

To be clear about the meaning of law, we begin at the beginning. First, the entire biblical story prior to the giving of the law on Sinai is a prologue. The Exodus account begins with the cry of oppressed slaves in Egypt and a loyal and compassionate God who hears their groaning. God is self-identified as "I will be who I will be," indicating that God is "that ultimate mystery who is free to be whoever and whatever God chooses to be, in whatever situation or circumstance."[12] At Sinai, God gives Israel the Torah (way, instruction, law), saying: "I am the LORD your God, who brought you out of the land of Egypt, out of the house of slavery" (Ex. 20:2). "Claim is based," says J. Gerald Janzen, "in faithful, gracious action. Law arises out of gospel, as its extension."[13] God's demands on the people Israel are expressed only after God's saving action on Israel's behalf has been recalled. Israel is justified by God's grace. Israel's sense of obligation is its response to unmerited benevolence.

Second, in the faith of Israel there is more than one term for what Christians call "law." Torah is one. Meaning "way, path, instruction," it includes more than law: narrative, ethical teachings, and religious concepts. Another is *halakha*, also meaning "way," but rich with connotations. Fundamentally, halakha is a process of interpreting and reinterpreting the law. Over time, old laws become irrelevant or fail to respond adequately to the voice of the vulnerable other in a new and different context. So each generation reinterprets its obligations. Halakha explicitly recognizes that God who gives the law also transcends it, and that no law is ever final. It is not fundamentalist with regard to law, a point to take into account. How long can some Christians confidently rely on ancient law in eternally denying rights to whole classes of people?

Christians have their own version of this, although we seldom recognize it. An increasing awareness of the vulnerable other is rousing Christian communities to rethink their attitudes toward law and to come up with some new laws. At least some are now more intentional about hiring and promoting women and minorities, and about policies and procedures designed to eliminate sexual harassment. To the extent that the church discovers its sense that the church is a church for the poor and the marginalized, it begins to take halakha seriously as disclosing God's will.

---

[12]J. Gerald Janzen, *Exodus* (Louisville: Westminster/John Knox Press, 1997), 34.
[13]Ibid., 142.

God, who is the God who will be who God will be, is free to disclose God's self through the law, itself a gracious gift, that requires us to love our neighbors as ourselves, to love the stranger as ourselves, and to invent ways of proactively standing up for all the vulnerable and protecting their well-being. Law in the service of blessing (well-being) is a blessing. When we understand the law properly, we can say with the psalmist: "I find my delight in your commandments, because I love them" (Ps. 119:47).

Jesus Christ and the Israel of God

The revelation of God in Jesus Christ has been variously characterized in relation to the revelation of the person of God in the history of Israel, the Torah, and the prophets. The revelation confessed by the New Testament is sometimes contrasted with that of the Hebrew Bible as the final with the provisional, the permanent with the transient, the perfect with the imperfect, the substance with the shadow. Indeed, some of these contrasts are found within the New Testament itself (e.g., Heb. 7–10). This way of putting the relationship calls into question the character of God: Why would God disclose God's self to Israel in a way that is imperfect, shadowy, temporary, and provisional, make with Israel an inferior and earthly covenant only to set all this aside at a later date? And why should Jews be criticized for being faithful to God's self-disclosure in the Torah and the prophets? Why should Christians place their ultimate trust in a God whom they thus characterize as untrustworthy?

Another possibility is to regard the revelation of God in Jesus Christ as the fulfillment and cancellation of the promises of God to Israel and the realization of the hope of Israel. The *adversus Judaeos* ("Against the Jews") literature of the church uses the terms "fulfill" and "abrogate" (cancel) interchangeably and synonomously.[14] This possibility also finds support in the New Testament, although not everywhere that it speaks of "fulfillment." Matthew speaks of Jesus Christ as having "fulfilled what had been spoken through the prophet" (2:17) or written in scripture. But he does so to tie the event

---

[14]For example, see Tertullian, "An Answer to the Jews," in *The Ante-Nicene Fathers* (Grand Rapids: Eerdmans, 1978), vol. 3, 151–73. At least seventy theologians of the ancient and medieval church produced such anti-Jewish tracts. A. Lukyn Williams' classical study, *Adversus Judaeos* (Cambridge: Cambridge University Press, 1935), is a fine study of the content of these tracts, although his explanations of the church's anti-Judaism are wanting.

of Jesus Christ tightly to the scriptures of Israel. He does not think that the covenant was canceled: "Do not think that I have come to abolish the law or the prophets; I have come not to abolish but to fulfill. For truly I tell you, until heaven and earth pass away, not one letter, not one stroke of a letter, will pass from the law until all is accomplished" (5:17–18). So, we may speak of "fulfillment" provided that we make clear that by doing so we do not mean God's cancellation of prior covenants. If God is not faithful to God's covenants with Israel, why should we presume that God will be faithful to God's covenant with us?

An exegetical comment is in order. John 1:17 has often been given an anti-Jewish, supersessionist interpretation. Here is the verse: "The law indeed was given through Moses; grace and truth came through Jesus Christ." In some translations the word "but" appears before "grace and truth." The NRSV is accurate here; there is no "but" in the Greek. The classical interpretation of this verse understands the relation between "law and Moses" on the one hand, and "grace and truth" and "Jesus Christ" on the other, as a contrast.

There are problems with the classical interpretation. First, God is the "giver" of both the law (*nomos*) and grace (*charis*); they were "given," God does the "giving." Second, the gospel of John never uses "law" in a negative sense. It is used in a wider sense, like the Jewish concept of Torah, to include the scriptures (10:34, 15:25).

This paragraph in John (1:14–18) speaks three times of grace and twice of "grace and truth." John is speaking out of the depths of his knowledge of the scriptures of Israel that speak of "grace and truth" more than twenty times. One of the more well known is Exodus 34:6–7, in which God proclaims:

The LORD, the LORD,
a God merciful and gracious,
slow to anger,
and abounding in steadfast
        love [*chesed*, grace] and faithfulness [truth],
keeping steadfast love for the
        thousandth
        generation...

The wider literary context of these verses explains their significance. The people have committed the sin of the golden calf while Moses was on the mountain receiving the Torah; God pronounced punishment on the people; Moses interceded with God and the punishment was averted; Moses' prayers to God lead up to the story of the renewal of the tablets that had been broken. In other words, the giving of the "law" (Torah) in the second set of tablets is nothing but grace and effects the restoration of the people. Torah, the law (teaching, way), means grace. God's proclamation in Exodus 34:67 is often reused in later texts as a quintessential way of characterizing God and God's mercy.

Note that God is "full of grace and truth," "keeping grace and truth for the thousandth generation." A rabbinic principle of interpretation held that there is no redundancy in the Torah. The double appearance of grace (chesed) is therefore significant. The second use adds an aspect not explicit in the first. God's grace is a stored grace, kept, promised for the future, for the thousandth generation. It is promised and kept not only for Moses and the people Israel, but also for all the Gentiles, among whom we may humbly name ourselves the recipients of God's grace.

Returning from our journey into exegesis, we note that defenders of the view that Jesus Christ was both the fulfillment and abnegation of the covenant with Israel stress that God's revelation to the Israel of God was prospective; it pointed beyond itself to a future consummation to which those who received it also looked forward. This future consummation, they say, has arrived in Jesus Christ, the revelation of God that discloses the meaning of the "Old Testament" revelation, of which the "New Testament" is the definitive exposition.[15] Christ stands at the convergence of all the perspectives of the Old Testament; in him all the diverse strands and fragments of revelation are gathered up into a single, significant pattern; in him the scriptures are fulfilled.

Of this view, it can be asked whether this revelation is not itself, in turn, prospective. Does it not point us forward to the eschaton, the *Basileia*, realm of God? What did Paul mean in Romans 8:18 when he said: "I consider that the sufferings of this present time are not worth comparing with the glory about to be revealed to us"? Or what did Jesus mean when he said "I will never again drink of this fruit of the vine until that day when I drink it new with you in my Father's kingdom" (Mt. 26:29)? The revelation of the God of Israel

---

[15]"Old" and "New Testaments" are here put in quotation marks because this very designation of the scriptures partakes of the traditional old/new dichotomy of the church's anti-Jewish, displacement ideology. Paul and the writers of the gospels simply referred to "the scriptures," a practice we should emulate.

in the Bible is always prospective or proleptic, a revelation of the God who calls us forward to God's promised future.

Another possibility is found in Paul. This option neither contrasts the revelation in Jesus Christ with that to Israel as the permanent with the transient nor claims that it cancels the promises of God to Israel. Rather, Paul suggests in various places that Jesus Christ functions differently for Jews and Gentiles. For Jews, he "*confirm(s)* the promises given to the patriarchs," and to Gentiles he opens up the possibility that they "might glorify God for his mercy" (Rom. 15:8–9). In him [Christ] every one of God's promises is a "Yes!" (2 Cor. 1:20). Paul never uses the term "fulfill" to state the relation between the revelation of God in Christ and that to the Israel of God. He finds scriptural warrants for his view in the Psalms, Deuteronomy, and Isaiah. Following Paul, one could develop an understanding of the decisiveness of the revelation of God in Jesus Christ as the event that makes clearest what had been meant all along, that further actualizes what had always been affirmed, but that in no way cancels or abrogates either God's faithfulness to Israel or Israel's place in God's heart. The revelation of God in Christ makes good on the original promise to Abraham that in his descendants all the Gentiles would bless themselves.

Any view of revelation that jeopardizes the faithfulness of God endangers the very faithfulness in God that it wants to promote. The view adopted in this systematic denies that the revelation of God in Jesus Christ can ever properly be turned into an instrument of curse and death against the Israel of God.

The New Testament offers three somewhat incompatible understandings of its relation to the Hebrew Bible. Therefore, the issue of how to understand that relationship cannot be settled simply by quoting the New Testament. When Daniel Migliore comments that "what God has done in the covenantal history with the people of Israel is not abrogated but confirmed and surprisingly enlarged in the new covenant in Jesus Christ,"[16] he is staking out a position on this issue, a position that is the only appropriate one to hold unless one wants to raise disturbing questions about the faithfulness of God. By contrast with Migliore, Gustaf Aulen argues the fulfillment/ abrogation solution in his systematic theology:

---

[16]Daniel L. Migliore, *Faith Seeking Understanding* (Grand Rapids: Eerdmans, 1991), 20.

The relation of Christian faith to the Old Testament religion is different from its relation to non-Christian religions, because, on the one hand, God's revelation of himself in Christ implies the fulfillment of the Old Testament religion; but the relation is the same, since, on the other hand, the revelation in Christ involves the fact that "the old covenant" is supplanted by "the new covenant."[17]

Here "fulfill" and "supplant" come to the same thing, and faithful Jews are placed in the same category as those who do not know the God of Israel.

Jesus Christ is the decisive self-disclosure of the God of Israel. Remembering the theological rule that we do all our theology and witnessing "to the greater glory of God," and remembering as well that God is not just any god but the God who is identified by pointing to all those things that God did in the history of the Israel of God, we interpret the revelation of God in Jesus Christ in the only context in which it makes any sense: the covenant between the God of Israel and the Israel of God. To confess faith in *Jesus* Christ is to acknowledge the stubborn facticity, the unbudgeable particularity of the Jew Jesus *in* whom we believe. To confess *Jesus* Christ is to confess faith in the one who takes form in the history of Israel and in the scripture of Israel. Paul argues (Rom. 10:5–13) that this Jew Jesus was the content of the Torah, which always was and is near to Israel. The promise and command, call and claim, of the God of Israel was disclosed to Jews and witnessed to by them for over a millennium before any Gentile heard the name Jesus of Nazareth. The Jew Jesus participated in and was shaped by a community and tradition going back to Abraham and Sarah. He was connected to, interrelated with, and constituted by a Jewish tradition of faith in the God of a singular promise and a singular command. He brings all that with him. Language about Jesus Christ only makes sense when it plays on its "home field" of the Hebrew Bible.

Why is it true to say that Jesus Christ is the decisive revelation of the God of Israel? The criterion of authentic revelation is the prophetic critique of idolatry. Does the revelatory event point beyond itself to God as ultimate, or does it claim ultimacy for itself? If it does the latter, it violates the prophetic standard and is idolatrous

---

[17]Gustaf Aulen, *The Faith of the Christian Church* (Philadelphia: Fortress Press, 1960), 26.

and false. If it, instead, points beyond itself to God, it is authentic and true. Jesus Christ as attested to in the New Testament consistently makes claims like this: "Whoever welcomes you welcomes me [said to the disciples as they go out on a missionary journey], and whoever welcomes me welcomes the one who sent me" (Mt. 10:40; Lk. 9:48, but the context is different). Or in the earlier form of the saying in Mark: "Whoever welcomes me welcomes not me but the one who sent me" (9:37; the obverse is in 10:16). Or: "Whoever believes in me believes not in me but in him who sent me" (Jn. 12:44).

Therefore, when we confess that "Jesus Christ is Lord," we will do so, as did Paul, "to the glory of God the Father" (Phil. 2:11), the God of Israel. Finally, the cross stands as the sign that all genuinely revelatory events point beyond themselves to God, the One who is ultimate, and do not claim ultimacy in themselves. No self-glorifying (would-be) revelatory event would undergo the scandal of being disclosed in humiliation and crucifixion. This is Luther's "theology of the cross," in opposition to all "theologies of glory." In the brokenness of Jesus Christ on the cross, all oppressive, demonic, and destructive idolatries are broken. In Tillich's metaphor, Jesus is "transparent" to God.[18] This metaphor might be better expressed in John Calvin's understanding of the scriptures as a lens through which our awareness of God is brought into clear focus.[19] We get ahead of ourselves but will come back to this when discussing christology and, particularly, incarnation, because it is God incarnate in Christ of whom we speak here, God taking the agony of the world upon God's self.

The church confesses that Jesus Christ is the decisive revelation of the God of Israel and as such is a gift to the church from the God of Israel and from the Israel of God. An implication of the doctrine of revelation is that what we know by way of revelation is what is given us to know. We do well to develop a certain humility before what is not given us to know. The main problem with all literalisms is their lack of humility. Revelation is one form of God's gracious love. The proper response to grace is gratitude, not arrogance.

---

[18]Paul Tillich, *Systematic Theology,* vol. 2 (Chicago: University of Chicago Press, 1957), 135.

[19]John Calvin, *Institutes of the Christian Religion* 1, ed. John T. McNeill, trans. Ford Lewis Battles (Philadelphia: The Westminster Press, 1960), 69–70.

An Unusual God, with Unusual Communities

When God reveals God's self, God discloses God's will, aim, intent, purpose for human beings. "I am the LORD your God, who brought you out of the land of Egypt, out of the house of slavery" (Ex. 20:2). This statement succinctly summarizes the first nineteen chapters of Exodus, all of which is prologue to God's giving of the Torah to Moses. The prologue functions to base Israel's obligations to God on God's gracious deeds on Israel's behalf.[20] Israel is to affirm God's rule over Israel by observing God's commandments (*mitzvot*). Prior to telling the story of God's giving of the Torah, Israel recites the history of God's gracious acts on its behalf so that keeping the commandments will be understood as Israel's response to God's unmerited good pleasure. Observing the Torah is the means of an intimate and loving relationship with God, of "communion with a loving and personal God."[21]God discloses to Israel a way to live that is the way of life, decidedly not the way of death.

Israel's very existence as a distinct people depends not on its own merit of any kind, but on an affair of the heart, a love. Says the Deuteronomist, "Although heaven and the heaven of heavens belong to the LORD your God, the earth with all that is in it, yet the LORD set his heart in love on your ancestors alone and chose you, their descendants, after them, out of all the peoples as it is today." (Deut. 10:14–15). Hence, Israel is to love God, walk in God's way, and keep God's commandments. Israel loves God by walking in God's way. God's Torah is born in love; God's love given voice in mitzvot.

Here we see the essential structure of biblical faith, which will be repeated in the New Testament. It is not a circle with one center, but an ellipse with two foci: the love of God freely offered to God's people and the command of God that they in turn love God and one another. The commandments, including the law of love of God and neighbor that Paul understands to summarize "all the law" (Rom. 13:9), are a form for expressing gratitude and are themselves a means of grace.

The extreme variety of mitzvot in the Hebrew Bible (orthodox rabbis count 613 of them!) is confusing to many Christians. We can understand this variety by remembering one principle: that God is

---

[20]Jon Levenson, *Sinai and Zion* (San Francisco: Harper & Row, 1985), 37.
[21]Ibid., 50.

sovereign over every aspect of life.[22] The Bible develops the fundamental commandments to apply them to concrete and particular situations. For example, because we are to love our neighbors as ourselves (Lev. 19:18), hired workers are to be paid promptly when the wages are due and not later. The reason is that the poor need the money (Lev. 19:13). This is why, in Jesus' parable of the vineyard (Mt. 20:1–16), the workers are paid immediately upon leaving the vineyard. The poor, along with the stranger, are particularly to be loved and treated justly; numerous laws seek to ease their lot and protect them from extortion. Land was to be periodically redistributed every seventh year, all debts canceled, and the widening gap between rich and poor to be reversed. Leviticus 25 describes the jubilee year with its clear effort to prevent homelessness and destitution in Israel, and Jesus begins his ministry (Lk. 4:19) proclaiming "the year of the Lord's favor"–good news to the poor, release to the captives, sight to the blind, and freedom for the oppressed.

Israel in covenant with God, says Walter Brueggemann, "embodied not only a theological novelty but also a social experiment as well."[23] The totalitarian, hierarchical social order of the surrounding city-states was rejected, and the Israelite order from Moses replaced it with a bold social experiment predicated on the claim that Israel's only identity came from allegiance to God. Its new order was socially egalitarian and politically decentralized, seeking to order society under God's intent (the kingdom of God, not some pharaoh) for human beings. Covenant, says Brueggemann, is a "subversive paradigm."[24]

Similarly, Alfred North Whitehead, speaking of Jesus, said: "So long as the Galilean images are but the dreams of an unrealized world, so long they must spread the infection of an uneasy spirit."[25] The realm of God into which Jesus invited "the lost sheep of the house of Israel" (Mt. 10:6) was a movement of the poor, the hungry, and those who weep (Lk. 6:20–21). Jesus' followers comprised a bunch of nobodies–the "children" or "little ones" of the time, the humble. He talked, shockingly, not just about a kingdom of the poor,

---

[22]Gerhard von Rad, *Moses* (New York: Association Press, 1959), 49.

[23]Walter Brueggemann, *A Social Reading of the Old Testament* (Minneapolis: Fortress Press, 1994), 18.

[24]Ibid., 43–54.

[25]Alfred North Whitehead, *Adventures of Ideas* (New York: The Free Press, 1933), 17.

but of the destitute. His kingdom was not for the rich; the camel cannot get through the needle's eye. With God, however, "all things are possible," and even the rich can be converted, just as Saul the oppressor became an apostle. It is a kingdom of weeds and undesirables; mustard is a weed and leaven is unclean. It is a kingdom of the nobodies, the beggars, the destitute, and it is here and now; it is a kingdom that is "in your midst," given freely by God, and one simply has to start living in it and on its terms rather than on the terms of the Roman occupier.[26] It was an alternative to the way of death embodied in the Roman crucifying power.[27]

A Few Helpful Hints for Thinking about Revelation

First, the event of revelation always involves an objective and a subjective pole. Something or someone is revealed to someone. We may refer to the objective side of the event as an "act of God." In revelation, God actively gives something or someone (God's own self) to the community. The subjective side of the revelatory event we will call "the response of faith," or simply "faith." Faith receives the gift of God's revelation, but never merely passively.

What is revealed may be said to be a proposition, an infallible teaching, the word of God, God's personal will or being (the grace and command of God). But revelation is always to someone, revelation is always received and interpreted. If revelation is to be properly understood, neither pole may be allowed to "swallow" the other. If the objective pole swallows the subjective, the recipients of revelation become automatons—perhaps robotic writers of inspired scripture. If the subjective pole swallows the objective, the event of revelation loses its edge—one can no longer ask what is disclosed. Extreme subjective interpretations of revelation lose themselves in talking about "feeling" and have all the intellectual content of a hiccup. Stress upon each pole enables us to affirm both that there is a "givenness" (or "giftedness") to revelation, and that what is given is always subject to interpretation by fallible human beings. Hence, reinterpretation, criticism, and self-correction of the tradition become both possible and necessary.

---

[26]This description of the rule of God is indebted to the work of John Dominic Crossan in, e.g., *Jesus: A Revolutionary Biography* (San Francisco: HarperCollins, 1993), chapter 3.

[27]If our understanding of revelation does not help us think critically about the social arrangements of the world in which we live, is it authentically biblical?

Revelation cannot be separated from interpretation. We cannot say, first there is revelation and then, later, the community interprets it. To name an event as revelatory is already to interpret it. There is no problem with this unless we believe that all interpretation is misinterpretation. But, then, how would that interpretation be anything other than a misinterpretation?

Second, faith, the receptive side of the revelatory event, will be characterized differently depending on how we understand the objective pole of the event or what is given. If the primary emphasis in what is given is on a proposition or doctrine, or set of propositions or body of doctrine, faith will primarily be understood as an act of intellectual assent to this body of doctrine. Theologians often use the Latin term *fides* as a technical term for this meaning of faith. Paul Tillich calls this the "intellectualist" distortion of faith and finds it characteristic of orthodox Protestant theology and fundamentalism; it is also present in some forms of sacramental theology.[28] Historically, faith as "assent" of the intellect to truths revealed by God is most frequently associated with Thomas Aquinas. However, if what is given is taken to be the word of God in the person of Jesus Christ, that is, if we hear Luther's proclamation that "God opened his heart to us in Jesus Christ," then faith will primarily be understood as "trust" rather than assent, as *fiducia* rather than *fides.*

For Luther this one Word is the sole center of scripture and what he really means by his term *sola scriptura* (scripture alone). This Word of God, he said, lies in the words of scripture as a baby lies in a cradle. We find the Word in the words of scripture, but we do not confuse it with the words of scripture. Rather, we interpret and criticize the words of scripture by reference to that to which they bear witness. In this way, Luther found revelation to be a liberating word, a word that liberated him (and us) from authoritarian views of scripture. Luther regarded Christ as "*rex scripturae*" (king of scripture) and as the ultimate source of all authority, not simply another authority. The word of God's justifying grace was the norm to which even scripture was subjected, and he was willing to toss out of the canon parts of scripture that did not *"um Christus treiben"* (strive with Christ, drive Christ into the heart). He wanted, in other words, a norm that stood in the service of freedom, one that was not authoritarian or oppressive, but one that defended the freedom of God to be for

---

[28]Paul Tillich, *The Dynamics of Faith* (New York: Harper & Brothers, 1957), 30–35.

God's creatures and for the freedom of interpreters of scripture and of tradition from authoritarianism. Revelation, understood as gracious, is opposed to all forms of oppression and authoritarianism.

Third, assuming that God is a person (in an analogical or "stretched" sense of the term), we may compare the knowledge gained in revelation to the knowledge people gain of one another in personal encounters. The philosopher Ian Ramsey developed his notion of "disclosure models" (as distinct from "picture models") of truth from situations of personal encounter to suggest that knowledge of God in revelation is like the knowledge of other persons. We may know a lot about another person, without really knowing that person. We come to know that person when he discloses himself to us, when he speaks and tells us who he is. Sometimes when people speak to one another, the situation "comes alive and is electrified," "eye meets eye," "the penny drops," "the ice breaks." The revelation of God is not unlike the situation in which we come to know another person—such knowledge is always a gift of self-disclosure. It must always be met with discernment and commitment; the situation cannot come alive nor "eye meet eye" without at least two persons being involved.[29]

Fourth, people who come to know one another often tell their life stories to each other. There is a narrative character to identity, and in the case of human beings that narrative character is critically important. We all have stories to tell, and if we do not know each others' stories, we do not know each other. Hence, the narrative approach to biblical study, the attempt to show how the biblical narrative renders a character—the character of God and the character of Jesus—is a promising way to deal with the objectivity of revelation.[30]

Two cautions need to be kept in mind with regard to narrative. One is that identity transcends, exceeds narrative. None of us can perfectly tell our individual stories, nor does everyone who hears our stories really know who we are. Another is that narratives necessarily exclude many parts of the story and the stories of many others in order to tell any story at all. In some respects, this is a reality of finitude: To tell any story is to tell a limited story. The story that tells all stories will never be written. For those whose stories are excluded this creates a problem.

---

[29]See Ian T. Ramsey, *Religious Language* (London: SCM Press Ltd., 1957), esp. 11–25.

[30]See, e.g., William Placher, *Narratives of a Vulnerable God* (Louisville: Westminster/John Knox Press, 1994).

This is why it is important that all the voices around the theological table are allowed to participate in the discussion of the narrative, because they will bring different suspicions with them, different questions that need to be asked and answered. We need to remember that Christians over the centuries could hear these narratives discussed in church and then go out and commit crimes against Jews and women as a result. Reading the narrative imaginatively through the eyes of those who have been victimized by misuses of it is quite important.

Fifth, rather than looking upon revelation as the antithesis of intelligibility, the sworn foe of theological inquiry and questioning, why not look upon it as what makes intelligibility and questioning possible? Alfred North Whitehead defined "rational religion" as that religion

> whose beliefs and rituals have been reorganized with the aim of making it the central element in a coherent ordering of life—an ordering which shall be coherent both in respect to the elucidation of thought, and in respect to the direction of conduct towards a unified purpose commanding ethical approval.[31]

Such a religion, he said, "appeals to the direct intuition of special occasions, and to the elucidatory power of its concepts for all occasions. It arises from that which is special, but it extends to what is general.[32]

H. Richard Niebuhr paraphrased Whitehead when he commented:

> Revelation means for us that part of our inner history which illuminates the rest of it and which is itself intelligible…The special occasion to which we appeal in the Christian church is called Jesus Christ, in whom we see the righteousness of God, his power and wisdom. But from that special occasion we also derive the concepts which make possible the elucidation of all the events in our history. Revelation means this intelligible event which makes all other events intelligible.[33]

---

[31]Alfred North Whitehead, *Religion in the Making* (New York: The Macmillan Co., 1926), 31.

[32]Ibid., 32.

[33]H. Richard Niebuhr, *The Meaning of Revelation* (New York: Macmillan, 1941), 93.

"Revelation means the point at which we can begin to think and act as members of an intelligible and intelligent world of persons."[34] Revelation yields concepts and generates thinking; the revelatory event is that event to which we ever and again return as we wrestle with whatever problems are generated for us in the intersection between our tradition and the situation in which we find ourselves having to do our thinking.

Sixth, Paul Tillich suggests that whatever constitutes the definitive revelation for us must pass the test of the prophetic principle: "A revelation is final if it has the power of negating itself without losing itself."[35] This is his doctrine of the cross. No medium of revelation may appropriately claim ultimacy for itself. When that happens, we have idolatry: a piece of finite and relative reality claiming in itself to be absolute and ultimate. Idolatry is always demonic and destructive. The definitive event of revelation points beyond itself to the One who is ultimate, to God.

> Let the same mind be in you that was in Christ Jesus,
> who, though he was in the form of God,
>   did not regard equality with God
>   as something to be exploited,
> but emptied himself,
>   taking the form of a slave,
>   being born in human likeness.
> And being found in human form,
>   he humbled himself
>   and became obedient to the point of death—
>   even death on a cross.
>
> Therefore God has highly exalted him
>   and gave him the name
>   that is above every name,
> so that at the name of Jesus
>   every knee should bend,
>   in heaven and on earth and under the earth,
> and every tongue should confess
>   that Jesus Christ is Lord,
>   to the glory of God the Father. (Phil. 2:5–11)

---

[34]Ibid., 94.
[35]Paul Tillich, *Systematic Theology*, vol. 1, 133.

Definitive revelation does not impose itself in an authoritarian, oppressive way on anyone. The name above every name that is bestowed on Jesus is the name of God: Yahweh is salvation. This revelation can only be appropriately received and understood "to the glory of God the Father," the God of Israel. Jesus Christ took shape among the people Israel and is a gift to us from the unconditional love of the God of Israel and from the Israel of God. One thing we cannot do with this gift of unconditional love is to turn it into a condition apart from which God is not free to love Israel or anyone else. Notice further that a nonauthoritarian understanding of revelation will be much more fruitful in addressing issues of religious pluralism than an authoritarian interpretation.

Is There One True Religion, or Are There Many?

Last, is there one true religion, or are there many? This is the way this question is usually posed today. To it, there are several logically possible answers. First, there is the exclusivist claim that Christianity is the only true religion, and that only Christians are granted salvation. This alternative is inappropriate to the Christian faith, to the gospel of God's love graciously given to each and all, and to the claim that the act of God in Jesus Christ is sufficient once for all unto salvation (Heb. 10). Christian faith, argues Christopher Morse, refuses "to believe that God is not free to speak wherever and as God chooses," and so rejects the idea that God is "exclusive to Christianity" and cannot be known elsewhere.[36]

Second, there is the inclusivist position that holds that indeed Christianity is the one true religion, but that the question of a person's ultimate salvation is separate from that person's participation in Christianity or personal confession of Jesus Christ. For this position, no one is outside of Jesus Christ, and God's act of atonement in him on the cross is sufficient once and for all for the salvation of all humanity. The strength of this position is that it defends the truth of Christianity without being exclusivist with regard to ultimate salvation. In this way it preserves the stress on the sufficiency of God's gracious love. The inclusive strand of Judaism has affirmed its own version of this option since the Babylonian Talmud: "The righteous from all the nations inherit the world to come" (*Sanhedrin*

---

[36]Christopher Morse, *Not Every Spirit: A Dogmatics of Christian Disbelief* (Valley Forge: Trinity Press International, 1994), 111.

105a). All people are included within the covenant with Noah and "have a place in the world to come" provided that they keep the seven commandments of that covenant. Six of these are negative commandments that can be kept while taking a nap.

Third, there is the pluralist option, according to which there are many religions or ways of salvation that are equally true (or equally false, it would seem), that salvation is available to all in their respective traditions, and that interfaith or interreligious dialogue can only proceed on this basis. This argument is not convincing. First, religions differ in their claims (and it is the claims that may be called "true") and sometimes contradict each other. Is the ultimate reality "God" as understood in Christian faith or "nothingness" as understood in Buddhism? If one of these is the case, the other would seem not to be. Second, to say that the claims of a religion are "true" implies that one has in mind a criterion of truth in the light of which this claim can be justified. What is this criterion and how, in the light of it, do we conclude that all religions are true? Pluralism never answers this question and often does not even raise it. Third, we get our idea of what a true religion is from our own, respective religions. Hence, to say that another religion is true implies at least two things: first, that we know it well enough to be able to make this judgment, and second, that we have articulated and defended the criterion in the light of which we do so.

For example, in spite of all the wonderful things we could say about Buddhist compassion, there remains a considerable difference between Buddhism and Christianity. Buddha sitting beneath the Bo tree, unassailable by "attachment" to the world, says, "He who loves fifty has fifty woes, he who loves ten has ten woes, he who loves none has no woes."[37] Christ in Gethsemane agonizes before the destructive powers of the world that will crucify him. "The difference," says Frederick Buechner, "seems to me to be this. The suffering that Buddha's eyes close out is the suffering of the world that Christ's eyes close in and hallow. It is an extraordinary difference."[38]

---

[37]From John B. Noss, *Man's Religions* (New York: MacMillan Co., 1957), 173, quoted in Frederick Buechner, *Now & Then* (San Francisco: HarperCollins, 1983), 53. (My thanks for this reference go to Sarah Barker.)
[38]Ibid., 53–54.

Probably the greatest difficulty facing the pluralist option arises from questions concerning praxis. We are willing to say that those forms of Christianity that justify and reinforce oppressive practices, such as racism, slavery, sexism, and anti-Semitism, are simply false. The gospel of God's all-inclusive love and all-demanding protection for the vulnerable denies that they are true. What, then, do we say about another religion that seems to systematically subjugate women or categorize human beings into a color-bound caste system? We might want to say that Christianity, for example, is true "in spite of" so much obvious untruth in its actual historical life. It is true by God's grace, and not in and of itself. Perhaps this is what we would want to say of other religions as well.

A fourth possibility, unfortunately without a label with which we can tag it, would hold two things: First, that inclusivism is right in unhinging the question of ultimate salvation from whether any religion is, is not, or might be true. That a child was born and died among the Apache community of North America fifteen hundred years before missionaries brought the gospel to the Southwest seems an insufficient basis for consigning it to hell. Also, doing so arguably contradicts the message of God's all-inclusive love. Second, some (which means at least one and possibly more) other religions might be true. What would be involved in reflecting on this latter statement? Consider this proposition: If the religion of Israel were untrue, then Christianity, which borrows all its ideas, themes, concepts, metaphors, historical narrative, and identifying marks of God from that religion, must also be untrue. If postbiblical Judaism, which shares these features with Christianity, is untrue, then Christianity must also be untrue. Even if one were to regard both biblical religion and Judaism as the "questions" to which Christianity is the "answer," then if the questions are "false," so is their answer. Of course, other religions regard themselves as having the answers that Christianity needs to hear.

Consider yet a fifth option. The claims that Christianity makes are true, but in confessing these claims Christians also confess that the church stands under the judgment of the revelatory events, and decisively that of Jesus Christ, to which it points. The claim, then, is that these revelatory events convey truth, and also that this truth is confessed by a sinful people who fail truly to live out and bear faithful witness to their own claims. The status of Christianity, then, among the religions of the world is that of a forgiven sinner, one who is both *simul iustus et peccator* (simultaneously justified and a sinner). Since in our history we have greatly mistreated members of other faiths–consider the Crusades, which brought death to village after village of Jews down the Rhine and Danube valleys and in Jerusalem and to Muslims in the Holy Land–this option should also command our attention.[39]

Interfaith and Interreligious Dialogue

The covenant of life and well-being that God makes with Noah and all his descendants (all the human beings), and with Sarah and Abraham and "all the families of the earth," is therefore a covenant with all the members of all the religions of the world. We stand in a covenantal relationship of responsibility to them, to be a blessing to them, to guard and protect their well-being. Ishmael, who is circumcised by Abraham but not a member of the people Israel, is nonetheless in covenant with both God and the children of Abraham. There is a covenantal pluralism, pluralism with a point of view that we have traditionally neglected. We should exercise our covenantal obligations toward members of other faiths by adopting toward them a stance of respect and approaching them in the spirit of conversation.

The way of faith at present stands before a fork in the road. One of these forks is the road to conversation between and among the religions or faiths of human beings. This is the way of life. The other is the old road of dispute, controversy, mutual denial, and hostility. It is the way of death. Early in its history, the church was a movement within Judaism. Paul the apostle, whatever his quarrels with his fellow Jews, sought to effect a new humanity of Jew and Gentile centered around Jesus Christ. Paul's letters provide us with no warrant for the existence of a Gentile church separated from the people Israel. But for most of its history, the church has been the church

---

[39]It was Karl Barth who suggested that, among the religions of the world, Christianity is a "forgiven sinner" (*Church Dogmatics*, 1/2 [Edinburgh: T. & T. Clark, 1956], section 17). For a collection of original sources representing most of the options on this issue, see *Christianity and Other Religions*, ed. John Hick and Brian Hebblethwaite (Philadelphia: Fortress Press, 1980). Schubert M. Ogden discusses the question in his *Is There Only One True Religion or Are There Many?* (Dallas: Southern Methodist University Press, 1992), although he does not separate the question of ultimate salvation from the issue of the truth or possible truth of other religions. Pamela Dickey Young's *Christ in a Post-Christian World* (Minneapolis: Fortress Press, 1995) deals with christology in relation to questions of both religious pluralism and feminism.

against the Israel of God. Its great theologians, such as Augustine, produced treatises bearing the title "Against the Jews," and its leaders worked hard for centuries at creating a Christian social identity that was other than Jewish, anti-Jewish, and better than Jewish. Christians were to understand themselves with regard to any matter in these ways.

The social policies of the churches as reflected in canon law and in the laws of the Christian Empire and the medieval states attempted to incorporate these Christian attitudes into the social, economic, and political fabric of Christendom. In Nazi Germany Hitler's lawyers found a precedent for every piece of their Aryan legislation in a law passed by a council of bishops (e.g., the law barring Jews from dining cars on trains cited the canons of Elvira in early fourth-century Spain that barred Christians from eating together with Jews). When laws and social pressure failed to convince all Jews to convert, Christians resorted to massive population expulsions from England, France, Spain, Portugal, the provinces of Germany, and Latin America. Pogroms (outbreaks of mass murder) began in earnest after the Crusades. In historical perspective, the Holocaust of our time was simply the largest and most recent of these pogroms. All in all, Christians (only nominal Christians, of course, not "true" ones) have murdered about half the Jews who have been born in the world in the last 800 years.

All this is said not to induce guilt. Christians today are not responsible for Luther's plea to the Elector of Saxony, in his last sermon, to expel all Jews from Ernestine Saxony, or for what Ferdinand and Isabella did in 1492 in ejecting all Jews and Muslims from Spain. If we Christians can see this, we can also see that Jews today are not responsible for what some Jews did in the year 30. We face choices with regard to how we talk about, approach, and deal with people of other faiths (and Christians can hardly deal with the New Testament from week to week without talking quite a lot about Jews). These choices are between approaches that lead to death and approaches that are life-giving, between those that bless and those that curse.

Regarding others as conversation partners, treating them with respect, being willing to learn and understand, being open to criticism and growth are good and healthy things. So is being able to criticize, to disagree where one must, but never understanding or approaching conversation as simply another form of warfare, a battle that, at all costs, must be won. When genuine conversation between members of different faiths goes on over time, interesting developments take place. One becomes more clearly aware of the depth and particularity of one's own faith and more genuinely appreciative of others and their differences. One becomes friends with those whom one would otherwise know only as the one-dimensional cartoon-style stick figures that one's tradition makes of them. One enters into a solidarity with those against whom one's own tradition has practiced evil. One learns the meaning of grace and forgiveness in surprisingly unanticipated ways.

"Today...I have set before you life and death, blessings and curses. Choose life" (Deut. 30:19).

Chapter 3

Light for the Path:
Scripture and Tradition

Scripture and Tradition: Authority and Interpretation

The contemporary church faces a dilemma in dealing with the authority of scripture and tradition. We seem unable to live with the authority of scripture or without it. On the one hand, scriptural authority is necessary to the church. A traditional mark of the church has been that the church is present where the "word is rightly preached." On the other, appeals to scriptural authority are often made, for example, in order to deny ordination to women, justify traditional and oppressive attitudes toward Jews, or to reject the teaching of evolution in high school biology classes.

A resolution affirming the authority of scripture recently came to the floor of the general assembly of a "mainstream" North American denomination. Sponsored by an evangelical group, the resolution, although revised by the denomination's theology commission, was rejected by a majority of the assembly's delegates. Some of its opponents argued that "authority is always used to oppress." Many members of the denomination were surprised when later they read the newspaper headline: "Denomination Denies Authority of Scripture."

This action of a contemporary church's general assembly makes clear the dilemma we face. Scriptural authority is, in some sense, essential to the church, part of its very being, its *esse*. Yet, uncritical affirmations of scriptural authority may result in worship of "the book" as holy in itself, in an authoritarian impulse (as in oppressive attitudes toward women, minorities, and gay men and lesbians), or in obscurantist rejections of science.

One particular biblical book, Exodus, illustrates this situation. No story is more pivotal to Judaism than that of Exodus and Sinai. Nor should any book be more crucial to how Christians understand themselves. Exodus, says David Tracy, "provides a proper context for understanding the great Christian paradigm of the life-ministry-death-and-resurrection of Jesus Christ."[1] Christianity misunderstands itself whenever it wallows in a privatized, depoliticized, and de-historicized faith. Exodus requires "a resolutely this-worldly spirituality as it demands a historical and political, not a private or individualist, understanding of Christian salvation-as-total-liberation."

Yet, with every text we also receive the effects of "its former receptions in theory and practice." Exodus and its message of liberation is accompanied by the evils committed upon the Canaanites and "murmurers" among the people Israel, by what happened to the Irish Catholics suffering under the rule of Cromwell, and by the "noble experiment" of the New England Puritans and the fate of the natives of North America.[2] Far from being a blameless text, Exodus reflects the patriarchal character of its society. Nor do the gospels come to us free of the "history of effects" associated with their use in Christian history, particularly the anti-Jewish effects that found their justification in the heavily negative images of Jews with which the gospels are replete.[3] In what sense, then, may we trust scripture and tradition (which latter includes the history of effects of scripture)?

---

[1]David Tracy, *On Naming the Present: God, Hermeneutics, and Church* (Maryknoll: Orbis Books, 1994), 67.

[2]Ibid., 68.

[3]The term "history of effects" (*Wirkungsgeschichte*) is from Hans Georg Gadamer. For a discussion of Gadamer's contribution to the perspective of this systematics, see Clark Williamson, "Process Hermeneutics and Christianity's Post-Holocaust Reinterpretation of Itself," in *Process Studies* 12/2 (1982): 77–93.

In What Sense Is Scripture Not Authoritative?

Scriptural authority, *in some sense*, is necessary to the church. Now we must ask two questions: In what sense is it necessary, and what sense of scriptural authority must we deny? By way of a preliminary answer to these questions, let us say this: As bearing witness to the way of life and blessing disclosed by God in the history of the people Israel and definitively in Jesus Christ, scripture is authoritative to the end or for the sake of that way of life and well-being. Whenever scripture is used in the cause of obscurantism, oppression, prejudice, racism, sexism, or antienvironmental purposes, it is not authoritative. In the first case, its use is a light to our path. In the second, it causes us to lose our way in the darkness of ignorance and prejudice.

"It was, after all," as Tracy rightly says, "the black slaves in the American antebellum South, not their white masters, who rightly interpreted the heart of the liberation narrative of Exodus."[4] Scripture and its authority are inseparable from the matter of their "right interpretation."

In order to serve the way of life and blessing, there is a sense of the authority of scripture and tradition that is hereby denied. What is denied is the old model of authority to which theologians refer as the "scripture principle." As described by Edward Farley and Peter C. Hodgson, the scripture principle was developed by Jews living in the dispersion during and after the exile in Babylon.[5] Living apart from the land of Israel, not having the temple, they substituted the written Torah (the first five books of the scriptures) and the institution of the house of study (the synagogue). This was a remarkable development in the history of Israel, providing Jews with a portable religion. Yet it was an ambiguous development.

The scripture principle is a large theological claim. It holds that scripture is a complete written "deposit" of truth that serves to legitimate all ritual and moral obligations. It locates revelation thoroughly in the past. There can be no new revelation. It holds that the text is equally valid in all its parts. It asserts that what God intended to communicate and what is expressed in scripture are indistinguishable. The texts are absolutely true and infallible.

---

[4]David Tracy, *On Naming the Present*, 71.

[5]Edward Farley and Peter C. Hodgson, "Scripture and Tradition," in *Christian Theology: An Introduction to Its Traditions and Tasks*, ed. Peter C. Hodgson and Robert H. King (Philadelphia: Fortress Press, 1985), 61–87. My description of the scripture principle follows Farley and Hodgson.

Jews managed to avoid being suffocated by the scripture principle by employing two ideas. One was that of the "oral Torah," the body of rabbinic interpretation that originally was not written down, but passed on from teacher to student and eventually resulted in the Mishnah and Talmud. Another was that of *midrash*, a word that means "to search out." Midrash was the method of reading the written Torah and finding its deeper meaning that came to be included in the oral Torah.

The later church adopted the scripture principle, in spite of misgivings on the part of some (Tertullian bitterly complained that "the Holy Spirit was chased into a book").[6]Obviously the church also revised the scripture principle by hyphenating the scriptures into an "Old" and a "New" Testament, granting only provisional validity to the "Old," and shifting the heart of the story from Torah to gospel. The method of interpreting scripture remained the same: prooftexting of the inspired "deposit" of truth and applying it to whatever was at issue.

This understanding usually lies behind claims that the scriptures are inerrant. Inerrancy can be articulated in a more nuanced way, so as to argue that if we interpret scripture responsibly and in the same way that it criticizes and interprets itself, it will not mislead us. This position, that scripture can be trusted because it contains its own self-correcting hermeneutic (method of interpretation), is the one that is here affirmed. The crucial difference between the two is simple: The traditional scripture principle is authoritarian and denies critical inquiry into scripture. The claim that scripture contains its own self-critical hermeneutic requires critical inquiry into scripture. If God, in scripture, can be questioned, cannot scripture also be questioned? Our definition of idolatry is this: An idol is anything or anyone that sets itself up as incapable of being questioned. Scripture is not an idol.

The next question is: In what sense do we affirm the authority of scripture and tradition? We affirm their authority when, and on the condition that, they are understood as containing and authorizing faithful self-questioning and self-revising. That is, when we understand what is meant in speaking of scripture as a "living book" instead of a "dead letter," we will find how scripture can genuinely

---

[6]Cited in Bruce L. Shelley, *Church History in Plain Language* (Word Books: Waco, Tex: 1982), 80.

be a light to our path and a lamp to our feet as we walk the way of life and blessing. Doing so will require us to understand the intermeshed nature of scripture and tradition in each other and their interpretation. Convinced that historical process is deeply embedded in scripture and tradition, of which a few examples will be given, we will employ some insights from process thought to look at the nature and interpretation of scripture.[7]

The Scriptural Process and a Norm of Appropriateness

We need a norm of appropriateness for guiding the interpretation of biblical texts. The lack of such a norm is a weakness in some forms of contemporary hermeneutics (methods of interpretation). The very strength of these hermeneutics, that they are aware of the developmental nature of meaning and desire to allow the various and sometimes conflicting motifs in scripture to come to expression, as Barry Woodbridge observes, "points to the need for some form of normative assistance."[8] He seeks this normative assistance in "the social context of interpretation and the possibility of the self-transcendence of this hermeneutic."[9] The social context of interpretation includes both the larger guild of biblical scholarship with which any responsible interpreter must be in conversation and the community of the church.

Woodbridge correctly notes that a large, diverse community of interpreters provides a corrective to interpretation. He accurately recognizes that interpretation is self-transcending, that no particular interpretation is ever the last word on the subject. However, neither communal discourse nor failure to have the last word guarantees that a criterion of appropriateness will be brought to bear on the results of interpretation. For example, and in spite of a very few exceptions, the community of interpretation in Nazi Germany

---

[7]Readers interested in orienting themselves to process hermeneutics are referred to the discussions found in the following sources: "New Testament Interpretation from a Process Perspective," *Journal of the American Academy of Religion* 47/1 (1979); "Old Testament Interpretation from a Process Perspective," *Semeia* 24 (1982); and William A. Beardslee's essay, "Recent Hermeneutics and Process Thought," *Process Studies* 12/2 (1982): 65–76. Also helpful for the questions it raises is David H. Kelsey's "The Theological Use of Scripture in Process Hermeneutics," *Process Studies* 13/3 (1983): 181–88, as is David J. Lull's introductory article "What Is 'Process Hermeneutics'?" *Process Studies* 13/3 (1983): 189–201.

[8]Barry A. Woodbridge, "An Assessment and Prospectus for a Process Hermeneutic," *Journal of the American Academy of Religion* 47/1 (March, 1979): 126.

[9]Ibid., 126.

supported an anti-Jewish reading of scripture. The larger community of the church had been long conditioned by the "teaching of
contempt" for Jews and Judaism to lend its support to or acquiesce
in that same interpretation.

An insight that makes it possible for us to arrive at a norm of
appropriateness stresses that scripture itself is the result of, embedded in, and results in a long historical process of interpretation and
reinterpretation. "Tradition" derives from its Latin root, *traditio*, "that
which is handed on." This "handing on" is no static procedure by
which we merely pass on, unrevised, what we earlier received. No
one has better seen the critical/constructive character of tradition
than Schubert M. Ogden:

> ...no religious tradition can long continue as a vital source
> of faith and life unless it is critically appropriated in each
> new historical situation. The importance of such tradition
> always lies in the precious freight of meaning it bears, not in
> the forms of expression through which that meaning is borne
> from the past to the present. All such forms are only more
> or less adequate to the actual occurrence of tradition, and
> they are to be retained, if at all, only because or insofar as
> they still make possible the "handing over" which the word
> "tradition" (*traditio*) originally signifies. Since whether any
> given forms of expression continue to serve this purpose is
> determined by our ever-changing historical situations, the
> more radical the changes from one situation to another, the
> more urgent and far-reaching the task of a critical interpre-
> tation of the tradition.[10]

Although Ogden's remarks are made in the service of defining
the contemporary theological task, they describe how the biblical
and post-biblical traditions themselves developed. The Bible, as
James Barr argues, "is the product of a long process of formation
and revision of *traditions*."[11] It is the "final precipitate from this long
fluid state of tradition."[12] Before there were "scriptures" in the sense
of "writings," there were traditions, both oral and written. Before

---

[10]Schubert M. Ogden, "Toward a New Theism," in *Process Philosophy and Christian Thought*, ed. Delwin Brown, Ralph E. James, Jr., and Gene Reeves (Indianapolis: Bobbs-Merrill, 1971), 173.

[11]James Barr, *The Scope and Authority of the Bible* (Philadelphia: The Westminster
Press, 1980), 58.

[12]Ibid.

there was a "Bible" there were books; the canon of the New Testament was late, only being formally established in the western church around the year 400. The Roman Catholic Church did not define its canon of the Old Testament until the Council of Trent (1545–1563) in response to Protestant rejection of the Apocrypha. But establishment of the canon did not so much stop the critical/creative development of church tradition as change its character, enabling other pre-canonical tradition to disappear from view and rendering the post-canonical tradition exegetical.[13]

Barr would revise the traditional model "God–>revelation –>scripture–>church" to this: "God–>people–>tradition–>scripture," with revelation "deriving from all stages alike" rather than being simply located in the past.[14] In light of his own remarks, however, his model should probably be revised to read: "God–>people –>tradition–>scripture–>post-scriptural tradition," with the latter understood as extending to the present and into the future and with revelation "deriving from all stages alike." Also, the people are involved in each stage. Barr recognizes that the standard way in which we approach scripture has been "dominated by *the past*," whereas the "functioning of the Bible is much more directed toward *the future.*"[15]

Because scripture and tradition are constantly involved in dialogue with the contemporary situation, process hermeneutics similarly claims that "what the text might come to mean can theoretically be more important than anything the text has meant in the past."[16] On one level, the Bible tells the story of the past; on a deeper level, it speaks of and for the future. Stories are never told of Sarah and Abraham, of the prophets, or of Jesus simply to relay information about past events, but to describe the life of faith today. Stories are told to indicate how God's word intersects contemporary events, or to re-present the voice of the living Christ to a community of contemporary readers/hearers (for centuries the Bible was read aloud, not silently to oneself; indeed, silent reading developed slowly).[17]

---

[13]Ibid., 59.

[14]Ibid., 60.

[15]Ibid.

[16]Barry A. Woodbridge, "An Assessment and Prospectus for a Process Hermeneutic," *Journal of the American Academy of Religion* 47/1 (March, 1979): 124.

[17]See Paul J. Achtemeier, "*Omne verbum sonat*: The New Testament and the Oral Environment of Late Western Antiquity," *Journal of Biblical Literature* 109/1 (Spring, 1990): 3–27.

Amidst all this interpretation and reinterpretation for new situations, the need for a norm of appropriateness is critical, lest interpretation go badly awry. "Tradition" means "to pass on." The word "traitor," which is related to a similar root (*traditor*), reminds us that a heritage can be passed on in ways that betray it. We find such a norm in what James A. Sanders calls "canonical criticism," which focuses on the "canonical process":

> The model canonical criticism sponsors as more nearly true to what happened, and what happens, is that of the Holy Spirit at work all along the path of the canonical process: from original speaker, through what was understood by hearers; to what disciples believed was said; to how later editors reshaped the record, oral or written, of what was said; on down to modern hearings and understandings of the texts in current believing communities.[18]

This canonical process was and is one in which the believing community "contemporized earlier value-traditions to their own situation."[19] The whole of scripture is such "adaptable wisdom," contemporized (reinterpreted) for different situations because in each situation people needed "to know ever anew *who they were and what they should do*," amid the changes of history, culture, and fortune.[20] This process of contemporization "was there from the start and continues unabated through and after the periods of intense canonical process of stabilization."[21] Phyllis Trible's comment, "All scripture is a pilgrim wandering through history, engaging in new settings, and ever refusing to be locked in the box of the past," nicely captures the sense of scripture and its subsequent interpretation as an adventure.[22]

Sanders finds a hermeneutic running through the biblical authors and editors, a hermeneutic that is the Bible's "self-corrective apparatus."[23] This self-corrective, self-critical hermeneutic guided the critical and new interpretations generated by the biblical

---

[18]James A. Sanders, *Canon and Community* (Philadelphia: Fortress Press, 1984), xvii.

[19]Ibid., 27.

[20]Ibid., 28.

[21]Ibid., 31.

[22]Trible is cited in Sanders, Ibid., 41.

[23]Ibid., 46; the following description of Sanders' canonical criticism depends on pp. 51–59.

communities over five different cultural eras of tumultuous change, from the Bronze Age to the Roman era. The conspicuous features of it are: (1) It is a *monotheizing* literature (as Israel was influenced by and borrowed from her neighbors, Israel struggled to monotheize what was borrowed, affirming God's oneness); Israel used a "broad theocentric hermeneutic," in which there were two axioms, (2) the *constitutive* axiom that bespeaks God's love for Israel or the church, and (3) the *prophetic axiom* that manifests God's love for *all* God's people (and creatures).

The constitutive axiom was brought into play when the community was in distress and needed to be reminded of God's special (but not exclusive) love for it, the prophetic when the community thought God loved it exclusively and needed to be reminded of God's love for each and all, as well as of God's command that justice be done to each and all. The constitutive axiom gives voice to God's singular love, graciously offered, the prophetic to God's singular command, understood as calling for the proper response to God's grace. (4) "*God betrays a divine bias for the weak and dispossessed.*"[24] This is a pervasive if not omnipresent axiom of biblical hermeneutics, and a necessary articulation of the prophetic axiom lest the latter be rendered abstract to economically and socially privileged readers. (5) It assumes that God always works through human sin and error (*errore hominum divina providentia*).

Canonical criticism enables us to affirm the developmental nature of biblical tradition without falling into the relativism in which such an affirmation might result. It allows us to affirm the authority of scripture without locking ourselves into rigid adherence to past interpretations that leave us unable to address a living word to the present. We can formulate the axioms of canonical hermeneutics more crisply by claiming that the good news that runs throughout scripture is the promise of the love of God graciously offered to each and all, and the command of God that we love God in return with all our selves and our neighbors (*all our neighbors*) as ourselves. Love for the neighbor implies and requires justice to the neighbor, lest love become the formal and empty sentimentality to which it has so often degenerated in Christian history. It is salutary, however,

---

[24]Ibid., 54; italics Sanders'.

to keep before us the reminder of God's bias for the weak and dis-possessed. So the gospel is an ellipse with two foci, the grace and command, gift and claim of God, neither of which may be forgot-ten, both of which are definitively made clear in Jesus Christ. This formulation, the theocentrically, and therefore christocentrically, understood gospel of the promise of God lovingly offered to each and all, and the command of God that justice be done to each and all, we shall take as our norm of appropriateness for guiding inter-pretation. We find this norm decisively, but not exclusively, mani-fest in Jesus Christ.

Scripture: Telling Stories against Itself

Genesis 16 tells the story of Sarai, Abram, and Hagar, "an Egyp-tian slave-girl." Sarai was unable to conceive, so she gave Hagar to Abram that by her she might have children (Gen. 16:3). She con-ceived, "looked with contempt" on Sarai, as a result of which Sarai "dealt harshly" with her, and Hagar fled into the wilderness. An angel of the Lord found her and said three things to her: Return to your mistress, submit to her, and I will multiply your offspring. Her son is named Ishmael because God has "heard" (*shamà*) her afflic-tion. "He shall be," said the angel, "a wild ass of a man..." (Gen. 16:12). "Her child," comments J. Gerald Janzen, "born in her servi-tude, will be free: He will be a wild ass of the wilderness, not a domestic; he will not be under anyone's power."[25]

There are two lessons to this story. The first is that the people who had been given and called to be a "community of promise and hope, of redemption and liberation...is itself capable of becoming a community of oppression." The second is that "Israel's story includes within it this episode which Israel tells against itself." Such stories contain "elements that should guard against that story becoming an ideological weapon against other peoples."[26]

The subsequent story, of Sarai's conceiving and giving birth to Isaac, also contains a surprise. In a patriarchal culture, the firstborn son of the father was the one to inherit. The rule of primogeniture meant that Ishmael as Abram's first born son should inherit. But God blesses Sarai, gives her a new name (Sarah), and says to Abraham "I will give you a son by her" (Gen. 17:16).

---

[25]J. Gerald Janzen, *Abraham and all the Families of the Earth: Genesis 12–50*, 45.
[26]Ibid., 47.

"With one stroke," comments Janzen, "God subverts two of the bases of patriarchal identity and power: (1) primogeniture is displaced, and (2) inheritance is tied to the mother as well as to the father." In the prior paragraph (Gen. 17:9–14), God introduced circumcision as the sign of an everlasting covenant. If in a patriarchal world, the male generative organ was "the instrument and symbol of conventional wisdom and power," then "circumcision may be the mark of a radical reconception of the wisdom and power at the base of God's new society and indeed of creation itself."[27] Patriarchal as the Bible is, in places it topples patriarchy, thus providing its own self-critique.

A Story of Blessing-in-Difference

We have inherited a major problem for biblical interpretation from the Christian tradition. Beginning in the second century, such thinkers as Justin Martyr (ca. 100–ca. 165) and Irenaeus of Lyon (ca. 130–ca. 165) created what R. Kendall Soulen calls "the standard canonical narrative."[28] A canonical narrative is "a framework for *interpreting* the biblical canon," a decision "about how the Bible 'hangs together' as a whole."[29] The standard narrative follows the classical creeds of the church: creation, fall, redemption. The basic story is one of God's creating the world, telling "how God having created the first parents [Adam and Eve] initially proposed to consummate or perfect and fulfill them by bringing them to eternal life."

But God's work immediately underwent a disastrous onslaught in the fall, which let loose the devastating forces of sin, death, and evil upon Adam and Eve and the good creation. Subsequent to this disaster, God "graciously resolved to engage humankind specifically as Redeemer in Christ," both to deliver from sin and perfect human beings.[30] How Christians understand the relation of creation and redemption, and the relation of the scriptures of Israel to the writings of the apostles to each other, is deeply shaped by this model.

In order to tell this story of creation–>fall–>redemption, the church needs Genesis 1 and 2 (creation), Genesis 3 (fall), and the

---

[27]Ibid., 51.

[28]R. Kendall Soulen, *The God of Israel and Christian Theology* (Minneapolis: Fortress Press, 1996), 19.

[29]Ibid., 13.

[30]Ibid., 15.

New Testament. Hence, the serious shortcoming of the standard narrative is apparent: "It makes God's identity as the God of Israel largely indecisive for shaping theological conclusions about God's enduring purposes for creation." The story supports a "Gnosticism of history," according to which God's redeeming action in Jesus Christ liberates Jesus' followers from the history of the God of Israel with the Israel of God. And the story "fosters and supports a triumphalist posture toward the Jewish people," a displacement, supersessionist posture. Its further costs are "a loss of biblical orientation for Christian theology," and a "loss of creative theological engagement with the hard edges of human history."[31]

As an alternative to the standard narrative, Soulen suggests that the story of fall and redemption presupposes a more basic story, that of an "economy of consummation based on the Lord's blessing."[32] God promises well-being that includes all of life (peace, economic sufficiency, health, safety, fertility, God's loving presence) and makes for the fullness of human life. The fullness of human life is a gift from the fullness of God's life.

Soulen's crucial insight is that God's aim to engender fullness of life necessitates "*economies of mutual blessing between those who are different.*"[33] Blessing is a gift from an Other who is God; it is to be received, not seized. Blessing is to be shared with others who are different, not hoarded. The two great blessings in Genesis are given to creation itself and to Abraham and "all the families of the earth." Adam and Eve, man and woman, are blessed in their difference from and relationship to one another; together they are blessed in their difference from and their relationship to "all the living things." God's blessing on Israel is for the sake of those who are not Israel, all the Gentiles. God gives Israel the Torah as a means of blessing and life; "I am setting before you today a blessing and a curse: the blessing, if you obey the commandments…, and the curse, if you do not obey…" (Deut. 11:26–28). The eschatological goal of God's efforts is "that future wherein the blessing promised by God in the past is finally realized in all its fullness."[34]

The church has long had difficulty accepting difference. Rather than looking upon difference as an occasion of mutual blessing, we have tended to look upon it as something alien and to be feared.

---

[31]Ibid., 17.
[32]Ibid., 115.
[33]Ibid., 116; italics are Soulen's.
[34]Ibid., 130.

Jews, women, racial minorities, members of other religions, nature itself, other kinds of Christians, all have been targets of our tendency to vilify and demonize the other.[35] Were we to relocate the Christian story within the larger context of God's purpose of blessing all creation with well-being and shalom, we might overcome our propensity to think that otherness is evil and learn, instead, that reconciliation is divine.

Interpretation: Examples

When we turn to the interpretation of particular passages, we should not to rush to label them "inappropriate" because they seem to violate the norm. There are in Paul, for example, several passages that clearly claim that we are judged by our works. In dealing with the various sins committed by some in the church at Corinth, Paul argued that transgression would bring suffering and death (1 Cor. 11:27–34), that punishment and exclusion should be meted out by the community, particularly for those who commit incest (*porneia*) (1 Cor. 5:5, 9–13), that reward and punishment would be meted out at the judgment (1 Cor. 3:5–4:6), and that Christians can lose their status by committing the sins of idolatry or sexual immorality (1 Cor. 6:9–10).

One could read all such passages (assuming that we have correctly understood them) as simply "works-righteous," and dismiss them as inappropriate. Or one could read them works-righteously and use them to affirm a "reward and punishment" understanding of the gospel. We need, instead, to remember a few things. First, neither Paul nor other biblical writers presented their thought as systematicians, always carefully balancing all the proper themes in one coherent statement. They wrote as homileticians or rhetoricians, saying whatever needed to be said to make the point. Because Paul's gospel affirmed both the singular grace and the singular command of God, it is not difficult to see that sometimes we find the one emphasis in some passages, the other in others. Paul does think, as E. P. Sanders says, "that Christians should behave correctly, and one of the words which he uses to indicate that behavior is 'law': they should fulfill the law."[36] Indeed, the whole law is summarized in the

---

[35]See Elaine Pagels, *The Origin of Satan* (New York: Vintage Books, 1995).

[36]E. P. Sanders, *Paul, the Law, and the Jewish People* (Philadelphia: Fortress Press, 1983), 113.

command to love the neighbor (Gal. 5:14), and Paul, the Pharisee, never forgot what was included in the summary. God is the gracious and primordial creator and consummator of our being and becoming, the one who calls us forward to a new and transformed life; God does not require us to become anything the possibility of which God does not graciously give to us. Yet God does have an aim in view for us, and missing it is sin. The inverse procedure would apply to any passage that articulated a view of grace devoid of any command on God's part. By itself, grace that requires nothing by way of response is not worth getting excited about, it is "cheap grace." Any such passage, should we find one, would have to be held in tension with the other pole of the gospel.

Concern with Credibility

We need to be concerned not only with appropriateness, but with moral and intellectual credibility as well.[37] These three criteria (appropriateness, credibility, and moral plausibility) are not separate from one another. We might better speak of one complex criterion with three relatively distinct aspects. The gospel of the promise of God's love freely and decisively offered to each and all in Jesus Christ and the command of God that justice be done to each and all is not only the norm of appropriateness, but clearly contains a strong moral component. So to say that an interpretation of scripture must be morally credible simply highlights part of what is involved in saying that it must be appropriate to the gospel.

What many see less clearly is that the gospel also requires us to make sense. By "making sense" I mean simply saying what we mean by what we say and giving reasons why that is worthy of being accepted. Doing so makes possible an ongoing conversation. We "make sense" within a community of interpretation. We do not come up with the final, definitive word for all time. Within the process of reinterpretation that goes on in scripture itself, sense-making is a central concern. One reason why Israel and the church reinterpreted their traditions from generation to generation was to "make sense" of the new situations in which they found themselves in the light of their traditions and to "make sense" of their traditions in the light of

---

[37]See, e.g., Schubert M. Ogden, *On Theology* (San Francisco: Harper & Row, 1986), 4–6.

their new situations. To accomplish this double task, they had to interpret the new situation in the light of the tradition, and they had to reinterpret the tradition in light of the new situation in order to accomplish the first task. Luke-Acts, for instance, clearly seeks to come to terms with the delay of the *parousia* as well as with the enduring power of the Roman Empire and reinterprets the apocalyptic thrust of the Christian tradition accordingly.

We can clearly see, in a microcosm, this kind of interpretation going on in Matthew 7:7–11 and Luke 11:9–13.[38] This passage is about prayer, and it *promises* that if we ask, it *will* be given us; if we seek, we *will* find, if we knock, it *will* be opened to us. Reasoning from the lesser to the greater, it argues: "If you then, who are evil, know how to give good gifts to your children, how much more will your Father in heaven give *good things* to those who ask him" (Mt. 7:11). I emphasize the words "good things," because in Luke these are virtually the only words that are changed from Matthew. In Luke the closing question reads: "If you then, who are evil, know how to give good gifts to your children, how much more will the heavenly Father give *the Holy Spirit* to those who ask him" (Lk. 11:13).

At this point, Luke, written later, differs from Matthew. Why would Luke make such a change? For the reason that if the content of the promise "Ask, and it will be given you" is "good things," Luke was probably aware that many people prayed to God for all sorts of good things and did not receive them. We know the same. Many pious Jews and devout Christians died in Auschwitz, praying for a deliverance that did not come; many Africans died in slavery praying for a liberation that came too late. Many a family has prayed for the life of a child, and regarded the prayer as "unanswered." Perhaps they thought God said no. Luke saw that if the promise of prayer was that God would give us all the "good things" for which we ask, then the promise seems to be false.

But Luke takes responsibility for the truth claims of the Christian faith and revises his understanding of the promise: It *is* true that if you ask, you will be given, that everyone who seeks finds. Yet, what we should ask for is not "good things," but "the Holy Spirit." If we understand how to pray as we ought, we will not ask God to give

---

[38]This discussion is dependent on Schubert M. Ogden's discussion of the same passages in *Rockefeller Chapel Sermons*, comp. Donovan E. Smucker (Chicago: The University of Chicago Press, 1966), 98–109.

to us the sorts of things that we are responsible for providing for ourselves. We will ask God for the one thing that God and God alone can give us, God's own personal presence to our spirits, the companionship of God's Holy Spirit. If we understand prayer appropriately, we know that its promise must be true. The process of reinterpretation internal to scripture is concerned with intelligibility for the sake of appropriateness, for the sake of the promise and command of the gospel. This concern for credibility does not stop with the close of the canon. As with appropriateness and moral plausibility, we must constantly subject our interpretations of the Christian tradition to critical review.

The people of the Bible "needed to know ever anew," said Sanders, "who they were, and what they should do." We need ever anew to know the same things: Who are we, and what should we do? We recall our earlier discussion of what Whitehead called "rational religion," and what H. Richard Niebuhr, paraphrasing him, called "revelation." Whitehead said that rational religion seeks to make possible "a coherent ordering of life...both in respect of the elucidation of thought and in respect to the direction of conduct towards a unified purpose commanding ethical approval."[39] After quoting this definition of rational religion, H. Richard Niebuhr spoke of revelation as "that special occasion" from which

> we also derive the concepts which make possible the eluci-
> dation of all the events in our history. Revelation means this
> intelligible event which makes all other events intelligible...
> revelation means the point at which we can begin to think
> and act as members of an intelligible and intelligent world
> of persons.[40]

Avoiding Unnecessary Abstractness

The virtual disappearance of the practice of reading aloud threatens to bring a certain abstractness into our interpretation of scripture. Too many interpreters are tone-deaf; they do not resonate to the music of the passage. Structural linguists remind us that, even now, written language is both rare (in comparison to the quantity of

---

[39]Alfred North Whitehead, *Religion in the Making* (New York: Meridian Books, 1960), 30.

[40]H. Richard Niebuhr, *The Meaning of Revelation* (New York: Macmillan, 1941), 93–94.

speech) and highly abstract. Written language is that of "sight," says Whitehead, speech that of "sound."[41] When someone speaks to us, we know how she feels about what she says by where she puts the stress in her remarks. Paul J. Achtemeier emphasizes that the culture of late Western antiquity, well into the early medieval period, was one of "high residual orality, which nevertheless communicated significantly by means of literary creations."[42] Modern scholars have been led "to overlook almost entirely how such an oral overlay would affect the way communication was carried on by means of written media."[43]

Not only has there long persisted in the church a preference for oral over written traditions but, for the first several hundred years of church history, the general practice was to read aloud.[44] Writings were written to be read aloud, were received orally and read aloud, and the "actual writing must have been accompanied by an oral performance of the words *as they were being written down*."[45] That most writing, as in the case of Paul's letters, was dictated to a scribe underlines this point. To read was to read aloud; Philip "heard" the Ethiopian reading from Isaiah (Acts 8:30). As late as the fourth century, the fact that Ambrose of Milan could read silently generated conjecture and remarks. "Reading was therefore oral performance *whenever* it occurred and in whatever circumstances. Late antiquity knew nothing of the 'silent, solitary reader.'"[46]

What this has to do with hermeneutics is fairly straightforward. Augustine, in his comments on biblical interpretation, reminds us that to understand a biblical text one must decide how to "pronounce" it.[47] This emphasis has returned in what Charles Blaisdell calls "tone of voice" exegesis.[48]

---

[41]Alfred North Whitehead, *Modes of Thought* (New York: The Free Press, 1938), 36.

[42]Paul J. Achtemeier, "*Omne Verbum Sonat*," 3.

[43]Ibid.

[44]Ibid., 15.

[45]Ibid.

[46]Achtemeier, "*Omne Verbum Sonat*," 17.

[47]Augustine, *On Christian Doctrine*, trans. D. W. Robertson, Jr. (Indianapolis: Bobbs-Merrill, 1958), 79, 81.

[48]Charles R. Blaisdell, who coined the expression "tone of voice exegesis," provides an example of its possibilities in "Speak to the Heart of Jerusalem: The 'Conversational' Structure of Deutero-Isaiah," *Encounter* 52/1 (Winter, 1991). The application, in what follows, of "tone of voice" exegesis to the story of the healing of the centurion's servant was made by Blaisdell in his sermon "A Gruff God?" preached at Christian Theological Seminary on October 4, 1988.

We see how "tone of voice" exegesis works by looking at the story of Jesus' healing of the centurion's servant (Matt. 8:5–13//Luke 7:1–10). The centurion tells Jesus that he need not come to his house to do the healing: "Only speak the word and my servant will be healed." The centurion reasons that "I also am a man under authority, with soldiers under me; and I say to one, 'Go,' and he goes, and to another, 'Come,' and he comes, and to my slave 'Do this,' and he does it." Jesus "was amazed" at the centurion's remarks and said, "Not even in Israel have I found such faith."

If we think about how to pronounce the story, how to emphasize it in reading it aloud, how would we inflect it? Where would the stress fall in the line: "Not even in Israel have I found such faith"? Is Jesus saying that he found no trust in God's healing power in all of Israel, or is he saying that in all of Israel he never found a Jew who thought God was a general? Would he not have found in Israel "instead a God who is described in Isaiah as enfolding Israel in her arms, as holding Israel up that it might walk, sustaining Israel that it might not be faint or weary"?[49] There are two theological and scriptural reasons for asking this question. One is that if healing (salvation) is dependent on having the right kind of faith, the text proclaims a works-righteous understanding of salvation. Another is that we are given reason, elsewhere, to believe that Jesus rejected precisely the understanding of things that this text puts in the mouth of the centurion:

> "You know that among the Gentiles those whom they recognize as their rulers lord it over them and their great ones are tyrants over them. But it is not so among you; but whoever wishes to become great among you must be your servant, and whoever wishes to be first among you must be slave to all." (Mk. 10:43–44; Mt. 20:26–27; Lk. 20:26)

The usual interpretation of the healing of the centurion's servant is both works-righteous and anti-Jewish. It buys "into a military model of the nature of God, a model full of threat and coercion, and…read[s] out scriptures in a way so wooden that it does us and them no honor."[50] A more sensitive interpretation might read the story as the gracious gift of healing (salvation) to the servant in spite of the centurion's clearly patriarchal understanding of power.

---

[49]Blaisdell, "A Gruff God?" 3.
[50]Ibid.

Locating Jesus in Context

This discussion leads naturally into the next feature of process hermeneutics. Because it rejects a misleading abstractness and affirms the socio-temporal relationality of all things actual, process thought turns a critical eye upon all attempts to understand the historical Jesus by way of isolating him from his context, which inevitably in this case means his Jewish context. We cannot understand anything out of context, and the first context for understanding Jesus is the covenant between the God of Israel and the Israel of God. The second is the Christian community to whom Jesus reveals the all-inclusive grace of the God of Israel.

To understand Jesus, therefore, we must set him in, not against, his circumambient environment in the Judaisms of the first century, particularly that of Galilee.[51] The famous "criterion of dissimilarity," which new-questers of the historical Jesus long used to decide which teachings in the gospels could be considered as actually having come from Jesus, methodologically ruled out, in principle, all sayings that Jesus had in common with the Judaisms of his time or before. By the same token it disallowed all sayings that could be considered as reflecting the interests and needs of the later church that collected the sayings.[52] The problem with using the criterion of dissimilarity to reconstruct the historical Jesus is that, as a result of it, "he becomes the embodiment of abstract principles that belong to neither history nor culture."[53] By overcoming the anti-Jewish abstractness of the historical Jesus methodologically alienated from what Bernard E. Meland calls his "communal ground of being," a process hermeneutic goes far toward overcoming the grounds for the "teaching of contempt" for Jews and Judaism that often come to expression in commentary on Jesus of Nazareth.[54]

---

[51]See Clark M. Williamson, *Has God Rejected His People?* (Nashville: Abingdon, 1982), chap. 1. See also Bernard J. Lee, *The Galilean Jewishness of Jesus* (New York: Paulist Press, 1988).

[52]For a clear definition and application of the criterion of dissimilarity, see Norman Perrin, *Rediscovering the Teaching of Jesus* (New York: Harper & Row, 1976), 43.

[53]Theodore J. Weeden, "The Potential and Promise of a Process Hermeneutic," *Encounter* 36/4 (Autumn, 1975), 318.

[54]For Meland's "communal ground of being," see *Fallible Forms and Symbols,* passim; for locating Jesus concretely in context as a corrective to christology, see Clark M. Williamson, *Has God Rejected His People?* chap. 1.

Interesting Propositions

Whitehead's theory of propositions holds, as do most such theories, that "a proposition must be true or false."[55] Nonetheless, being true or false is only one of the jobs of a proposition. More basically, propositions "are the tales that perhaps might be told about particular actualities."[56] As such, "its own truth, or its own falsity, is no business of a proposition."[57] Truth is the business of judgments, which test propositions in a variety of ways in order to determine which are true. "In the real world it is more important that a proposition be interesting than that it be true. The importance of truth is that it adds to interest."[58]

Process hermeneutics employs Whitehead's understanding of the role of propositions to interpret biblical texts, regarding these texts either as housing propositions or as being, themselves, complex propositions. As such, biblical texts function as proposals for ways of understanding features of "objective reality, as important for the reader's 'forms of subjectivity.'"[59] The text, altogether apart from whether in this or that respect its proposition is true, nonetheless invites the readers and hearers to understand themselves differently in relation to whatever feature of objective reality the text sets forth as important. The text may purport to describe historical events, the significance of Jesus, a miracle, the power of God, the patience of God, the importance or relative unimportance of being a member of the community (as in "I have other sheep that do not belong to this fold" [Jn. 10:16]).

While we cannot be indifferent to questions of truth, there are times when it is more important that a scriptural proposition be interesting than that it be true. An example is the way the book of Acts depicts Paul

> as one who remains a faithful observer of the law of Moses from the Damascus road to Rome, even to the point of seeing to the circumcision of the half-gentile Timothy (16:1–3) and the observance of the Nazirite rites (21:17–26). These

---

[55]Alfred North Whitehead, *Process and Reality* [Corrected Edition], 256.

[56]Ibid.

[57]Ibid., 258.

[58]Ibid., 259.

[59]David J. Lull develops this aspect of process hermeneutics: "What Is 'Process Hermeneutics'?" *Process Studies* 13/3 (Fall, 1983): 193.

texts propose that the reader think of Paul, precisely in his capacity as the Christian evangelist to gentiles *par excellence*, as at the same time the exemplary Pharisaic Jew.[60]

Whether this picture of the "historical Paul" is true, as David Lull says, "has defied solution." Still, it is highly interesting; the considerations it arouses with regard to Christianity's continuity with Judaism have an "importance independent of the truth of the proposal."

What is going on in the text, or between the text and the reader, is that Luke's "*proposed* picture of Paul...serves to invite approval of the author's conviction that continuity between Christianity and Israel's Scriptural religion is germane to the church's identity and self-creation."[61] This latter, a matter of theological self-understanding, is quite true, regardless of the truth or falsity of certain empirical-historical claims of Luke, such as that Paul studied in Jerusalem with Gamaliel (Acts 22:3). The theological significance of Act's proposal is that it enables the church today to reclaim its rootedness in and indebtedness to Judaism as well as to reconstitute itself in solidarity with the people Israel, for whom it has so long preached contempt. A proposal's interest for us and our self-understanding as Christians is not limited to questions of its truthfulness.

Contemporizing of Tradition

Canonical texts are always "contemporized" traditions. This means that interpretation proceeds on the model of a conversation with the text, and the logic of conversation is the logic of question and answer. The interpreter asks questions of the texts, and the text, in its turn, puts questions to the interpreter. The interpreter goes to the text with an interest, and the fact that the interpreter goes to this text (e.g., the Bible) shows that the interpreter is in its "effective history" or "field of force."[62] Sanders' expression "contemporized traditions" makes us remember that the text itself was an answer to a question, a question that must be surfaced if the text is to be understood.

---

[60]Ibid., 193.

[61]Ibid.

[62]The relation between Hans Georg Gadamer's "effective history" (*Wirkungsgeschichte*) and John B. Cobb's "field of force" was argued by Williamson in "Process Hermeneutics and Christianity's Post-Holocaust Reinterpretation of Itself," *Process Studies* 12/2 (Summer, 1982): 81.

A text without a context is just a pretext. Different texts, written at different times and places, to differing circumstances, seek to answer different questions. As new questions arise, new answers are forthcoming. These new answers, or texts, are contemporized to new situations. Although there is no scholarly certainty on the point, there is evidence that during his lifetime Jesus and his disciples understood themselves as concerned exclusively with "the lost sheep of the house of Israel," and not at all with Gentiles. Matthew preserves traditions according to which, when Jesus sent out the Twelve, he charged them to "go nowhere among the Gentiles, and enter no town of the Samaritans, but go rather to the lost sheep of the house of Israel" (10:5).[63]

The early church that wrote the scriptures was able to retain these evidences of its early "limitation" to Jews in the very document that ends in the great commission to "make disciples of all nations" (Mt. 28:19). It should be noted that the term "all nations" is *panta ta ethne*, "all the Gentiles." The "only to the house of Israel" passages reflect a question and answer from the early part of the first century; the great commission reflects a question and answer from the latter part of the first century. In between, the tradition had been creatively transformed in continuity with itself but "without the obligation of *conformity*" to the past; it could give a new answer to a new question arising later "without the *rejection* of tradition."[64] Biblical interpreters who understand that tradition is itself a process of creative and self-critical transformation need not be put off by the apparent contradiction between the limitations of the Jesus movement to the house of Israel and the calling of the church to go to all the Gentiles. In each case, tradition is contemporized to a different situation and made to answer a different question. In each case, the mission is to make known the promise and command of God to each and all; in the one case to all the house of Israel, including its lost sheep, in the other to all the peoples. In either case, the message is inclusive. What has changed is the scope of inclusiveness.

This latter comment discloses that a relatively clear statement of the norm of appropriateness need not be taken to imply that there is an absolute, unchanging essence to Christianity. Rather, the meaning of such words as "all" is itself contemporized to different situations at different times and places. Abstractly, "all" means "the whole

---

[63]See, e.g., Bernard J. Lee, *The Galilean Jewishness of Jesus,* 67ff.
[64]Lull, "What Is 'Process Hermeneutics'?" 195.

of," with none left out. Concretely, "all" can grow in meaning. That God loves "all," in the early Jesus movement, meant that God loved the whole of the house of Israel, including especially its "lost sheep." Later in the Jesus movement, "all" took on a larger meaning. Now the church saw that God's love for all had to be taken in the light of God's initial promise to Abraham that his seed would be a light to the Gentiles; God loves even or especially the lost Gentile sheep. In our own time we have clearly learned that the "all" whom God loves is a rather larger "all" than we had previously taken it to be; now it includes especially women and African Americans and the barrio dwellers of Latin America, to name but a few. For some Christians, after a long tradition inclining them to the contrary, even Jews are especially loved by God.

This does not mean that there is an absolute, unchanging essence to Christianity. Rather, it illustrates the distinction that Schubert Ogden develops, from Stephen Toulmin, between the "field-invariant force" of criteria of appropriateness and adequacy and their "field-dependent standards," which Ogden later refers to as their "context-invariant" and "context-dependent" aspects.[65] It probably suffices to say that the "force" of such criteria is "context-transferrable," without getting too worked up over how universally invariant they are.

A similar relationship exists, David Lull suggests, between the letters of Paul and the letter of James. James, writing some time later, was aware of Christians who held that "faith without works" is salvific (2:14). They seem to have thought that they agreed with Paul, who had argued that justification is by faith "apart from works of law" (Rom. 3:28). But in their time and place, the question that Paul was trying to answer was no longer being asked, and the situation he had addressed was no longer pressing. Paul was striving to gain an equal place for his Gentile followers within the Jesus movement without requiring them to submit to the ritual practices of circumcision and the food laws, practices that served as the "identity markers" or "membership badges" of the Jewish people, and which to Paul indicated that the grace of God is not available outside the boundaries of that people.[66]

---

[65]See the discussion in Ogden, *The Reality of God* (New York: Harper & Row, 1966), 38 ff., and *On Theology* (San Francisco: Harper & Row, 1986), 5–6.

[66]See James D. G. Dunn, *Jesus, Paul, and the Law* (Louisville: Westminster/John Knox Press, 1990), 11–12.

In James's time, Christianity was, as Lull says, "well on the way to becoming a gentile religion, separate from Judaism," and there was little if any pressure to conform to Jewish ritual requirements. Now the question about "faith without works" was being raised by people "whose lives exhibited moral laxity."[67] In this situation, James could not possibly be satisfied with a hermeneutic of "mere conformity to tradition," because such conformity was precisely what had produced the "heresy" of thinking that faith need not be active in love. So, James "contemporized" tradition, in a way that was more faithful than conforming to it would have been, and transformed it to enable it to answer the new question.

Summary

By way of a quick review, we have tried to lay out the introductory groundwork of our approach to process hermeneutics. We began with the need for a norm of appropriateness, described the nature of scripture itself as an instance of tradition, as the final precipitate of a long process of revision and reinterpretation and subject to further reinterpretation, sought to show scripture's self-critical hermeneutic and adopt it as our norm of appropriateness, indicated why a concern for credibility is of critical importance to the gospel itself (hardly just to be well adapted to "modernity"), and sought to show how to avoid a misleading abstractedness by contextualizing Jesus and Paul, being attentive to the tone of scripture, and by looking at texts as proposals and at the contemporizing of tradition.

Because of the social, temporal, historical nature of scripture and tradition, the various methods of ideology criticism and political interpretation are helpful. As a matter of fact, much of what has gone before in this chapter is unintelligible without the presupposition of at least some of these. The church throughout its history has succumbed to the temptation to interpret scripture in ways that are death-dealing, not life-giving, to various groups of God's beloved children. Scriptures have been interpreted to show the inferiority of women and to justify so treating them, to show the emptiness of Jewish faith and life and justify the social, economic, and political subordination of Jews, and to justify claims about the racial inferiority of Africans and so their enslavement. Ideological criticism asks

---

[67]David J. Lull, "What Is 'Process Hermeneutics'?" 196.

the question: Who benefits from this interpretation? Theology also asks: Who is glorified by this interpretation? If those who benefit and are glorified are white, male, and Gentile, and the mistreatment of others is justified, what we have on our hands is ideology, the distortion of truth in the interests of power, not authentic faith. All our interpretation should be done to the greater glory of God and for a blessing to the poor and oppressed, the nobodies to whom Jesus ministered.

Light for the Path

The point of this discussion of scripture (and tradition) is to help the church see that and how scripture and tradition play authoritative roles. They do that, and do it appropriately, when we live with them long enough and understand them well enough that scripture can become for us again a "living book." If this discussion has succeeded, whatever the merit of any particular part of it, it has taken the Bible away from you as a "dead letter," and given it back as a living book. The way that God gives and calls us to walk is the way of life and blessing, not death and curse. We are to carry the scriptures with us as we walk; and, with their help and the inspiration of the Holy Spirit, we are to wrestle with them in relation to the contexts, promises, and difficulties of our times.

Chapter 4

God the Creator and Redeemer of Life

Problems with the Traditional Model of God

The God of the Bible creates, re-creates, and ultimately redeems life. This God, whatever other so-called "gods" might be like, loves life, rejoices in it, is concerned about it, not only creates it for the purpose of blessing it, but saves it, and in between discloses to God's covenanted people the way of life that they are to follow as an alternative to the death-dealing ways so prevalent in the world.

Yet, we have a major problem. Much formal theology defines the God of traditional Christian theism as unqualifiedly impassive. This means that God is in no sense affected by feeling for others, in no sense passible. It interprets God as so completely immutable as to deny that God can in any sense be affected by what happens to others. God becomes in all respects eternal and necessary, with the result that it is only on pain of incoherence that we can speak of God as genuinely temporal or in any sense contingent, as would be required if God were genuinely, not merely nominally, related to what is contingent (such as you and me). The tradition makes God so utterly absolute as to make it impossible to speak of God as genuinely related to us, as in covenant, because "the absolute" cannot be related.

Meanwhile, the church in its worship, hymns, and prayers clearly said and assumed quite different things about God. For example, a God to whom we pray is assumed to "hear," to be affected by, prayer. Yet, the formal tradition argued otherwise, as in this example from the Westminster Confession of 1646:

> There is but one only living and true God, who is infinite in being and perfection, a most pure spirit, invisible, without body, parts, or passions, immutable, immense, eternal, incomprehensible, almighty, working all things according to the counsel of his own immutable and most righteous will, for his own glory; most loving, gracious, merciful, long-suffering...[1]

If necessity, changelessness, the lack of becoming, and relationality define what it is to be supremely real, then it is no wonder, as Langdon Gilkey claims, that along with this in Christendom went a progressive loss of the sense of the "reality, value, or meaning of the changing, temporal, material world, and of earthly human and historical life in time."[2]

The doctrine that God is *in all respects* immutable and impassible (incapable of change or being affected) severely hampered traditional theology in its task of formulating an appropriately Christian doctrine of God. This doctrine, imported from Hellenic thought and religion, was simply assumed by the patristic writers and never argued either biblically or theologically. That God must be in *some* respects immutable and impassible is an important emphasis in articulating God's faithfulness and constancy (God's *hesed*). Process theologians argue that God is immutable (or absolute, necessary, and eternal) with regard to two aspects of God's life: God's existence and God's essence. In other words, that God is (God's existence) and who God is (God's character) are necessary. What is contingent or relational in God is God's experience of the world.

If God were in all respects mutable, God might cease to be or cease to be God. But to assert that God is in all respects immutable/

---

[1]John Leith, ed., *Creeds of the Churches* (Richmond: John Knox Press, 1973), 197.

[2]Langdon Gilkey, "God," in *Christian Theology: An Introduction to Its Traditions and Tasks,* ed. Peter C. Hodgson and Robert H. King (Philadelphia: Fortress Press, 1985), 93.

impassible is to exempt God from involvement in time, history, and relationships. Yahweh's "immutability" is intrinsically a relation to God's creatures; Yahweh is faithful through history, not exempt from history. Most classical trinitarian theologians assumed otherwise, not only Arius but also Athanasius, his major opponent at Nicaea and afterward (see his *On the Incarnation of the Word*).[3] The dispute between Arius and Athanasius was not whether to place a buffer between God and creation, but where to place it. Arius placed it between God and the Logos; Athanasius placed it between the Logos incarnate in Christ and the body of Jesus that "suffered" as the Logos could not. This traditional assumption not only undercuts the doctrines it seeks to interpret (such as the incarnation) but suffers from an uneasy relation to the biblical witness. Jaroslav Pelikan claims that this assumption of total impassibility represents "a more subtle and more pervasive effect of dejudaization" of Christianity than is found in the anti-Jewish tracts of the church fathers.[4]

As an alternative to this traditional model for God, we will here consider a neo-process theological understanding of God as more appropriate to the biblical witness and more adequate to the deep concern of the God of the Bible for the life of human beings and the world.[5] This understanding of God, formulated particularly by Whitehead and Hartshorne, develops the idea of God as a unitary being who not only acts upon but is acted upon by, who interacts with, the world. Such a concept of God corresponds better to the "Christian 'story' of God's involvement with the world than the traditional philosophical idea of God."[6] In the Christian faith the

---

[3]Athanasius, *On the Incarnation of the Word* in *Christology of the Later Fathers*, vol. 3 of The Library of Christian Classics (Philadelphia: The Westminster Press, 1964), 55–110.

[4]Jaroslav Pelikan, *The Emergence of the Christian Tradition (100–600)*, vol. 1 of *The Christian Tradition* (Chicago: The University of Chicago Press, 1971), 21–22.

[5]I use the term "neo-process" to indicate that, while I both appreciate and appropriate many themes, concepts, and metaphors from process thought for the purpose of doing theology, I think that theology's conversational relation to philosophy also requires some criticism and revision of philosophy on its part. My revisions of process thought in this chapter will focus mainly on the doctrines of creation *ex nihilo*, which process philosophy is widely assumed to deny, and of the Trinity, which is underdeveloped in process theology. Other "neo-process" thinkers are: Langdon Gilkey, *Reaping the Whirlwind* (New York: Seabury Press, 1976); Robert C. Neville, *A Theology Primer* (Albany: SUNY, 1991); and *The High Road Around Modernism* (Albany: SUNY, 1992); and Thomas E. Hosinski, *Stubborn Fact and Creative Advance* (Lanham, Md.: Rowman & Littlefield, 1993).

[6]Hosinski, *Stubborn Fact and Creative Advance,* 238.

doctrines of creation for the sake of blessing, sin, redemption, judgment, and eschatological culmination have the form of a story or narrative structure. God creates, the creatures fall into sin, God re-creates or redeems, God trans-creates (calls God's creatures forward into God's future for them), and ultimately God transforms the world in the eschaton. This "story of God" reflects the experience of the people Israel and the church of God's dynamic interaction with the world. Biblically, it is simply not the case that God is in all respects infinite, eternal, immutable, and impassible. Instead, God is the "living God" who cares passionately about God's creatures.[7]

A Learned Ignorance

The Christian tradition developed what it called a "negative theology" (*via negativa*), a term that can have two different meanings. One of these meanings we need to reject; the other one serves as an important reminder to us that we who speak of God are human beings, and that all our speech, all our concepts, metaphors, and models, are said of God "as it were" (a characteristic Jewish qualification on all talk of God).

The first meaning of "negative theology" is that in all our statements about God we do not so much say what God is as what God is not. So we say that God is "infinite," not in order to specify anything about God, but to note that God is "not finite" (which is all that the word "infinite" means). We call God "eternal" to say that God is "not temporal." Yet this is a high price to pay in our talk of God, if our language is to be appropriate to the gospel of God's love graciously offered to each and all in Jesus Christ and God's command that justice be done to each and all. When we say that "God is love" (1 Jn. 4:8), surely we intend to say more than that God is not non-loving. The church in its wisdom also developed a "positive theology" (*via positiva*), to which we will turn later.

The second meaning of "negative theology" is that all our models and metaphors are inadequate to give voice to the mystery of God. By "mystery" I do not mean that we posit some general sense of mysteriousness and ascribe that to God. Rather, the God who reveals Godself to us through the history of Israel, the Torah, the

---

[7]For other efforts of mine to discuss the doctrine of God, see Clark M. Williamson and Ronald J. Allen, *A Credible and Timely Word* (St. Louis: Chalice Press, 1991), 15–38, and Clark M. Williamson, *A Guest in the House of Israel* (Louisville: Westminster/John Knox Press, 1993), 202–32.

prophets, and Jesus Christ is mysterious. This is the living God who will be whoever God will be and who thereby transcends and escapes our categories. Analogously, the way we know another person is by her self-disclosure to us of who she is, yet she is never reducible to our descriptions of her, correct though those descriptions may be. She is capable of surprising us. Our knowledge of God is what Nicolaus Cusanus (1401–1464) termed "a taught ignorance" in his work by that title (*De Docta Ignorantia*).

Experience with seminary students over several decades indicates that they turn surprisingly agnostic when the time comes to think about God, declaring that "the finite cannot comprehend the infinite," so any ideas one might have about God are just as good as any others. Such agnosticism has its roots either in intellectual laziness or in a theological despair at ever getting things right. In either case, it is sorely mistaken. Our task is not to overcome what Bernard Meland called the "fallibility" of all our forms and symbols for God.[8] It is to come up with ways of talking about God that are appropriate to the revelation of God attested to in the biblical witness. All ways of talking of God are arguably inadequate. Yet, some are more clearly inadequate than others. There are ways of talking about God that are more appropriate to the norms of the Christian faith than others and that are also more helpful in the face of the challenges that confront us in the death-dealing times in which we live.

Neo-Process, Relational Models of God

Now we turn to a more positive use of metaphors and concepts from our experience, one tempered by the reminder that all our talk of God is "as it were." Process thought differs from classical thought in that the latter took objects of ordinary perception as its paradigmatic cases of reality. In this way, an object such as a gray stone came to exemplify the two basic categories of interpretation of classical thought. "Gray" was understood as an attribute or property of the underlying reality of the stone, which in turn was conceived as a "substance." Hence, reality was understood in terms of unrelated substances undergoing only external and accidental adventures of change as indicated by alterations in their attributes (when

---

[8]Bernard E. Meland, *Fallible Forms and Symbols* (Philadelphia: Fortress Press, 1976).

wet, the stone would be a darker gray). So God could be conceived as a substance of whom we could know only the attributes and who was independent of time and relationships, eternal, necessary, immutable, and impassible in all respects.

Classical theology, the theology of ancient, pre-Christian Greeks, was "an exact antagonist of biblical faith."[9] Greek thought regarded time, in the words of John Dewey, as "the tooth that gnaws; it is the destroyer."[10] The ultimate concern of Greek religion was to overcome time and the realities of chance and death that came in its wake. It attempted to do this by identifying the divine with timelessness as such. When the question had to do with what can save us from the ravages of time, the answer came in the form of an escape from time by union or reunion with the timeless God who is in all respects eternal and in no respects temporal. The defining characteristic of God became God's total exemption from time, history, becoming, and relationships. Hence, God must be immutable, impassible, incapable of being affected, and these in all, not merely some, respects.

On the contrary, Yahweh, the God of Israel, "was eternal by his faithfulness *through* time." The Greek gods, however, were eternal by virtue of being utterly timeless. "Yahweh's eternity is thus intrinsically a relation to his creatures—supposing there are such—whereas the Greek gods' eternity is the negation of such relation."[11] It is from this sense of the word "negation" that the first meaning of Christian "negative theology," described above, derived. The traditional theology of the church merged this understanding of God as in all respects impassible and necessary with the God of the Bible. The result was to formulate an understanding that undercut all the symbols that it was used to interpret, such as the incarnation. The suffering of Christ on the cross can disclose nothing of God, because God is, by definition, incapable of suffering. So it was the man Jesus who suffered, not the impassible Logos incarnate in him.[12]

---

[9]Robert W. Jenson, "The Triune God," in *Christian Dogmatics*, vol. 1, ed. Robert W. Jenson and Carl E. Braaten (Philadelphia: Fortress Press, 1984), 115.

[10]John Dewey, "Time and Individuality," in *Philosophers of Process*, ed. Douglas Browning (New York: Random House, 1965), 208.

[11]Robert W. Jenson, "The Triune God," 116.

[12]This is exactly the claim made again and again by early theologians of the church. See Athanasius, *The Incarnation of the Word*, in *Christology of the Later Fathers*, vol. 3 of the Library of Christian Classics, ed. Edward Rochie Hardy (Philadelphia:

God discloses God's name to Moses as "I will be who/what I will be," and subsequently shows the capacity to act in new and surprising ways. Hence, we have a biblical way of talking of God as perfectly self-surpassing. In the light of further disclosures of God's vulnerability to suffering, we have a biblical way of talking of God as not only perfectly self-surpassing, but also, in virtue of God's faithfulness to God's promises to God's creatures, of God as genuinely in relationship to them and us.

The neo-process relational model of God begins with a different starting point. It takes our awareness of our own experience as subjects as the basis of our fundamental concepts. Totally unlike the traditional notion of substances, which are nontemporal and nonrelated, the "very being of the self is relational or social; and it is nothing if not a process of change involving the distinct modes of present, past, and future."[13] Because it is affected by, and interacts with, others who change and become, the self is both temporal and social.

If we develop a model of God from this basic awareness of the self, then God would be genuinely social and temporal, affected by others as well as effecting (creating) them, and "different from the wholly timeless and unrelated Absolute of traditional theism."[14] The categorically unique status of God—God's perfection or what it is that makes God God and different from, as well as in some respects like, us—would no longer be understood in terms of God's utterly timeless, static being, but as God's being "the self-surpassing surpasser of all."[15] God is the One who effects and is affected by all others, who interacts with all others. God's faithfulness, that God cannot fail to be, or to be God in whatever circumstance, here takes the place of what the tradition regarded as God's total immutability. Because God does not change in these ways, God is affected by and vulnerable to events in nature and history.

Westminster Press, 1954), 71. He reiterates the point in his *Orations Against the Arians,* in *The Christological Controversy,* ed. Richard A. Norris, Jr. (Philadelphia: Fortress Press, 1980), 92–93.

[13]Schubert M. Ogden, *The Reality of God* (New York: Harper & Row, 1966), 57.

[14]Ibid., 58.

[15]Charles Hartshorne, *The Divine Relativity* (New Haven: Yale University Press, 1948), 20.

What God Does

First, God creates everything that is. Whitehead began to write about God because he had concluded that the metaphysical analysis at which he had arrived left us with the same problem faced long ago by Plato. That problem was that if the world is finally analyzable into two realities, creativity and possibility, the question is: How are they ever gotten together? Why is there anything at all? Whitehead first decided that God must function as the "principle of concreteness" who would grade the possibilities into relevance for the ongoing flux of creativity. Otherwise, nothing actual could occur.[16] Later, as his thought developed, he concluded that God had to be thought of not as a "principle," but as an actuality, an agent.

Neo-process thinkers develop this aspect of Whitehead's thought further than he did by affirming the doctrine of creation ex nihilo. Whitehead called God an agent or an actuality because of one of the most basic principles of his thought, the "ontological principle." It holds that actualities or agents are the only reasons, that if you look for a reason you must look for an actuality, an agent. This is the hardheaded principle of empirical thought. Finally, all reasons for why things are the way they are have to do either with decisions made by past agents or decisions made by contemporary agents.[17] Yet Whitehead did not follow through consistently with this insight, or at best did so only intermittently.

For instance, he made two claims that, logically, move him in the direction of a doctrine of creation ex nihilo. He commented, late in *Process and Reality*, that God both "exemplifies and establishes the categoreal conditions."[18] Previously he had said only that God is the "chief [i.e., perfect] exemplification of the metaphysical categories." In that formulation, God would seem to be subject to metaphysical categories that exist independently of God's decision making. But according to the ontological principle, metaphysical categories cannot be their own explanation; they require explanation by reference to the decision of an actual agent. Late in *Process and Reality*, Whitehead realizes this and claims that God establishes the conditions that God perfectly exemplifies. Later yet in his developing

---

[16]Alfred North Whitehead, *Science and the Modern World* (New York: New American Library, 1925), 160.

[17]Alfred North Whitehead, *Process and Reality: Corrected Edition* (New York: The Free Press, 1978), 24.

[18]Ibid., 344.

thought, he argues that "apart from God, the remaining formative elements [creativity and pure potentiality] would fail in their functions. There would be no creatures..."[19]

Nonetheless, even in this remark there remains the ambiguity that apart from God there are "the remaining formative elements." What accounts for them? If, indeed, actual agents are the only reasons, only God can account for all the things necessary for there to be a world: creativity, forms of definiteness, and actual things of whatever kinds. Logically, Whitehead's philosophy requires to be completed by a doctrine of creation ex nihilo understood as a limit concept and made clear by what it denies.

By implication, so would any process metaphysic, such as Hartshorne's, that is also an event metaphysic and that argues, as Hartshorne does strenuously, for the critical role of the ontological principle. We shall return to the doctrine of creation ex nihilo in the discussion of creation, providence, and evil.

So, God creates us and everything that is. God's creativity is not simply a once-upon-a-time creation, but an ongoing creativity that calls every moment of the life of the world into being. God creates human beings, in particular, in such ways that we are blessed with a depth of experience of appreciative value that we call the past, present with us in contemporary experience as a great cloud of witnesses. The more of the past we are able to appreciate, the richer our present experience, the greater the range of our possibilities (because of the forgotten alternatives that we remember), and the more significant our freedom.

God creates us as free, partially self-creating, self-determining creatures. To be a human being means, among other things, to decide how to understand and constitute ourselves. We do this in community and tradition, to be sure, but inescapably we do it. The only question is whether we take responsibility for such deeply personal and radically existential decisions or whether we hand them over to others. But process thought claims that the more you let Christ into your life, the freer you are. "It is by God's grace that I experience a call to be more than I have been and more than my circumstances necessitate that I be; it is by God's grace that I am free."[20]

---

[19]Whitehead, *Religion in the Making*, 100.
[20]John B. Cobb, Jr., *Talking about God* (New York: The Seabury Press, 1983), 53.

So, without God neither we nor anything else would have received the gift of life; without God we would not have the richness
of life; without God we would not be free. But God not only effects
(creates) the world; God also interacts with it, is acted upon by the
world that God has created. God's relation to the world is not merely
nominal to God. God is not only unsurpassably active in the sense
of "doing all that could conceivably be done by any one individual
for all others," but God is "unsurpassably passive, being open to all
that could be conceivably done or suffered by anyone as something
that is also done to God."[21] What we do to "the least of these," said
Jesus, we do to God.

Typically, we speak of God creating, redeeming, reconciling,
sanctifying God's creatures, and of human beings as capable of being aware of and benefiting from God's creative activity on our behalf. God acts redemptively toward us in each moment of our lives,
creating us out of the mess and ambiguity of the past that each of us
brings with us as part of ourselves to that moment. God takes this
past into account, laden as it is not only with good, but with the
realities of sin, evil, and narrowness of outlook. God offers us once
again God's creative love, loving us into genuine freedom (love for
God and the neighbor) and freeing us into genuine love. Because
God is really related to us, God knows our situation, and God's love
is offered in ways that are timely and relevant. God's ongoing creativity is redemptive.

God Redeems the World

God acts redemptively throughout the scriptural narrative, and
we will take up this theme more fully in the discussion of christology.
It is important to note that God acts redemptively in order to make
good on God's primary purpose, that of bringing about the reality
of well-being, blessing, among God's creatures. That well-being can
only be received as a gift from an Other, can only be had by being
shared with an other, it blesses humanity and nature, women and
men, the Israel of God and the Gentiles, in mutuality and in difference, and is always under threat from the revolts of sin and evil.
Apart from understanding God's primary purpose in creating and
re-creating us and all that is, there is no way to understand why

---

[21]Schubert M. Ogden, "The Metaphysics of Faith and Justice," *Process Studies*
14 (1985): 86.

God's redemptive work is important. Why is it worth the bother to God to act redemptively in Jesus Christ? To what end? To that of the sanctification, the blessing, the well-being of all God's creation.

God's Reconciling Love

God's creativity is reconciling. Whenever the apostle Paul speaks of God's love as "justifying," it is always in the context in his letters of a social conflict within the congregation to which he is writing. Martin Luther's term for justification was *Rechtfertigung,* "setting right." "Justifying" and Rechtfertigung are gerunds, verbal nouns, that identify the kind of love that is God's. God is a right-setting God, a God who intends to set things right. As individuals, we need to be reconciled with ourselves, to be liberated from the deep self-rejection that makes it difficult, if not impossible, to accept our neighbors. As members of groups, we need to be reconciled with other groups from which we have been alienated. Ephesians speaks of God's reconciling activity as breaking down the "dividing wall" between Jews and Gentiles, between the "insiders and outsiders" of God's house. We are reconciled by God in Christ to one another and to God (Eph. 2:11–22).

The aim or purpose of God's creating, redeeming, and reconciling love freely offered to us is that we may be sanctified, led to live new and transformed lives. We are a blessing to the world, to our neighbors, to the extent that living new and transformed lives engenders in us a willingness to do deeds of loving kindness, deeds that "mend the world" (*tikkun olam*). By actively sharing the way of life and blessing with the world, we at least bear witness in word and deed to the possibility of an alternative to the ways of death that dominate our secular history.

Why God Created/Creates the World

God creates the world and us for a reason; God's providence has a purpose. Whitehead thought that this purpose was to engender strength of beauty (intensity) in all of God's creatures and particularly in humans.[22] Jonathan Edwards, the great Puritan theologian, took seriously this question: Why did God create the world? He argued that there is an infinite fullness of "all possible good in God, a fullness of every perfection, of all excellency and beauty, and of infinite

---

[22]See Whitehead, *Process and Reality, Corrected Edition,* 105.

happiness."[23] In creation, this fullness of well-being, beauty, and happiness flows forth in abundant streams and multiplies. God's purpose in creating the world was "to communicate of his own infinite fullness of good"; this is what "moved him [God] to create the world."

God created the world in order to share with it the blessing of God's fullness of all possible good and beauty, to bring the world to well-being that the world might thereby glorify God. "The chief end of human beings," so went the old catechism, "is to glorify God and enjoy God forever." It is the beauty of God, a beauty found in God's internal relationship of mutuality and respect among a community of distinct persons, that is to be a blessing to human beings. The more that we reflect God in our lives, the more beautiful we are, and the more well-being we receive from, as well as give to, others.

We bring this point into the perspective of the rest of the outlook of this systematic by noting that God creates the world in order to sanctify all things. It is an eccentricity of church history that the Puritans reestablished the institution of the Sabbath.[24] European Christianity, acting out of its deep anti-Judaism, rejected the Sabbath and effectively had only nine of the ten commandments. Let us revisit Exodus 20:8–11:

> Remember the sabbath day, and keep it holy. Six days you shall labor and do all your work. But the seventh day is a sabbath to the LORD your God; you shall not do any work— you, your son or your daughter, your male or female slave, your livestock, or the alien resident in your towns. For in six days the LORD made heaven and earth, the sea, and all that is in them, but rested the seventh day; therefore the LORD blessed the sabbath day and consecrated it.

Exodus relates the Sabbath (the day of rest) to creation. The creation story provides the basis for the Sabbath. The Sabbath is instituted in creation, reinstituted at Sinai. God's institution of the Sabbath discloses God's ultimate purpose for all creation: the sanctification, the blessing of well-being, of all things. The Sabbath as a day not only reflects God's purposes in creation, but has

---

[23]Jonathan Edwards, *Dissertation on the End for Which God Created the World,* in *The Works of President Edwards,* 4 volumes (New York: Leavitt and Trow, 1843), vol. 2, 206.

[24]For an early example of antagonism toward the Sabbath, see the *Letter of Barnabas,* in *The Ante-Nicene Church Fathers,* vol. 1 (Grand Rapids: Eerdmans, 1979), 146–47.

eschatological significance as well. It discloses the presence of God in the world; it is a foretaste of the end, when all shall be well, and all manner of things shall be well. Of course, the Puritans placed the Sabbath on the first, not the last, day of the week. But unlike the anti-Jewish tradition, this was not a rejection, but an eschatological affirmation of the Sabbath. The beauty and holiness, the infinite fount of excellences, were overabundant and could not be contained by the seventh day. They were beginning to fill the other days, as the kingdom of God, by God's grace, is coming.

The one commandment of the Sabbath is that we must avoid all work. We are commanded to loaf systematically, to spend time in face-to-face relations with our loved ones, to take a walk and enjoy God's good creation, to play a game with our children, to take time to hug our spouses, to engage our neighbors in conversation, to have a picnic in the park, to enjoy and serve the well-being that is God's purpose for all creation. Were we to join the more Orthodox Jews in their refusal to drive a car on *Shabbat*, we could give the ecosphere a rest and quit, at least for a day, overworking it.

Gender and God-Language

God as Father

In our time, a critical issue pertaining to how we talk about God has to do with the use of the traditional metaphor "father" for God. Many people are profoundly troubled by this way of talking about God. Women theologians make the point that to speak of God exclusively as father serves to make women invisible or second-class within the community. If God is male, the argument goes, the male is God. Another point in this argument is that for those (both men and women) whose experiences with their fathers were quite negative, to speak of God as "father" raises a significant barrier between them and God, possibly making it impossible to love and serve God.

Theologically, God is other than us, categorically unique. God loves and cares for us as only God can do. Fathers and mothers, at their best, love us as fathers and mothers do, but God loves us as God and God alone can do. All human love is both limited by finitude, the ordinary limitations to which we are all subject, distorted by sin, and self-centeredness. God's love is neither conditioned nor distorted. It is pure and unbounded. Hence, there is no reason not to speak of God's love for us in the language of either mother-love or father-love. Mothers and fathers can both serve as appropriate, if finally inadequate, symbols for God. All our symbols point to what is more than they can express.

The gospels vary considerably in the extent to which they have Jesus refer to God as "Father." He calls God "Father" five times in Mark, but over one hundred and ten times in John. The latter tells us more about the language of John than that of Jesus. Nonetheless, it is appropriate to pray to and speak of God as father. The metaphor "father" means that God creates the world, that God cares about us, provides for us, and rescues us. Also, "father" is a personal and familial metaphor, as is "mother." God the Father creates life, redeems it from self-destruction, and ultimately saves it.

Paul uses the expression "God the Father" to make clear that he is speaking of the God of Israel. In reading Paul, we need to remember that the large numbers of Gentiles in his congregations brought with them the religious understandings of their cultures. They already knew, so many of them thought, all about God, the Spirit, how life is to be lived, and what it means to eat the flesh and drink the blood of a savior. Except that Paul felt the need to correct and instruct them on all these points, including their understandings of "God."

No metaphor that we may use for God is ever free from ambiguity. We use any metaphor for God properly when we add the proviso, "as it were." Male or masculine metaphors clearly need rethinking, particularly after the long patriarchal epoch of Christianity. Yet there are good examples of judges, warriors, and kings. In evaluating a metaphor, we need to look at the context in which it was originally used and how it functioned, what was meant with it. The early martyrs of the church, for example, were executed because they would not confess that "the king (Caesar) is God." In their refusals they appealed to another king, One who does not kill, but loves and even died for his subjects. For them Christ the King was not the projection onto heaven of an earthly king. Quite the opposite, Christ revolutionizes and undercuts the brutality and death-dispensing ways of earthly kings.

God as Mother

The Christian tradition, including the biblical tradition, provides significant resources for talking about God as mother or as a woman who may not be a mother. The tradition of negative theology reminds us that all our metaphors for God are fallible. God never was regarded literally as father. In the early third century the apologist

Minucius Felix in his *Octavius* argued that we should call God "parent," to avoid confusing outsiders as to what we mean to say about God.[25] One of our Advent hymns, "Of the Father's Love Begotten," in its original Latin first line reads: *corde natus ex parentis,* "of the parent's love begotten." This awareness could loosen the grip that "father-language" has on us and free us to consider alternatives.

The scriptures are a source of forgotten alternatives. The mystery of God's freedom, as testified to by the biblical writers, transcends the biological distinctions between male and female and the cultural distinctions of masculine and feminine. The self-revelation of God to Moses in Exodus 3 points to a metaphor of God as "helper," and in Genesis 2, when Eve is said to have been created as the "helper" of Adam, the biblical tradition uses for Eve a word, "help," that "is generally applied to God who is par excellence the succor of those in need and despair."[26] Adam and Eve, created together in God's image, are theomorphic in their co-humanity and are given the responsibility to care for the rest of God's creation as God's helpers.

The image of God as a mother bird is present in scripture: "Hide me in the shadow of your wings," prays the psalmist (Ps. 17:8). "All people may take refuge in the shadow of your wings" (Ps. 36:7). "In the shadow of your wings I will take refuge" (Ps. 57:1). "Like birds hovering overhead, so the LORD of hosts will protect Jerusalem" (Isa. 31:5). Matthew 23:37 and Luke 13:34 attribute to Jesus the statement about Jerusalem: "How often have I desired to gather your children together as a hen gathers her brood under her wings, and you were not willing!"

Names and images of God as wife or mother also appear. The psalmist appeals to God's motherly compassion, and the love of God is compared with a mother's love for her child or a wife's affection for her husband (e.g., Ps. 131:2; Ps. 49:14–15). "You forgot the God who gave you birth," declares Deuteronomy 32:18. The Hebraic tradition used several names in the female gender for God: *Shekhinah* to refer to the all-present One, Torah to refer to God's teaching for us; *Chokmah* to name God's wisdom, often personified as Woman Wisdom. The "spirit" of God, *ruach,* is feminine. When

---

[25]Minucius Felix, *The Octavius,* in *The Ante-Nicene Fathers,* vol. 4 (Grand Rapids: Eerdmans, 1979), 182–84.

[26]Letty Russell, *Human Liberation in a Feminist Perspective—A Theology* (Philadelphia: Westminster Press, 1974), 99.

Jesus says, "Take my yoke upon you, and learn from me; for I am gentle and humble in heart, and you will find rest for your souls. For my yoke is easy, and my burden is light" (Mt. 11:29–30), he is paraphrasing Sirach 51:26, a statement about Woman Wisdom: "Put your neck under her yoke, and let your souls receive instruction."

No terms are used more often of God in the Bible than such words as "compassionate" (*rahamim,* compassion) and "steadfast love, loving faithfulness" (*hesed,* loyalty). The roots of these conceptions are in "the ethics of loyalty between family and clan members. 'Kindness' is the loyalty one shows to one's 'kind' or kin." The ethics are grounded "in a compassion arising out of common ancestry (*rehem,* 'womb')."[27] The primal, initial context in which all of us live is the womb of our mothers. There we grow and are cared for in relational empathy. There our well-being is guarded and developed. God loves us with a mother's love; the womb-like love of Yahweh is the matrix of our lives.

Hence, God can be appropriately imaged as both mother and father, provided that we remember that God loves all her children, us included. Our neighbors, including all those strangers of other races, ethnic groups, faiths, and languages, whose appearance and demeanor are different from ours, are the children of a loving God, borne in the same compassionate matrix. They are the neighbors whom God has given us to love. In loving and doing justice to them we honor the God who is the ground and end of their and our being, and who is affected by everything we do or fail to do to her children.

Father, Son, and Spirit?

Those for whom "father" language for God is problematic often seek other ways to speak of the Trinity, such as "Creator, Redeemer, Sanctifier." This solution to the problem is unhappy because it reflects an inappropriate understanding of the Trinity, one frequently found in patristic writers. Lurking behind talk of God as "Creator, Redeemer, Sanctifier" is the notion that each person of God has a smaller sphere of influence than the former person. Thus, God the Father creates and governs the world, God the Logos relates to all human beings, and God the Spirit sanctifies Christians and attaches

---

[27]J. Gerald Janzen, *Abraham and all the Families of the Earth,* 75.

them to Christ and the church (Schleiermacher). This view is inadequate to the biblical witness according to which the Spirit is the source of life of all persons everywhere and makes the Spirit the private preserve of Christians and the church. The *adversus Judaeos* literature systematically affirmed the absence of the Spirit from the people Israel who are "carnal," in contrast to the church that is "spiritual," the "new, spiritual" Israel as opposed to the "old, carnal" Israel of the flesh.

The function of the doctrine of the Trinity in the church is to regulate our use of language in talking about God. The point is not that every Christian pastor has to reinvent the Trinitarian wheel, but to pay attention to how we speak of God. Consider the old Trinitarian rule: *opera dei ad extra indivisa sunt* ("the external works of God are indivisible"). This rule is violated when we speak of God the Father as creating, God the Word or Son as redeeming, and God the Spirit as sanctifying. This may be a problem when we substitute for the traditional way of speaking of God as "Father-Son-Spirit" the expression "Creator-Redeemer-Sanctifier." Modalism/Sabellianism so spoke of the three "personae" of God as subsequent modes of God's action. The Cappadocian theologians (Basil the Great, Gregory of Nazianzus, and Gregory of Nyssa) took this horizontal (sequential) "trinity" and turned it upright (vertically) and compared the three "hypostases" ("persons") to three links of a chain: When you grab the chain by any one link, you grab the whole chain. In any moment of relation to God, one is related to each and all of the persons. God is in every moment the giver, the gift, and the giving of God's self-disclosure.

Rather than dividing up the functions of God in a Sabellian manner, it would be better to adopt William Placher's suggestion to speak of God as "Father, Son and Holy Spirit, one God, mother of us all."[28]

As to creating, redeeming, sanctifying, the Bible speaks of God creating, God creating through the Word (Logos), of the Spirit present at creation brooding upon the face of the waters. Redeeming is spoken of as the creation within us of a new spirit, making us new creatures. Jesus sends his disciples the Spirit, but God sends the Spirit to

---

[28]William C. Placher, *Narratives of a Vulnerable God* (Louisville: Westminster/ John Knox Press, 1994), 61.

Jesus at his baptism. The Bible is a lovely mess on this point; it will not allow an easy sorting out of the separate roles of the three persons. If the doctrine of the Trinity is a way of summarizing the content of revelation (and it is), it must be arguably adequate to that content.

God as the Ultimate Companion

One of the first thinkers to criticize the traditional model of God in Christian theology was Alfred North Whitehead. He disliked its monarchical character. Its God "stood in the same relation to the whole World as early Egyptian or Mesopotamian kings stood to their subject populations."[29] Thus it was, according to Whitehead, that when Christianity became established in the fourth century, "Caesar conquered."[30] In spite of the fact that the Galilean origin of Christianity "dwells upon the tender elements of the world, which slowly and in quietness operate by love," the church continued to fashion "God in the image of the Egyptian, Persian, and Roman imperial rulers."[31] It "gave unto God the attributes which belonged exclusively to Caesar." God was thought of as Aristotle's "unmoved mover," as an imperial ruler, or as a ruthless moral energy. Yet, says Whitehead, "love neither rules, nor is it unmoved; also it is a little oblivious to morals."[32]

Because he thought that the nature of God is dipolar, that God not only effects but is deeply affected by what happens to God's beloved children, Whitehead argued that God saves the world by taking into God's life all of God's children. Ultimately, all of them are saved. This aspect of God's life is expressed by Whitehead as "the tender care that nothing be lost."[33] God is the ultimate Redeemer of the world, redeeming it by suffering with it and granting it meaning and worth beyond itself in God's life.

Thus, he came up with the metaphor for God as "the great *companion*–the fellow-sufferer who understands."[34] God spoke to Moses, says Exodus, "as one speaks to a friend" (Ex. 33:11; see also 2 Chr. 20:7; Isa. 41:8; Jas. 2:23). God is our ultimate companion,

---

[29]Whitehead, *Adventures of Ideas* (New York: Macmillan, 1933), 169.
[30]Whitehead, *Process and Reality*, 342.
[31]Ibid.
[32]Ibid., 343.
[33]Ibid., 346.
[34]Ibid., 351.

not just another companion. God is the one companion on whom we may ultimately rely never to fail to do for us all that God can possibly do for us and in whom we may place our radical trust to take our lives into God's care and keeping. The word "companion" derives from the Latin words *cum* (with) and *panis* (bread). A companion is one with whom we break bread. At every Lord's supper, Jesus is our companion who breaks bread with us. God in Jesus Christ befriends us and befriends the whole world. "I do not call you servants any longer," said Jesus, "but I have called you friends..." (Jn. 15:15). Jesus invites us to be his friends and creates a new dimension of receptivity in us. Sallie McFague suggests that God's friendship for us is God's liking us: "A friend is someone you like and someone who likes you."[35] Friendship is an adult relationship in which we have "to grow up and take responsibility for the world."[36] We cannot do otherwise, if we are to be friends of the One who is Friend of all.

Such responsibility is wearying, which is where the grace of the Friend plays a critical role. One breaks bread with this Friend, and bread is nourishing. The love of God the Friend is a refreshing, sustaining love. The commanding love of God the Friend enables and empowers us to take up the responsibilities for the world of God's other friends.

God the Trinity: The History of Salvation

This discussion of the doctrine of the Trinity will take place in two steps. First, we will talk about God's involvement in human salvation. Traditionally Christians have called this "the economic Trinity," meaning by that term God's "building up the house of salvation." The Greek words for house (*oikos*) and law (*nomos*), from which we get our word "economy," are here put together for a theological use. The economic Trinity is, simply, the history of the God of Israel with the Israel of God and the Gentiles. Second, we will talk about the "immanent" or "ontological" Trinity, that is, God in God's own being. The immanent Trinity is an attempt to speak of God in a manner appropriate to what has been disclosed to us about God in the history of salvation. It is a way of answering the question: If God does this sort of thing, what is God like?

---

[35]Sallie McFague, *Models of God* (Philadelphia: Fortress Press, 1987), 160.
[36]Ibid., 165.

The Economic Trinity: How Christians Name God

The way in which the church names God is expressed in its doctrine of the Trinity. God is the God whom we meet in the history of salvation in several roles. God creates and continually recreates the world and us with the purpose of blessing and sanctifying that world. God redeems the world out of its estrangement and sin; in Christ, by God's grace, we are made "new creatures" (2 Cor. 5:17; Gal. 6:15). God sanctifies the world toward the future that God has in store for it. God is the Spirit who creates, redeems, and ultimately reconciles. These three ways of speaking of God's activity are not simply laid out historically in a sequential fashion, because in each moment of our lives God creates us anew, redeems us out of the narrowness and stupidity of the past, and calls us forward toward God's future with all God's friends.

There is suffering and vulnerability in God and God's relationship to the world. The scriptures often depict God as being in turmoil over the sin and evil of the world, so deeply is God affected and so profoundly does God care. The New Testament's central way of characterizing this suffering and vulnerability of God is in the story of the crucifixion of Jesus. God hands over God's only son, as Abraham had been willing to do with Isaac (a story of which the gospel-writers are aware as they write of the crucifixion), and the Son in obedience undergoes death on the cross. Both the Father and the Son suffer, the one grief and the other death. Their grieving mutual love bears the consequences of the sins of the world; God once again and decisively takes them upon God's self so that we do not have to bear them. As Jürgen Moltmann puts it: "Any one who talks of the trinity talks of the cross of Jesus, and does not speculate in heavenly riddles."[37]

The doctrine of the Trinity is the church's way of asserting that the God it worships is the God of Israel and of the Israel of God. The Trinity names or identifies the God who is incarnate in Jesus Christ and active in the Holy Spirit as the God of Israel and of the scriptures. It is a way of summarizing/describing the activity of God in the history of salvation, God as related to the world and history.

It is a common mistake among theologians writing about the history of the doctrine of the Trinity to begin the discussion in the

---

[37]Jürgen Moltmann, *The Crucified God,* trans. R. A. Wilson and John Bowden (New York: Harper & Row, 1973), 207.

early fourth century with Arius' teaching that the Logos incarnate in Jesus Christ was subordinate to God, a creature, and of a different substance than God.[38] To begin the discussion at that point misses a large part of its significance.

Well before the fourth century two major complications for the Christian understanding of God were posed by extremely Gentile and anti-Jewish versions of "Christian" teaching: (a) Marcion (ca. 100–ca. 160) argued that the Creator and Redeemer were not one but two gods and that the redeemer, clearly the superior of the two, was not the God of what Marcion named the "old" Testament. Here it is God the "father" who is "subordinate" to the redeemer. (b) Gnostic, docetic christologies argued that the God who "seemed" (*dokeo*) to take on a body in Jesus was the supreme being who came to "save" us from the creator God of the Jews who "trapped" us in material bodies. Saturninus, for example, said: "Christ came to destroy the god of the Jews."[39]

In his *Against Praxeas*, Tertullian (ca. 160–ca. 225) argued that Praxeas, a Monarchian, "did a twofold service for the devil at Rome: he drove away prophecy, and he brought in heresy; he put to flight the Paraclete, and he crucified the Father" (*Ante-Nicene Fathers*, 3, 597). In response to Praxeas' Monarchianism, Tertullian coined the term "trinitas" and developed the western trinitarian formula, "tres personae in una substantia" (although the meaning of "substantia" in Tertullian is far from clear, the legal sense of the term–i.e., my "substance" is my controllable assets–was quite important to Tertullian). Tertullian also insisted on the divine "economy" (*oikos*= house, *nomos*= law; the "law of building a house"; theologically, the history of the building up of salvation). What we think of God must be derived from and rooted in the history of salvation.

Therefore the question, "Who is God?" or "Which God is incarnate in Jesus Christ?" is answered by saying: The God who created the world, liberated Israel from captivity in Egypt, was with Israel in the wilderness, in the entrance to the land of Canaan, who "dwelt" with Israel in the ark of the covenant, in the temple, who went with Israel into exile, the God whose "dwelling" (the root meaning of

---

[38]Catherine Mowry LaCugna, "God in Communion With Us," in *Freeing Theology*, ed. Catherine Mowry LaCugna (New York: HarperCollins, 1992), 85.

[39]Robert M. Grant, *Gods and the One God* (Philadelphia: Westminster Press, 1986), 107.

shekhinah = presence) is with us even in the valley of the shadow of death, the God who became flesh in Jesus Christ and "dwelt among us, full of grace and truth," this "Emmanuel" (God with us), and this God who eschatologically will ultimately redeem God's good creation—this is the One of whom we speak when we name/identify God as "Trinity." If we wait until Arius arrives on the scene to identify the trinitarian problem, we miss a major point of the doctrine, that it names/identifies the God whom Christians worship as the God of Israel.

There are three issues immediately apparent: (1) If we say that "In Christ God was reconciling the world to himself" (2 Cor. 5:19), of which God are we speaking, the God of Israel or some other understanding of God that we import (from where)? (2) If salvation occurs through Jesus Christ, how is this possible unless God is graciously operative both in and through Jesus Christ and in and upon us as the Holy Spirit? (3) If we say that God is our "savior," what do we mean by "save, savior," and so forth? With regard to the meaning of salvation, note that those who denied that the God incarnate in Jesus was the God of Israel also had radically different understandings of "salvation" from those found in the Bible. Whereas, for the scriptures "salvation" could never be separated from the hoped-for liberation of this world from all forms of oppression (even if salvation also could never simply be reduced to liberation from this-worldly oppression), for the Gnostics salvation consisted of abandoning this world for a salvation reserved for the spiritually "elite" who are eligible for it (Gnosticism's elitist connection with racism has been pointed out frequently).

The first question, "Who is God?" has been dealt with before: The God who saves us in Jesus (whose very name "Yahweh is salvation" should be clue enough) is the God of Israel to whom Jesus prays and witnesses ("Hear, O Israel: the Lord our God, the Lord is one"—Mark 12:29, the *Shema*). Jesus' prayer at Gethsemane to "Abba, the Father" (Mk. 14:36) reflects Abrahamic and Jewish traditions.

What do we mean by "salvation"? The love of God graciously offered to us makes possible our salvation. God is the subject of all the salvation verbs in the Torah/Christ story, although God often works with such human agents as Moses. We can be saved, re-created (become new creatures) only by our Creator; salvation is by God's gracious initiative. We have an inherent trinitarian structure of thought: *God saves us* through Jesus Christ; God saves us *through Jesus*

Christ; God saves us through Jesus Christ *by the operation of the Holy Spirit upon us.* Jesus Christ is the gracious gift to the church from both the God of Israel and the Israel of God in whom and in whose scriptures Jesus Christ took shape. Our ability to appropriate this gift of God is itself possible only by God's gracious efficacy upon our spirits by the Holy Spirit; the church is a creation of the Holy Spirit (Acts 2). We cannot "know" God apart from some construal of God through a finite medium of the divine ground and end of our being and becoming, nor can we so know God by any innate or natural human ability to do so apart from God's gracious direction; hence, the salvific self-disclosure of God happens both through Jesus Christ and the Spirit of God. This is the "economy" of salvation. The "economic trinity" refers to God's activity or operation in the world, the "immanent trinity" to God's being considered not apart from, but in distinction from God's activities in the world.

Salvation is di-polar, involving both redemption and emancipation (i.e., liberation from this-worldly oppression). Redemption is liberation from sin, ignorance (idolatry), death (and the fear of death), judgment and condemnation, meaninglessness and emptiness. The grace of God is: God's empowerment of our salvation; God's seeking and finding us as the lost ones; God's benevolent disposition toward and action on behalf of people trapped in evil; God's forgiveness of sins; God's reassuring us as to God's reality and meaning when damnation takes the form of meaninglessness; God's placing us in a community of redemption and reconciliation when abandonment and isolation is the form of human hurt; God's supply of strength when weakness is characteristic of human effort; God's yes in the gospel to every no of the world within, the world among, and the world around; God's presence to us as eternal in the midst of the temporal; God's promise and power of life at the moment or in the fear of death. Grace is intrinsic in all that God has made. God's supreme gift of grace is Jesus Christ, a gift which "redeems" us from understanding ourselves in any ultimate way other than in terms of the love of God graciously given to us.[40]

Redemption is not reducible to, but entails, emancipation. Those who understand themselves as loved by God understand themselves

---

[40]This paragraph was inspired by notes taken on a lecture given by Joseph Sittler in 1958.

also as under the radical command of the God who loves all others, so that we shall in turn love God with all our selves and our neighbors as ourselves. In the biblical context, the latter means a proactive approach to social justice on behalf of the poor, the weak, the oppressed, widows, and orphans in their affliction, "the least of these," that we are commanded to meet their needs as the very needs of Jesus Christ. Salvation by grace is made possible by the unfathomable love and total claim of God disclosed in the history of the God of Israel with the Israel of God, in Exodus, the Torah, and the prophets and with decisive clarity in Jesus Christ, who took shape in the people Israel.

Christians might learn something about the meaning of salvation from our Jewish brothers and sisters. Jews distinguish between personal salvation and social-public redemption. Salvation has to do with the well-being of persons, well-being in all its dimensions. The psalms in particular emphasize God's gracious ability to provide salvation to persons. Covenantal promises often have to do with communal well-being. Prophetic promise and criticism are addressed to the people as a whole. Messianic expectation is for a renewed public life. In no case do Jews earn either redemption or salvation. But Judaism does underline the importance of opportunities in personal life for the response of faith and opportunities in political life in which God's redemptive power may be allowed to work. Opportunities to perform deeds of loving kindness are graciously given to us, just as God's grace always makes possible the turning of a person to God in repentance.

Two further important points that we should appreciate are these: First, Judaism refuses to believe that this world of war, tension, genocide, in which two-thirds of the world's populace goes to bed hungry every night, is God's promised redemption. Redemption and its final disclosure or achievement lie in the future and will not come about without the participation of God's covenant partners. Second, all human beings, not only Jews, are graced by God with their own opportunities of faithful turning to God and joyful performance of deeds of loving-kindness. The "righteous from all peoples inherit the world to come."[41]

The point of the doctrine of the Trinity, then, is itself "trinitarian": (1) the one God, whom we know in Jesus Christ, is the God of Israel;

---

[41] *Sanhedrin*, Babylonian Talmud, 105a.

(2) through Jesus Christ, and in the Spirit, the God of Israel graciously saves us and creates in and with us a community of the Spirit; and (3) God is always and everywhere the gracious Savior of all God's creatures.

The point or intent of the doctrine of the Trinity is to stress that Christian faith in God is faith in Jesus Christ (that Jesus Christ is Lord is the constitutive assertion of the Christian faith). This faith gets its firsthand character from the fact that it is faith in the Holy Spirit. The historical anchor of Christian faith is Jesus Christ; the continuing, present-living, revelatory aspect of Christian faith testifies to the active, gracious presence of the Holy Spirit. We know God by God's grace through Christ, by virtue of the gracious activity upon us of God's Holy Spirit; both Christ and the Holy Spirit are *homoousios* with God, that is, the spirit operative upon us is the Spirit of God. As we make this last point, we are aware of and reject the tendency in the Christian tradition to restrict the work of the Spirit to Christians and to deny that the Spirit is universally active.

Let us summarize this discussion of the economic Trinity. The doctrine of the Trinity is a symbol that matures over time as a people reflect on their experience with the God of Israel disclosing God's self to them in Jesus Christ in the power of the Spirit. "Christian experience of faith," as Elizabeth Johnson says, "is the generating matrix for language about God as triune. Conversely, the Trinity is a legitimate but secondary concept that synthesizes the concrete experience of salvation in a 'short formula.'"[42] If we fail to keep the doctrine of the Trinity firmly grounded in this concrete historical experience, theorizing about it "can degenerate into wild and empty conceptual acrobatics."[43]

We turn now to the immanent Trinity, a discussion of God's inner life, hoping always to remember to say what we say "as it were." How do we make the move from a discussion of the experience of God in history to that of God's being? In this way: We have three experiences of God and three kinds of possible relationships with God. Hence, we infer that we may speak of three relevant corresponding distinctions in God. We do this on the assumption that God is faithful and true, that God does not mislead us when God reveals God's self.

---

[42]Elizabeth Johnson, *She Who Is* (New York: Crossroad, 1994), 198.
[43]Ibid.

The Immanent Trinity: God's Life as Blessing and Well-being

As with our earlier discussion of the doctrine of creation out of nothing, this discussion, too, is from the perspective of neo-process theology or a theology that finds process thought an engaging conversation partner. It is a long-standing criticism of process theology that it has not developed a doctrine of the Trinity, although some process theologians have sought to address this shortcoming.[44] The difficulty that process thought faces in this regard is owing to its concentration on the topics of becoming and relationality at the microcosmic level of the smallest actual things of which reality is made up, actual entities. Were process thought to concentrate with equal vigor on developing its macrocosmic understanding of persons, this difficulty might be overcome.[45]

We begin with a theological premise and an observation about ordinary experience. The premise is that the best metaphor we have for speaking of God is that of person. God is personal. We call this a metaphor, because in some senses God is not literally personal, that is, God is not like human persons in several important respects. God is not limited or sinful and does not have eyes and ears. In other respects, God is both like and unlike human persons. God knows, hopes, feels, acts, and reacts, but always perfectly and not imperfectly, and is in communion with all others, not only some others.

The observation from ordinary experience is simply this: We have no analogy in our experience for the concept of a single person existing in absolute autonomy with no essential relations to other persons. All the persons we know, or can ever hope to know, come bundled in social and communal relationships with other persons. Persons do not first exist singly and then decide to enter relationships. Relations to other persons are primary to the existence of every individual person. Scratch any person you know, and down deep you will find relations to that person's parents.

---

[44]See, e.g., Robert Cummings Neville, *A Theology Primer* (Albany: State University of New York Press, 1991), chap. 4. For Joseph Bracken's work, see his "The Holy Trinity as a Community of Divine Persons," *Heythrop Journal* 15 (1974): 166–82, 257–70, and his *The Triune Symbol* (Lanham, Md.: University Press of America, 1985).

[45]This is analogous to the argument of George R. Lucas on the concept of freedom in his *Two Views of Freedom in Process Thought* (Missoula: Scholars Press, 1979).

Only in communion with other persons, argues John Macmurray, is each of us enabled to become a person.[46] A person is "a person-only-in-relation-to-other-persons." We have no experience, no knowledge of self-sufficient individuals.

The point has to do with intelligibility. It is usually presumed that the doctrine of the Trinity does not make sense, whereas a simple monotheism according to which God is one person does make sense. But, if we are utterly lacking any analogue in our experience for the idea of one person existing altogether apart from relation to other persons, the presumption is without foundation and strictly nonsensical, lacking any meaning conceivably derivable from experience.

The Politics of the Trinity

We receive the most important reflections on the Trinity from theologians primarily concerned with faith as a way of life and blessing and as a witness against the death-dealing ways of the world. Juan Luis Segundo is convinced that one of the idols that holds Latin Americans in bondage is the idea of God as absolutely independent of the world, an absolutist abstraction bearing no resemblance to the biblical story of God's engagement with history. Such a view is a projection on to God of what is wrong with our society: other-worldliness, passivity, and individualism.[47]

Feminist theologians like Anne Carr regard the "mystery of God as Trinity" as expressing the excellences "of mutuality, reciprocity, cooperation, unity, peace in genuine diversity that are feminist ideals and goals derived from the inclusivity of the gospel message."[48] Her language is reminiscent of Jonathan Edwards' remarks about God's life being full of "every excellence and beauty." God's internal life embodies the blessing and well-being of genuine community and compassionate love among coequal persons that undercuts all ideas of domination and oppression. Thus the Trinity, Carr contends, includes "qualities that make God truly worthy of imitation, worthy of the call to discipleship that is inherent in Jesus' message."[49]

---

[46]John Macmurray, *Persons in Relation* (London: Faber and Faber, 1961), 159.
[47]Juan Luis Segundo, *Our Idea of God* (Maryknoll: Orbis Books, 1974), 178–79.
[48]Anne Carr, *Transforming Grace* (San Francisco: Harper & Row, 1988), 157.
[49]Ibid.

By the Oaks of Mamre

Genesis tells us that Abraham and Sarah were in their tent "by the oaks of Mamre" (Gen. 18:1–15). Three "men" visited and Abraham offered them hospitality, water to wash their feet, bread and cakes from the finest flour, and a roasted calf. One of the men promised that he would return "in due season," and that Sarah would have a son. Sarah laughed "to herself," only to discover that one of the "men" was the Lord.

What this story of hospitality has to do with the Trinity is just this: An acclaimed icon of the Trinity is the fifteenth-century painting of this scene by the Russian artist Andrei Rublev. His icon portrays three angels sitting around a table on which is a chalice. A house and a tree are in the background. Like other icons of the Trinity, Rublev's was elicited by the story of Abraham and Sarah by the oaks of Mamre.

Catharine Mowry LaCugna, one of the more creative trinitarian thinkers of our time, takes this icon and story as the starting point for her discussion of the Trinity.[50] The point of the doctrine of the Trinity has to do with uncommon hospitality and an open communion of persons. The tree in the background is the tree of life and the house is the temple, Sarah and Abraham's tent transformed into a place where God may dwell.

Although the three figures, Yahweh and the two men (angels), "are arranged in a circle, the circle is not closed. One has the distinct sensation when meditating on the icon that one is not only invited into this communion but, indeed, one already is part of it."[51] The Trinity is a communion of equal persons (coequal, the tradition liked to say), and we are invited into such communion. In the beginning, says Leonardo Boff, is communion.[52] That is, we are invited out of communities of domination and into the kind of communion practiced by Jesus: "You know that among the Gentiles those whom they recognize as their rulers lord it over them, and their great ones are tyrants over them. But it is not so among you; but whoever

---

[50]Catherine Mowry LaCugna, "God in Communion with Us," in *Freeing Theology*, 83–114. See also her *God For Us: The Trinity and Christian Life* (New York: HarperCollins, 1991).

[51]Ibid., 84.

[52]Leonardo Boff, *Trinity and Society*, trans. Paul Burns (Maryknoll: Orbis Books, 1988), 9.

wishes to become great among you must be your servant" (Mk. 10:42–43; Mt. 20:25–27; Lk. 22:25–27).

The development of the doctrine of the Trinity was made possible, according to LaCugna, by several theological steps: distinguishing between being and personhood, thinking of God as self-differentiated, and making person and not substance the major category for understanding reality. In other words, the idea of person, of being-in-relation-to-another person, is the appropriate metaphor for God instead of ideas of substance, self-sufficiency, or of God as essentially unrelated and patriarchal.

The politics of the Trinity are discerned when we see that God's unity and life are situated "in the communion among equal though unique persons, not in the primacy of one person over another."[53] We speak of God as one in order to make clear that God is not divided, not double-minded. We speak of God as three to affirm communion in God. Life is blessing and well-being when all relations of domination and oppression are expelled. Communion among persons is the divine order and the intended human order of well-being. The fundamental intent of the doctrine of the Trinity is to protect an understanding of God as a profound relational communion. A relationship (not merely a relation) of authentic communion among God, human beings, and all God's creatures is the aim of God's work in the world. It also calls radically into question and theologically undercuts, although hardly defeats, all human political and social arrangements that would subordinate women to men, Jews to Christians (as Christendom did in many ways, not the least through canon and secular law), one race to another, two-thirds of the hungry world to the one-third that is comfortable.

God's life is one of hospitality, blessing, and well-being among a communion of equal persons, and persons are only found and only prosper in such communion. God graciously offers the blessings of God's life in self-disclosure to the world, in the history of the Israel of God and the church for our sanctification. But as God did not liberate Israel from oppression without the cooperation of Moses, neither does God work God's will in the world without God's covenant partners. God's power to work well-being in the world is the power of a covenantal, communal God, not the power of a divine autocrat.

---

[53]Ibid., 88.

God's Power

Biblically, as Jon Levenson makes clear, God's power is not total or God's victory over evil and disorder complete. God reveals God's self as a covenant-making God who calls and claims us as God's covenant partners in realizing God's purposes in the world and history. If we are to think of God, in relation to the biblical witness, we have to locate God's love, power, and justice in relation to one another and not consider them separately as abstract properties that we choose, randomly and capriciously, to affirm of God in whatever sense we choose and with meanings drawn from just anywhere we please. God's power and justice are the kind of power and justice appropriate to God's love; God's love, the kind of love appropriate to God's just purposes and power.

Biblically, God is "lord in covenant" with God's people. God is a covenant-making God (covenant-making = a primary form of God's grace). Between the creation and flood stories in Genesis, as Jon Levenson points out, there was neither human righteousness nor God's utter immutability (which many biblical stories belie), but only God's *covenantal faithfulness*, God's respect for the solemn pledge that God made to Noah (in the utterly gracious covenant with all people and even "the living things"). God's activity in the Bible limits, but does not eliminate, chaos and evil; life remains precarious. It was precisely when the people Israel had the greatest reasons, from their experience, to doubt God's power that Israel celebrated God's power. God's victory "must be interpreted in the light of the historical experience of the torching of his cult sites, the absence of miracles, the blaspheming of God's name, the defeat of his partners in covenant, and the general collapse of his mastery over the world."[54]

God is not omnipotent in the sense of being wholly in control either of the world or of the human heart. "Rabbi Hanina said: 'Everything is in the hand of heaven [God] except the fear of heaven.'"[55] What guarantees that evil will not finally triumph is God's covenantal faithfulness and the faithfulness of God's covenant partners in the task of actualizing God's purposes in the world. God and the

---

[54]Jon D. Levenson, *Creation and the Persistence of Evil* (San Francisco: Harper & Row, 1988), 19.

[55]*Berakot*, 33b.

community in covenant interact with one another. God's purposes can well be at odds with many purposes of other agents in the world.

God is a God of love, justice (including judgment, wrath), and power. That God is depicted as profoundly disturbed by human sin shows how vulnerable God is to it, and how profoundly related to us. The oneness of God (oneness not as utterly "simple," static, and unrelated) requires that God's love, power, and justice be understood so that God is not at odds with God's self. Unless our understanding of each of these terms is biblically informed, and unless each term is related to the others, our talk about God will be a muddle. Questions: How can God love us, yet be angry and wrathful toward us? How is God both all-powerful and loving at the same time? What kind of power do we attribute to God? If any and all kinds, how is this the power of love? If God is love, why does God's love seem not to be dominant in the world? How do you answer the theological question of a parishioner whose child has died: "Pastor, why did God do this to me?"

God's love, seen definitively in Christ, shows a God who, in love, seeks us out for reconciliation with God, ourselves, and one another; this love is freely, graciously given to us. The ministry, crucifixion, and resurrection of Jesus Christ are where this love appears, most decisively in the cross. This cross-bearing love is a love that has its own purposes and is willing to go to the cross for them.

God's love is against what is against love (Tillich); it is in radical opposition to evil and radically *for* reconciliation. God's wrath is the "strange work" (*opus alienum*) of God, whereas God's love is God's "proper work" (*opus proprium*). The way of God revealed in Torah and Christ is the "way of life" and is in opposition to the "way of death"; "I came that they may have life, and have it abundantly" (Jn. 10:10). God's love is in conflict with, contends against, everything that is evil and destructive. Hence the cross: So far does God go in the struggle against evil. God's wrath or anger is not aimed at the destruction of sinners but their transformation and redemption. It is important to remember this even, indeed particularly, with respect to oppressors. The book of Acts is the story of an oppressor, Saul, who became an apostle. Justice as the will of God (not vengeance that seeks to destroy and is part of the way of death) is the form of God's love; justice is the social form of love (Tillich, Niebuhr). Love without justice is empty; justice without love can become injustice (e.g., vengeance).

God and Ethics

In case it is not clear, let us do one more take on the topic of God and ethics. We consider a few home truths. First, if God is utterly immutable and impassible, then you and I and what we do make literally no difference to God. If, however, God is the One to whom all things happen, if everything that happens to each of God's creatures happens also to God (because those creatures are perfectly included in God's life), then what happens matters. Notice those three words again: What happens matters. What happens matters ultimately, because it happens to the One who is ultimate. God, therefore, is the reason why we should be moral, why we should love our neighbors as ourselves. God is the answer to the question, Why care at all?

Second, God always and already does everything for all of God's creatures (including us) that it is possible and appropriate for God to do. However, here we have to pay the price of saying that God is not one finite agent among and alongside others. Finite agents (such as you and I) can do things that God cannot do. We can make a peanut butter sandwich. Can God? We can take the peanut butter sandwich across the street and give it to a hungry person. God cannot. Here's the principle: If it's the sort of thing that you and I can do, then we're responsible for doing it. And that extends to some fairly big-ticket items, such as trying to make the church a genuinely inclusive community of women and men and trying to reverse the tide of its traditional anti-Judaism.

Chapter 5

Creation, Providence, and Evil

Creation Matters to God

The doctrine of creation has not only to do with "first things," looking backward to the beginning, but also with present life and future hope, not only for human beings, but for all creatures. The range and meaning of the doctrine of creation are expressed by the apostle Paul in his statement: "For from him and through him and to him are all things" (Rom. 11:36). God's creative activity embraces beginning ("from"), ongoingness ("through"), and *telos* (end, aim, goal: "to"). "All things" are from God, through God, and to God. This does not imply a monocausal universe in which God is the only cause and therefore both responsible and indictable for evil. There are other agents in addition to God (including tumors, viruses, bacteria, politicians, dictators, your parents, yourself), and these agents are capable of acting in ways other than God would have them act. Yet apart from God there would be nothing other than God. God's activity creates, sustains, and ultimately (eschatologically) causes the return to God's life of all that is. Our final end is in God. This world, albeit of God's good creation, is not our final home.

131

Therefore, we do not limit our understanding of salvation to liberation from oppression in this world. But this is the world that God creates, sustains, cherishes, and will, ultimately, redeem. What happens in it is ultimately important because it is important to God, who is ultimate. Therefore, it is promised not only a salvation in time, but a redemption beyond time. We shall try to make clear that, for these reasons, we are commanded to work for the liberation of our neighbors and of the rest of creation from oppression.

Some Rabbinic Wisdom

How the doctrine of creation functions in Judaism teaches us something about how it should function for Christians. In traditional Judaism there is a blessing for every occasion of life. For example, when one of us sees another person who is sexually attractive, the blessing to be said is: "Blessed art thou, O Lord our God, who has made us in thy image." This blessing does not deny the goodness of sexual attraction; it celebrates it as having been created by God. But it takes sexual attraction and sanctifies it, transforms it into something that can contribute to the well-being, the blessing of all God's creatures. To remember that a sexually attractive person is made in God's image is to be reminded that such a person is not a thing to be manipulated for one's pleasure, not a toy with which to play, not an employee who can be harassed, not a vessel for the release of one's overcharged sexual energies. Hence, the story of creation has to do with how we intend our neighbors, and not only our human neighbors, but all the "living things" as well. What posture shall we take to them? Will we treat them with respect as creatures of God; will we guard and protect the well-being of the stranger, of those who are "different" from us; can we affirm and rejoice in such difference as created and valued by God? Will we be a source of blessing and well-being to the neighbor and to nature, or a source of curse and death?

Let us look at a rabbinic passage.

> Only one single man [Adam] was created in the world, to teach that, if any man has caused a single soul to perish, Scripture imputes it to him as though he had caused a whole world to perish, and if any man saves alive a single soul, Scripture imputes it to him as though he had saved a whole world. Again, but a single man was created for the sake of

peace among mankind, that none should say to his fellow, "My father was greater than your father"; also that the heretics (*minim*) should not say, "There are many ruling powers in heaven." Again, but a single man was created to proclaim the greatness of God, for man stamps many coins with one die, and they are all like to one another; but God has stamped every man with the die of the first man, yet not one of them is like his fellow. Therefore every one must say, "For my sake was the world created."[1]

The rabbis make three points about the meaning of creation. First, because God makes us all in God's image, to cause one person to perish is the equivalent of causing "a whole world to perish." Killing is awesomely evil. Conversely, to save a human life is to save "a whole world." Saving a life is awesomely redemptive. The one is curse and death, the other life and well-being. Second, racism and ethnocentrism are denied because all human beings, said the rabbis, have one and the same forebear. No one's ancestry is superior to anyone else's. No ethnic group, community, race, class, or individual is justified in thinking itself superior to any other. Nor may it look condescendingly on others as inferior. All of us have the same human parents and all of us are morally equal to one another. Third, not one of us is like another. Being all made in the image of the God who will be whoever/whatever God will be, we are not shaped by the same cookie cutter. We are individually unique, and our differences are to be cherished, affirmed, and appreciated. My son is not me in miniature. He is his unique, creative self, and our mutual well-being is enhanced when I love him for himself and not as a reflection of my ego.

These considerations are presented as a foretaste of the orientation of this chapter on the doctrine of creation (including some discussion of providence and evil). We will deal with our topic as practical wisdom for the living of life in relation to urgent questions pressed upon us by our context. Those will be the questions raised by the ecological crisis of our time: What has the doctrine of creation to say about our responsibilities to this earth, this *eretz* of God's good creation?

---

[1] *Sanhedrin*, Babylonian Talmud, 37a.

Science or Theology?

The creation story (or stories; there are two in the first chapters of Genesis), coming as it does at the opening of the Torah, has been extraordinarily important to Jewish thought and life. Yet the rabbis of the Mishnah and Talmud were little concerned with the "scientific" status of the story. Instead, they understood the story in relation to the spiritual and moral insights that they drew from it. That God created the world means that the world has value and meaning to God and, therefore, to us. The world is not merely the result of an accident (we would say, a "big bang").

Avoiding Category Blunders

The doctrine of creation is an affirmation/confession of faith about creation. It is not a "scientific" explanation of how things came to be or an alternative cosmological theory among others. Scientific hypotheses (such as the current favorite, the "big bang," and the recent addition of the "great attractor"–a hypothetical mass of dark matter pulling the universe "sideways") have all the validity/invalidity appropriate to such statements. Such a hypothesis is proposed and then used for the systematic collection of evidence pro and con, its verification or falsification. Eventually, every scientific hypothesis will be falsified and replaced by another and, thus, do its work: that of producing interesting research. Each hypothesis is dropped when the difficulties that accompany it become too many and the benefits it produces become too few.

A category blunder occurs when we treat an idea from one field of discourse as if it belonged to another, in this case when we regard a statement of faith as if it were a scientific proposal or hypothesis. When Basil Fawlty of the British comedy series "Fawlty Towers" responded to his car's mechanical failure by beating it with a stick, treating a machine as personally responsible for having broken down, he committed a category blunder. Science deals with hypotheses that can, within limits, be experimentally tested. It may ask, for example, "How was the world created?" Did it start with a bang? Theology's questions and answers are tested publicly enough, but by theological criteria, not the criteria of science. Theology seeks to ask and answer the Why? questions: Why is there anything at all? Why be moral? Why care about truth? Why love the neighbor? If everything began as nothing more than the result of an explosion (although a very big one!) and promises to end in nothing more promising than a "black hole," and if that is the ultimate truth (so far as science, at any rate, can say), then what difference does it make whether or how I live my life? If Carl Sagan is right about the "cold beauty" of the intergalactic dance as the final truth of the universe, true as that may be scientifically, it is cold comfort to human beings.

This is not to say that theology never wishes to disagree with science with regard to how things happen. For science, God is not an agent who needs to be taken into consideration as a cause in any scientific explanation. For theology, at least for any process or neo-process theology as well as others, there is no situation in which God is not operative as a causal agent. For Darwin, it was not necessary to invoke God to account for the evolution of novel forms of biological life. For this theology, God is the reason why there is novelty. When theology disagrees with science, it is a matter of its worldview or ontology—its claim, for example, that the world exists because it is created from moment to moment by God.

Limit Questions and Answers

It is helpful to regard the doctrine of creation as an answer to what Stephen Toulmin calls a "limiting question."[2] Consider Blaise Pascal's (1623–1662) agonizing reflection on himself in relation to the immensity of the universe:

> When I consider the briefness of my life, swallowed up in the eternity before and behind it, the small space I fill, or even see, engulfed in the infinite immensity of space which I know not, and which knows not me, I am afraid…Who has set me here? By whose order and arrangement have this place and this time been allotted me?[3]

Notice Pascal's paraphrase of Psalm 8:3–4: "When I look at your heavens, the work of your fingers, the moon and the stars that you have established; what are human beings that you are mindful of them, mortals that you care for them?"

For Pascal the very immensity of the universe discovered by seventeenth-century science, plus its coldness and indifference to human beings and the concerns of the human heart, caused him to

---

[2]Stephen Toulmin, *Reason In Ethics* (Cambridge: Cambridge University Press, 1964), 205–11.

[3]Ibid., 209–10.

react with uncertainty, fear, wonder, and what Toulmin calls a "desire for reassurance." It is Pascal's finitude, the limits, spatial and temporal, to his existence, that occasion his question. A limiting question is a question that arises in one field of discourse (e.g., ethics), but cannot be answered (i.e., without being begged) within the rules of that field of discourse (e.g., why should I care about being ethical?).[4] A limiting question is a metaquestion. Pascal was not, in other words, asking for a "scientific" answer to his question. In a context designed to deal with proximate matters, he asked a question of ultimate meaning and importance.

Like Pascal, Paul Tillich interpreted the question of God and God's being as the existential question arising from the "anxiety of finitude" (Pascal's "I am afraid") and interpreted God and God's creativity as the "answer" to the question of the source of faith or the courage to be in the midst of a problematic (i.e., creaturely) situation.[5] The anxiety of nonbeing (the "fear of death"; cf. Mt. 10:31 "fear not") is overcome with faith in God as the source of the courage to be. "Perfect love casts out fear" (1 Jn. 4:18). This is not the claim that, chronologically, we first ask such a question and then invent/discover/have revealed to us its answer. It is a logical claim about the status and meaning of a doctrine. A limiting question is answered by a limiting concept, what we might call an "existential" concept (but not a concept that is reducible to existential matters). An existential concept (as I define it) is at the same time a theological concept, an ontological concept, and a moral concept. An existential concept has to do with how we understand ourselves (this is what makes it existential) in relationship to God, the world in which we live, and all our neighbors (including not only people but also the woolly-worms and the rest of creation as well). Such a concept attempts to answer the questions: Who are we? Who is God? How are we to understand the world in which we live? How are we to live in the world that we so understand? Thus the doctrine of creation also answers questions about the world, the neighbor, and how we should live.

---

[4]Paul Tillich, *Theology of Culture* (New York: Oxford University Press, 1959), 3–9.

[5]Paul Tillich, *Systematic Theology*, vol. 1 (Chicago: The University of Chicago Press, 1951), part 2.

Creation and God's Love

The doctrine of creation's answer to these questions is: You and everyone/everything else are those beings whose very existence is owed to God's gracious, primordial love. God is the creating, re-creating, and ultimately redeeming God of a singular promise and a singular command: the promise that God's love is freely given to you as to all others and the command that you are in turn to love God with all your self and your neighbors as yourself. The world in which we live, with all its mixture of good, evil, and sheer happenstance, is essentially good; we are to live in that world according to the "way of life" and not the "way of death." We do not kill those who are created in God's image.

William James, in an essay called "The Will to Believe," suggested that we have a "right to believe" such answers to limiting questions.[6] James later said that he should have called his essay "The Right to Believe," and denied that we can, "by just willing it, believe that Abraham Lincoln's existence is a myth…"[7] What he said in this "essay in justification *of* faith" was that under tightly defined conditions we have a "right" to believe certain statements.[8] The conditions are: that the proposed statement must be live, forced, and momentous. A live issue, as distinct from a dead one, is a possibility for us (we may be asked to believe that the moon is made of green cheese, but it is not a live issue). A forced issue is one that, because it cannot be settled by logic or by the empirical procedures of science (neither by logical demonstration nor empirical verification or falsification), we simply must choose one way or the other. It is also one where not to choose to believe is to choose not to believe ("Whoever is not for me is against me," said Jesus) and where choosing is part of what it means to affirm the statement. A momentous issue is one that makes all the difference to how we understand ourselves and to what we understand we ought to do. It makes a practical, moral difference. Here is an example from ordinary life: When you were first attracted to the person you love, the proposition that she/he might love you was live, forced, and momentous. Had you

---

[6]William James, *The Will to Believe* (New York: Dover Publications, Inc., 1956), 1–31.

[7]Ibid., 4.

[8]Ibid., 1.

demanded logical and empirical demonstration of her/his love, you would have been taken for a boor. "Faith in a fact," says James of such facts as our lover's love for us, "can help create the fact." God and God's primordial, creative love is something in which we have a right to believe and that is momentously important with regard to how we then live our lives. Accepting that God loves us does not create the gift of God's love, but is necessary to our receiving it in a transforming way.

Creation out of Love

Biblically, God's creating activity has a beginning, a continuation, and a goal. This beginning, continuation, and end have as much to do with Jesus Christ and the Spirit as with God the Father. The Word was in the beginning with God, and through the Word were made all the things that were made (Jn. 1). The Spirit brooded over the face of the waters (Gen. 1), and at the end, in the new Jerusalem, Jesus and the Spirit are both present along with God the Creator. The God of creation is also the God of redemption; creation had a beginning but not, so far, an end. God's creating activity throughout the history of the Bible is usually a re-creating activity in which God struggles with and against hostile powers and seeks to breathe new life into the "dry bones" of God's people. Creation is "new creation" (2 Cor. 5:17). Faith in Christ actively lives forward toward the completion of creation in the *eschaton*.

Creation expresses God's love. It is the life-giving activity of God's creative love. "God *is* love" (1 Jn. 4:8) and the "first" place we see this love is in God's creative activity. "First" here is logically, not chronologically, first. First, Israel saw God's goodness in the exodus/ Sinai complex of events; second, it interpreted the whole history of the world, including its creation, in that covenantal perspective. Creation is understood covenantally. Human beings are created so as to be capable of knowing/covenanting with God and, at the same time, of sinning, turning away from, and deceiving themselves about what has been given them to know.

Creation, the Covenant, and Human Beings

The creation stories are stories about the God of Israel, the God who liberated Israel from oppression in Egypt and forged a covenant with Israel at Sinai. One cannot read the creation stories of Genesis 1 and 2 without noting some interesting peculiarities. One is that all those things that were worshiped by the religions surrounding the people Israel are here explicitly mentioned as having been created by God. They are creatures. Another is that all the conditions necessary for Israel's receiving and living on the terms of a covenant of moral responsibility with God are here explicitly staked out. Adam and Eve are in right relationship with each other, their environment (the garden), and God. They are created in the *imago dei* as persons in covenant with one another. It is this covenantal relationship that "images" the covenant-making God. How they are to relate to each other and the environment is made clear. In their relations to nature and one another they are bound to God. God is the initiator of this covenant and provides means for the human beings to carry it out. It is, therefore, a gracious covenant.

What the Doctrine of Creation Denies

The doctrine of creation denies certain other claims. First, it denies that the world is God, that it somehow "emanates" (issues, flows) from God. The doctrine of creation affirms that God transcends and is different from (categorically) the world. "Transcend" does not mean removed, away, "up there," but affirms that God is free in relation to the world. God's freedom is not caprice, but must be held in close relation to God's love; God's creativity expresses God's love; God's love is creative (as well as re-creative and ultimately redemptive). "Transcend" distinguishes God from the world; it does not separate God from the world. The living God of the Bible is constantly talked of as the God who interacts with God's creation and God's people.

Second, it denies that the world is evil because it was fashioned by God out of recalcitrant matter. Gnosticism, docetism, and Marcionism presumed the Platonic understanding of God as the demiurge who created the world by shuttling back and forth between the "world of ideas" (pure forms of definiteness) and "matter" (pure creativity; matter as "alive": hylozoism). This God, considered by Gnostics as "inferior" to the Supreme Being, "trapped" spirits in material bodies from which they had to be saved. Hence, the church came to affirm that God created the world ex nihilo ("We believe in one God, the Father Almighty, creator of heaven and earth and of all things visible and invisible"). The "invisible" things included matter and the Platonic ideas.

Therefore, matter and the world are not evil (although evil occurs in the world), but good, because they are created and valued by God and redeemable. Because creation itself is good, however much sin and evil characterize its course, redemption can occur in history, and an eschatology of fulfillment (not destruction) is possible. This life is good, because it is a gift from God's primordial love.

These denials are part of what is meant by referring to the doctrine of creation ex nihilo as a limit concept. When we step beyond it as a limit concept, we seem inevitably to fall into contradictions. To speak in temporal terms of God's timelessness "before" God created, to say what God "was then," is, to say the least, confusing. It is equally confusing to posit the infinity of time and assert that it grows in quantum units. Perhaps it is best to regard the doctrine as a "protective" teaching (the whole of point 2) designed to "build a fence around the gospel" (somewhat akin to the rabbinic development of the oral torah to "build a fence around the torah").[9]

Another part of what we mean by calling creation a limit concept is that it is an idea of momentous importance for how we understand the world in which we live, how we understand ourselves, and how we understand how we ought to live in the world. It is an immensely practical idea with practical consequences. Ignoring the doctrine of creation, antithetically, also has momentous consequences of a destructive character.

The Whole Creation Groans in Travail

Virtually every issue of the daily newspaper brings new information about the threat to planet Earth. Hardly anyone can be unaware of the impending environmental crises with which the earth itself is faced. On October 1, 1998, the World Wide Fund for Nature reported that in the twenty-five years from 1970 to 1995, a third of the world's natural resources had been consumed. Freshwater ecosystems disappeared at a rate of 6 percent a year and were reduced in number by one half during this period. The natural forest cover fell by one half percent per year, meaning that the amount of forest lost annually was equal in square miles to the size of England and Wales or to Norway. Carbon dioxide emissions increased by about three times in the same period, while between 50 and 60 percent of 227 measured species of fish, birds, and mammals were in decline.[10]

"All life involves robbery," comments John Cobb, "but modern social life is grand larceny."[11] Cobb lists a number of environmental

---

[9] *Pirke Avot,* 1,1.

[10] This report was communicated online at http://www.forests.org/.

[11] John B. Cobb, Jr., *Process Theology as Political Theology* (Philadelphia: Westminster Press, 1982), 122.

catastrophes, some long in the making, such as the destruction of half of the farmable land on the Continent since neolithic times, deforestation, destruction of habitat, the fact that there is no way to dispose of nuclear waste. Nonetheless, he argues, "it is not too late for a moral choice."[12] It is not required of us that we continue depleting the ozone layer, finish up for good and all with the rain forests, and further heat up the weather systems.

Nature falls victim to what Cobb calls the "religion of economism" in which economists are priests, advertisers are evangelists, faith is properly placed in growth, laity are consumers, the shopping mall is the cathedral, the competitive spirit is virtue, and inefficiency is the only known form of sin. The morality of economism is expressed in the slogan "Shop till you drop." Economism turns both nature and people into things. The latter become "human resources," and nature is just a commodity to be mined or harvested, valuable only as it contributes to the insatiable appetite of the ideal of growth.[13]

We have, says Kathryn Tanner, "turned the earth into a commodity for human purposes." Our ways of producing and consuming "in the industrialized nations proceed as if the earth were an infinitely malleable object of human mastery readily bent for any human use, or as if the harm done by human enterprises to the earth and its life-forms were of no real importance or concern."[14] Tanner proposes that a Christian theology of creation has in it resources that can help us, as Christians, to address the environmental crisis. These resources are primarily found in the scriptures, in the covenantal ecology of Israel and its re-presentation in the New Testament.

God gives well-being to God's creatures, to receive as a gift from one and to share with another. God gives well-being to Adam and Eve to share with one another, although they are different, and to

---

[12]Ibid., 123.

[13]John B. Cobb, Jr., "Economism or Planetism: The Coming Choice," *Earth Ethics* 3 (Fall, 1991). For other important works on theology and ecology see: John B. Cobb, Jr., *Sustainability* (Maryknoll: Orbis Books, 1992); Charles Birch and John B. Cobb, Jr., *The Liberation of Life* (Cambridge: Cambridge University Press, 1991); Jay B. McDaniel, *Earth, Sky, Gods & Mortals* (Mystic: Twenty-Third Publications, 1990); and Jay B. McDaniel, *Of God and Pelicans* (Louisville: Westminster/John Knox Press, 1989).

[14]Kathryn Tanner, "Creation, Environmental Crisis, and Ecological Justice," in *Reconstructing Christian Theology*, ed. Rebecca S. Chopp and Mark L. Taylor (Minneapolis: Fortress Press, 1994), 99.

share with the "living things" from whom they differ. God blesses Abraham and Sarah and their descendants, and God wishes for them well-being with the Gentiles from whom they differ. Blessing, well-being, is God's aim for us. It is to be received as a gift, not grasped, and to be shared with those who are other than us, not hoarded as though it were ours to control. The ecological crisis is a crisis for theology not only because it endangers the ecosphere on which we depend for our human existence. It is a crisis because it shows us that we have not been a blessing to nature, but a curse; we have brought death to that which God wanted to produce and multiply. Sin is sin because it is detrimental or destructive to the well-being that is God's intent for all God's creatures.

Nature Matters to God

In the scriptures, particularly in the Hebrew Bible, the realm of nature is located in God's covenant history with the Israel of God. There is what Richard Austin calls "*a biblical ecology.*"[15] Land, as well as people, can be oppressed, and liberation includes both land and people. "The words *covenant* and *promise* apply to the range of created life as well as to human beings."[16] Unlike religions that regard nature as "sacred," the Bible attributes holiness only to God, but it includes nature in the covenant of moral responsibility. Of course, God may freely choose to reveal God's self in, through, and by means of nature and any natural object, such as a mountain. Places, for example, may be derivatively sacred by relation to God, as may all of nature.

The goodness of creation is the message of Genesis 1. Seven times God sees what God has made and calls it "good" or "very good." After each creation God pronounces its goodness. "This is," says Sallie McFague, "an amazing statement. God does not say that creation is good for human beings or even, more surprising, good for me, God, but just good, in fact, very good."[17]

---

[15]Richard Cartwright Austin, *Hope for the Land* (Atlanta: John Knox Press, 1988), 4.

[16]Ibid., 5.

[17]Sallie McFague, *Super, Natural Christians* (Minneapolis: Fortress Press, 1997), 165.

Genesis 1 and 2 describe two aspects to what Carol Johnston calls "the original human vocation."[18] Human beings are to "have dominion," which does not mean to exploit nature, but to relate to it as God does, who "restrains chaos to bring forth an ordered biosphere." Second, human beings are given a garden, a restricted range of duty, to till and keep. "The message of Genesis," remarks McFague, "is not domination but appreciation."[19] Beyond the garden (as later beyond the tilled fields of Israel) are the wild things and their habitat. Johnston points out the psalmist's testimony to God's providence for the wild things:

> You make springs gush forth in the valleys;
> they flow between the hills,
> giving drink to every wild animal;
> the wild asses quench their thirst.
> By the streams the birds of the
> air have their habitation;
> they sing among the branches.
> You cause the grass to grow for the cattle,
> and plants for people to use,
> to bring forth food from the earth,
> and wine to gladden the human heart,
> oil to make the face shine,
> and bread to strengthen the human heart.
> The trees of the LORD are watered abundantly,
> the cedars of Lebanon that he planted.
> In them the birds build their nests,
> the stork has its home in the fir trees.
> (Ps. 104:10–12, 14–17)

Martin Buber gave eloquent expression to the Jewish land tradition. The land is a "land of promise," he reminds us, to be understood as a gift from the God of Israel to the Israel of God. It "was at no time in the history of Israel simply the property of the people."[20] Rather, it was both gift and command: command to make of it what God intended for it.

---

[18]Carol Johnston, *And the Leaves of the Tree Are for the Healing of the Nations* (Presbyterian Church, USA: Office of Environmental Justice, 1997), 5.

[19]McFague, *Super, Natural Christians*, 166.

[20]Martin Buber, *On Zion: The History of an Idea*, trans. Stanley Godman (New York: Schocken Books, 1973), xix.

From the beginning, the destiny of human beings is tied up with the soil, and the fate of the soil is bound up with that of human beings. First, there was a fertile earth, an *Adama*, but no human being, no *Adam*, to serve and tend it. Then God creates human beings and puts them in the garden growing in the *Adama*. Humanity "and the earth are united one with the other from the beginning and to the end of time."[21] In the story, the human beings sin and God curses the earth; it and we are bound up with one another for good or ill, and its fate is affected by our conduct. Yet its fate is, in turn, our fate, a sobering thought in the age of ecological catastrophe in which we live. The communion between the earth and us is moral in character.

After it has become clear that human beings sin—Adam and Eve fail to trust God, and Cain kills Abel—God returns everything to its original condition in which waters cover the face of the earth and starts again with Noah. "The story of Noah's ark," says Johnston, "could be named the first endangered species project, in which God rescues the many species from the consequences of human sin, and begins again with the Rainbow Covenant."[22] God makes this utterly gracious covenant with Noah, his descendants (all human beings), "and with every living creature that is with you, the birds, the domestic animals, and every animal of the earth with you, as many as came out of the ark" (Gen. 9:9–10). This is an "everlasting covenant between God and every living creature of all flesh that is on the earth" (Gen. 9:16).

There are four major aspects to the biblical land tradition. First, all human dealings connected with the environment ("land" includes air, water, and soil as well as all their inhabitants) are to be engaged in honestly. Tracts of land are not to be endlessly added to one another, producing a growing disparity between the rich and the poor. People are not to be thrown into homelessness, a point to remember when we later comment on the economic dislocation in the land of Israel under Roman rule. Job refers to the unjust usurper of land who has caused the death of its owners, saying that the land cries out against him and its furrows weep (Job 31:38). Amos criticizes those who make excess profit on harvest and who "bring the poor of the land to an end" because they "practice deceit with false balances" (Am. 8:5).

---

[21]Ibid., 11.
[22]Johnston, *And the Leaves of the Tree*, 2.

Second, the land given to Israel is to have "a sabbath of complete rest" every seventh year (Lev. 25:4) when fields cannot be sown or harvested or vineyards pruned. Israel's claim to the land is relaxed and its yield made available to all the hungry (Ex. 23:11). The land "rests" from work and celebrates a holiday dedicated to God. "The idea," says Buber, "is that the earth is from time to time to be free, so as not to be subjected to the will of man, but left to its own nature, to be like a no-man's land."[23] The land belongs to God; our relationship to it is to be one of responsible communion, and we are not to dominate it recklessly.

The land is given a Sabbath rest every seven years, "so that the poor of your people may eat; and what they leave the wild animals may eat" (Ex. 23:11). Concern for the recovery of the land from being tilled is accompanied by a concern for the poor and the wild animals. This does not mean that the poor could forage freely only one year out of every seven. That would hardly relieve their hunger! J. Gerald Janzen suggests that the actual practice was for the fallow year to "rotate among various Israelites," so that "the poor and the wild animals would annually have some place to enjoy this 'moveable feast.'"[24]

The tradition of Sabbath rest is central to the biblical ecology. We, our family members, our employees, and our domestic animals, all have a right to loaf and cease trying to improve each shining hour. The Sabbath introduces into our ethic of responsibility "a sacramental dimension of communion with God and creation through the Sabbath peace, or the *shalom* of God."[25]

Every seventh day and every seventh year were Sabbaths. Every fiftieth year was a jubilee in which liberty was proclaimed "throughout the land to all its inhabitants" (Lev. 25:10). All slaves were to be freed, all debts cancelled. When Jesus proclaimed "an acceptable year of the Lord" in which the captives and oppressed would go free, he reaffirmed and reenacted the jubilee tradition in his own Sabbath presence.

Third, that God gave a land to Israel means that God gave a land to every people. In a covenantal perspective, landlessness is bad. For a people, landlessness means exile, homelessness, and suffering. Landedness is necessary to living the kind of responsible life

---

[23]Buber, *On Zion*, 15.
[24]Janzen, *Exodus*, 176.
[25]Johnston, *And the Leaves of the Tree*, 13.

that God gives and calls us to live. Other people also have their lands, regardless of whether they recognize that their land is a gift from God. "Did I not bring Israel up from the land of Egypt, and the Philistines from Caphtor and the Arameans from Kir?" (Am. 9:8). God has also brought other peoples into their present domains.[26]

Fourth, the land was given to Israel for a reason: so that "by you all the families of the earth shall bless themselves" (Gen. 12:1–3, author's translation). Israel is to be a blessing by living in *eretz Israel* (the land of Israel) a life based on God's disclosure of the "way of life" in the Torah, a social-moral life manifesting God's redemption in a liberating and restored human life. The land of Israel is the "storied place," the actual, earthly turf which Israel is given and called so to live.

This biblical ecology stands in contrast to the situation inherited by the people Israel at the start of their history in the land of Canaan. Constant warfare among the petty tyrants of Canaanite city-states in the thirteenth and twelfth centuries B.C.E., with its destruction of wells, springs, fields, forests, and scorching of farmlands, produced a devastated environment. Later the people Israel came to hope for a time of shalom when all could sit under their own vines and fig trees and no one could make them afraid (Mic. 4:4).

Consequently, in the subversive covenant with Moses, we note that (a) vengeance is prohibited (Deut. 32:35–36), (b) only God could call Israel to war and no civil authority could, and (c) the structures of political hierarchy and social stratification that oppressed both human beings and nature were rejected (Jer. 9:23–24). As to the land specifically, "the land is mine [says the Lord]; with me you are but aliens and tenants" (Lev. 25:23). "Indeed, the whole earth is mine, but you shall be for me a priestly kingdom and a holy nation" (Ex. 19:5).

> I will make for you a covenant on that day with the wild animals, the birds of the air, and the creeping things on the ground; and I will abolish the bow, the sword, and war from the land; and I will make you lie down in safety...On that day I will answer, says the LORD, I will answer the heavens and they shall answer the earth; and the earth shall answer the grain, the wine, and the oil, and they shall answer Jezreel; and I will sow him for myself in the land. (Hos. 2:18, 21–23)

---

[26]See the discussion in Janzen, *Abraham and All the Families of the Earth: Genesis 12–50,* 85.

The New Testament presupposes the covenant between the God of Israel and the Israel of God as the context in which its own language makes sense. When Jesus proclaims a jubilee year, that proclamation includes more than we have customarily taken into account. The "acceptable year of the Lord" is one in which "debts are forgiven, slaves go free, land reform is carried out, and the fields are given a Sabbath rest for the health of the soil."[27] Carolyn Merchant has abundantly substantiated the fact that there is a close connection between the oppression of human beings and the exploitation of nature. Nature and women, nature and minorities, share the same fate.[28] Biblical Israel knew that we cannot separate the liberation of the oppressed from the liberation of oppressed nature. Human beings and nature together are to share in well-being. Jesus' parables take up the wisdom tradition with its concern for nature and the basic things of life—the lilies of the field, the sparrows, bread and wine. The eschatological vision of the new Jerusalem describes "the river of the water of life" flowing through the middle of the city with the "tree of life" on either side of it: "And the leaves of the tree are for the healing of the nations" (Rev. 22:2).

Several classical theological ideas are pertinent to our topic. Carol Johnston points to two that encapsulate the relation among God, human beings, and creation that we have been describing. She takes the teaching that Jesus is the "second Adam" to mean that Jesus "restores human beings to their vocation to participate with God in tending the creation for the sake of its flourishing, but this time through the work of reconciliation." Throughout the scriptural plot, God has moved to reestablish right relations among human beings, nature, and God; in Jesus God so acts again. The second is that not only human beings are the objects of God's redeeming love; God saves all of nature. Jesus sends out his disciples to proclaim the good news to "the whole world," the entire *cosmos* (Mk. 16:15). John proclaims that Jesus came because "God so loved the *cosmos* that he gave his only Son," so that "the *cosmos* might be saved through him" (Jn. 3:16–17, author's translation).

Political and liberation theologians have long been concerned with the indivisible salvation of the whole world. Important as

---

[27]Johnston, *And the Leaves of the Tree,* 27.
[28]Carolyn Merchant, *The Death of Nature: Women, Ecology, and the Scientific Revolution* (San Francisco: Harper & Row, 1980).

personal salvation is, persons are persons-as-related not only to other persons but to the God who is the Friend of all the world and desires its salvation as well. Theology today must recover the ecological horizon that the scriptures seem never to have lost. The ecological outlook is necessary, says John Cobb, "if we truly care about the indivisible salvation of the whole world."[29] Theology in the West has long been anthropocentric, excluding nature from its sphere of responsibility. In the modern period this was partly due no doubt to the widespread use of the metaphor of machine for understanding nature. This metaphor, along with other modern habits of thought (such as regarding nature as entirely a construct of human subjectivity in Kant), has spelled disaster for our understanding of our relation to creation and has made difficult a recovery of the biblical ecology. It is time for nature to return to our field of vision, for us to "see" it in its distress and in relation to God's intent for both nature and us to enjoy well-being.

Third, the doctrine that we are justified by grace makes clear, as Paul Tillich argued, that we are accepted by God and that this acceptance comes to us as a gift.[30] It means that we are valuable to God as who we actually are, warts and all, valuable as such. It means also, as the doctrine of sanctification implies, that we are to be transformed by God's love and accept others as we have been accepted. We do not have to dominate the world of nature to be acceptable to God and to ourselves; indeed, we could accept nature as that part of God's good creation to which we have covenantal responsibilities.

The Difference That the Doctrine of Creation Makes

When William James talked about ideas as helpful in the business of knowing what to do next, he meant that an idea is the difference it makes in how we interpret the world in which we live and in how we intend to live in that world. As the cultural anthropologist Clifford Geertz puts it, a religion is a symbol system or form of culture by means of which people perpetuate and develop their understanding of, and attitudes toward, life. It is a fusion containing two aspects: a worldview and an ethic. It is not merely (a) an understanding of the world in which we live, because it always carries with it a sense of

---

[29]John B. Cobb, Jr., *Process Theology as Political Theology*, 112.
[30]Paul Tillich, *Systematic Theology*, vol. 3 (Chicago: The University of Chicago Press, 1963), 222–26.

devotion and commitment. But it is never merely (b) ethics, because the source of its moral and faithful vitality lies "in the fidelity with which it expresses the fundamental nature of reality."[31] The Christian faith, in other words, has two sides to it: a side in which we understand how things are in their ultimate significance and a side in which we understand how we ought to act in a world that we so understand.

Hence, the "cash value" of the doctrine of creation, or any other doctrine, lies in the changed behavior that should result from viewing the world of nature as a gift to us from the gracious love of God, as included in the covenant along with God and humanity, and as a world about which God cares deeply. The changes that viewing nature in the light of the covenantal ecology of the scriptures should entail are essentially two: learning to "see" nature as loved by God and vulnerable to our activity, and caring for it in such a way as to liberate it from the oppression to which we have subjected it.

God's Providence

God's providence *(pro* = ahead, *video* = to see) is an idea that has traditionally been discussed under three headings: those of God's preservation by which God conserves all creatures; God's cooperation by which God also concurs in the actions of these creatures so intimately that every human action is also an action of God; and God's government by which God fulfills God's purposes by "guiding" the creatures (Tillich: God's "directing creativity"). The latter two have been the topics of fierce debate throughout Christian history. How God so cooperates with our actions that we can meaningfully be said to be "free" and hence responsible has been the focal point of this debate. God's government came under the difficulty of being apparently irreconcilable with the idea that God seems to create creatures that are in turn at least partly, but genuinely, free (choosing and self-determining) as well as with the fact that there is no discernible pattern of this government in history.

Traditionally, the doctrine of providence has been distorted by the assumption that God is "in control" of whatever happens. This covenantal and neo-process theology argues, to the contrary, that many things are not, this side of everlastingness, under God's control.

---

[31]Clifford Geertz, *The Interpretation of Cultures* (New York: Basic Books, 1973), 126.

The covenantal God interacts and struggles in travail with God's at least partially free and creative covenant partners. "Control" is not part of the covenantal gameplan.

Therefore, God's providence is best thought of as God's continuing creativity as God is involved with, is affected by, and interacts with God's partly free creatures. This denies two alternative views: (a) that life and history manifest the "eternal return" of the same old stuff and (b) that the meaning of history lies in the fact that we are on a track of continuous progress toward a perfect future that will occur in this world and its history. Query: Does the assertion that salvation is liberation from some form of this-worldly oppression, along with the implicit or explicit denial that there is any ultimate, eschatological redemption,[32] assume that some form of this second view is the case? (This idea, popular in the period of modernist theology and modern optimism, has been effectively negated by the history of the twentieth century, a genocidal "dark ages" if ever there was one, in which we all now live not only after Auschwitz but also after Hiroshima. The ultimate goal, rather, is life in and with God; this world is not our final home.) God, who is faithful in covenant, provides for us as only God can provide. God, who is faithful in covenant, provides for us (God's free and wandering covenant, partners) as only God can provide for such partners. God constantly does for us all those things that only God can do. God's covenant partners are responsible for doing all those good things that can be done by finite and local agents such as we.

Providence and Evil

The doctrine of God runs into its greatest difficulties in connection with the reality of evil. This is particularly so for the traditional ways in which God has been understood. The "problem of evil" is a formal, logical problem, arising from a clash of premises. The premises are something like this: (1) God as all-powerful can unilaterally direct the course of events; (2) God as all-loving cares about God's creatures; (3) God as all-knowing is certainly aware of evil; (4) yet, there is evil. There seems no explanation for evil, since the world is made from absolutely nothing by an omnipotent, omnibenevolent God. Nor does this same God exterminate evil, which an omnipotent God could do and an omnibenevolent God would do.

---

[32]Rosemary Radford Ruether, *Sexism and God-Talk* (Boston: Beacon Press, 1983), 235–58.

This logical problem is a dilemma the way out of which can only be found by denying one of the premises. Either God is not all-powerful or does not have the requisite kind of power (God either self-limits God's self when God gives the kids the keys to the car, or God simply cannot have unilateral power). Or God is not all-loving (perhaps God has a Jungian "dark side"). Or because of God's lack of power, God's love does not seem to be sovereign in the world. Or God is not all-knowing, slightly dumb (this is the "God is a klutz" point of view). Or there is no evil (everything that "seems" to finite minds to be evil will turn out to have been good when it contributes to the harmony of harmonies in the great eschatological wash–this is also said by a finite mind: How does it know?). Not wishing to "limit" God, some opt for the last choice: There is no evil, really, because all evil contributes to a greater good. This last strategy is increasingly abandoned in the twentieth century; few theologians have the stomach to deny the reality of evil while standing in a slave graveyard in the American South or at the children's memorial at Yad Vashem where one and a quarter million candle flames commemorate the children killed by the Nazis because they had the "wrong grandparents," an ancestor who decided to be faithful to the God of Israel. Who can say, in the presence of the burning children and the slaves whose graves have no markers other than loose stones scattered about, that there is no evil?

Yet, some theologians can deny or trivialize evil. Steven Davis, an analytical philosopher and evangelical theologian,[33] uses the "free will defense" to protect the omnipotent God from the "problem of evil."[34] Davis claims to solve "the logical problem of evil" by noting that "it will turn out better in the long run that we act freely, even if we sometimes err, than it would have turned out had we been created innocent automata, programmed always to do the good." He denies the distinction between natural and moral evil, all evil being attributed to "free moral agents who choose to do evil."[35] He likens evil to the suffering he had to endure on his high school football team under coaches who were "hard, loud, and unbending."[36] Yet, this "suffering we endured was for a purpose, that we were being prepared to perform on the football field as well as we possibly could..."[37] This works, provided we are ready so to render trifling

---

[33]Stephen T. Davis, ed., *Encountering Evil* (Atlanta: John Knox Press, 1981), 69.
[34]Ibid., 70–71.
[35]Ibid., 78.
[36]Ibid., 98.
[37]Ibid.

something like the death of millions of people in World War II. But the point is not quantitative: This trivializes the death of one child.

Davis' more profound mistake, particularly from a theologian who calls himself "evangelical," is one to which we will return. It lies in assuming that we learn about who God is and what God's will is from football coaches. A properly Christian theology contends that we learn what we know of God from the gospel, the self-disclosure God makes of Godself in the history of Israel, in the Torah, and the prophets, definitively in Jesus Christ. Whatever we learn theologically from football coaches must be scrutinized in light of these norms.

The formal problem of evil arises only if, in a monumental act of absentmindedness, we forget the covenantal context of the biblical story of God. This story begins with the concrete experience of evil as slavery and oppression of the Hebrew people in Egypt and celebrates God's liberation of this people from it. Exodus and Passover, crucifixion and resurrection are the "pattern" for biblical thinking about evil. In the Bible, there is evil, God's love opposes it, and God seeks to overcome it with good. There are also many agents in the world, such as Pharaoh, who pursue their own courses. Similarly, feminist theology begins with an analysis of oppression, as do African American theology and liberation theology. So Reinhold Niebuhr's theology began in the Depression in Detroit, and Tillich and Barth got their awakening theological shocks from World War I. Good theology does not start *in illo tempore* (in those days or "once upon a time") when all was sweetness and light, but *in medias res* (in the middle of things) where evil is real. It does not trivialize evil or deny it. It does not particularly ask how evil is possible. It asks, instead, How is good possible and how can we mend the world?

There are two kinds of evil: natural and moral. "Natural evil" happens when a tornado strikes a church, killing all the folks attending Sunday school. Hurricanes, the movement of tectonic plates resulting in earthquakes, volcanoes pouring lava over villages, tidal waves killing 150,000 people: All are examples of natural evil. Some natural evil may result from human sinfulness, as when we despoil the supportive environment on which we depend; much does not. It happens, a result of senseless agencies that are heedless of their capacity to kill and destroy. Reducing all evil to "moral evil" is a too-simple solution that tries to get God off the hook. God created this world in which tectonic plates move and high winds blow.

"Moral evil" results from sin. Segregation results from the sin of racism; sexism, from the bias against women. Self-centeredness, greed, sloth, treating others as things to be used rather than as persons to be loved, all these are capable of having harmful ramifications beyond what we easily imagine.

Evil, the "Will of God," and the Doctrine of Revelation

No statement is heard more often at funerals, whether of the aged and suffering for whom death was a release, or of the young and promising who could have lived useful lives, than "it was God's will." "God decided to take her." Those who are tempted to use this kind of language about God face a major decision: From where will we gather our understanding of God and God's intentions for us? Is God's purpose for us disclosed in the general run of things, with its regular diet of savagery, recklessness, heedlessness of others, amorality, and immorality? Or is God's will for us decisively disclosed in Jesus Christ? If we decide that God's will is disclosed in everything and anything that happens, instead of in Jesus Christ and the story of Israel, then we will either deny that God is who God is disclosed to be in Jesus Christ, or we will camouflage God's antagonism to evil and thus deny the gospel of God's gracious love and God's command of justice.

So we have to choose. Those who choose to assert that God's aims for us are disclosed in everything that happens do not need the decisive revelation of God in Jesus Christ. Those who choose to assert that God's ways, however evil, are disclosed in the general run of things and go on to rationalize that "God's ways are higher than our ways," choose to ignore the disclosure of God's way to us in the history of Israel, the Torah, the prophets, and Jesus Christ. It is this God whose ways are not our ways. Consequently, if we choose the revelation of God in the exodus, at Sinai, and in Jesus Christ, we contradict the claim that God's will is disclosed in the general carelessness and ambiguity of whatever happens. We deny that God's will is disclosed in what insurance companies call an "act of God."

Evil and God's Covenant Will

Speaking of the Sinai covenant, God says: "...today I have set before you life and death, blessings and curses. Choose life..." (Deut. 30:19). The covenant comprises a dialectic of grace (God's initiative) and human responsibility (God's command). The covenanting

God graciously empowers God's covenant partners to do what God gives and requires of them to do: to choose life, to defend the imago dei that is every human being against the forces of death and evil. God is the God who promises to resist evil, and who elects first a people and then a church and calls them to the goal of the sanctification, the blessing of life. God seems to be the kind of God who has decided to share power with God's covenant partners. Hence, it is inappropriate to attribute to God total power and then talk of God's "causing" or "permitting" evil.

A post-Shoah theology, while it regards such questions as the one that closed the last paragraph as important, takes on other questions as more important. They have to do with such practical-moral issues as that of resistance to evil, opposition to all forms of evil that can be opposed. If the churches show no great interest in discussing theological understandings of the problem of evil, it is sadder still that they show even less in resisting it.

Consider this case study of evil: In 1942, the Nazi operatives calculated that if they worked the average Jewish prisoner to death over a period of nine months, their profit margin per prisoner would be 1,631 Reichsmark. The margin was enhanced by cutting down on the daily food ration and collecting the gold teeth and recycling for commercial uses the bones and ashes of the cremated prisoners. Consider that in 1944 the same operatives concluded that by clubbing Jewish children to death rather than gassing them, they could save one half Pfennig per victim. Consider that the whole Nazi attempt to make the world *Judenrein* ("clean of Jews") was an attempt to remove the covenant people and, hence, all memory of God's covenant from the face of the earth. In the presence of the burning children, it is difficult to say that God "permitted" this assault on the imago dei, without the very words turning to ashes in our mouths. The freedom of agents other than God is real. Evil is real. Our freedom to resist it is also real, as is our responsibility.

Faith in God's Providence

Trust in God's care is not simple resignation to the general run of things (as if the general run of things revealed God's aims for us). Nor is it the view that God's job is to make us happy (the way of "loving" God that treats God as a tool to be used rather than as a, or rather, *the* person to be served). Augustine of Hippo used to argue that our loves are distorted when, among other things, we love persons, who are ends in themselves, as things to be used, and things as though they were persons to be served rather than tools to be used. Awareness of our environmental sins sharply reminds us that, indeed, we all too easily regard even nature merely as a "thing" to be used.

Rather, trust in God's providential care, in spite of the seeming absence of such care in what often seems to be "the God-forsakenness" of the present, is a radical assurance or reassurance. It is a limit statement, perhaps, for times when we are at our limits, saying that there is no situation, no matter how dire, in which God does not participate, and in which we are effectively outside of God's love and care.

An image from Melville's *Moby Dick* is haunting. The novel culminates in the scene in which the whaling crew, after an almost disastrous pursuit of the whale, tries to make it back in their small craft to the mother ship. Storm and darkness cut them off from the ship, and they are thrown viciously about by the wind and waves. They fail to find the mother ship and the other whaling boats.

> There, then, he sat, holding up that imbecile candle in the heart of that almighty forlornness. There, then, he sat, the sign and symbol of a man without faith, hopelessly holding up hope in the midst of despair. (*Moby Dick*, p. 225)

That is the picture: above, darkness; beneath, the sea; around, loneliness and terror. Yet a light shines in the darkness. There is also in *Moby Dick* another ship that now and then sailed across the path of the *Pequod* (named for a tribe of native Americans almost totally exterminated; it and *The Rights of Man* both sank). The other ship was the *Rachel*, whose name alludes to words from the prophet Jeremiah.

> Thus says the LORD:
> "A voice is heard in Ramah,
> lamentation and bitter weeping.
> Rachel is weeping for her children;
> she refuses to be comforted for
> her children,
> because they are no more." (Jer. 31:15; see also Mt. 2:18)

Rachel, like so many biblical characters before her, "refuses" to be reconciled to the loss of her children, murdered by Herod. Such refusals are part of the faithful questioning that is honored by the biblical witness.

Rachel, mourning and searching for her missing children, reminds us of a few factors working against evil: people who care to search for survivors and God presiding over the world with "a tender care that nothing be lost."[38] In the end, the love of God is finally redemptive. It is Rachel, saving her children from death in the midst of evil and death, shouting a loud "No!" to evil, who points us to God, whose suffering love, struggling in travail with an immoral and amoral world, never gives up on us and finally takes us into God's care and keeping. In this world, God struggles against evil, seeking to overcome it with good; in the eschaton, God folds us into God's protecting embrace. So we trust, whatever may happen, in spite of "the sufferings of this present time" (Rom. 8:18), that nothing "will be able to separate us from the love of God in Christ Jesus our Lord" (Rom. 8:39).

The reality of evil in the history of Israel caused Israel to introduce into its faith a new idea: that of the general resurrection. After the army of Antiochus IV Epiphanes executed Jewish mothers (and their sons) who had their children circumcised (the mothers were hanged and the sons hanged around the mothers' necks [1 Macc. 1:60–61]), Jewish faith introduced the idea of resurrection: "Many of those who sleep in the dust of the earth shall awake…" (Dan. 12:2–3).[39] Eventually, it was affirmed of "the world to come" (not a this-worldly future–that is "the days of the Messiah") that "all Israel has a share in the world to come"–that is, not only those on the scene at the time (Mishnah, *Sanhedrin* 10:1; this tractate is concerned with the idea of resurrection). Eschatology (the doctrine of "last things") has to do with the final triumph of God's purposes of life and well-being.

---

[38]Alfred North Whitehead, *Process and Reality* (Corrected Edition), 346.

[39]On the efforts of Antiochus to stamp out Jewish faith, see Marti Steussy, "Judaisms in the Time of the Second Temple," in Clark M. Williamson, ed., *The Church and the Jewish People* (St. Louis: Chalice Press, 1991), 7.

Chapter 6

Neighbors Along the Way: Humanity

The Human Question

We human beings are a question to ourselves. Who are we? What is the meaning and destiny of our lives? What are we to do? How are we to understand ourselves in relation to this world in which we live? How are we to understand the world, in which we have to decide who we are and what it is that we are given and called to be and do? How are we to understand ultimate reality, God, and ourselves in relationship to God? Who are these other people, how are we to relate to them, and what are we to do about and with them?

To the community of faith, given and called to walk the way of life in service of God and the neighbor, the question that human beings are and ask of themselves presents itself in at least two ways. How are we to understand ourselves, we who are given and called to be a blessing to each other, to serve each other's well-being? And how are we to understand these other people, these strangers, who do not participate in our way of being human, but who may be participants in another religious tradition or in no religious tradition whatsoever? We will look first at this second question.

Neighbors Whom God Has Given Us to Love

As the community of faith seeks to walk the way of life in an increasingly crowded world, it encounters other people, strangers to it and its way of life. Who are these people? How are we to understand them? What should be our characteristic attitudes and actions toward them? The thesis of this post-Shoah theology is simple: All these strangers are our neighbors on planet Earth, neighbors whom God has given us to love, whose well-being is given to us to guard and protect, those toward whom we are to see that justice is done. Strangers are different from us, alien, foreign. In the parlance of postmodern thought, they represent "otherness." They think and act differently; they bring their questions with them. To love strangers is to love questions, and to love questions is to love strangers. Yet we are commanded: "You shall love the alien as yourself, for you were aliens in the land of Egypt: I am the LORD your God" (Lev. 19:34). We are freed by God to love these strangers, knowing that as we have been freely loved we are freed to love.

This thesis denies that all those who are different from us are to be understood as an "alienated other." Historically, all religious traditions have failed to understand others on their own terms. This failing is hardly unique to Christianity, but as this is a theology for Christians, we are obligated to address our own problems. There is no honest way to evade the fact that we have had a strong tendency to project onto other groups traits, characteristics, and faults that we find reprehensible. Projecting these faults onto others neatly allows us to avoid the self-criticism, repentance, and openness to the transformation graciously offered us by God that is at the heart of biblical faith. In the history of the church, women, Jews, heretics, members of other religions, and minorities have all been victimized by our tendency to define them as less than fully human or to demonize them. Today, homosexuals are similarly vilified.

Doing theology without any alienated other is necessary if the purpose of our way of life is to be a blessing to, serving the well-being of, our planetary neighbors. But it is a goal more easily stated than achieved. We will later look at some contemporary indications that this remains a problem for much contemporary theology.

Understanding Ourselves Appropriately

It is not only the case that we have difficulty understanding and acting appropriately toward our neighbors who are different from us. We also have had a terrible difficulty understanding and interacting appropriately with each other within the church. Sexism, racism, and anti-Judaism have created a deeper rupture within the church than has any other source of division (anti-Judaism signals the first great ecumenical rupture). We must take this into account in our developing understanding of human beings, of who we are in relationship to God and the neighbor and what God gives and calls us to be and do. Sexism, heterosexism, racism, anti-Judaism, attitudes toward "pagans," heretics, and "infidels" do not exhaust our difficulties with understanding what we as Christians should understand about ourselves and our neighbors as human beings. Another challenge is that in our postmodern, consumerist economy there are many proposals for how we should understand ourselves. Often we buy into them because they are simply part of the fabric of our society. These cultural forces work hard to convince us that they know best what it means to be a human being.

An Alternative Understanding of Humanity

Where we take our definition of humanity from is a critical question. According to the understanding of human beings found in the economist understanding of liberal capitalism, human beings are naturally aggressive competitors. Each person is a threat to all others. My neighbors are my competitors. It is our nature to fear one another. We live with the anxiety that at any moment we may be attacked and robbed of our property or deprived of it by some trick. Our prevailing concern is to survive, to maximize our possessions, and to chase after our interests.

We may have once believed that all human beings are essentially good, that together we constitute a family of sisters and brothers, that our destiny is to live in reconciliation with one another, or that we are watched after by a God who is graciously disposed toward us. But the insight of capitalism has been that only when we cease being mystified by fairy tales and let ourselves be guided by enlightened self-interest can we assure our safety by a government that protects the rights of all by limiting the power of each.

In such a worldview, it is irrational and utopian to be concerned about peace, social justice, fresh air, clean water, disarmament, a sustainable society, and a living wage. The rule of life is competition, curbed only by the competitiveness involved in the war of each against all. Loving your neighbor as yourself results in neurosis, or worse, failure to compete efficiently, which is capitalism's definition of sin.

Contrary to this, Christians are given to believe that human beings are created for relationships of love and justice, that God not only watches graciously over us, but is engaged in travail with us, that matters of compassion and solidarity (the social name for love) are, far from being utopian, the only realistic alternative to the way of death represented in the war of each against all, and that our destiny is intended by God to be one in which the war of each against all will finally be overcome (Rev. 21:4). Christian faith is an alternative possibility, and sometimes in its conversation with the situation, its answer is no. However gentle, it is nonetheless a resolute no. The market does not determine the worth and value of any human being. The "bottom line" is not the only norm, nor is it a moral norm.

Humanity in the Bible

What does the biblical witness have to tell us with regard to what it means to be a human being? We begin at the beginning, first with the Hebrew Bible, then with the New Testament.

First, the Hebrew Bible knows nothing about autonomous humanity in the modern sense of not only free but self-sufficient.[1] Human nature is determined entirely by our relation to God, to nature, and to other people (which includes the relationships of well-being that God wants us to have with God and each other), a relation that preserves the distinction between God and humanity, between the Creator and the creature. The belief that human beings are created in God's image (the *imago dei*) defines our relation to God and to the rest of nature. We are not divine or descended from God. We are created for and called to a unique companionship with God, one another, and the world. This companionship involves responsiveness to God's freeing us to love and loving us into freedom. Covenant is a controlling metaphor for the Bible: We are created to be the kinds of beings with whom God can enter into covenant and

---

[1]G. Ernest Wright, *The Biblical Doctrine of Man in Society* (London: SCM Press, 1954).

who live in covenantal responsibility with one another and the environment.

Because God transcends nature, our duty is not defined in terms of a mystical identification of ourselves with nature so as to achieve harmony with it. Humanity is a psychophysical organism that, as a whole, is related to God. There is in human beings no immortal part that can survive death on its own account. Human beings are good, indeed "very good," because we are cherished by God. But all human beings, not only our kind, are so treasured, and so are all of God's other creatures, whom God also pronounces "very good." We are created for a covenant relationship of life and blessing with one another and with God.

The Ugly Word: Sin

Sin is revealed for what it is by what it opposes: Sin is our opposition against life, against well-being, against the freedom to love God with all our selves and our neighbors as ourselves, against the love that frees us to do so, against being loved, against God, and against God's gift to us of abundant life. Apart from the revelation of God's gracious love, the nature and character of sin are not clear. God's self-disclosure, and therefore the disclosure of the nature of sin, occur throughout scripture and with decisive clarity in Jesus Christ. We see sin clearly when we clearly see what it opposes and the depth and virulence of its opposition. We see sin clearly when we see it in ourselves first, and know that we are *simul iustus et peccator*, at one and the same time justified and sinners. It is idolatrous to project sin onto others and regard them judgmentally as if we had the status to make such judgments. This is the sin of arrogance, committed by the self-righteous.

Because of our creatureliness and in the absence of faith, we are in a state of anxiety. Human beings are sinful, but being sinful is not part of the definition of human beings. It is not necessary that we sin. Sin is something we freely do, even when, as in the case of systemic sins, we are not quite aware of our complicity, and something from which we can be freed. We are all "recovering sinners," precisely because we are not necessarily sinners. God is not a cosmic prankster who creates us as sinners in order to give us the pointless injunction not to be so.

The Hebrew Bible does not theorize about sinfulness and knows nothing about the loss of our likeness to God (the image of God). It knows a lot about sinfulness. Its most remarkable analysis of the human situation is Genesis 3–11. We sin because we wish vainly to assert our autonomy over against God. Adam, Eve, Cain, Lamech, the builders of the tower all exhibit this. In Genesis 3–11, sin (murder, violence, and injustice) so pollute the earth that God sends a flood and makes a new start with Noah, Noah's children, and all the "living creatures" who are included in the Noachic covenant. Psalm 143 petitions God not to judge the psalmist, because "no one living is righteous before you." Psalm 51, a confession of sin and plea for mercy, is radical: "Indeed, I was born guilty, a sinner when my mother conceived me." This psalm articulates the Augustinian motifs of biblical faith: "Create in me a clean heart, O God, and put a new and right spirit within me" (51:10).

The prophets provided a searching analysis of sin as estrangement from and rebellion against God. This corresponded to their convictions about God's holy, loving, and righteous will. Our creaturely weakness is not the direct cause of sin so much as the temptation that can occasion sin. The sin of Adam and Eve was the effort to be "like God"; the sin of the builders of the tower of Babel was that there was no limit to their ambition. The prophets criticize kings, in one case a Babylonian, for saying: "I will ascend to heaven...I will make myself like the Most High" (Isa. 14:13–14).

Sin takes several forms. It is self-centeredness, manifesting itself as arrogance (arrogating to ourselves a status that is God's, regarding ourselves as the ground and end of our own being and meaning). It is sloth, not thinking highly enough of ourselves as loved by God and given and called to the possibility of a life of blessing and well-being (sloth amounts to a rejection of oneself as created in the imago dei). It is avarice, envy, lust, and anger, those sins against the neighbor that destroy the neighbor's well-being and refuse the possibility of a life of blessing and reconciliation with our actual human associates. Karl Barth's view of sin is extraordinarily helpful: In contrast to the humility of Christ, sin is pride (which I prefer to call arrogance); in contrast to the majesty of Christ, it is sloth; and in contrast to the truth of Christ it is a lie. "Epigrammatically," he says, "and to be taken *cum grano salis*, we might say that falsehood is the specifically Christian form of sin."[2] These are not three separate forms of sin: "Proud and slothful, he [meaning any human being] is necessarily false as well."

---

[2]Karl Barth, *Church Dogmatics*, IV, 3.1, 368–69, 372.

That sin is a lie is a particularly important insight. We cannot lie unless we know the truth. The truth that Christians have been given and called to know has to do with the unfathomable love and grace of God that have disclosed to us the conditions of life and well-being and done so throughout the history of the God of Israel with the Israel of God and with manifest clarity in Jesus Christ. Only those to whom this has been given to know can lie about it. And we let ourselves believe the lies that the systemic sins of our world drum into our heads. We will return to this point in our following discussion of original sin.

The Unity of Humanity

The scriptures think of humanity as one whole; all human beings have the same parents. Israel's privilege and responsibility are because of God's grace and on behalf of "all the Gentiles" and because of no superiority on Israel's part. It is a particular election within a universal inclusiveness. Israel is called to be a representative human community and, as such, experiences to the full the responsibility of being involved in historical existence.

This insistence denies all racism. Jewish legends about the creation of Adam illustrate this point. According to one, God took dirt "from all four corners of the earth," so that a human being, whether from east or west, north or south, would be at home anywhere. The legend continues, the dirt was of different colors—red clay, black loam, white sand, and yellow soil—so that no race of human beings could ever be told "you do not belong here."[3]

Paul agreed when he declared at Athens that God had "from one ancestor made all nations to inhabit the whole earth" (Acts 17:26). In the table of the peoples in Genesis 10, the Hebrew people take their place among all the others. When Abraham is summoned to his special destiny by God, God promises that by him "all the families of the earth shall be blessed."

God is equally concerned with Ethiopians, Philistines, and Syrians as well as with Israel (Am. 9:7). Said Isaiah on behalf of God: "Blessed be Egypt my people, and Assyria the work of my hands, and Israel my heritage" (Isa. 19:25). This inclusive outlook reaches its pinnacle in the picture of the Servant of the Lord in Second Isaiah (42:6) who is to be a "light to the nations"; in the vision of a unified

---

[3]Louis Ginzberg, *The Legends of the Jews,* vol. 1: *From the Creation to Jacob* (Philadelphia: Jewish Publication Society, 1909), 54–55.

humanity with its religious center in Jerusalem (Isa. 2:2–4; Mic. 4:1–3); and in the books of Jonah and Ruth. Gentiles (and Gentile women) are listed in the genealogies of the Messiah, and in Genesis 9 God makes a covenant (Noah) not only with all humanity, but with all the "living things." Israel was unaware of the kinds of distinctions with which the Greeks divided humanity into Greeks and barbarians. If Israel was chosen from among the nations, this was not because of any merit, but because of the unfathomable will of God. In Job 31:13–15, the distinction between slave and master is denied.

Human Worth

Human beings have several characteristics, of which the first is worth. This is not a value that we expropriate for ourselves, but a gift from God. It is a blessing, part of our well-being, to think well of ourselves; but it is only so as a gift, not as a form of self-congratulation. As made in the image and likeness of God, we have worth both as God's gift and because we matter to God. In a number of places the self is designated by the words for "honor, glory," notably so in Psalm 8:3–4:

> When I look at your heavens, the work of your fingers, the moon and the stars that you have established; what are human beings that you are mindful of them, mortals that you care for them? Yet you have made them a little lower than God, and crowned them with glory and honor.

In themselves, human beings are fragile. The classic affirmation of the value and worth of fragile, breakable, irreplaceable people is in Psalm 103:13–17:

> As a father has compassion for his children,
> so the LORD has compassion for
>   those who fear him.
> For he knows how we were made;
>   he remembers that we are dust.
> As for mortals, their days are like grass;
>   they flourish like a flower of the field;
> for the wind passes over it, and it is gone,
>   and its place knows it no more.
> But the steadfast love of the LORD
>   is from everlasting to everlasting.

The same comparison of human beings to grass or to dust and ashes is found in Isaiah, Jeremiah, 2 Chronicles, the Psalms, and

Genesis. Paul the apostle talks in several places about human weakness, a Pauline theme too often overlooked. Human frailty is reflected in our liability to disease, in the fact that our strength diminishes with age, and in our mortality. We are the beings who have to die and know it. As a result of our vulnerability and mortality, we experience anxiety and fear; the fear of death (Tillich's anxiety of nonbeing) is a major factor to be confronted in coming to terms with a biblical understanding of human being and human sinfulness. Do we sin out of sheer malevolence, or are there objective factors in the human condition (the snake already in the garden) that are the occasions of temptation?

In the New Testament, the person, male or female, is the creature whose body is made alive by God's breath, whose divine image can be defaced (but not effaced) by sin and redeemed by Christ through the Holy Spirit, and whose historical destiny is defined from birth to death by relationships. The legacy of the Hebrew Bible is generally carried over into the New Testament in that humanity is viewed as a totality, with terms such as heart, soul, flesh, or spirit denoting the entire person from a particular point of view. Human beings are sexual, and flesh is intrinsically good, so long as one does not boast in it.

Since all New Testament writers assume the human dilemma lies in disobedience rather than in materiality, the crucial differences among them arise in conceptualizing sin and its cure. There is a tendency to divide the world between saints and sinners along moralistic lines—found in Revelation and the pastoral epistles. There is a tendency toward moral gradualism through obedience to moral norms found in Luke, Matthew, and James. There is a doctrine of relationship, according to which the line between saint and sinner is marked by faith in God or lack of faith—typical for the historical Jesus (on most reconstructions) and the Pauline and Johannine traditions; this line runs down the middle of every person.

Each approach to sin implies a different sense of human destiny and a different meaning of salvation. Since the last option has the strongest claims to originality, consistency with the event of Jesus Christ, and appropriateness to the gospel of God's gracious love, it will be developed more fully here.

Discipleship and Servanthood

That "no one can serve two masters" (Mt. 6:24) presupposes that human beings are created for covenantal relationship with one another, with God, and with the rest of creation. We are determined by whom or what we serve, whether God or mammon (or something else). "Serve" here has the meaning of "love." You are what you love. You are what you love because in deciding what to love you constitute yourself as such a person with such a love. Freedom is not absolute autonomy, but release from idolatrous forces that distort life. Paul's attack on justification by works of the law (he means "ritual works") would apply to any attempt to seek justification by any kind of works. His critique, and the struggle in the letters to the Hebrews and Colossians against the veneration of cosmic forces, all aim at restoring humanity to proper servanthood. The images of stewardship (Mt. 25:14–30, Lk. 17:10), discipleship (Mk. 6:8–11), sonship (Gal. 4, "adulthood"), and being begotten by God (Jn. 3) imply high levels of independent initiative for those who know God's will.

To stand fast in freedom (Gal. 5:1) is to fulfill one's destiny through service in love, to reject continuously all conformity to the world, while being impelled by grace to render service to the world (Rom. 12:1–2). For those set free by Christ, socially imposed subservience is no longer determinative, and equality is the result:

> There is no longer Jew or Greek, there is no longer slave or free, there is no longer male and female; for all of you are one in Christ Jesus. And if you belong to Christ, then you are Abraham's offspring, heirs according to the promise. (Gal. 3:28–29)

Paul makes clear in Galatians 4 that these "heirs" are not "minors," but mature children of God ready for grown-up responsibility and freedom.[4]

Finitude and Ethics

Freedom does not include release from the essential conditions of bodily historical existence. We remain "body"; our life is "in the flesh." Paul did not think of a real self in contrast with fallen flesh, for these were categories borrowed from his opponents and hence redefined in the context of Pauline theology. So constitutive is bodily existence that each person must find an appropriate way to express

---

[4]See Martin Luther, *The Freedom of a Christian,* in *Martin Luther: Selections from His Writings,* ed. John Dillenberger (Garden City, N.J.: Anchor Books, 1961), 42–85.

sexual inclinations (1 Cor. 7). Each must work for daily bread
(1 Thess. 4:11–12). The alienation that these relationships produce
is overcome by Christ, but we remain finite. Thus, although there
are remarkable efforts to overcome inequalities, Paul once found it
necessary to reimpose traditional sex roles temporarily in the face
of Gnostic demands to eradicate such finite factors from Christian
self-identity (1 Cor. 11:2–16). Each person's sexual gift must be exercised in "holiness" and display the love of Christ (1 Cor. 7:4).

The love ethic (Jn. 13) requires the full use of our sagacity. The
gift of the Spirit unleashes, rather than subordinates, the use of the
intellect (1 Cor. 14). Human beings are the creatures who move
toward God's future (Phil. 3; Heb. 13), whose deeds and values face
judgment and whose virtues can never be an occasion of boasting
(Eph. 2:9). Even the most exalted spiritual or theological insights
are finite and need eschatological fulfillment (1 Cor. 13:12). To be
human requires faith rather than perfect certainty, hope rather than
present fulfillment. As pilgrims, we are to "[go] out, not knowing
where [we are] going" (Heb. 11:8). With adversity our expected lot,
we remain vulnerable until the eschaton.

Reconciliation and Resurrection

Salvation involves reconciliation in, rather than release from finitude. Each person repeats the choice of Adam to sin by disregard-
ing individual limits (Rom. 5:12–21). The essence of sin is not
rule-breaking, but alienation—the refusal of the creature to acknowledge the Creator and to love the neighbor. Alienation is a matter of
what Augustine termed the self that was *incurvatus in se ipsum*—curved
in upon itself. One can be curved in upon oneself in more than one
way—in arrogance and *hubris* (self-elevation) or in self-pity, bathos,
sloth, self-disparagement. "Flesh" in this context denotes the tendency to mistake one's accomplishments for the good or to make
oneself the center of reality (concupiscence, in the tradition). The
human dilemma is not weakness per se, but mistaken strength, which
relates closely with Paul's critique of misguided zeal (Rom. 10:1–4)
and Jesus' opposition to unbridled anger (Mt. 5:21–26). The cross
reveals the depth of this alienation, and the resurrection gives the
power that we need to break free from it (Rom. 3:21–26).

When people receive this gospel and are reconciled with God,
the righteousness of God is restored (Rom. 1:17–18), and we regain
our rightful role in the creation (Rom. 8:12–23; 12:1–2; 1 Cor. 6:3).

We take up responsibility in the world and extend reconciling love into our economic, family, and political obligations (Eph. 5:21–6:9; 1 Pet. 2:13–25; 1 Cor. 7; Rom. 13:1–7). We are set free to enjoy creaturely existence (Mt. 11:19; Phil. 4:8) and to find "rest" in our encounter with God's word (Heb. 3:7–4:13). Thus restored, we exhibit an alert, resourceful vitality as we move in hope toward the fulfillment that only God can provide (Mt. 24; Phil. 3:8–16; Heb. 11–12). We are reconciled to the exigencies of historical life and can face death with courage, expecting the resurrection. Yet we live on this side of God's final judgment, as justified sinners dependent on God's grace and, at best, only fragmentarily and occasionally manifest the newness of life by which we are called and claimed.

In short, human beings are created, sustained, called, and claimed for God's future by God's gracious love. They are those beings who can understand themselves in any ultimate sense in terms of, and only in terms of, God's love freely given to them and, in turn, as called to love God with all themselves and their neighbors as themselves.

Some Contemporary Issues

The question of what constitutes an appropriate Christian theological understanding of what it means to be a human being is a theological theme that shifts and develops over time. The issues and possibilities presented by the context in which we live have to be addressed by Christian teaching. Feminist and African American theologians call into radical question traditional Christian understandings of what it means to be human. They do so from their experience of inherited doctrines as oppressive or manifestly inadequate to their experience. Women theologians correctly claim that there is a gender bias in traditional anthropology, and African American theologians note that racist assumptions have too often shaped Christian thought.

The dualistic model of traditional theological ways of thinking about human beings, in which the soul was regarded as of more value than the body, and the body as a "seducer" of the soul, has been tremendously injurious for women. When males are regarded as more "rational," and females more "carnal," women are viewed as potentially seductive of men, causing them to sin. Such a view regards women as more to be feared morally than men. Females are not intrinsically evil, but morally more dangerous. Thomas Aquinas argued that women are hierarchically subordinate to men in status and deficiently exhibit human nature.[5] Women participate less in the image of God, he contended. He was guided by Aristotle's biological understandings of the role of women and men in procreation and concluded from them that women should not be ordained because they were defective males. If we are called to love our neighbors as ourselves, such understandings need revision. The appropriate direction for change is to argue that it is human beings as created for covenantal love and mutual respect, for being a blessing to each other, that is meant by saying that we are created in God's image.[6]

Understanding what it means to be a human being is related to other major Christian doctrines. How we understand God, the world (creation, providence, and evil), salvation, and so on, are part of the picture. Also, our theological understanding of human existence must be in conversation with understandings of human beings in such sciences as psychology and sociology. The philosophical perspective we bring to the discussion (tacitly or explicitly) plays its own role: What do we assume about reality and, hence, human reality that colors the way we construe the Christian witness? Our unexamined Stoicism, individualism, consumerism, and culture-bound visions of the good life need to be looked at critically.

Because of the conversational character of theology, we cannot think about human beings by proof-texting the Bible, mining it for "what the Bible says" about women or homosexuals, and then using the result of such proof-texting in an authoritarian manner to settle contemporary issues. We have to think theologically in our context, as the writers of scripture did in theirs. The deeper insights of the scriptures, that all human beings are loved by God, that God calls the creation of human beings "good," that we are given and called to serve the well-being of each other, that we are embodied and

---

[5]See Thomas Aquinas, *Summa Theologicae,* part 1, question 92: "The Production of the Woman," ed. Fathers of the English Dominican Province (London: Burns, Oates and Washbourne, 1914).

[6]Some important feminist theologies are: Rosemary Radford Ruether, *Sexism and God-Talk* (Boston: Beacon Press, 1983); Letty M. Russell, *Human Liberation in a Feminist Perspective–A Theology* (Philadelphia: Westminster Press, 1974); and Anne E. Carr, *Transforming Grace* (San Francisco: Harper & Row, 1988).

sexed and that this, too, is "good," that the one thing God said was "not good" was that Adam was alone (Gen. 2:18), that Jesus Christ is God's gracious gift to the ungodly who are without a judgmental leg to stand on, all these will guide our thinking.

Some Propositions about Human Beings

Human beings are created. Human life is limited (subject to weakness, ignorance, illness, and mortality), but not reducible to the result of inscrutable fate or chance (a mere accident of evolution–although we are evolved creatures). Creation is not the corrupted or emanated form of an ideal world, but the object of God's communicative love–and it is good by God's creating of it. Human beings are not ultimately tragic figures (as in classic Greek tragedy), nor ultimately pathetic (as in much twentieth-century drama, e.g., Willy Loman). Human beings are good, are sinful, and are redeemable. Still, human existence, as finite, is dependent on God as the ground and end of all being and is also subject to all manner of causes operating efficaciously upon it in the world–bacteria, viruses, weather, and so on.

Human beings come equipped with libidos, sweat glands, metabolism, sometimes grow bald, get flat feet, and are found in all shapes and sizes. They are capable of incredible acts of love and self-transcendence, as well as unspeakable evil.

Human beings are social and political. Far too many Christians, especially in America, think of human beings individualistically. One gets the impression that all the social roles we play, all the relationships in which we participate, are like the sides of a banana that can be peeled off, enabling us to get to the "real person" beneath the roles and relations that make up our being. As a result, often we are unaware of all the many ways in which we are inherently related to one another, to nature, to God, and to the societies, cultures, and institutions that do so much to shape our understandings of who we are and how we are to relate to each other.

This has not always been so in the Christian tradition. For many earlier thinkers, human life was social and corporate (this is radically so for the Bible), exemplified more in the public sphere than in "private" religion. In America we have had a lot of the privatizing of religion, which goes along with certain political assumptions about the individual as the aim or end of the body politic and its organizations. "The topic of religion," said Whitehead, "is individuality in community," not individuality by itself.[7] We need to de-privatize our understanding of human beings in order to do justice to the political and communal character of life. The communally worshiping church reflects its faith in a covenantally related God. Zeal for the unity of the church is a hope for the unity of humanity. Christian unity as usually treated is so trivialized as to be malicious. Responsibility for public, communal life is not an occasional theme in Christian theology, but a constant melody.

Human beings are created for covenant. Human beings are essentially related to God, one another, and the rest of the created order (the natural environment). The God of Israel breaks with all culturally accepted definitions of "god" in Canaanite society (gods who are preoccupied with their "rule") and opts for faithful interrelatedness, steadfast solidarity. Yahweh identifies a faithful covenant partner, responding to the groans of an oppressed people (Ex. 2:24–25). This is an irreversible move, one that is definitional for God and for God's covenant partners. Covenant is possible not because the covenant partner is worthy, but because God commits Godself to new kinds of solidarity with that partner. "This God has given up power in the certainty that real saving power is found in uncompromising faithfulness, the very posture the other gods in heaven could not countenance."[8] Hence, covenant is never properly understood as enforced legality with dangerous power coercing our agreement. Covenant is definitional for human beings: We are created for proper relationships with God, ourselves, one another, and nature. Covenant is a social prescription for hope—what human life might yet be like ("your will be done on earth, as it is in heaven") and a subversion of all present worldly ways of organizing life that oppress, subjugate, and enslave the imago dei.

Human beings are sexual. In some parts of the Christian tradition, sexuality per se is viewed as evil. Does agape stand in final opposition to eros? Is agape best defined as "self-sacrificial love"? Does it oppose eros, or can it transform eros and libido? Is it "regard for the other as other," respectful of the personhood and dignity of the other, so

---

[7]Alfred North Whitehead, *Religion in the Making* (New York: Living Age Books, 1960), 86.

[8]Walter Brueggemann, *A Social Reading of the Old Testament*, ed. Patrick D. Miller (Minneapolis: Fortress Press, 1994), 45.

that agape can redeem relationships of eros, libido, and philia?[9] Laboring under the weight of a profoundly negative tradition, Christian thought has to forge new meanings in sexuality and, in overcoming heterosexism, understand anew what it means to be human beings as males and as females. The tradition had a hard time overcoming its acceptance of Aristotle's definition of woman as a "misbegotten male" and its own preference for Genesis 2 and Eve's being "second" over Genesis 1 according to which Adam and Eve are both created in the image of God in their cohumanity. The tradition has had such a difficult time talking credibly about sexuality at all that one wonders how it can discuss sanely any controversial issues relating to sexuality.

Not all human beings are heterosexual. The question of the status of gay men and lesbians in the church today is a controversial issue. We discuss it in light of the conviction that human beings are created by God for covenant relationship with God and one another, in the image of God, that all human beings are justified and ultimately reconciled with God and one another by the act of God in Christ, that we are given and called to be transformed by Christ and not conformed to the world, and that God made us who we are, as we are, embodied persons enlivened by God's spirit.

Some favorite proof-texts from the Hebrew Bible. Many churches today refuse to ordain gay men and lesbians who are "open and practicing," requiring of their clergy "fidelity in marriage and celibacy in singleness." Typically this practice is justified by proof-texting a few verses from disparate parts of the Bible, with the added assumption that it is clear that these texts condemn homosexuality. Defenders of this practice frequently claim that the sin of Sodom was homosexuality, but "the test of Sodom," says J. Gerald Janzen, "turns on the question of hospitality."[10] "Gang rape of guests," comments Marti Steussy, "is offensive regardless of sexual orientation." She points out that Ezekiel 16:49 did not see Sodom's sin as

---

[9]Paul Tillich's *Love, Power, and Justice* (New York: Oxford University Press, 1954), chap. 2, is a groundbreaking reflection on the relation of agape and eros, one that does not simply see them as inherently conflictual. Sallie McFague, *Models of God* (Philadelphia: Fortress Press, 1987), builds on such developments to use eros and philia as metaphors for God's love: "Agape, the love that gives with no thought of return; eros, the love that finds the beloved valuable; and philia, the love that shares and works for the vision of the good...all of them in different ways attest to the oneness of love, so evident in sexual union, as 'that which drives everything that is towards everything else that is'" (131).

[10]J. Gerald Janzen, *Abraham and All the Families of the Earth*, 61.

homosexuality: "This was the guilt of your sister Sodom: She and her daughters had pride, excess of food, and prosperous ease, but did not aid the poor and needy."[11] The Sodom story (Gen. 19) is not helpful to the discussion because it describes an activity, gang rape, that everybody agrees is wrong.

Here is a good place to make an important point: The scriptures do not have a concept of homosexuality as an orientation. Whenever they talk about homosexuality or about what some interpreters have taken to be homosexuality, the reference is always to behavior, as in the story we just considered.

Those who regard homosexuality as a sin and support fidelity in marriage and celibacy in singleness do not tell certain biblical stories. They do not tell of Solomon's seven hundred wives and three hundred concubines, nor of the fact that the scriptures do not criticize him for his one thousand female companions. He is censured, rather, because some of his wives led him to fail to be "true to the LORD his God" (1 Kings 11:4). Nor is David criticized for loving Jonathan. Jonathan loved David, we are told, "as he loved his own life," and at Jonathan's death David sobbed: "Greatly loved were you to me; your love to me was wonderful, passing the love of women" (2 Sam. 1:26).

Were David a contemporary Christian, he could not be ordained.[12]

Where the scriptures differ from the practice of the contemporary church, as Christopher Morse makes plain, is in this: A practice constitutes sexual infidelity when it violates faithfulness to the covenant with God.[13]

The legal codes in scripture assume patriarchy—the rule of the fathers—and are concerned with matters of purity and property. For example, Leviticus 18:6–18 spells out forbidden relations. Marti Steussy points out that the operative principle in the list, however, is that of violation of privilege. The list does not forbid fathers to "uncover the nakedness" of their daughters. Leviticus 18:19–24 includes a prohibition of homosexual activity: "You shall not lie with a male

---

[11]Marti Steussy, class lecture on "Sex and the Bible," for Introduction to the Hebrew Bible, Oct. 23, 1997.

[12]Obviously, the relationship between David and Jonathan need not have been homosexual; it has, however, long been so interpreted.

[13]Christopher Morse, *Not Every Spirit*, 276.

as with a woman." But here the operative principle, according to Walter Brueggemann, in the whole list of banned practices is that the male "seed" shall not be wasted.[14]

The following relations are banned: with a menstruating woman (the seed cannot sprout); with a kinsman's wife (the field is being seeded by someone else); by sacrifice to Molech (a waste); on a man (pointless if seed is not to be wasted); with an animal (equally pointless). In this list, lesbian relations are not banned; they do not waste male seed. Judith Plaskow notes that while the Talmudic rabbis condemned male homosexuality, they "indicate no knowledge of homosexual orientation in the modern sense." Also, the Talmudic rabbis regarded lesbianism less seriously "because it involves no intercourse and no 'wasting of seed,'" and therefore "brought no legal penalty."[15]

Jon Berquist points out that such passages make assumptions having to do with the nature of the household in ancient Israel. A household had one adult male and other people including women and children, some older adults needing to be cared for, slaves, and servants. Each household was economically self-sufficient. "The key to understanding sexual behavior," he says, "is that the male head of the household owned the sexuality of those inside the household, but was forbidden to have sex with members of another man's household."[16] This explains why father-daughter and father-son incest shine by their absence from the list of prohibited behaviors. This does not mean that ancient Israelites regularly practiced such incest; it does mean that the relations that are forbidden are those with women whose sexual function is the legal property of another man.

Marti Steussy asks this question: "We tend to regard the Bible as a collection of morals (statements about what you should/shouldn't do) but there are demonstrable ethics (underlying reasons) associated with those morals. Does a moral still apply if its ethic has been rejected?"[17] Jon Berquist claims that the kind of sexual ethics just described are "unhelpful in thinking about contemporary sexuality."[18]

---

[14]Cited in Steussy, ibid.

[15]Judith Plaskow, *Standing Again At Sinai* (San Francisco: Harper & Row, 1989), 182.

[16]Jon Berquist, April 14, 1998, correspondence with the author. Judith Romney Wegner agrees with Berquist on this point; see her "Leviticus," in *The Women's Bible Commentary* (Louisville: Westminster/John Knox Press, 1992), 41.

[17]Steussy, "Sex and the Bible."

[18]Berquist correspondence.

Some favorite proof-texts from the New Testament. Fred Craddock proposes that we take seriously an often overlooked question in dealing with the New Testament's statements about homosexual behavior. We should look, he proposes, at how the earliest Christian communities discussed the topic, and learn again to hear biblical texts conversing about the topic within their particular religious, cultural, and political contexts.[19] We should note first, he points out, what the New Testament does not do. It does not use as instructions for Christians any passage from the Hebrew Bible that bears directly upon homosexuality. It never refers to the life of Jesus as providing a model for how to deal with or relate to homosexuals. It never quotes a saying of Jesus concerning homosexual behavior. It cites no early Christian prophet as giving a "word from the Lord" on the topic. It contains no list of household duties (such as that in Eph. 5:22–6:9, for example) that "offers any advice, warning or command related to homosexual conduct."[20]

The New Testament does contain lists of vices, lists developed to denounce and, hence, use as a moral bulwark against the surrounding culture. Such lists are found in Mark 7:21–22; 1 Timothy 6:4–5; 2 Timothy 3:2–4; 1 Corinthians 6:9–10; Romans 1:24–31; and 1 Timothy 1:9–10. The last three contain "the only clear references to homosexual behavior in the New Testament."[21] Since Craddock wrote his article in 1979, the clarity of some of these references has been called into question. Yet we discuss all of them, because proof-texters appeal to all of them.

What does Paul make of these vice lists, once he has quoted them? Of the vices listed in 1 Corinthians 6:9–10, he says to his readers: "And this is what some of you used to be. But you were washed, you were sanctified, you were justified in the name of the Lord Jesus Christ and in the Spirit of our God" (1 Cor. 6:11). The list serves to provide a contrast with what the church is given and called to be. Also, the list contains ten vices; it is far from clear that Paul meant that the Corinthians had been guilty of all ten. Paul does not use the list to discuss homosexual behavior. A further difficulty is

---

[19]Fred Craddock, "How Does the New Testament Deal with the Issue of Homosexuality?" *Encounter* 40/3 (1979): 197.

[20]Ibid., 199–202.

[21]Ibid., 203.

that the term often translated "homosexuals," *arsenokoitai*, literally the "soft ones," was widely used to refer to men who deck themselves out in order to attract women![22] Greek culture apparently regarded homosexual encounters as evidence of being macho, not soft. 1 Corinthians 6:9 seems less clear than it once did.

Another vice list is found in Romans 1:24–31:

> For this reason God gave them up to degrading passions. Their women exchanged natural intercourse for unnatural, and in the same way also the men, giving up natural intercourse with women, were consumed with passion for one another. Men committed shameless acts with men and received in their own persons the due penalty for their error. (1:26–27)

To interpret these verses as condemning homosexuality overlooks the introduction and the conclusion of the passage. The introduction makes it clear that the long list of bad behavior that follows happened because people turned away from God and exchanged the glory of God for images (Rom. 1:20–23). The conclusion contradicts the proof-texting use of the passage: "Therefore you have no excuse, whoever you are, when you judge others" (Rom. 2:1). "All the world is indicted," says Craddock, "every mouth is stopped from boasting, and the word of grace is awaited."[23] Beverly Gaventa comments that this passage affirms that homosexual behavior is no more or less sinful than self-righteousness; hence, we cannot use it as a basis for calling homosexual persons sinners.[24]

First Timothy 1:9–10 uses the same term, *arsenokoitai*, as did 1 Corinthians 6:9–10, and hence is subject to the same difficulty of interpretation. But even if one takes it as clearly referring to homosexual behavior, Craddock's observation is to the point: All we have is a list. "There is no charge, no counter charge, no discussion, no instruction to a congregation, no discipline, no embrace, no affirmation of love, no call to obedience."[25]

---

[22]Berquist correspondence; he refers to Robert Brawley, ed., *Biblical Ethics and Homosexuality: Listening to Scripture* (Louisville: Westminster John Knox Press, 1996).

[23]Craddock, "How Does the New Testament Deal with the Issue of Homosexuality?" 206.

[24]Beverly Gaventa, "Romans," in *Women's Bible Commentary* (Louisville: Westminster/John Knox Press, 1992), 316–17 (my thanks go to Jon Berquist for pointing me to this work).

[25]Craddock, "How Does the New Testament Deal with the Issue of Homosexuality?" 207.

The result is that Romans 1:24–31 is the only New Testament text that clearly mentions homosexual behavior, and the conclusion that it draws from its list of vices is simply this: "Therefore you have no excuse, whoever you are, when you judge others; for in passing judgment on another you condemn yourself…" (Rom. 2:1). Using any of these texts to draw any other conclusion than Paul himself draws is unscriptural.

A Constructive Alternative

Where does all this leave us? Just here: "What the Bible says" about sexuality and sexual practice is much less clear than generally supposed. The proof-texts cited in defense of anti-gay and lesbian stances have lost their obviousness, and the only clear case in the New Testament contradicts such usage. The ethical reasoning lying behind some passages from ancient Israel (preservation of male seed; the father's ownership of the sexuality of members of the household) is no longer convincing. The one thing clearly condemned—violation of fidelity to the covenant with God and one another—is a point on which there should be no disagreement within Christian circles (except for supersessionists who think that God violates covenants!). Lastly, all parties to the discussion should be clear that they reject behavior, whether hetero- or homosexual, that violates the integrity and well-being of another person.

The current practice of the church in denying ordination to persons whose sexual orientation is gay or lesbian is incoherent, contradicting the gospel of Jesus Christ, and immoral because it is destructive of the well-being of those who are made in the image of God.

Earlier we pointed out that the scriptures do not have the concept of homosexuality as an orientation. It is now time to pick up this point. Being gay or lesbian, as best we can know, is not a choice, preference, or decision. The best argument for this claim comes from the experience reported by heterosexuals. Neither I nor any of my male heterosexual friends can recall ever having "decided" to be heterosexual. Since having fallen in love with our sixth-grade sweethearts, all we know is that we have just "been" this way. Each of us has also always been either right- or left-handed. Being right-handed is not a choice, or a decision for which I can be held morally accountable. It is just the way I am, more like the color of my eyes, for which I am also not responsible, than like deciding to go into the ministry. So is my heterosexuality; it is just the way I am created.

There's the rub, or part of it. "In what amounts to a tragic cruelty joke," says Christopher Morse of gay men and lesbians, "their being human as God has made them and their being faithful as God calls them are presented as antithetical."[26] The other part of the rub is that the only alternative the church offers to gay men and lesbians is "celibacy in singleness." Here the church directly contradicts the spirit of the remark made by God about Adam before Eve was created in Genesis 2:18: "It is not good that the man should be alone." How does the church require what God declares "not good"?

Christian faith denies, says Morse, "that the way God makes us, in creation, including our sexuality, is ever a cruelty joke." It also denies that God calls us to "a life of lonely repression," devoid of affection and relationship to others, and denies that who we are called to be in salvation contradicts what we are given to be in creation.[27]

The promise and challenge held out to the church today is to come to see sexuality in a way it has hardly ever seen it before: as a part of who we are and of what enables us to reach out beyond ourselves to others, as a primary component of the new and transformed lives that we are given and called to live as Christians. Can the church be mature enough to place the issue of homosexuality in this framework? If our sexuality indeed is a given, not something that we choose, then is it not one of those "gifts" that we have from God (via whatever genetic or otherwise biological means that are yet to be determined) and hence neither something about which to boast nor to refuse? We should raise for the church the question Judith Plaskow asks of Judaism: Are we willing to affirm the value "of each of us being able to find that place within ourselves where sexuality and spirituality come together?"[28] Or will we continue to see to it that the only available paths to the Christian life systematically exclude some from following them?

Gay men and lesbians are human beings, made in the imago dei. It is past time to say so. Part of what that means is involved, along with other matters, in the following propositions.

---

[26]Morse, *Not Every Spirit*, 280.
[27]For these points in Morse, *Not Every Spirit*, see 281–82.
[28]Plaskow, *Standing Again At Sinai*, 208.

Human Beings Are Equal

The scriptures go a long way toward overcoming ethnocentrism and the various dualisms into which Hellenistic culture divided human beings (Greeks and barbarians, slave and free, male and female, with the latter of each pair "less" than the former). The Christian message proclaims that in Jesus Christ God accepts all persons as potential heirs of God or "fellow citizens of the kingdom." Hence, all inherited theological doctrines that argued that some people contain in themselves more of the imago dei than do others are rejected. Any claim or implication that any human beings, because of race, gender, ethnicity, skin color, culture, sexual orientation, religious tradition, or whatever, are less than fully human is hereby denied.

Human Beings Are Part of Nature

Christian tradition has tended to cut off human beings from the natural order. This has given us too great a sense of our importance over the rest of nature and has assumed that God values us at its expense. Part of our sin of arrogance has been the brazen denial that we are dependent on a matrix of relations without which we would not even have air to breathe. It has also contributed, more indirectly than directly but quite really, to the rapaciousness displayed toward nature in what Tillich calls the "Protestant-bourgeois" era.[29] Ecological awareness has helped to restore this more unified biblical picture of humankind-in-and-of-nature. It prompts us to look at sin as an arrogant refusal to admit that we are a dependent part of an interdependent ecological system.

Human Beings Are Moral

Created for covenantal relationship, we receive from God the ability to esteem God's moral attributes (love, mercy, justice, holiness, etc.) and to make decisions and develop a moral sense or conscience. This moral capacity is part of our real, limited freedom. Christian existentialists stress the ever-renewed decisions of faith and love as the quintessential precondition for authentic life.

---

[29]See James Luther Adams, "Tillich's Concept of the Protestant Era," in Paul Tillich, *The Protestant Era,* ed. James Luther Adams (Chicago: The University of Chicago Press, 1948), 273–316.

Maturing in the Christian life, however, as in any committed relationship, means not having to decide anew every day whether to love God or one's spouse. Theology needs to reclaim the stress that the creation story in Genesis articulates the conditions for the covenant, as well as the understanding that because of God's steadfastness, human beings can also be steadfast.

Human Beings Are Fallen

In putting it this way, we deliberately avoid saying that "human nature is fallen." That way of speaking brings with it two unfortunate implications. One is that there is something called "human nature," some Platonic essence we all have in common. I would like to suggest that as made in the image of the God who is free to be whomever/whatever God will be, we need a "negative anthropology." It is not yet clear what we might become. This Platonic assumption is also radically questioned by the observation that all the different cultures and religions of the world are alternative ways of being human. It is further questioned by the additional observation that it is human beings who construct these cultures and religions. (That human beings construct religions does not deny that God discloses God's self to us in revelation unless one chooses to argue that religion is nothing but a social construction.)

The other unfortunate implication of saying that "human nature is fallen" is that it is our very nature to sin. Salvation, consequently, would require the annihilation of human nature. Like the tragic Vietnamese village, it would have to be destroyed to be saved. Some salvation! Sin is not definitional of human beings. It is not necessary that we sin. We are free not to sin, even though we fail to avoid doing so. Christian theology must deny determinism in its understanding of human beings. It is not unknown, even in these narcissistic days, that sometimes people appropriately feel guilty for having sinned. Were determinism true, both the sin and the feeling of guilt would be determined, mistaken though the latter would be.

It is more helpful to think of the fall in this way: All human beings are born into a fallen world and, unless we are open to the transforming grace of God, we become sinners. How is this so, how does it work? A post-Holocaust theology, like a feminist theology, takes sin with radical seriousness and understands it as historically and socially originated. We are born into and shaped by a sociocultural world whose beliefs, values, institutions, and practices make us who we are long before we can even begin to think critically about them. Yet we can come to see it for what it is and become responsible for trying to change it.

As an autobiographical example, I was born into the world of the mid-South where segregation and Jim Crow laws were as thorough as was the apartheid system in South Africa. Blacks and whites used separate water fountains, attended separate schools and churches, sat in separate parts of the bus, visited the zoo on different days, and faced markedly different economic prospects. We did nothing together and were denied almost all possibility of getting to know each other. The theory supporting this social system and practice held that blacks were naturally inferior to whites (being less fully human), like children, except that, unlike children, blacks could not grow up. Their comparatively greater poverty and lack of economic attainment, assured by the system of segregation, was taken as evidence of their inferiority. All this shaped our values, our psyches, and our self-understanding. Born as human babies made in God's image, we became sinners.

We are not born carrying a load of original sin. But we pick it up with remarkable quickness. A racist society, made by people who were racists, in turn makes people into racists. To grow up in such a society and, by the grace of having had a few faithful Christian teachers (as well as some excellent non-Christian teachers!), to learn to see it as a lie is to learn what it means to be lonely. Sin in this sense, original or inherited sin, is not something for which we are guilty, but something whose victims we are because of our human vulnerabilities. We are damaged not only by racism, but by all the other systemic sins that make up our world and go into the making of us. This is why Rita Brock says that "sin is not something to be punished, but something to be healed."[30] It is precisely because of our relationality, our openness not only to other persons but to the influences of institutions, cultures, and ingrained attitudes, that we can be deeply harmed.

Marjorie Suchocki reminds us of the contributions to the understanding of original sin made by the work of Walter Rauschenbusch and Reinhold Niebuhr. Rauschenbusch argued that sin is transmitted to us by our immersion in a social system that is either sinful or capable of great sin. "We draw our ideas, our moral standards, and

---

[30]Rita Nakashima Brock, *Journeys By Heart* (New York: Crossroad, 1988), 7.

our spiritual ideals from the social body into which we are born; these are mediated to us by the public and personal institutions that make up the society."[31] The most powerful institutions of the society are driven by economics, by greed; Rauschenbusch argued: "The problem of sin is that it is profitable." There is money to be made in the marketing of cancer-causing cigarettes, of death-dealing instruments of war, in selling handguns, in slum housing. The value system of such a society exalts evil, justifies it, provides it with an ethic. "Each generation corrupts the next."[32]

What Reinhold Niebuhr added to Rauschenbusch was a more deeply realistic view of groups and institutions as profoundly hypocritical and only rarely capable of self-criticism and self-transformation. He does not spare churches, as institutions, from this same criticism; the only difference there is that the hypocrisy is more blatant. Both contend that sin is mediated to society and to persons by the very mechanisms of society.

As such, it is profoundly personal and deeply structural. The powers and principalities, now understood as the magnitudes that govern our lives in so many dimensions, tempt us to believe the lie (e.g., the lie that the meaning of life is to be found in the possession of material goods and that our moral responsibility is to shop till we drop) and to be slothful, not to resist the injustices or challenge the lies.

The tendency of middle-class American churches is to treat sin, when it is talked about at all (and we are cautioned that talking about it is not conducive to church growth, because it is not a happy topic), as an individualistic, privatized matter. Sin is individual peccadilloes and sexual straying. Contrary to this, for the Bible and the greater part of the Christian tradition, sin is not only profoundly personal (persons are not unrelated individuals), but deeply structural. The great insight of the social gospel movement in liberal Protestantism and of the liberation theologies is that personal sins alone do not build the prison in which so much of humanity is caught. The crimes of the poor in the ghetto are, indeed, crimes, but so is the ghetto. And the crimes of the poor cannot be understood apart from the structures of consistent and often violent marginalization inflicted upon them.

---

[31]Marjorie Suchocki, *The Fall to Violence* (New York: Continuum, 1995), 114.
[32]Quoted in Suchocki, ibid., 114–15.

The death-dealing ways of our civilization that result in the deaths of 1,800 children per hour for lack of simple nutrition and elementary medical care cannot be blamed simply on individual sins. It is related to the powerful impact of economic and political realities and forces that can be named. The kinds of ecological disaster represented by destruction of whole swaths of rain forest is similar. The impact of such forces could be resisted, but is not. Personal sin figures into this discussion as the reason why we do not resist the powerful and destructive forces of the world. The sin of the churches is their almost unanimous silence on what one rabbi, Yeshua ha Notsri, called "the weightier matters of the law" (Mt. 23:23).

According to the doctrine of original sin, everyone participates in this fallen world, though whether each is "guilty" has been a debatable point. Theologians have disagreed about the cause, locus, and degree of this disorder. They have disagreed about its effect upon the imago dei, which characterizes human beings as created by God. But all agree that the central theme of Christian anthropology is the fact of, and the remedy for, this disordered reality and broken image.

It is appropriate to describe human existence, in its contradictions and ambiguities, as irreducibly mysterious, as dignified and miserable, as human but less than human. To refer to "mystery" is not to plea for theological silence; it is to warn of the dangers of excessive confidence and precision in theological anthropology.

How we assess the human situation is the most critical part of our theological anthropology. If we see the human situation before God and with one another as serious but not perilous, we will see human beings as only in need of moral correction and education, and little more. That we do need correction and education is not disputed. The more we see the human situation as in deep crisis, the greater and deeper is the divine response of grace and forgiveness required. In the latter case, our christology will have to make of Jesus Christ more than an example or symbol of God's goodwill toward us. Jesus Christ will have to be seen as the one in whom God declares God's acceptance of humanity in its lack of humanness, thus making it possible for us in our estrangement to appropriate the gift of a new and transformed life.

All Those Strangers Along the Way

Traditionally, Christians have only, with difficulty and all too rarely, been able to look upon all those "other, different" people in the world as neighbors whom God has given us to love. The closed-off, ethnocentric self-understanding of historical Christianity was often able to tolerate the stranger, if at all, only as a potential candidate for conversion. The stranger was permissible as long as we could sustain the assumption that, one day, she would become one of us, like us, and in no significant way any longer a stranger. In the political structure of Christendom, for example, Jews were the only religious minority that had any rights or protections. Paradoxically, they might have been better off without such protections, had they emigrated (as did the Church of the East—the Nestorians) to a less threatening environment. When Jews were seen to be resistant to conversion, Chrysostom declared them "fit only to be slaughtered," and Luther advocated burning their houses, synagogues, and holy books, putting them to work at forced labor, and, if necessary, expelling them from the country.[33]

The closed-off, absolutist, ethnocentric theology of Christendom cannot finally permit others to be in the world. One of the biggest challenges to contemporary Christians is to learn to welcome strangers. Their ways of being human, by sheer contrast with ours, will cause us self-doubt and self-questioning. Openness to strangers requires openness to questioning and a willingness to be questioned, because strangers are questions to us and bring their questions with them. Nonetheless, the moral measure of Christian theology will increasingly be taken by its capacity to welcome strangers and to guard their dignity and well-being.

---

[33]On Chrysostom, see *Homily I Against the Jews,* in *Jews and Christians in Antioch,* ed. Wayne A. Meeks and Robert L. Wilken (Missoula: Society of Biblical Literature, 1978), 89. As to Luther, see his *Concerning the Jews and Their Lies,* in *Disputation and Dialogue,* ed. Frank E. Talmage (New York: KTAV, 1975), 34–36.

Chapter 7

Jesus Christ: Pioneer of Our Faith

The Creative Transformation of Christ

Jesus and His Context

That the church always has and responds to a context when it makes the Christian witness, and no less so when it does that christologically, is made clear by the history of theology. That Jesus of Nazareth lived and acted in a context, that his ministry of teaching and acting responded to the most pressing issues of that context, is not so clear to most Christians. When we look at the historical Jesus, the prophet from Nazareth in his own time and place, we discover a person who is deeply involved with, responding to, the urgent and compelling condition of his own people in the land of Israel.

Agreement among New Testament scholars, even among those whose work focuses exclusively on the historical Jesus, is rare, infrequent as snowfall on the fourth of July. This discourages theologians from attempting to say anything about the historical Jesus and may account, to some extent, for a tendency to prefer the "Christ of faith" to the "Jesus of history." Nonetheless, for the sake of honesty, if nothing else, theologians need to come clean on what they think or assume about the historical Jesus. I will try to do this here, within a brief compass.

One important distinction must be made for the sake of clarity. To locate Jesus in his context is not to provide a sufficient reason for saying that "therefore he is the Christ." To note that Jesus was a Jew in his time and place, that he gathered a following, thought the rule of God the King was coming to Israel under Roman oppression, understood himself as having a critical role in introducing that rule, and so forth, does not allow the conclusion "therefore he is the Christ." One could say the same things, in all probability, about John the Baptist, but no one would suggest that "therefore he is the Christ." To say that he was "a Jew of his time and place," as he was, is to say something that we could say of any other Jew of any time and place. What we are doing here is inquiring historically into who Jesus was, this Jesus whom we confess to be the Christ. We return to him "not least to find ways of being Christian which highlight his care for the weak and powerless, the sinners and the marginalized."[1] We return to him partly to demonstrate that no way of witnessing to him can be used, as they too often have been, to wreak havoc on people or harm their well-being.

The Roman Context

What did it mean, to ordinary people, to live in the Roman Empire? That is the question we need to answer if we are to be clear about Jesus' context. We now benefit from two decades' worth of scholarship on the economic, social, and political situation in Galilee and Judea during the first half of the first century.[2] This period was

---

[1]N. T. Wright, *Who Was Jesus?* (Grand Rapids: Eerdmans, 1992), 25.

[2]See, e.g., K. C. Hanson and Douglas E. Oakman, *Palestine in the Time of Jesus: Social Structures and Social Conflicts* (Minneapolis: Fortress Press, 1998); Richard J. Cassidy, *Jesus, Politics, and Society: A Study of Luke's Gospel* (Maryknoll: Orbis, 1978); Ernst Bammel and C. F. D. Moule, eds., *Jesus and the Politics of His Day* (Cambridge: Cambridge University Press, 1984); Richard A. Horsley, *Jesus and the Spiral of Violence* (San Francisco: Harper, 1987); Richard A. Horsley and John S. Hanson, *Bandits, Prophets and Messiahs* (Minneapolis: Winston, 1985); Calvin J. Roetzel, *The World That Shaped the New Testament* (Atlanta: John Knox, 1985); Douglas E. Oakman,

once glorified as the Pax Romana, the "Roman Peace." Norman Beck points out that this is the view "from above," generated for the benefit of the rich supporters of the Roman historians who produced it. It functioned both to justify and advance their privileged position.[3]

The view "from below," from the perspective of the underclasses, is rather different. The result of living in a land held in subjection by the Roman Empire was the economic exploitation of its people for the benefit of the city of Rome. Taxation, exaction, and expropriation were the order of the day. The prime goal was to protect the status of the upper classes in Rome and the upper classes (through whom Rome ruled) in the rest of the empire. Peace was secured for the city of Rome by shifting war to the borders of the empire (e.g., Syria). Rome ruled primarily by scaring people to death; the army was neither everywhere nor far away.

The socioeconomic structure of a society like that in Judea and Galilee was distinguished "by an abysmal gulf separating the upper from the lower classes."[4] The ruler and the governors constituted about one percent of the populace, but owned about half the land. In an agrarian society, this resulted in massive landlessness and unemployment. Priests could own about fifteen percent of the land. Below both groups were generals and bureaucrats, and below them merchants who could develop some wealth and influence.

Subordinate to these groups were the peasant farmers, two-thirds of whose crops were devoted to the support of the small upper classes. "If they were lucky they lived at subsistence level, barely able to support family, animals, and social obligations and still have enough for the next year's seed supply."[5] Below them were the artisans, such as carpenters (including Jesus?), who came from the unnecessary

---

Jesus and the Economic Questions of His Day (Lewiston, N.Y.: Mellen, 1986); Luise Schottroff and Wolfgang Stegemann, *Jesus and the Hope of the Poor* (Maryknoll, N.Y.: Orbis, 1986); John E. Stambaugh and David L. Balch, *The New Testament in its Social Environment* (Philadelphia: Westminster, 1986); Michael Walsh, *The Triumph of the Meek* (San Francisco: Harper, 1986); Norbert F. Lohfink, *Option for the Poor* (Berkeley: Bibal, 1986); Norman A. Beck, *Anti-Roman Cryptograms in the New Testament* (New York: Peter Lang, 1997); Klaus Wengst, *Pax Romana and the Peace of Jesus Christ*, trans. John Bowden (Philadelphia: Fortress Press, 1987).

[3]Norman Beck, *Anti-Roman Cryptograms in the New Testament*, 7.

[4]John Dominic Crossan, *Jesus, A Revolutionary Biography* (San Francisco: HarperCollins, 1994), 25.

[5]Ibid.

members of the peasant class who had been forced off their farms and had to develop some craft. At the very bottom were the "expendables," beggars, outlaws, hustlers, day laborers, prostitutes, and slaves.

How would such dispossessed people hear the parable in Matthew 20:1–16 about a vineyard owner who hired laborers for his vineyard "early in the morning," again "about nine o'clock," again about noon, once more at three o'clock, and yet again at five o'clock? Would they notice that the vineyard owner observed people "standing idle in the marketplace" each time he left the vineyard? How would they hear the statement that he paid each one a full day's wage? Does not the setting of this parable, a vineyard near a marketplace full of men standing around idle, sound like the day-labor office in the inner city?

The people Israel did not need Jesus to tell them to love one another; they already knew that. They did not need him to instruct them on getting their sins forgiven; God had taken care of that in quite adequate ways. They wanted jobs, food for the family, relief from destitution, the ability to live as faithful Jews in the land promised for that purpose. They were in captivity in their own land, in exile at home, under occupation by an emperor who claimed to be god but was not. They wanted bread and freedom, not hot air.

Jesus, the gospels tell us, was born "in the days of Herod [the Great], king of Judea" (Lk. 1:5; Mt. 2:1). They do not tell us, no doubt because their readers did not need to be told it, that when Herod died, enormous social and political revolution broke out all over the land. The popular military leaders, drawn from the impoverished classes, were Judas in Galilee in the north, Simon in Perea in the east, and Athronges in Judea in the south. Armed revolt arose from the peasant classes and broke out in all important regions of the country. Three Roman legions plus supplementary troops were required to suppress the rebellion, which ended only when two thousand rebels were crucified outside the walls of Jerusalem.[6]

In outline, this was the situation under Roman occupation: First, the time was one of massive social and political turmoil. Roman soldiers frequently acted violently toward the people. Taxation, exaction, and expropriation of money and land created unemployment and destitution ("blessed are you poor"). Stress between

---

[6]Ibid., 22.

different classes of Jewish people—rich versus poor, Essenes versus the temple priests, violent rebels opposed to those with other strategies for survival—ran high. Apocalyptic prophets baptizing people in the Jordan where Joshua entered the land, reenacting his liberation of it, found followings.

Second, expectations that Israel's God would act, would return as king, mounted. Perhaps God would send a messiah, a prophetic messiah, a priestly messiah, a teaching messiah, a military messiah— some kind of liberator, please!—to announce the revolutionary inbreaking of God's kingship. Some decided not to wait for God to act and carried out their own plans for revolution; they failed and were killed in battle or crucified. Others intensified their observance of the traditional laws, the Essenes those of priestly purity at Qumran, the Pharisees their liberalized version of the same in their own households.

Third, the hope of Israel for liberation from bondage, the story of the exodus and Sinai, was reenacted several times a year in liturgies and pilgrim festivals. No feast was more important in this regard than Passover, a pilgrim festival celebrated in the Jerusalem temple under the watchful eyes of the Roman legion stationed next door in the Fortress Antonia. There is no way to depoliticize the meaning of Passover for Jews, not today when all those who are under oppression are prayed for, and certainly not then and there under their own oppression from Rome. Caesar was the new Pharaoh. Would God once again deliver the people? Would someone come announcing that only God is king, thus demoting Caesar?

"It was to this people," says N. T. Wright, "that Jesus came. It was these whispers that he heard in the lanes and backyards of his native Galilee. It was these aspirations that he found himself called to fulfill."[7] Yet he did not fulfill them in the expected ways.

The Jewish Context

An alternative to be avoided, in seeking to understand Jesus' relationships to the various movements in the Judaism of his time, is that of trying to get at his teachings by way of the "criterion of dissimilarity." Long honored in the seminars of Jesus scholars, this criterion has now fallen into disrepute. As Norman Perrin defined it, the criterion holds that:

---

[7]N. T. Wright, *Who Was Jesus?* 95.

The earliest form of a saying we can reach may be regarded as authentic if it can be shown to be dissimilar to character-istic emphases both of ancient Judaism and of the early Church...[8]

The problem with this criterion is obvious. There are few if any sayings or actions of Jesus that do not fall within the range of the Judaisms of his time or before, and nothing that the gospels de-scribe him as saying and doing that the church did not preserve or attribute to him (indeed, that is how we know them). A serious ap-plication of the principle would give us a character who had no history, no context, and who made no impact. He would not have made any sense to his contemporary Jews and could have gathered no following. He could not have differed meaningfully enough from any group for anyone to see that he was different or was about some-thing important.

Such a criterion would give us at best either a non-Jewish or an anti-Jewish Jesus, but not a Galilean prophet whose teachings are in the wisdom tradition and who declared a jubilee year for his follow-ers. He might have been a friend, as both Norman Perrin and Langdon Gilkey chose to affirm, of the contemporary "quislings" of his world.[9] Unfortunately, the term "quisling" comes into our vo-cabulary from Vidkun Quisling, a former Minister of War and, un-der the Nazis, the head of a nationalistic, pro-Nazi and anti-Semitic "National Meeting" political party in Norway. The Nazis made him the head of their new government in Norway in the spring of 1940.[10] A quisling is a bizarre kind of "liberator." Christians need to put our anti-Jewish Jesus behind us in a massive act of repentance.

To understand Jesus it is necessary to see him in his Jewish con-text (as well as in the Roman context and as one in whom the church came to believe). We can only do so by avoiding twin dangers. One is so to oppose him to his context that he becomes a complete anomaly, a mere aberration. The other is so to submerge him into it that he has a less distinct identity than any other Jew of the time of whom we know, such as John the Baptist.

---

[8]Norman Perrin, *Rediscovering the Teaching of Jesus* (New York: Harper & Row, 1976), 39.

[9]See Langdon Gilkey, *Message and Existence* (New York: The Seabury Press, 1979), 165.

[10]See Raul Hilberg, *The Destruction of the European Jews,* 355.

The way ahead in Jesus research is pointed by scholars who try to understand Jesus in his context. The first word the church ever heard about Jesus was in the context of the story of the Israel of God with the God of Israel. To remove him from that context is to lose him. The scholars to whom we will pay attention include Paula Fredriksen, Howard Clark Kee, E. P. Sanders, John P. Meier, James H. Charlesworth, James D. G. Dunn, Geza Vermes, and N. T. Wright. What distinguishes them is that they seek to situate Jesus within his Jewish context.

Jesus and John the Baptist

We have reviewed the situation in the land of Israel under Roman occupation. Into this situation of Roman domination, denying to the people Israel the ability to live in the land according to God's *torah,* came John the Baptist. He worked in the Judean wilderness, a refuge from Roman control and a reminder of the hope of Israel. The wilderness recalled the desert where Israel had lived with Yahweh prior to entering the land of promise. Here the Qumran community chose to wait for the messianic age, the end of Roman rule, and a new temple priesthood.

Here John the Baptist preached his message of the coming new age. The earlier occupation by Antiochus IV Epiphanes had produced the hope for the restoration of Israel under the rule of God. Under Roman occupation a similar development takes place, producing a revival of the prophetic hope or of "Jewish restoration theology."[11] Jewish restoration theology expects the redemption of Israel and the Gentiles by God's action in establishing God's rule over human life. It is more helpful to speak of "Jewish restoration theology" than of eschatology or apocalyptic because with these terms one continually has to stress that they deal with real politics in metaphorical language, a point that keeps escaping us and needs endless repetition.[12]

John's preaching was political, proclaiming the coming of One who would bring God's rule. "Even now the ax is lying at the root of the trees" (Lk. 3:9). Calling John "political" does not mean that he

---

[11]The term is Paula Fredriksen's. See her *From Jesus to Christ* (New Haven: Yale University Press, 1988), 18.

[12]See the discussion in N. T. Wright, *Jesus and the Victory of God* (Minneapolis: Fortress Press, 1996), 96–98.

was a militarist ready to assemble an army to attack the Tenth Legion. He was political in the sense that to proclaim that only God is king is to proclaim that Caesar is not. "'No king but God' was the revolutionary slogan of the day."[13] If the proclaimer of the message were gentle as a lamb, trusting in God to effect change, and practicing the total rejection of all violence, Rome would still not be pleased, and less so if the preacher got a following.

The gospels (Mk. 6:17–29, Mt. 14:3–12, Lk. 9:9) and Josephus tell us of John's execution by Herod. Familiar as Christians are with the gospel account, Josephus' is of interest. He depicts John as a "good man" who "exhorted the Jews to lead righteous lives...and so doing join in baptism." But, when people responded to him in large numbers, Herod became dismayed.

> Eloquence that had so great an effect on humanity might lead to some form of sedition, for it looked as though they would be guided by John in everything that they did. Herod decided therefore that it would be much better to strike first and be rid of him before his work led to an uprising.[14]

The gospels tell us two things about Jesus' attitude to John. First, when asked "By what authority are you doing these things?" Jesus retorted: "I will ask you one question: answer me, and I will tell you by what authority I do these things. Was the baptism of John from heaven [God], or was it of human origin? Answer me" (Mk. 11:27–30; Mt. 21:23–25a; Lk. 20:1–4). Here Jesus points to John as drawing his authority from the same source as does Jesus.[15] Second, "I tell you, among those born of women, no one is greater than John; yet the least in the kingdom of God is greater than he" (Lk. 7:28// Mt. 11:11). "No one born of women is greater than John" is tolerably high praise. To say that the least in the kingdom is even greater indicates that Jesus regards John as heralding the rule of God that Jesus declares is "among you." For Jesus the kingdom is not only future, but here and now.[16]

---

[13]N. T. Wright, *Who Was Jesus?* 97.

[14]Josephus, *Jewish Antiquities*, 18, 117–18; cited in Geza Vermes, *Jesus the Jew* (New York: Macmillan, 1973), 50.

[15]See Hendrikus Boers, *Who Was Jesus?* (San Francisco: Harper & Row, 1989), 42.

[16]John Dominic Crossan, *The Historical Jesus* (San Francisco: HarperSanFrancisco, 1991), 283.

Like John, Jesus was committed to the restoration of Israel under God and the torah and therefore apart from Roman domination. Like John, Jesus met his death at the hands of the Roman overlord, in the person of Pilate rather than Herod. Roy Eckardt rightly argues that Jesus was the "Champion of Israel."[17]

Jesus and the Pharisees

What exactly the Pharisees at Jesus' time were like, and what his relations with them were, are incredibly complex matters and have yielded a wide variety of results. That there were two different groups of Pharisees between whom the gospels do not distinguish, the followers of Shammai and Hillel, does not make things easier. Another difficulty is created by these two facts: First, many of the teachings of Jesus are closely parallel in spirit, and sometimes in exact wording, to those of the Hillelite or "liberal" Pharisees.[18] Second, the gospels clearly depict Jesus and "the Pharisees" as in frequent conflict, particularly prior to the time that Jesus enters Jerusalem.

Because the similarity in teachings between Jesus and the Hillelite Pharisees is probably unfamiliar to most readers of this book, I point to three instances as illustrative. Matthew reports that Jesus instructed his followers to "love your enemies…so that you may be children of your Father in heaven; for he makes his sun rise on the evil and on the good, and sends rain on the righteous and on the unrighteous" (5:44–45). The Talmud preserves this saying: "Greater is the day of rainfall than the day of resurrection for the latter benefits only the pious, whereas the former benefits pious and sinners alike."[19] This has to do with attitudes toward "enemies" and "sinners."

A story is told of Hillel that when he was a young man he was found on the Sabbath, near death, covered with snow, apparently having fallen asleep on a roof listening through a window to the sages' teaching. The rabbis Shemaiah and Abtalion saved his life, profaning the Sabbath in doing so. From that event, Hillel is said to

---

[17]A. Roy Eckardt, *Reclaiming the Jesus of History: Christology Today* (Minneapolis: Fortress Press, 1992), 63–88.

[18]Jacob Neusner, *From Politics to Piety* (Englewood Cliffs, N.J.: Prentice-Hall, 1973), 13.

[19]Quoted by David Flusser, "A New Sensitivity in Judaism and the Christian Message," *Encounter Today* 5/1 (Winter, 1970): 6.

have learned that the Torah and Sabbath are for people, not vice versa. Later Rabbi Jonathan ben Joseph, quoting Exodus 31:14, "[The Sabbath] is holy for you," interpreted it: "This means it is given to you, not you to the Sabbath."[20] Jesus made the same point.

The last has to do with attitudes toward Gentiles. The story is told that a Gentile came to Shammai, saying, "You may convert me if you can teach me the Torah while I am standing on one foot." Shammai threw him out of the room. He then went to Hillel and made the same statement, to which Hillel responded: "Do not do to your neighbor what would be hateful if it were done to you. This is the whole Torah, all else is commentary. Now go and study it."[21] Shammai may have been offended because of either the impudence of the request or because he thought that Gentiles were "impure." Hillel seems not to have been offended on either count (if we can assume the story's historicity, but that's a problem with all our stories, including those of Jesus).

Also worth noting is that some Pharisees were quite capable of being self-critical. Self-criticism is a great Jewish tradition, as witness the prophets. The Talmud preserves a humorous list of five types of Pharisees whom it calls "the scourge of the Pharisees." Some Pharisees are: egotistical (showing off their piety), so humble they walk with mincing steps, bleeding from the forehead because they are afraid of being tempted and so walk with their eyes closed, bent over (to prove their humility), so incessantly seeking good deeds to do as to be pests.[22]

Jesus, the Pharisees, and "Purity Laws"

Several contemporary scholars who seek to resituate Jesus within a Jewish context assert that he came into conflict, particularly with the Pharisees, over the issue of "purity laws." James D. G. Dunn contends that "*the purity of the meal table was an important concern among many of the Pharisees of Jesus' time,* or at least within a significant faction of the Pharisees."[23] Recognizing that many references to the Pharisees in the gospels are later revisions, he nonetheless claims

---

[20] *Yoma* tractate, 85b.
[21] *Shabbat,* 31a.
[22] Talmud, *Sota,* 20ff.
[23] James D. G. Dunn, *Jesus, Paul and the Law* (Louisville: Westminster/John Knox Press, 1990), 65.

that at Jesus' time a significant group of Pharisees passionately defended Israel's status as the people of God by insistence on the purity laws. Dunn rejects discredited notions of Pharisees as legalistic, works-righteous, or particularly hypocritical.[24] Purity laws functioned to maintain social boundaries, self-differentiation from other groups. This was their social function, and Jesus sought to re-create the people of God without drawing boundary lines that would include some and exclude others.

Marcus Borg contends that the function of the "purity system was to create a world with sharp social boundaries."[25] The system separated rich and poor, pure and impure, sinners and the righteous, male and female, Jew and Gentile. The Pharisees, he argues, were devout, not hypocrites, but they were concerned to extend "the more stringent priestly rules of purity into everyday life." Jesus was motivated by "an alternative social vision: a community shaped not by the ethos and politics of purity, but by the ethos and politics of compassion."[26] He throws considerable light on many of Jesus' teachings and actions, such as his meals with the nobodies, the destitute, with this interpretation. Jesus' politics of compassion was not "an indictment of Judaism"; it "was the voice of an alternative consciousness within Judaism."[27]

Borg's is an appealing vision of Jesus. But it may not be quite right. The Pharisees were about what Protestants have long called "the priesthood of all believers." In saying that the family table can be as holy as the temple altar, that every table is the Lord's table, the Jew is "acting as if every Israelite were a priest."[28] The ordained are not the only people who can pray. This is not altogether a bad idea. Also, the Levitical law concerning impurities makes it clear that the remedy for impurities (including the most serious) was to let the sun go down and to take a bath (Lev. 22:2–7). Since the sun sets on the pure and the impure, and anyone can take a bath, the social boundaries would not seem to be terribly sharp. Jacob Neusner complicates

[24]Ibid, 69, 71.

[25]Marcus Borg, *Meeting Jesus Again for the First Time* (San Francisco: HarperSanFranciso, 1994), 52.

[26]Ibid., 52–53, 65, n. 24.

[27]Marcus Borg, *Jesus* (San Francisco: Harper & Row, 1987), 160.

[28]Jacob Neusner, *A Rabbi Talks with Jesus* (New York: Doubleday, 1992), 125.

matters further by asking this question: "What, in accord with the law of Torah, can I do if I am pure, but not do if I am not pure? The answer is mainly, if I am pure, I can come to the temple; if I am not pure, I cannot."[29] But after the sun has set or one has taken a bath, one can go to the temple. The social boundaries may well not have been so sharp as Borg asserts.

Some Pharisees in the early first century were deeply committed to the purity laws; Saul, before his encounter with the risen Christ, certainly was (Gal. 1:13–14). The answer as to why they were is found by looking at history. In 198 B.C.E. Syria (the Seleucids) took Judea as a colony into its empire. In 175 Antiochus IV became king and named himself Epiphanes, "God made manifest." When the Jewish people in Judea revolted against his rule, his army responded by killing about 80,000 people in three days (2 Macc. 5:11–14). Antiochus himself plundered the temple, tore down the curtain, and entered the Holy of Holies.

He took one more step: He tried to put an end to Judaism. He ordered all Torah scrolls to be destroyed, banned circumcision and observance of the Sabbath, and had a swine sacrificed on the altar:

> The king sent an Athenian senator to compel the Jews to forsake the laws of their ancestors and no longer to live by the laws of God; also to pollute the temple in Jerusalem and to call it the temple of Olympian Zeus…The altar was covered with abominable offerings that were forbidden by the laws. People could neither keep the sabbath, nor observe the festivals of their ancestors, nor so much as confess themselves to be Jews…For example, two women were brought in for having circumcised their children. They publicly paraded them around the city, with their babies hanging at their breasts, and then hurled them down headlong from the wall. (2 Macc. 6:1–2, 5–6, 10–11)

First Maccabees 1:60–61 claims that, pursuant to a decree from Antiochus, his soldiers "put to death the women who had their children circumcised, and their families and those who circumcised them; and they hung the infants from their mothers' necks."[30]

---

[29]Ibid.

[30]From the translation in Lawrence H. Schiffman, *Texts and Traditions: A Source Reader for the Study of Second Temple and Rabbinic Judaism* (New York: KTAV, 1998), 157.

In the early first century, Roman occupiers put their own pressure on Judaism and Jewish identity. Emperor Caligula instigated a long crisis by insisting on erecting a statue to himself in the temple in the year 40.

Hence, some Pharisees, probably those whom N. T. Wright calls "hard-line Shammaites," stressed the purity code as an alternative political agenda, one that zealously insisted on Jewish identity and refused to assimilate and disappear into the larger Hellenistic culture.[31] Strong emphasis would have been placed on the Sabbath, the dietary laws, circumcision, and the temple as the "clearest marker-posts for the symbolic world of Israel."[32] This "angry zeal," also characteristic of many violent revolutionaries of the time, served as a protection against Gentiles and a reinforcement of ethnic boundaries.

Recalling Borg's "politics of compassion," we should have some compassion for Jewish victims of Syrian and Roman oppression. We should have some compassion for those who kept the Jewish community alive amidst terrible times. We might even have some compassion for Pharisees, vilified as they have been down through the Christian centuries. Had Antiochus succeeded in stamping out Judaism, the Christian faith could not have arisen.

Abraham and All the Families of the Earth

Let us recall the basic plot line of the biblical narrative. The promise was that the people Israel would be a blessing to the Gentiles. Jesus' proclamation and activity proclaimed that only God was king, that Caesar was not. But God's kingdom, present and coming, "would be characterized not by defensiveness, but by Israel's being the light of the world; not by the angry zeal which would pay the Gentiles back in their own coin…, but by turning the other cheek and going the second mile."[33] God's rule is here, Jesus said and showed, "*but it's not like you thought it was going to be.* How so? When Israel's God acts, the Gentiles will benefit as well."[34] Acting out of the deepest tradition of the people Israel, Jesus' movement included

---

[31]N. T. Wright, *Jesus and the Victory of God,* 393.
[32]Ibid., 389. For a discussion of these matters in relation to Paul, see my *A Guest in the House of Israel,* 98–100.
[33]N. T. Wright, *Jesus and the Victory of God,* 389.
[34]N. T. Wright, *Who Was Jesus?* 98.

"*all the wrong people.* He went into low dives and back alleys. He knocked back the wine with the shady and disrespectable. He allowed women of the street to come and fawn over him."[35]

The Mirror Image: Two Kings, Two Kingdoms, Two Meals

In a literary masterstroke, the gospel of Mark tells one after the other two stories of two kings, two banquets, and two kingdoms. He first describes a banquet Herod Antipas (one of the sons of Herod the Great and local ruler of Galilee and Perea) gave to celebrate his birthday—a typical Hellenistic activity. The guests included "his courtiers and officers and...the leaders of Galilee" (Mk. 6:21), the rich and powerful. Entertainment was provided by at least one dancing girl, Herod's daughter, Herodias, and perhaps others. What Mark does not tell us, but that we can provide from our knowledge of such banquets, is this: that the guests reclined to eat, being treated like royalty, and that the ones serving the meal would have been the slaves, women, and nobodies of the time. The highlight of the dinner was the display of the head of John the Baptist, requested by Herod's wife and given to Herodias for having "pleased" the guests with her dancing.

The next banquet story is the one known as the feeding of the five thousand (Mk. 6:30–44). In this story the poor, the hungry, and the mourners who were attracted to Jesus were assembled "in a deserted place" (a point repeated three times so that we will not miss the parallel to God's feeding of Israel in the desert). Jesus' disciples wished to send them away to nearby towns to buy food for themselves, but Jesus countermanded their desire with a simple imperative: "You give them something to eat." Most translations say that Jesus had the people "sit down" to eat, but the Greek makes clear that they were told to "lie down" (*anaklithenai*). This not-so-small point indicates that the poor and the nobodies were treated like royalty. Jesus broke and blessed the bread and divided the fish, which the disciples then served to the nobodies. Jesus and the disciples did the work of the women and the nobodies, while the nobodies were treated like royalty.

Unlike Herod's, Jesus' kingdom was one in which those who would be greatest of all must be servants of all. It was one in which nobodies were included on terms of respect. In the mirror image

---

[35]Ibid., 99.

that Mark here holds up, everything in Jesus' kingdom is the reverse of Herod's kingdom. These two stories, the latter of which is usually simply taken as a "miracle" story, make things clear as to Jesus' relation to the powers-that-be of his time.

Jesus set out to restore the Jewish people in a situation of occupation and internal exile, being in the land of Israel, the place for faithful living, under Roman domination. His movement was for the poor, the hungry, and the mourners, whose poverty, hunger, and weeping are well accounted for by Roman practice. His activities of feeding them, treating them as royalty when doing so, of creating a community of service instead of domination ("whoever would be greatest among you must be servant of all"), make clear how he went about doing this. He called disciples and in that sense started the church on its way (this is not to say that he anticipated bishops, beeswax candles, and all the rest of it).

It is easy enough to see how Jesus' followers began talking of him as "Messiah." Meaning "the anointed one," the messiah, whether a king, warrior, prophet, priest, or teacher, was expected to effect the rule of God on earth. With the messiah would come *shalom,* "well-being." Oppression would end, swords would be beaten into plowshares, history would manifest God's redemption of it from sin and violence. Early Christians said this of Jesus in light of a redefinition of messiah as one who serves, one who is vulnerable even to death on a cross, one who rejects all violence (including retaliatory violence, who "turns the other cheek"), and ratchets down the rhetoric of vengeance. He did not just preach it. He did it. They also said it dialectically, in anticipation that Jesus would return and finish what he had begun. "I consider that the sufferings of this present time are not worth comparing with the glory about to be revealed to us," said Paul (Rom. 8:18). The "glory" is Jesus' return, his second coming. Present sufferings indicate that redemption is far from complete—a good Jewish point that we had best not relinquish.

Crucifixion

It is also easy to see why the ruling powers of the time, chiefly Caesar's governing and military officials and the local groups through whom they ruled, the oligarchical Sadducees and major priests of the temple, would want to be rid of Jesus. The fate of John the Baptist shows that anybody who offered an alternative to the rule of Caesar, whether mediated through Herod or Pilate, was destined to have a short career.

So it was with Jesus of Nazareth. He gathered a following, proclaimed and enacted the kingdom of God, God's way of ruling, that was the mirror-image opposite of the Roman kingdom. He fed the hungry, included the poor and those left in mourning by Rome, provided a welcome for the nobodies. Finally, he took his movement to Jerusalem and carried out a demonstration in the temple, at Passover, under the nose of the onlooking Tenth Legion (the Fortress Antonia, housing the Tenth Legion, overlooked the temple courtyard). He was crucified, a punishment reserved to Roman authority for putting down insurrections in the provinces. His was a nonviolent movement, proclaiming God's actual and coming lordship. But the only thing Pilate understood was sedition. So he asked, "Are you the king of the Jews?" All he could see was a threat to Roman domination.[36] He was both right and wrong. Right in that the gospel is opposed to all domination, all destruction of the well-being of people; wrong in that he was not dealing with a military movement.

To speak of Jesus' context is misleadingly simple. His context is defined by three intersecting realities: the Roman Empire (Lk. 2:1 tells us that Jesus was born during the reign of the Emperor Augustus); the various movements that comprised the Judaism (or Judaisms) of his day; and the community of faith, the followers of Jesus, who became the church that believed in him. All these are the complex context of Jesus. Only when we have some sense of his relationships to them do we have Jesus in an understandable context.

Resurrection

But the story does not end with Pilate's action against the One who sought to restore the redefined people Israel and reclaim for it the promise that it would be a light to the Gentiles. It does not end with Pilate's blow against life and well-being. The early church that wrote the New Testament presupposes and proclaims that God has vindicated Jesus against the death-dealing ways of the world. The entire New Testament rests on the presupposition of the resurrection.[37] The resurrection explains the New Testament; the New Testament does not explain the resurrection. The resurrection is

---

[36]See Ellis Rivkin, *What Crucified Jesus?* (Nashville: Abingdon Press, 1984), 69–77.

[37]A point made well by Gustaf Aulen, *The Faith of the Christian Church,* 72.

God's answer to Pilate's brutality and to the death-dealing ways of all oppressive powers and principalities. It was because of Christ's obedience even unto death on the cross that God "highly exalted him and gave him the name that is above every name, so that at the name of Jesus every knee should bend,…and every tongue should confess that Jesus Christ is Lord, to the glory of God the Father" (Phil. 2:9–11).

Marc Chagall's painting *Yellow Crucifixion* depicts Jesus hanging on the cross wearing around his waist not a loincloth, but the prayer shawl of an observant Jew. This dramatic painting reminds us that the one who died for our sin is a member of the people Israel, *Yeshua ha-Notsri* (Jesus of Nazareth), the one whom God raised from the dead and who is now the living Lord of the church. When the church affirms that the Christ who was raised still bears the marks of the crucified Jew who died on a Roman cross, it puts us on notice that the risen Christ will not now do anything out of character with what the Jew Jesus did in relation to his followers. As Jesus then confronted his followers with the promise and command of the God of Israel, so Jesus now confronts his followers with the same promise and command.

Jesus lived his life in opposition to evil, to the death-dealing ways of the world. In the end, the death-dealers killed him, as they had John the Baptist and Judas the Galilean and as they later would Simon Bar-Kochba. Jesus was not the only Jew to die for the sanctification of the divine name at Gentile hands or, sadly, the last. This is the real problem that the crucifixion and resurrection present to us. Jesus died a witness to the truth of God's promise to give life and well-being to all God's creatures; "I came that they may have life, and have it abundantly" (Jn. 10:10). Yet not only was he killed, but, as N. T. Wright so movingly puts it, "on the first Easter Monday evil still stalked the earth from Jerusalem to Gibraltar and beyond, and stalks it still."[38]

Too often neglected in discussions of Jesus' resurrection is what resurrection meant in the context of Israel's exile—whether long ago in Babylon or subsequently, when Israel is in exile in the land of Israel under brutal repression. In Ezekiel's vision, the valley of dry bones represented Israel in exile. God promised Ezekiel that the

---

[38]N. T. Wright, *Jesus and the Victory of God,* 659.

dry bones could live again: "Thus says the Lord GOD: I am going to open your graves, and bring you up from your graves, O my people; and I will bring you back to the land of Israel" (Ezek. 37:12). Ever since Ezekiel's time his metaphor of corpses coming to life "had been one of the most vivid ways of *de*noting the return from exile and *con*noting the renewal of the covenant and all creation."[39] We may not abstract the resurrection of Jesus from the promise of the God of Israel to the Israel of God for the latter's restoration, nor from Jesus' commitment to that promise.

So, in the great "in spite of" of faith, the early disciples announced to the death-dealing powers and principalities that their days were numbered. Death and curse are still real; there is a considerable mopping-up operation to be done. But God in Christ has absorbed their heaviest blow, as God will have to absorb it ever and again on the butcher block of history, and has vindicated Jesus. In Christ we are free from the fear of death, free from the power of the death-dealers to scare us into slothful submission, if only we can trust God.

Jesus, Teacher and Practitioner of a Wisdom "From Below"

How did the church ever develop a high christology? How did it come to see Jesus as God incarnate? To get a sense of this, we look to Jesus as a teacher and practitioner of wisdom.

Jesus as a teacher of wisdom stood in the wisdom tradition of the people of Israel. Over time, this tradition had increasingly become a teaching of dissident or subversive wisdom. Jesus is to be understood in relation to it. The wisdom tradition begins with the book of Proverbs, which represents the conventional or establishment wisdom of Israel. It is wisdom from above, wisdom produced by or for the well-to-do, who had the leisure for education and reflection. It is wisdom for a time when things work, when people can expect wise actions to produce beneficial results, when we reap what we sow. Job moves in the direction of a dissident wisdom, a wisdom for the person who decidedly does not reap what he sows. By the time we get to Ecclesiastes (*Koheleth*) things have become even more dissident. Ecclesiastes is a wisdom for a time not when one person's

---

[39]N. T. Wright, *The New Testament and the People of God* (Minneapolis: Fortress Press, 1991), 332; his whole discussion from pp. 320 to 334 carefully argues this point.

boat seems to have sunk unfairly, but when the ocean has become so turbulent that all the boats are sinking.

Three items about wisdom are important in considering Jesus. First, there are kinds of wisdom teachers, ranging from conventional establishment wisdom to dissident wisdom of a counterorder. The wisdom teaching of Jesus, of which there is much, is that of a counterorder, a wisdom "from below," in solidarity with the destitute and oppressed. Second, many of Jesus' wisdom teachings in the gospels are direct quotes from prior wisdom tradition or slight paraphrases of them. Third, the personification of wisdom is quite important. In Proverbs 1–9 the role of Woman Wisdom is stressed in creation, providence, and moral instruction. Proverbs locates behind the voice of the wisdom teacher an "even more authoritative and revelatory voice, that of Woman Wisdom, who is teacher, sage, Queen of Heaven, the child of God, and the mediator between heaven and earth."[40]

The importance of the personification of wisdom cannot be overemphasized. Over time wisdom comes not only to represent an attribute of God or God's creation, but is used to talk about the central focus of Israelite faith–Torah. Then, it becomes a way of talking about Jesus, both in the gospels and in the christological hymns. Wisdom is identified with Torah and Jesus with Wisdom. He incarnates Wisdom/Torah. In the gospels Jesus speaks primarily in a wisdom manner or in prophetic or eschatological adaptations of the wisdom form *mashal* (parable).

Consider just some of these parallels between Sirach and the gospels.

> One becomes rich through diligence and self denial, and the reward allotted to him is this: when he says, "I have found rest, and now I shall feast on my goods!" he does not know how long it will be until he leaves them to others and dies. (Sir. 11:18–19; see Lk. 12:13–21, the parable of the rich fool)

> Come to her like one who plows and sows...Put...your neck into her collar. Bend your shoulders and carry her...Come to her with all your soul, and keep her ways with all your might...For at last you will find the rest she gives. (Sir. 6:19, 24–25, 26, 28)

---

[40]Leo Perdue, *Wisdom and Creation* (Nashville: Abingdon Press, 1994), 78.

Put your neck under her yoke, and let your souls receive instruction. (Sir. 51:26)

"Take my yoke upon you, and learn from me; for I am gentle and humble in heart, and you will find rest for your souls. For my yoke is easy, and my burden is light." (Mt. 11: 29–30)

If they make you master of the feast, do not exalt yourself; be among them as one of their number. (Sir. 32:1)

"For who is greater, the one who is at the table or one who serves? But I am among you as one who serves." (Lk. 22: 26–27)

Jesus' teachings were directed to "you poor…you who hunger… you who weep now." "It is easier for a camel to go through the eye of a needle than for someone who is rich to enter the kingdom of God" (Mk. 10:25; Mt. 19:24; Lk. 18:25). This is wisdom of a counterorder. It deals with a typical wisdom theme—wealth—but rather than seeing riches as a blessing from God (as do Proverbs and Job), it sees them as blocking the door to the realm of God. When one percent of the population owns half the land, forcing many into destitution and day-labor, wealth looks pernicious. That old preacher's dodge—the nonexistent needle gate—is a fiction.

These few examples illustrate the three points made above: Jesus' wisdom was that of a counterorder; he taught in profound continuity with the Jewish tradition and its dissident wisdom; and either he or his disciples identified him with Wisdom personified: "Take my yoke upon you." Jesus also taught by means of parables, apparently his major means of discourse, a prophetic adaptation of the modes of wisdom speech.

Now, here is the big question to which we may be moving toward an answer: How did Jesus' Jewish disciples come to talk of him as Wisdom or Word incarnate, as the incarnation of the Logos of God? Logos was what happened to wisdom (*chokmah*) when Hebrews began to speak Greek. First, it becomes *sophia* as in "wisdom is vindicated by her deeds" (Mt. 11:19), then *logos* (as in "in the beginning was the Word [Logos]" [Jn. 1:1]). Whether the masculine *logos* replaced the feminine *sophia* because of matters of gender or the popularity of *logos* in the Hellenistic world and its usefulness as gathering up the meanings of both "word" and "wisdom" is a much-debated question. Since English is one of the few languages in which linguistic gender has anything to do with sex, it is not clear that this shift was motivated by sexism. Nonetheless, all this feminine language for God reminds us that God transcends gender.

In the Hebrew Bible, a person was often presented not merely as telling parables, but as being a parable. The nation serves as a parable (Deut. 28:37; Ps. 44:14; 2 Chron. 8:20). But in Psalm 69:11 a particular individual is a parable. Certain prophets not only tell parables, but become parables. Not merely bearers of a message, they act out, embody, the word they are given to say. Ezekiel and Jeremiah do, as does Hosea through his marriage to Gomer. Now, with these *analogia scripturae* before us, consider Jesus of Nazareth in the light of this remark from Leander Keck:

> Jesus concentrated on parabolic speech because he himself was a parabolic event of the Kingdom of God. Jesus is himself a parable. He not only tells shocking stories but leads a shocking life toward a shocking end. Precisely the offensiveness of the historical Jesus is congruent with his parabolic function, for he arrests the flow of trust and thoughts and thereby invites us to reorder them, that is, to reorder ourselves...It is not just the words of Jesus that call [us] to repent, but the man as a whole.[41]

In the gospels, at places where we do not expect a high christology, we note with surprise that, at the end of several sections of teaching material, Jesus is presented or presents himself as the very embodiment of Wisdom, one who is vindicated by his deeds, one who seeks the lost, one who laments over Jerusalem, as a mother over her children. The "highest" christologies are the hymns quoted in various documents. These are fundamental expressions of Wisdom christology. Consider Philippians 2:6–11 (other wisdom-christology hymns are: Col. 1:15–20; Heb. 1:2b–4; Jn. 1:1–15). Here we have a story about the exaltation of the humble One who had humbled himself willingly. We find preexistence language, servant language, humility and exaltation language (as we do in Sirach and the Wisdom of Solomon). Here, Wisdom, who was present at creation, and Christ become merged as God, and "God...gave him the name that is above every name, so that at the name of Jesus [translation: Yahweh saves] every knee should bend,...and every tongue

---

[41]Leander Keck, *A Future for the Historical Jesus* (Nashville: Abingdon Press, 1971), 246–47.

should confess that Jesus Christ is Lord, to the glory of God the Father" (Phil. 2:9–11).

That is how Jesus' Jewish followers began to talk of him as the incarnation of the Logos, self-emptyingly (*kenosis*) incarnate as one who serves and as the crucified and risen Christ. This is not a Hellenistic deification of an individual—as Caligula having himself declared a god by the Roman Senate—but a Jewish identification of *Immanuel,* God-with-us. God's dwelling has always been "with" God's people. It is a Jewish thing that John does when he proclaims that in Jesus God "dwelt" with us, that God's *shekhinah* was among us, full of the grace and truth that had always characterized God.

As God sank a carnal anchor in the world with the people Israel, so God sinks a carnal anchor in the world in Jesus of Nazareth, this particular member of the people Israel. The gospel is no more separable from him than is the Torah from Israel. Here begins a trajectory that leads to Nicaea and Chalcedon.

Jesus as Confessed in the New Testament

In the New Testament, Jesus is confessed in a wide variety of ways, as "Son of Adam," "Messiah," "Lord," "Son of God," "God with us." We can despair or rejoice in this variety of confessions, and which we do says as much about us and our moods as anything else. The variety of New Testament witness, its richness, almost wastefulness of praise, is a great gift to the later church that finds it necessary from time to time to turn to various aspects of the New Testament's confession.

We can sort our way through the diversity of confession by remembering, first, that it is Jesus who is confessed, not his ideas, ideology, faith, experience of God, teaching, or practice. It is faith in Jesus that we find in the New Testament, not a concern with the faith of Jesus. The New Testament, for all its variety, never confesses merely the significance of the historical Jesus. We believe in Jesus, not in Jesus' belief, that is, we do not believe with Jesus. Jesus was not merely the first of the believers, or merely the first and best of the believers.

It follows, therefore, that it is always the present status of Jesus that is confessed—not what he was, but what or, better, who he is. The confession that Jesus is the Christ always uses the present tense— "Is"—not "was" the Christ, or Son of man, or Son of God, or Lord, or Word incarnate. Christians confess faith in the living Jesus. This implies the resurrection, not simply as a past fact, but as testimony to the living Jesus and to the vital character of Christian faith in its encounter with the living Christ through preaching, the sacraments, and the "least of these" who present to us the needs of Christ.

It is always Jesus whom Christians confess. It is Jesus the Jew from Nazareth, rabbi Yeshua ha Notsri, this actual historical person who is confessed to be the Christ, Son of God, Lord. The Jesus who both was, and continues to be, the Christ, Lord, Son of God. The risen Christ bears the marks of crucifixion on his body.

The New Testament does not feel constrained to confess Christ in exactly the same ways in which it had previously done so. The "old time religion" was never good enough for it. Rather, it always confessed Christ so as to make plain to the community the gospel of the love of God freely offered to it and the command of God that those so loved must in turn love God with all their selves, and their neighbors as themselves. The gospel of Jesus Christ was the context-invariant force of its christologies; the concrete ways in which Christ was imaged varied from context to context in order to serve human need and the way of life.

Jesus through the History of the Church

Jesus has been confessed differently throughout the history of the church. Each significantly new context calls forth from the community of faith a new way of confessing its faith in Christ. So it was in the early church; so it has been throughout the rest of the church's history. Jaroslav Pelikan describes eighteen different "Christs" and christologies.[42] Confessions framed in one context do not remain the same when the context changes; new situations call forth new forms of confession.

Each new setting in which the church lives poses to it a new question (or questions) to be faced, a new problem to which the community of faith must respond. For the Christian faith to remain a "way of life" by which we may fruitfully live in the present, this question must be answered. The transformative, creative work of

---

[42]Jaroslav Pelikan, *Jesus Through the Centuries* (New Haven: Yale University Press, 1985).

tradition is most evident in the manner in which the image of Christ is transformed from one set of circumstances to another. Jesus Christ is the incarnation of the creative, not the stagnant, Logos of God and, hence, the embodiment of creative transformation.[43]

Some who remember living through World War II tell striking stories about churches they recall. When every lamppost on the street carried a propaganda poster of a bloodthirsty Japanese depicted with fangs, the bulletin board in the church narthex featured a picture of Kagawa, a Japanese Christian regarded as saintly for his work with the poor. When supporting the war effort involved even the neighborhood children collecting tin cans, the entryway into the church carried a poster of Christ as the Prince of Peace.[44] Faithful witness addresses the major issues in its context. It does this particularly in what it selects to say about Jesus Christ.

The thesis of this discussion of christology is that how the church interprets, images, and symbolizes Jesus Christ in any given context reflects its most profound understanding of what God gives and calls it to be and do in the only situation in which it can bear witness to the way of life and well-being. Jesus is the pioneer of our faith in the sense that he is always calling us to respond to the claim that the gospel of God lays upon us in whatever new context we find ourselves.

A few examples from church history will clarify the point. Prior to Constantine's legitimation of the church, the church faced the agony of persecution from the empire. The primary model of Jesus Christ throughout this period was that of the Christ who suffered a sacrificial death. Parallel to that, the ideal Christians were the martyrs who witnessed to their faith in Christ even at the cost of their lives.[45] In that context, how they imaged Christ told them who God was (One who suffers with them), who they were, and what they ought to do.

---

[43]See the discussion in John B. Cobb, *Christ in a Pluralistic Age* (Philadelphia: The Westminster Press, 1975).

[44]Kagawa's picture was in the church attended by T. J. Liggett, friend and colleague. The poster of Christ as the Prince of Peace was placed there by my grandfather, J. Murray Taylor, who was the pastor of the Hollywood Christian Church, where I was brought up in the Christian faith.

[45]This discussion is indebted to that of William A. Clebsch in *Christianity in European History* (New York: Oxford University Press, 1979).

After Constantine legitimized the church, being a Christian was not only the thing to do, but a route to success and fortune in the empire. At this time, the image of Jesus that gained ascendancy was that of the Christ who conquered temptation, and the Christian ideal became the monk who withdrew not so much from the world as from the world in the church.

One last example comes from the seventeenth and eighteenth centuries, when the problem facing the church was that of the breakdown of Christendom. Christians sought to address this crisis by reestablishing Christian unity by developing the religious capacities of people. This effort took two forms, those of the moralists and the pietists. The former regarded moral behavior as the basic expression of religion. Accordingly, they sought to elicit from the life of Christ the axioms for a moral life that would overcome divisions among Christians. Consequently, by "Christ" they meant Jesus as the model of moral behavior, and the ideal of Christian living became that of the imitation of Christ. Meanwhile, the pietists thought that religion was primarily given voice through the expression of pious feelings. Hence, the model Christian was a person with a warm heart, and Christ became Jesus the friend with whom a transforming unity could be effected.

In our time, and for some time preceding it, Christ has been Jesus the Liberator. The model Christian has become the one whose life embodies solidarity with the oppressed. Resistance against authoritarianism in some form or other has been constant in all revisionary theologies since the eighteenth century. The variable in revisionary theologies has been its analysis of the kind of oppression from which liberation is sought. The first-century radical rabbi who announced an "acceptable year of the Lord" for his followers and who ministered to the poor, the hungry, and the grieving now directs the justice of God against all oppressors of humanity and of nature. Paul first declared Christian liberty through Christ: "There is no longer Jew or Greek, there is no longer slave or free, there is no longer male and female; for all of you are one in Christ Jesus...For freedom Christ has set us free. Stand firm, therefore, and do not submit again to a yoke of slavery" (Gal. 3:28; 5:1).

These are only a few examples; obviously there are more. Along the way we will comment on the major classical and modern ways of doing christology. Later we will return to the liberation model for doing christology, seeking to develop it further for our context and its multiple challenges.

Classical Christology: Athanasius

The question(s) that classical christology sought to answer were essentially three: They were the existential problems of death, ignorance (idolatry), and sin (alienation from God and one another). Their christological answers were that Jesus Christ is the life of the world (who delivers us from death), the light of the world (who delivers us from ignorance), and the savior of the world (who redeems us from sin). As we cannot do these things for ourselves, they must be done by God. Hence, it is God who was in Christ reconciling the world to Godself. But as salvation must occur in at least one human life, God had to be present in a truly human being.

Alfred North Whitehead commented on the Alexandrian theologians, of whom Athanasius was one, that they "have the distinction of being the only thinkers who in a fundamental metaphysical doctrine have improved upon Plato."[46] Plato expressed God's relation to the world merely in terms of the world's "dramatic imitation" of the ideas that God contemplates. The world, for Plato, "includes only the image of God and imitations of his ideas, and never God and his ideas."[47] Arius' solution, that it was not God but a created image of God that was incarnate in Christ, "is orthodox Platonism, though it be heterodox Christianity." Against Arius, the orthodox theologians decided

> for the direct immanence of God in the one person of Christ. They also decided for some sort of direct immanence of God in the World generally. This was their doctrine of the third person of the Trinity...in the place of Plato's solution of secondary images and imitations, they demanded a direct doctrine of immanence.[48]

Thus they affirmed the presence of God in Jesus Christ; this is the greatest strength of classical christology.

Nicaea (325) insisted that the Logos or Son, incarnate in Jesus, was of one essence (*homoousios*) with God the Father. The two primary assumptions of classical christology were that it must be God who is present and active in Jesus Christ, because only God can

---

[46] Alfred North Whitehead, *Adventures of Ideas* (New York: The Free Press, 1967), 167.

[47] Ibid., 168.

[48] Ibid., 168–69.

save, and God must be present and active in a genuine human being, because we are the ones who need to be saved. Arius denied that God was present in Christ. Apollinarius denied that the one in whom the Logos was incarnate was a complete human being (lacking a human mind, which had been replaced by the Logos). The upshot of the discussion was Chalcedon (451), which affirmed that Jesus Christ is "truly God and truly man," "acknowledged in two natures, without confusion, without change, without division, without separation...the distinctive character of each nature being preserved and combining in one person (*prosopon*) or entity (*hypostasis*)." The *person* of Christ was that of the *Deus Homo*, the divine human being. The *work* of Christ was to do what only God could do—restore fallen humanity to the original image of God in which it was made and so redeem it from death, sin, and ignorance (idolatry).

Others thought, with some justification, that it is not possible to have "nature" without "person" (*ousia* without *hypostasis*) or universals without particulars. This assumption led, on the one hand, to Nestorianism (dualism in Christ's persons, or two persons—one human and one divine—perfectly cooperating with one another) and on the other to Monophysitism (which gave us Christ as only one person and that divine—e.g., Apollinarius).

Yet, Chalcedon says that in Christ we have two natures, but only one person—so that there is in the Christ of Chalcedon a human nature, but no separate or distinct human hypostasis. Later councils affirmed that Jesus had both "two minds" and "two wills," thus struggling to avoid denying the humanity of Jesus. Some problems with classical christology are that:

(a) it was expressed in the kind of metaphysical terms, especially involving immutability, that undercut the symbol (incarnation) that it sought to articulate;

(b) it never overcame the problem of subordinationism—such metaphors as "son" are inherently or clearly subordinationist, and when two persons "proceed" from a third, but not vice-versa, they remain subordinate to the one from whom they "proceed";

(c) it never gave a coherent account of how Jesus Christ was fully human, finally decreeing as orthodox doctrines that look suspiciously like those that got Nestorius excommunicated ("two minds, two wills") at the sixth ecumenical council; and sometimes forgot entirely that his humanity was particular and therefore Jewish;

(d) Luther's doctrine of justification by grace alone was aimed at overthrowing, not answering, the traditional question: How does

Christ make possible our reunion with God? For Luther, Christ is God's free gift to us and is our fellowship with God. Luther's theology sought to answer the question: How can I find a gracious God?

(e) classical christology was unable to articulate its faith in Jesus Christ without saying, at the same time, "and the Jews be damned." See, for example, Athanasius, "An Answer to the Jews," that follows his christological essay, "On the Incarnation of the Word." Thus it fails to articulate adequately the grace and faithfulness of God (who is the God of Israel) and what Paul calls the "faithfulness of Christ," and so falls into works-righteousness. Paul's discovery of the triumph of grace, that if justification by the grace of God alone is not true for Jews, it is not true for us, passed unnoticed by most of the church for most of its history;

(f) classical christology was developed in relation to an understanding of salvation (soteriology) according to which we can be saved only by participating in the sacramental system of the church. Salvation meant immortalization of the mortal, divinization of human beings. Christ "became what we are that He might bring us to be what He is Himself." Grace was available to believers through the sacramental system, through the church, and through the priesthood; it was channeled grace. Gregory of Nyssa was not atypical when he argued that sin is a "poison," disintegrating human nature. So he interpreted the sacraments as an "antidote" or "medicine" that counteracts the poison.[49] This understanding makes salvation dependent on the church and the priesthood through which salvation is channeled. Ideology critique would suggest that we not overlook that such an understanding is in the interest of the priesthood. Those who do not do the "good work" of joining the church and participating in the sacraments are excluded from salvation, of which the church is the only broker.

Despite these problems, the intent of classical christology, to express the saving presence of God in Christ, remains an essential part of any adequate christology. If we cannot affirm the action of God in Christ, then our christology (such as it is) will probably take a works-righteous turn in which the human Jesus in his faith and/or practice becomes a model to be emulated and nothing more. Such a christology will be all demand and no grace.

---

[49]See Gregory of Nyssa, "Catechetical Oration 37," in *Documents in Early Christian Thought*, ed. Maurice Wiles and Mark Santer (Cambridge: Cambridge University Press, 1975), 194–96.

Modern Christology

The first thesis of this discussion of modern christology is that such christology has made two great gains: It has rediscovered the humanity of Jesus of Nazareth, and it has developed a christology of Jesus the Liberator. The second is that these projects remain ongoing tasks. We must deal both critically and constructively with ways in which earlier modern and contemporary theologians have done christology.

For most modern theologians, those in the eighteenth century and afterward, classical christology collapsed under its own weight. One seldom finds modern theologians engaging in a sustained argument against traditional christology, presumably because they did not think it necessary to do so.

The tradition never gave an account of the humanity of Jesus, leaving that humanity as "an-" or "en-hypostatic," the person of Jesus being constituted by his divinity–two natures, one person. His humanity was somehow miraculous or more than human or peculiarly passive in relation to his divine nature; thus, Jesus did not exercise a fully human freedom, nor was the immutable and omniscient Logos subject to the conditions of finitude. In modern eyes, traditional christology never escaped Docetism, the doctrine that Jesus merely "seemed" (*dokeo*) to be human. The contribution of modern, revisionist christologies is their conviction that being human entails unreserved participation in finitude and freedom. The idea that Jesus shared in the preconceptions of his times, that he was a person of his time and place, a Galilean Jew of the first century, that his self-understanding grew gradually ("he increased in wisdom"–Lk. 2:52)–these are distinctly modern propositions. Modern christology turned to the Jesus of history to do its christology. The way it did so, however, has its own problems.

Modern christology looks for the divinity of Jesus in the unique quality of his life on earth. In classical christology, the "uniqueness" of Jesus was that his person was composed of two natures, human and divine. In much modern christology, the only way to establish the uniqueness of Jesus is to contrast him utterly with his historical context. We tried to provide a corrective to this fault in our earlier discussion of Jesus. A major weakness of modern christology is that the distancing of Jesus from his Jewish context becomes more pronounced than before.[50] Thus, we get a picture of Jesus' life as

---

[50]See R. Kendall Soulen's penetrating analysis of this development in his *The God of Israel and Christian Theology* (Mineapolis: Fortress Press, 1996).

lived in opposition to Jews and Judaism, of his teachings as taught against Jews and Judaism, of his death at the hands of Jews and Judaism, because of his teachings, and of his resurrection as God's vindication of him over and against Jews and Judaism.

The person of Christ in modern christology is no longer that of the *Deus-Homo*. His person is that of a historical human being, who knows God perfectly; he is the perfect believer, constantly has the "abba experience." Whereas for the tradition, the Logos was subjectively incarnate in Christ (the divine subject united with the human subject), for modern christology God is objectively incarnate in Jesus. God is present to the consciousness of Jesus as the object of Jesus' faith. In a stroke, Jesus shifts from being the one in whom Christians believe to the one who is himself the "perfect believer," with whom we believe.[51] No contention is dearer to the heart of modern christology than this one, and we find it from Schleiermacher's insistence on Jesus' "perfect God-consciousness" to arguments in support of the uniqueness and constancy of Jesus' "abba experience."[52]

The work of Christ is redefined in modern christology. In the tradition, this work was to deliver humanity (or at least believing humanity) from death, sin, and ignorance. In modern christology, Christ's work is to liberate humanity from authoritarianism. Authoritarianism was particularly of concern for all the thinkers of the new movements of freedom associated with the Enlightenment. Bad religion is dictatorial religion that imposes an alien law on people. Although the "real" targets of liberal Protestants were Roman Catholicism and Protestant Orthodoxy, it was Judaism, more than anything else, that came to typify bad religion in their eyes. A characteristic of anti-Judaism is that it uses an external, fictive enemy as the brush with which to tar real enemies who are internal to the church. Christ becomes the one who saves us from Judaism.

It is difficult to make this point too strongly. In whatever ways modern and contemporary christologies define oppression, they

---

[51]A more sustained analysis and criticism of modern christology can be found in Williamson, *A Guest in the House of Israel,* 174–88. This critique was suggested by and developed from that penetratingly set forth by Schubert M. Ogden in *The Point of Christology* (San Francisco: Harper & Row, 1982).

[52]See, e.g., James D. G. Dunn, *Unity and Diversity in the New Testament* (Philadelphia: The Westminster Press, 1977), 184–89.

usually select Judaism to typify it. Since Christ is always understood to oppose oppression, Christ becomes more anti-Jewish than he was in the prior tradition.

All distinctly modern christologies are, and always have been, liberation theologies. Where they have differed, over time, is in their analyses of the particular oppression from which we need to be delivered. For them, salvation is a this-worldly process in which we are emancipated from oppressive structures. Initially, these had to do with authoritarian religion. Later, a wide variety of forms of cultural oppression, bureaucratic manipulation, economic exploitation, sexual and racial oppression, and so forth, became the targets of liberation.

Let us pause to make a distinction. The modern insistence that salvation through Jesus Christ entails opposition to any and all forms of oppression is unarguably correct. The affirmation of freedom is one of the great contributions of modern theology, and we should appreciate and develop this emphasis, even while noting that Christian freedom and Enlightenment freedom are not identical with each other. It is self-contradictory to claim to love one's neighbor as oneself and to allow that neighbor to suffer from any form of oppression. But two fallacies require attention: (1) the reduction of salvation to emancipation from this-worldly oppression and (2) the continuing identification of Jews and Judaism with the oppressors. For example, Susannah Heschel and Judith Plaskow, Jewish feminists, criticize Christian feminists for their contention "that the Jews introduced patriarchy and violence into the world."[53]

This identification of Jews and Judaism with oppressors runs through most contemporary christologies whose authors have not become aware of the ideology that they unintentionally repeat. The most practical thing one can do about an ideology is to know what it is and understand how it works to reflect and reinforce practices that are not only injurious to our neighbors, but contradict the good news we are given and called to proclaim.

---

[53]Susannah Heschel, "Christian Feminism," *Tikkun* (May/June, 1990): 27. Heschel returns to the subject with further documentation in "Denigration of Judaism as a Form of Christian Mission," in *A Mutual Witness,* ed. Clark M. Williamson (St. Louis: Chalice Press, 1992), 33–47. Judith Plaskow discusses the same problem in her "Christian Feminism and Anti-Judaism," *Cross-Currents* 28: 306–9. Katharina von Kellenbach, *Anti-Judaism in Feminist Religious Writings* (Atlanta: Scholars Press, 1994), uses ideology critique to look at a wide range of feminist writings.

Kant and Hegel

Immanuel Kant and Friedrich Hegel are the philosophers who most profoundly impacted liberal, nineteenth-century Protestantism. Each stood for freedom in philosophy, religion, ethics, and history, and Hegel developed a philosophy of history in which freedom was the central category. Both were firmly committed to the emancipation of human beings from authoritarianism, with Kant defining the meaning of Enlightenment as "man's release from his self-incurred tutelage."[54] The point of Enlightenment was that we have the "courage to think" (*sapere aude*) and free ourselves from the authoritarianism that asks us to turn our minds over to someone else.

Kant regarded Judaism as the antithesis of the freedom he celebrated. Religion for him consists in the fact "that in all our duties we look upon God as the lawgiver universally to be honored," and the way religion is determined "hinges upon knowing *how God wishes* to be honored and obeyed."[55] God may be understood to command "either through laws in themselves *merely statutory* or through *purely moral* laws."[56] Judaism is Kant's premier example of a merely statutory religion, Christianity of a "purely moral" one. A statutory religion is authoritarian because knowledge of its laws can be gained "not through our own reason alone but only through revelation," whereas "pure moral revelation, through which the will of God is primordially engraved in our hearts, is not only the ineluctable condition of all true religion whatsoever but is also that which really constitutes such religion."[57]

Because they are radically divergent, "the Jewish faith stands in no essential connection whatever with" Christianity.[58] Christianity derives no spiritual patrimony from Judaism that was "a collection of mere statutory laws upon which was established a political organization." Genuinely moral values cannot be Jewish, because morality requires freedom that Judaism, a merely statutory religion, rejects. Because of its statutory character, Judaism "is not a religious faith at all."[59]

---

[54]Immanuel Kant, "*What Is Enlightenment?*" trans. and ed. L. W. Beck (Chicago: University of Chicago Press, 1955), 286.

[55]Immanuel Kant, *Religion Within the Limits of Reason Alone,* trans. Theodore M. Greene and Hoyt H. Hudson (New York: Harper & Brothers, 1960), 95.

[56]Ibid.

[57]Ibid.

[58]Ibid., 116.

[59]Ibid., 117.

Yet among this people "there suddenly appeared a person whose wisdom was purer even than that of previous philosophers, as pure as though it had descended from heaven."[60] Kant virtually renders this appearance miraculous. Consequently, Christianity utterly forsook "the Judaism from which it sprang, and grounded [itself] upon a wholly new principle."[61] Hence, Christianity supersedes Judaism, the signs of the covenant being dispensed with, and Jesus' appearance among Jews is a complete novelty; he taught a freedom unknown to "slavish" Jews.

Hegel understood Christianity as a synthesis of the beauty of Greek religion with Kant's emphasis on freedom; to this, Judaism was the antithesis. Contrasted with Christian beauty, Judaism is ugly, stressing disunion rather than union, hostility rather than friendship to nature.[62] At Jesus' time, Jewish faith was "ordered and compressed in dead formulas, and nothing save pride in this slavish obedience to laws not laid down by themselves was left to the Jewish spirit," additionally embittered by Roman occupation.[63] Exclusivist in religion, "they utterly abhorred and despised all surrounding peoples."[64] Abraham's leaving Ur of the Chaldees was "a disseverance which snaps the bonds of communal life and love."[65]

Jesus' relation to the Jews is predictable. He who was one with God was utterly rejected by them:

> How were *they* to recognize divinity in a man, poor things that they were, possessing only a consciousness of their misery, of the depth of their servitude, of their opposition to the divine, of an impassable gulf between the being of God and the being of men? Spirit alone recognizes spirit.[66]

"Faith in something divine," says Hegel, "cannot make its room in a dunghill. The lion has no room in a nest, the infinite spirit [God] none in the prison of a Jewish soul."[67] Jesus came not to bring peace,

---

[60]Ibid., 74.

[61]Ibid., 118.

[62]Friedrich Hegel, *On Christianity: Early Theological Writings,* trans. T. M. Knox (New York: Harper & Brothers, 1961), 9–10.

[63]Ibid., 68–69.

[64]Ibid., 78.

[65]Ibid., 185.

[66]Ibid., 265.

[67]Ibid.

but a sword that would cut himself and his disciples off from Judaism.[68] We cannot fail to point out the mutually contradictory evaluations Hegel offers of the "disseverances" of Abraham and Jesus.

Hegel's chief influence on theology was in the support he provided for historical analyses of the Bible and church history and for the attempt to develop christology "from below" based on the empirical-historical Jesus. For Hegel, the infinite is in the finite, as the finite is self-transcending; therefore in the very humanity of Jesus where the finite is most clearly self-transcending, the infinite is most fully realized. Thus by historical investigation of Jesus' humanity, we uncover his divinity.

One Example of Liberal Christology

To make clear the model and logic of liberal christologies, we will look at one: that of Adolf Harnack's highly influential book *What Is Christianity?*[69]

Harnack tried, by historical-critical method, to get at both the "main features" of Jesus' message and his "character" or "person" by way of the synoptic gospels. Aware of the difficulties in using the gospels as sources of historical knowledge, Harnack knew that "we are unable to write any life of Jesus."[70] Yet he was convinced that he could discern the main features of Jesus' teaching, how his life issued in the service of his vocation, and the impression he made on his disciples. In spite of admitting that we cannot write a life of Jesus, Harnack insisted that Jesus "lived in religion, and it was breath to him in the fear of God; his whole life, all his thoughts and feelings were absorbed in the relation to God."[71] This claim was important to Harnack, because he knew that all of Jesus' teachings were already present in Judaism. What counts, he said, is not novelty of teaching: "Words affect nothing; it is the power of the personality that stands behind them."[72] The romantic-psychological age with its concern with "personality" much influenced Harnack.

Harnack knew that the Pharisees were credited with having taught virtually everything that Jesus proclaimed. Unfortunately, according to him, they also possessed much else:

---

[68]Ibid., 286.

[69]Adolf Harnack, *What Is Christianity?* trans. Thomas Bailey Saunders (New York: Harper & Brothers, 1957).

[70]Ibid., 30–31.

[71]Ibid., 35.

[72]Ibid., 48.

As regards piety, the spring of holiness had long been opened; but it was choked with sand and dirt, and its water was polluted. For rabbis and theologians to come afterwards and distill this water...makes no difference. But now [with Jesus] the spring broke forth afresh, and broke a new way for itself through the rubbish.[73]

Jesus compares favorably to the "rubbish," as to Hegel's "dungheap." Jesus' preaching of the acceptable year of the Lord to the poor, the broken-hearted, and captives was "a definite signal for contradiction" of the prevailing religious system. It brought him into opposition with the official leaders of Judaism, who were aware of God's presence only in the law, whereas Jesus "saw and felt Him everywhere."[74]

Jesus sifted the elements of the Jewish tradition, discarding everything Jewish in it and keeping only that which was genuinely religious and universal. Harnack consistently caricatures Judaism, claiming that the Pharisees and priests "had little feeling for the needs of the people" and "held the nation in bondage and murdered its soul."[75] Jesus' teaching embodies a higher righteousness and a new commandment: His overcoming of Judaism is Harnack's doctrine of the work of Christ who saves us from bad religion, that is, Judaism.

The other aspect of Harnack's christology is his doctrine of the person of Christ. This becomes the person of the historical Jesus "who himself was what he taught," all of whose life, thought, and feelings were absorbed in the relation to God. Harnack was inattentive to the problem that such claims cannot possibly be warranted by the historical-critical method that he claimed to use. What is important about such claims is that they provide the reason why, for Harnack, it is true to say that Jesus is the Christ: because he was the perfect believer. Harnack redefines the classic terms: "It is 'knowledge of God' that makes the sphere of Divine Sonship."[76] God is objectively incarnate in Jesus' consciousness as an object of knowledge, "feeling," and faith.

The pay-off of Harnack's theological anti-Judaism comes in his interpretation of Paul: "Someone had to stand up and say, 'The old

---

[73]Ibid., 48.
[74]Ibid., 50–51.
[75]Ibid., 103.
[76]Ibid., 128.

is done away with'; he had to brand any further pursuit of it as a sin; he had to show that all things were become new."[77] By implication, Jews who continue to pursue Judaism are sinners.

The model of modern, liberal christology (with some critical comments appended) is as follows:

(a) The *work of Christ* was to overcome inauthentic, authoritarian religion (identified with Judaism); as this model is subsequently pressed into service, the description and analysis of oppression/authoritarianism/hierarchy, and so on, will change as contexts change.

(b) The *person of Christ* was the empirical-historical Jesus (the Jesus who can supposedly be reconstructed behind the texts with the use of the historical-critical method), interpreted as the perfect believer; because he was what he taught, he is the warrant for what he did. This is in spite of the fact that we cannot possibly justify claims about what Jesus "always" felt. Nor do the gospels provide us with so much as half a line on such matters. That Jesus had aims is clear; they were to proclaim and enact the rule of God. How he "always" felt is not accessible to us, even if it were important.

(c) Jesus is, hence, inappropriately made over into the first of the believers, the one with whom we believe, no longer the one *in* whom we believe *with* the apostles (it is important to get the prepositions straight).

(d) This empirical-historical Jesus with his teachings and practice of liberation is the norm of christology and Christian theology. Taking this step raises at least two issues: (1) Is it appropriate to make Jesus the norm of theology? Is Jesus not more than any mere norm? Is Jesus, perhaps, better understood as our Savior, however much what that means remains to be unpacked? (2) If we make the historical Jesus our norm, then do we have to read back into him whatever we feel it necessary to read out of him? For instance, in order to argue the case of feminism, does one, therefore, have to legitimate feminism by appeal to the historical Jesus? Can that be done without falling again into the traps set by historical-Jesus christologies, including the trap of anti-Judaism?

---

[77]Ibid., 175.

(e) When the understanding of the Judaisms of Jesus' time held by Harnack are shown to be fallacious, as they have been by a spate of writers too numerous to mention, what happens to his case for the uniqueness of Jesus?[78] Does loving our neighbors mean that we should not tell lies about them?

Liberating Jesus

The expression "liberating Jesus" is nicely ambiguous. It has two senses. The first is that we need to liberate Jesus from the anti-Jewish grip in which we have held him for so long, making him into one whose teachings were against Jews and Judaism, whose life was lived in conflict with Jews and Judaism, whose death came at the hands of Jews and Judaism, and whom God raised in vindication over Jews and Judaism. Jesus needs liberating from Christian anti-Jewish ideology. Christology needs liberating, as well, from its inherited ideologies.

Second, Jesus liberates us (or God in Jesus liberates us) from sin, evil, and commitment to the death-dealing, curse-bringing ways to which we find ourselves addicted, by which we are narcotized. But only a liberated Jesus can be a liberating Jesus. The doctrine of the atonement or "work of Christ" has always had to do with liberation, whether or not it has been explicitly interpreted to do so. The oldest, that of Christ as a ransom paid to the devil, makes this clear. The metaphor of ransom means that we are "kidnapped" by sin and evil. We are held against our will because we are enticed, addicted, unable to free ourselves from our entanglements with evil. We rationalize and legitimize evil; what we do not do is face it. Christ enters the precise spot of our addiction to evil and makes clear that evil's demonic demand on us is phony, illegitimate, devoid of the authority it falsely claims for itself.

Our enslavement, our craving for death and curse (our joy of mall shopping and our indifference to Third World makers of the garments we buy), means we cannot live up to God's perfectly legitimate requirements of us. We fail in all sorts of ways to honor God's intent and love our neighbors as ourselves. We suppress,

---

[78]We should have known better at least ever since George Foot Moore's *Judaism in the First Centuries of the Christian Era,* 3 vols. (Cambridge: Harvard University Press, 1927–30).

conceal from ourselves our unwillingness and inability to exist in relationships of mutual blessing and well-being, of love and freedom, with God and the neighbor. So the second metaphor of atonement, Anselm's in his *Why God Became A Human Being,* holds that God in Christ frees us to love and loves us into freedom in spite of our unfree refusal to love God with all our selves. Christ bears for us the burdens that we accrue so that we may be liberated to love.

The effect of sin and evil, enslavement, addiction, neither loving God the ultimate with an ultimate love nor loving our neighbors as ourselves, is that our affections are tied up, bound. So the third metaphor of atonement, associated with Abelard, is that Christ frees us to relationships of warmth and affection by the contagion of a love that is warm and affectionate.

So, Jesus is liberating Jesus; that is who he is and what he does. He liberates us to love ourselves appropriately, to love God with all of ourselves and our neighbors as ourselves. He liberates us to understand ourselves in any ultimate sense as loved by God and therefore given and called by God to love God and our neighbors/strangers in return.

For far too long we have characterized Jesus as the bright and shining light contrasted with its alienated other—the dark, negative, Pharisaic, works-righteous, legalistic Judaism that he opposed and that, in its malevolence, put him to death. Thus, he became the confirmer, the legitimator of the death-dealing, curse-bringing ideology of anti-Judaism. The record of the church's history on this point is open to be read. That is why, in order to liberate Jesus so that he can be "liberating Jesus" again, we have to reappropriate his Jewishness. Perhaps if we can accept that he was one of them, not one of us, that he is other than, different from, us, then we can finally learn to appreciate and affirm otherness and difference.

Only a Jesus liberated from anti-Judaism can be "liberating Jesus." So let us remember several points about the one whom we confess to be the Christ.[79] First, his name, Jesus, is theologically significant. This name, *Joshua* in Hebrew, *Yeshua* in Aramaic, means "Yahweh saves" or "Yahweh is salvation." To be confronted by Jesus Christ is to be confronted by the God of Israel, Yahweh, and the Israel of

---

[79]One of the better, but remarkably unheralded books on Jesus is that of Gerard S. Sloyan, *Jesus in Focus: A Life in Its Setting* (Mystic: Twenty-Third Publications, 1983). Its influence is reflected here and throughout this chapter.

God (the Jewish people), of whom Jesus of Nazareth (*Yeshua ha Notzri*) was and is one. It is God who has graciously acted in and through the ministry of Jesus to save us, which is what Matthew meant when he repeated this connotation of the name: "You are to name him Jesus, for he will save his people from their sins" (1:21).

The land itself, the *eretz Yisrael,* is a major factor in the story of Jesus. Neither he nor the Israel of God can be understood apart from it. It is that "storied place" that God gave to the people as a gift for the purpose that in it they would be free to be a witness and a blessing to the Gentiles.[80] Nothing helps as much to understand the historical context of Jesus' times as a visit to the land of Israel. One sees the archaeological excavations of such large Roman cities as Sepphoris, Tiberias, and Beth Shean, cities that Jesus avoids on his journeys, and the model of first-century Jerusalem that depicts its Roman domination and Hellenization in the Fortress Antonia and the Hippodrome (horse racetrack). This actual piece of earthly turf was to be Israel's spiritual home. We can neither take Jesus out of the country nor the country out of Jesus.

More specifically, Jesus was a person of Galilee, of northern Israel. He was a non-Judean Jew committed to his fellow Jews, "the lost sheep of the house of Israel" (Mt. 15:24). Jesus reflects some of the concerns of the northern prophets Elijah and Elisha to whom Luke compares him (4:24–27). Like them he fed large crowds and was a healer of body and mind. The bond of empathy between women and Jesus reminds us of that between women and the "man of God" in northern Israel (see the Elijah stories in 1 and 2 Kings).

Jesus was a wandering teacher, committed to the renewal of Jewish life under the Torah and through the promise to Abraham that the people Israel would be a blessing to the Gentiles. Under the "internal exile" that Roman domination imposed, this renewal was both critical to the people Israel and threatening to Rome. His roaming about the countryside was itself important, proclaiming the freedom of his gospel of God's rule open to all the lost sheep, not "brokered," as John Dominic Crossan puts it, by any town or group or even by his disciples.[81] This concept of a "brokerless kingdom" is

---

[80]For the concept of Israel as "storied place" see Walter Brueggemann, *The Land: Place as Gift, Promise, and Challenge to Biblical Faith* (Philadelphia: Fortress Press, 1977).

[81]John Dominic Crossan, *Jesus: A Revolutionary Biography,* 54–74.

at odds with the later church's tendency to set itself up as the universal broker of salvation. We have seen that Jesus' teachings are highly parallel to those attributed to Hillel and the liberal Pharisees. "From early Jewish writings we could easily construct a whole gospel without using a single word that originated with Jesus."[82]

The movement that Jesus led was both inclusive and egalitarian. There were no lines between who was "in" and who was "out," no ritual requirements for joining, no apparent concern for ritual purity (in strong contrast to the Qumran community). It was aimed at all the lost sheep, the destitute and nobodies, and included people of both genders. In the gospels, the risen Jesus continues and expands the inclusiveness of this movement with the command to the disciples to go "to all the Gentiles" [*panta ta ethne*] (Mt. 28:19). It was egalitarian in this sense: "You know that among the Gentiles those whom they recognize as their rulers lord it over them, and their great ones are tyrants over them. But it is not so among you; but whoever wishes to become great among you must be your servant" (Mk. 10:42b–43).

André Trocme and John Howard Yoder long ago showed how Jesus' teaching and practice of God's rule "borrowed extensively from the prophetic understanding of the jubilee year."[83] This entailed "a visible socio-political, economic restructuring of relations among the people of God, achieved by his intervention in the person of Jesus as the one anointed and endued with the Spirit." The Jesus movement was a radical alternative to the prevailing Rome-dominated model. "As a radical rabbi Jesus was far more of a political figure" than the more privatized christologies of the contemporary church admit.[84]

Jesus was like the *hasidim* of Galilee. The term "hasid" is related to the noun *hesed*, "steadfast love/loving kindness/faithfulness," used numerous times in the scriptures to refer to Yahweh's gracious faithfulness. God's hesed is a Jewish way of talking about what Christians call "grace." A *hasid* (a Galilean "man of deeds") typically rose above all demands of the law to come to the aid of people in need. The hasidim did not only good deeds, but deeds of power. In an

[82]David Flusser, "Jesus, His Ancestry, and the Commandment of Love," in James H. Charlesworth, ed., *Jesus' Jewishness* (New York: Crossroad, 1991), 171.

[83]John Howard Yoder, *The Politics of Jesus* (Grand Rapids: Eerdmans, 1972), 36.

[84]Ibid., 39, 100.

arid climate Honi the circle-drawer would appeal "to the Abba in heaven" to send rain; and the Abba would.

Jesus is reported to have performed healings, exorcisms, and feedings. He answers John the Baptist's question, "Go and tell John what you hear and see: the blind receive their sight, the lame walk, the lepers are cleansed, the deaf hear, the dead are raised, and the poor have good news brought to them" (Mt. 11:4–5). One thing that ancient healers did was to remove the social ostracism from the disease.[85] For example, today the stigma of having AIDS is almost as bad as having the disease itself. Never once in more than forty healing stories does Jesus ask: "How did you get this disease?"

Jesus' ministry was neither one of words nor of deeds alone. It was a ministry of deeds interpreted by words, words acted out as deeds. He did not only talk about God's rule or content himself with proclaiming that he was the bread of life. Galilean peasants knew all about rule; they suffered from it daily. And they knew all about bread; they just did not have enough of it. They knew kingdom as tax and debt, malnutrition, homelessness, and going crazy (demonic possession). Jesus could have talked about being the bread of life until he was blue in the face. No one would have listened. It was because he acted it out as a kingdom of a different order that they could hear him. Like the prophets of scripture, his word was also deed, his deeds were expressed in words. "Jesus willed his public activity to be a dramatic acting out of his message of God's welcome and forgiveness extended to the prodigal son."[86]

Jesus of Nazareth was a Jew of his time and place. As Paul the apostle said of himself in Philippians 3:5, Jesus was "a member of the people of Israel,...a Hebrew born of Hebrews." For Paul the universality of the gospel itself made it requisite that Jesus be a Jew. Jesus' Jewishness was a necessary condition whereby the peoples of the world, the Gentiles, could have access to the gracious gift and irrevocable calling of the God of Israel. Only one who took shape in the Israel of God could mediate the blessings of the God of Israel to the outsiders of God's house. Every time we encounter Jesus Christ, in the word of preaching, in the sacraments, or in the needs and hurts of "the least of these," we are laid bare before the God of Israel, the Creator and Redeemer of the world.

---

[85]Crossan, *Jesus: A Revolutionary Biography*, 80–82.

[86]John P. Meier, "Reflections on Jesus-of-History Research Today," in Charlesworth, ed., *Jesus' Jewishness*, 93.

Images of the Liberating Jesus

How the church images Jesus Christ in each of its historical contexts gives expression to its deepest sense of what God gives and calls it to do in response to the challenges it faces in that context. Jesus is always contextualized, always contemporized. He is always with his followers and with the hurting of the world, in whatever context they find themselves. This is what it means to speak of him as the living, risen Jesus. He does not just reside in the past. Had he not been an actual figure in a concrete Jewish past, we would today entertain no thoughts about what he gives and calls us to do with regard to, say, all his women followers or the desperate situation of all those folks who constitute the inner city underclass.

Thus, we have images of Jesus as "the black Messiah" or Jesus as the leader of an inclusive and egalitarian community. We could enumerate further examples, but the point is clear. All this is well and good. Jesus affirms the worth and dignity of people of color, many of whom are today, on the world's terms, the "nobodies," the destitute of our society. Jesus is for their liberation, and with them in their suffering. So he is with women as those people who, in every society, bear a greatly unequal burden of oppression and domination.

Jesus, liberated from the oppressive ideology of anti-Judaism, can function as the Liberator of all from oppression. Liberated from anti-Judaism, he acts in character on behalf of all the nobodies. If we can appreciate and affirm the otherness of Jesus, his difference from us, his Jewishness, perhaps we can allow Jesus to empower us to affirm and enjoy all those other differences and not turn them into new forms of segregation. Only a Jewish Jesus can liberate us from drawing our own lines of purity to guard us against the poor, the dirty, the uneducated, the scruffy, and those who are sexually different from us.

Chapter 8

The Spirit of New Life

Some Preliminary Considerations

The Meaning of "Spirit"

Spirit is a word that can mean anything we want it to mean. People talk about team spirit, the spirit of the age (the latest fad or cultural trend), the spirit of *Playboy*, school spirit, the spirit of Lincoln, the spirit of the Confederacy, the spirit of IBM, or the spirit of the Führer. Let us stipulate a linguistic rule: Spirit is always "spirit of _____." Spirit is not an attribute that applies equally and in the same senses to God, us, political parties, communities, or times. Whatever spirit means is defined by how we fill in the blank. Spirit is always the spirit of some particular person or group, for example, the spirit of my friend Gerry or the spirit of our congregation. To be theologically clear as to what we mean by "spirit," we speak of "the Spirit of God" or "the Spirit of Christ." For the same reason, we need to keep Spirit and word or gospel closely connected to each other.

The Lord and Giver of Life

Christian faith is a way of life and well-being, a way walked through history. The Creed of Constantinople, adopted in 381, affirms: "And [we believe] in the Holy Spirit, the Lord and life-giver, Who proceeds from the Father, Who is worshiped and glorified together with the Father and Son, Who spoke through the prophets."[1] God creates life and discloses the way of life to us in God's self-revelation of God's will for human beings. God is also the source of our new or re-newed life, renewed amid the brokenness and ambiguity that sin introduces into our history with God and one another. God calls us forward into new adventures on the way of life pointed toward God's rule over all of life. The thesis here is: "God is Spirit" (Jn. 4:24), and the activities of God the Spirit are trinitarian in character.

But that is jumping ahead of the game. Because we are well advised to see how our language works when it plays on its "home field," we begin our reflection on the Holy Spirit by looking at the scope of the biblical witness to the Spirit. Having been informed by that, we will then make some theological comments on God the Spirit.

The Spirit Blows Where It Will

We will look at what the entire scriptures have to say about the Holy Spirit. We do this in order to resist the way in which the *Adversus Judaeos* tradition of the church has distorted the doctrine of the Holy Spirit. Anti-Judaism is a systematic hermeneutic that systematically misconstrues every doctrine it touches. "Most traditional Christian pneumatology [doctrine of the spirit]," says Michael Lodahl, "has also shared in the anti-Judaic bias."[2]

The effect of anti-Judaism on the doctrine of the Spirit was not only to assert that the church is the locus of divine presence, but to identify the Spirit with, and restrict it to, the church. This is an *exclusivism of the Spirit*. "It has claimed that the Church is the possessor of God's Spirit, and that *the Jews in particular* have forfeited the blessings of God's presence because of their rejection of Jesus."[3] We find this interpretation not only among the church fathers, but in important contemporary theologians as well. Thomas F. Torrance illustrates it:

> Now the coming of the Creator Spirit as at Pentecost is the point where man's own sinful creativity has to be broken...

---

[1]All the creeds of the churches are gathered together by John H. Leith in his *Creeds of the Churches* (Richmond: John Knox Press, 1963).

[2]Michael Lodahl, *Shekhinah/Spirit* (New York: Paulist Press, 1992), 6. Lodahl's work is the major treatment of the Holy Spirit in post-Holocaust theology.

[3]Ibid., 16.

At that point he is either re-created and emancipated from himself for genuine faith in God, or he lapses back in conflict with the Spirit into his own self-willed existence and becomes even more securely imprisoned within his own inventions...

Is that not the story of the recalcitrant Jews face to face with Jesus? Out of their own distinctive piety and attitude to existence they had forged their own conception of the Messiah...Then when at last the Messiah actually came the conflict between their own image of God and that mediated by the Messiah was so intense that instead of surrendering to the creative impact of his Spirit upon them, they crucified the Messiah, and in a desperate attempt to force the hand of God they even resisted his Holy Spirit.[4]

There has been a strong tendency in the history of the church to restrict God's activity as *life-giving spirit* within the periphery of Christianity. Friedrich Schleiermacher, a pivotal figure in the history of modern theology, did precisely this when he defined the Holy Spirit as "the common Spirit animating the life in common of believers." In the context it is utterly clear that these are Christian believers.[5] The Spirit is the "Common Spirit of the new corporate life founded by Christ." God's omnipresent indwelling, dwelling in each creature as the creative ground and end of its life, has often been denied. Christopher Morse argues that the "arrogance of such a perspective cannot be reconciled with the gospel message of God's universal dominion of love as the basis of the injunction to love one's neighbor."[6] This jaundiced approach to the Holy Spirit is hereby denied. Faithfulness to the biblical witness requires its rejection. The Spirit blows where it will. It is not the exclusive possession of the church.

The thesis of this discussion of the Holy Spirit is that because the Hebrew Bible is the home field of Christian language, we must look at the entire sweep of the biblical witness to the Holy Spirit and not only to that of the New Testament. From the broadly based biblical testimony we shall find that a rather different understanding of

---

[4]Thomas F. Torrance, *Theology in Reconstruction* (Grand Rapids: Eerdmans, 1975), 255–56.

[5]Friedrich Schleiermacher, *The Christian Faith,* ed. H. R. Mackintosh and J. S. Stewart (Edinburgh: T. & T. Clark, 1928), 560–74.

[6]Christopher Morse, *Not Every Spirit,* 174.

the Spirit emerges, one that recognizes the presence and activity of the Spirit of God not only in Judaism, but in all human movements of liberation and self-transcendence and in the church as well.

One pay-off of this stance is the implications it holds for how the church understands and undertakes its mission. The Division of Overseas Ministries of the Christian Church (Disciples of Christ) states as one of its basic premises that:

> God has never, in any time or place, been without witness. One who is more fully known in Jesus Christ has been and is at work in the creation of community, the sharing of love, the seeking of freedom, the search for truth, the reactions of wonder and awe in the presence of nature's power and beauty and creativity, and the awareness of the worth of persons.[7]

The Spirit and the Trinity

The Spirit, said the creed of Constantinople, is "worshiped and glorified together with the Father and the Son." At the conclusion of our earlier discussion of the Trinity, we said: In the beginning was communion. The Trinity is a community of persons existing with one another in perfect mutuality, perfect love, and perfect freedom. God as Trinity is also universally active. The scriptures and the tradition (at its best) affirm that all life everywhere is a gift of the life-giving Spirit. The Spirit creates community between and among human beings, and between human beings and the nonhuman beings with whom we are in a covenant of moral obligation. When there is widespread peace among all creatures it will be because "the mouth of the LORD has commanded, and his spirit has gathered them" (Isa. 34:16). The Spirit recreates community, reconciles us to one another, and so is appropriately spoken of as the creator of the community known as church (Acts 2). This preaching, community-gathering, and vitalizing are no less than God's presence at work among us. The Spirit today calls us to accept and actualize new relationships of mutuality and respect between and among the various religious and ethnic communities of humanity. The Spirit gives and calls us to a praxis of love.

---

[7]"General Principles and Policies of the Division of Overseas Ministries" (St. Louis: Christian Board of Publication, 1981), 16.

Spirit in the Biblical Witness

Metaphors for the Spirit

The Hebrew and Greek terms *ruach* and *pneuma* have a number of equivalents in the scriptures. "Wind" is often a metaphor for spirit in the scriptures, and in particularly important ways in the New Testament, especially in Acts 2:1–13 where the ingathering of scattered Israel and the creation of the church is described. First, the spirit is *ruach Yahweh*, the spirit of Yahweh. The people Israel testify that the spirit of Yahweh liberated them from slavery in Egypt (Ex. 15:8–10), this same Yahweh who is the lord and giver of life: "The spirit of God has made me, and the breath of the Almighty gives me life" (Job 33:4). The ruach Yahweh is the Creator Spirit, was present at creation ("a wind from God swept over the face of the waters"– Gen. 1:2), and is explicitly talked of as creator: "By his wind the heavens were made fair" (Job 26:13).

Another image for spirit is "breath." Throughout the Bible the ultimate source of life is God; and spirit comes to be associated particularly with the life created by God (Gen. 1:2; cf. 2 Macc. 7:22, Lk. 8:55–the story of the healing of the daughter of a leader of the synagogue: "Her spirit returned and she got up at once"). To breathe is to live by God's gift and grace. Hence, every human being is related to God, obvious as it is that all human beings do not so understand themselves.

"Soul" is another biblical metaphor for spirit. For the Hebrews, human beings are of the earth, flesh; yet as the creatures of God they are living souls marked out for a special relationship and destiny with God. This is not, repeat *not*, a soul/body dualism in which the body is mere temporary housing for the soul, its earthly Tupperware container until the soul departs for higher climes. In the postexilic period "spirit" became a virtual synonym for "soul" and "heart," the seat of intelligence and emotion in human beings. Human characteristics are described in "spiritual" terms, such as the quiet or humble spirit. The highest reaches of human life are set within the framework of a divine dimension (Isa. 54:6–7: "For the LORD has called you like a wife forsaken and grieved in spirit,...with great compassion I will gather you"). God not only creates heaven and earth; God forms the inner life of people–our spirit, our "real" personality (Zech. 12:1: "Thus says the LORD, who stretched out the heavens and founded the earth and formed the human spirit within..."). This meaning of spirit is widespread in the New Testament.

We cannot miss the universal implication of these metaphors: The ruach Yahweh, God's Spirit, is creatively present wherever there is life. Spirit, as God's personal presence and activity in the world, is active in all times and places.

Spirit in the Biblical Narrative

The biblical story concerns the one, living God, whose spirit was *active in creation:* "A wind from God swept over the face of the waters" (Gen. 1:2). The spirit is active in *maintaining human life* (the metaphors of breath and soul). The spirit of God acts in every situation, whether in nature or history. Extraordinary endowments for leadership, particularly *prophecy*, are due to the "invasion" of the spirit. When David spoke as a prophet, he claimed: "The Spirit [ruach Yahweh] of the LORD speaks through me" (2 Sam. 23:2). Second Isaiah declares: "And now the Lord GOD has sent me and his Spirit" (Isa. 48:16). Ezekiel claims that the Spirit "falls upon" him and "enters" him, "enraptures" him and tells him what to say (Ezek. 2–11).

The prophetic word is not merely a word *about* the future; it is a word that *creates* the future, that opens up an alternative future. "For as the rain and the snow come down from heaven, and do not return there until they have watered the earth, making it bring forth and sprout…, so shall my word be that goes out from my mouth; it shall not return to me empty, but it shall accomplish that which I purpose" (Isa. 55:10–11). The work of the prophets is God's continuing creative, redemptive, reconciling work–calling Israel forward to become the Israel that God gives and empowers Israel to become.

Also, *wisdom* and discernment are special gifts of the Spirit. Joshua was full of the spirit for wisdom (Num. 27:18). The Wisdom of Solomon beautifully expresses the close relationship between the divine Spirit and wisdom: "Who has learned your counsel, unless you have given wisdom and sent your holy spirit from on high?" (9:17).

The Spirit is God active in all history, and chiefly in Israel's. It is immanent because transcendent, coming forth from the life of God who deals directly with human beings. Spirit stresses the presence, the nearness of God: "Where can I go from your spirit? Or where can I flee from your presence?" (Ps. 139:7). As the Mishnah developed, Spirit came to be spoken of as *Shekhinah,* the all-present one. "R. Hanina b. Teradion said: If two sit together, and words of Torah [are spoken] between them, the Divine Presence rests between them…"[8] Christians are familiar with this saying in an earlier and different form: "For where two or three are gathered in my name, I am there among them" (Mt. 18:20).

Spirit in the Life-Praxis of Jesus

The biblical story depicts the Spirit active in the life and ministry of Jesus. First, the birth and childhood narratives in Matthew and Luke reflect Christian belief that the Spirit was particularly active in relationship to Jesus. The Spirit was graciously present to Jesus at his conception, baptism, temptation, first sermon, exorcism of demons, his healings, transfiguration, resurrection, and the giving of the great commission.

In his conception by the Spirit, we find the claim that Jesus Christ is a gift to the church of the creative, life-giving Spirit of the God of Israel, as the genealogies stress that he is a gift to the church of the Israel of God, the faithful of all the generations. The Spirit descends upon Jesus at his baptism, his temptation, and at the critical hour when his ministry begins, to fit him for his unique vocation of being a servant to the people Israel (Rom. 15:8) in order that the Gentiles might glorify God for his mercy (Rom. 15:9). In the great commission (Mt. 28:19), the apostles are instructed to make disciples of all the Gentiles (*panta ta ethne*), baptizing them "in the name of the Father and of the Son and of the Holy Spirit." Jesus' ministry begins in Luke in the synagogue at Nazareth when he reads from Isaiah 61:1–2:

> "The Spirit of the Lord is upon me, because he has anointed me to bring good news to the poor. He has sent me to proclaim release to the captives and recovery of sight to the blind, to let the oppressed go free, to proclaim the year of the Lord's favor." (Lk. 4:18–19)

The Spirit acted in the creation of the church at Pentecost (Acts 2:1–17). The apostles were filled with the Holy Spirit that came "like the rush of a violent wind," giving them the power to speak in the languages of the Parthians, Medes, Elamites, Mesopotamians, Judeans, Cappadocians, Egyptians, Libyans, in all the languages (*heterais glossais*–not "tongues," but "other tongues") of the known

---

[8]*Pirke Aboth,* 3.2 in *The Mishnah,* trans. Herbert Danby (London: Oxford University Press, 1933), 450.

world. They spoke intelligibly to all the peoples of the world about "the mighty acts of God" in the story of Israel and of Jesus. Out of its diversity and without suppressing that diversity, one community is formed; a universal community; a spiritual community (because created by the Holy Spirit); and a holy community, a *communio sanctorum* (because created by the Holy Spirit). It is also a *communio peccatorum*, a community of sinners. When the church later defined itself in the creed of Constantinople (381) as "one, holy, catholic and apostolic," it derived its definition from Acts 2. The church is one, inclusive of all its cultural diversity; holy, because created by the Holy Spirit; catholic, because universal; and apostolic, because it lives by proclaiming the apostolic message of the good news of God. Also, the church is not only created in the beginning, but lives and spreads and grows through the work of the Spirit, manifest throughout the Acts story.

The meaning of "spirit" in Acts as it relates to individual members of the church is stated by Peter: "Repent and be baptized...and you will receive the gift of the Holy Spirit" (2:38). Baptism into the community of faith is indistinguishable from the gift of the Holy Spirit. All members of the church receive the gift of the Spirit.

Paul

For Paul, there are many meanings of the term "spirit," and Christian life is life "in the Spirit." Christians are to live by an ethic of the Spirit; if you live in the Spirit, walk in it. What we are commanded to do by way of deeds of loving-kindness is always something that God's Spirit already empowers us to do. Our task is to become what God has already given us the possibility of being. Because of confusion among his first-generation Gentile converts, Paul constantly wrestled with misconceptions of what it means to be "spiritual," to have "spiritual gifts," and to be justified by grace rather than by any "work of the law." So he stresses that the virtues of sanctified Christians are the harvest of the Spirit cooperating with us as we seek to obey the Lord. These virtues of the Spirit are: "love, joy, peace, patience, kindness, generosity, faithfulness, gentleness, and self-control" (Gal. 5:22–23). To the Corinthians, who are much impressed with their abilities to speak in tongues, he says "well, okay, but never without an interpreter and only a few at a time," but meanwhile remember that "If I speak in the tongues of...angels, but do not have love, I am a noisy gong or a clanging cymbal" (1 Cor. 13:1).

Love is the greatest gift of the Spirit–it has been shed abroad in our hearts through the Holy Spirit that has been given to us (Rom. 5:5). This ethic of love or of the spirit or of grace leads to an ethic for the participant in the church: Christians form a *koinonia* in the body of Christ; they constitute the family of God, they participate in the Spirit that fashions a community; Christian virtues are therefore also ecclesiastical. Love means love of our sisters and brothers. True spiritual worship (Rom. 12) has to do with how we present our "living bodies" in the mundane activities of ministering, teaching, exhorting, giving, leading, exercising compassion and cheerfulness. Paul makes us aware that every member of the community has some kind of gift, some *charism,* from the Holy Spirit, even such a "boring" gift as that of administration. What all gifts of the Spirit have in common is that they "build up" the community. That is why love is the greatest gift of the Spirit.

John

In the gospel and letters of John, we find a number of characteristic claims about the Spirit. Jesus, the Wisdom or Logos of God made flesh, is the one upon whom the Spirit rested and remained, who received the Spirit by being endowed by God with completeness of spiritual power and insight and, hence, is God's Son. His words are "spirit and life," for in him we encounter the maker of heaven and earth. Christians are those who have experienced rebirth, the birth of the Spirit; those who decide to believe in Jesus Christ are born of God, are God's children. See Ezekiel 36:25–27: "I will sprinkle clean water upon you…a new heart I will give you, and a new spirit will I put within you…my spirit." This gift, symbolized by wind, cannot be automatically induced; it is not under the church's control or possession. Only when we so understand these matters can we worship "in spirit and in truth" (Jn. 4:23). Worship must be seen in the context of love for one's neighbor and orthodoxy (particularly against heresies that deny the humanity of Jesus: Gnosticism and docetism). John's emphasis on the Spirit runs counter to allowing the growing reality of the book in Christian life to introduce legalism and creedal forms without life (see Jn. 14:26 and 15:26f.). John's gospel promises in these verses that the Advocate will continue to teach the church, and the truth of the gospel will come alive in subsequent generations.

Not only does God give the Spirit, but the Spirit may be predicated on God's very nature: "God is spirit" (Jn. 4:24). Hence, in

Christianity all provincialism of place, book, and ethnicity are transcended—at least, in principle. Christianity in its history has exhibited every possible provincialism and has often reduced the people (*laos*) of God simply to another ethnic group (*ethnos*). By implication all provincialism of sexism and racism are also transcended, although sexism and racism remain persistent realities in the concrete life of actual congregations. As Spirit, God is also the Truth and Love; in which respects God is revealed in Jesus Christ, who as the "word become flesh" (*Logos sarx egeneto*) is full of "grace and truth" (Jn. 1:14). The love that Christians must manifest as those who live in communion with the Father and the Son is a fruit of the Spirit who abides in them. The love of the Father for the church means Christ's presence in them, a presence realized by the coming of the Spirit (Jn. 14:18). Also implied in "God is spirit" is that God is active in the world like the wind, unseen but not unknown. God is not a mere immanent principle in the world, nor is God aloof from the affairs of Earth or the needs of people. All this defines God as spiritual and the Spirit as divine.

The Spirit is the Paraclete, the Comforter, the Advocate, the one whom we may call to our aid. As disciples of Christ in this world we may not expect to bear the Christian witness without undergoing tribulation and persecution. But we shall find peace despite tribulation because the Spirit is our Comforter (*con + fortis* = with strength). The Spirit strengthens us in our weakness (also often in Paul). The Spirit, hence, is both Champion and Teacher of the church, taking up the same office that the incarnate Lord had discharged.

For the New Testament as a whole, the church is a distinctive society: It shares a new and common life (2 Cor. 3:6; Rom. 8; Jn. 6:63). It shares a new and common love (Gal. 5:22; Col. 1:8; Rom. 13:8; Heb. 13:1; Jn. 15 [the "vine" chapter]). It must therefore be one; its unity is made a reality by the Spirit. As "the unity of the Spirit...There is one body and one Spirit" (Eph. 4:34). It is apostolic, yet served by a charismatic ministry. This charismatic ministry eventually gives way to a more formal system by the late-first to mid-second century.

Thus, the grand sweep of the original Christian proclamation was from the beginning when the Spirit moved upon the face of the waters and the Word was with God, to the unending end when God will be all in all (Rev. 21:22–22:5). In this whole drama, the Spirit of

God is active throughout all creation, in Israel, in Christ, in the church, and in the world.

The Spirit and the Life of the Church

We will discuss here three questions pertaining to the role of the Spirit in the life of the community, the church. Subsequently we will attend to issues raised for the church by our contemporary context.

The "Frozen Chosen" and the Holy Spirit

One of the typical functions of religion is to provide stability to people. Stability is not, as such, bad. Yet insistence on stability may be a church's first and last line of defense against the work of the Spirit. God is not the God of the status quo. God is the God who called Abraham and Sarah out of the status quo into God's future for them. God is the God who called a motley crew of Galilean fishermen away from business as usual into a movement of the kingdom. Abraham, Sarah, and Peter could have said, "But we've never done it that way before." Thanks to the work of the Spirit, they did not.

Sometimes new good threatens old good. The possibility of new life for a congregation may come only at the price of significantly changing its ways. The community needs freedom, freedom to become, to change, to grow, to respond to new challenges, to love the new and quite different neighbors that now live in its immediate vicinity. Will the community freeze up in the icy grip of a past, perhaps a glorious past, and justify the epithet "the frozen chosen," or will it respond in faith and hope to the transcendence that now confronts it?

The same dilemma faces clergy, ministry students, and theologians: Will we be tempted forever to live by a willfully unexamined tradition, or will we respond to the urgent challenges and issues troubling thoughtful people in our time? Are religious practices and institutions the main bulwarks against a hopeful future? Is God the chief maintainer of the status quo? Is it possible for the church to be a genuinely moral community, responsive to the ethical crises of its time, or is stability, particularly institutional stability, the one god whom it will serve? Can the church be a light to the world, can it protect and enhance the well-being of its neighbors? If so, how?

In facing these questions, our temptation is to rush to the moral imperative, to become hortatory, preachy. "Must" and "ought" tend to be the operative vocabulary. Moral harangues miss the deeper difficulty: that love is dependent on faith and hope, and faith and hope are in short supply. Faith, radical trust, is what is needed. Anxiety and dread in the face of dizzying, disorienting change engender reactions of resistance, hanging on to stability. So a church may commit spiritual suicide, deny its own most fundamental beliefs, turn its back on those neighbors whom God gave it to love, be they women, minorities, members of other religions, or gay men and lesbians.

Trust in the Holy Spirit, the Spirit who blows through the windows of the musty institution, who brings in a breath of fresh air; this trust will enable a church to respond faithfully to its challenges. It is the trust that, in spite of everything, contrary to all appearances, we are confident that the future is in God's hands. We can allow our deeper moral insights to lead us into places where we fear to go. The stories of Abraham and Sarah, and of the apostles, come again to life. Liberation from captivity to our past, from enslavement to what once may have worked, but does so no longer, is an old enough message, but one that bears repeating.

Literalism and the Spirit

"The wind blows where it chooses, and you hear the sound of it, but you do not know where it comes from or where it goes" (Jn. 3:8). The biblical metaphors for the Spirit, wind and breath, make it bluntly and straightforwardly clear that we cannot objectify God, cannot turn God into an object that we can control. Wind and breath are, like God, invisible (Rom. 1:20; Heb. 11:27). This is why they are such appropriate metaphors for God. God is not like the objects of our sense-perception, the ketchup bottle on the shelf between the coffee and the oregano. We can see and control the ketchup bottle, leave it in place and pick up something else, put it where we wish. God is neither seeable nor controllable.

The temptation of all literalism in religion is to forget or deny this point. The error, indeed the heresy, of literalism is to objectify and seek to control God. The purpose of objectifying God, reducing God to a thing, is to control, to gain power over God. The same purpose is served whenever human beings or nature are reduced to things, objectified. The justification is then in hand to control and manipulate them. God transcends, escapes our conceptual schemes, our assertions of biblical inerrancy in which we insist on an identity between the objective words of scripture and the word of God, and our desires to control God through ritual.

Throughout its history the church has struggled with the temptation to identify the Spirit so strongly with the letter of scripture that the letter has protected the church from the Spirit. Appeals to biblical inerrancy and, ironically, to the doctrine of the inspiration of scripture, are guilty of this. The problem with inerrantists is not that they take scripture seriously or regard it as authoritative. The problem is that the word of God is looked upon as an objective fact, a datum subject to our control, a law that can be used repressively (always an illegitimate use of torah) to put down whatever just cause is afoot at the time. All efforts to control, tame, domesticate, and manage God's Spirit are attempts to control the ways of God, to deny that God's ways are inscrutable (Rom. 11:33). The doctrine of the Holy Spirit repudiates all efforts to turn God into a thing or to deify a thing, such as the letter of scripture. God is faithful to God's promises for blessing and well-being, in ways that we constantly find surprising, in ways that to our normal expectations are paradoxical.

Subjectivism and the Holy Spirit

Displeased as fundamentalists may find themselves with the prior point, their diametrical opposites, those who prefer to forget the authority of scripture and the importance of the word, will be unhappy with this one. When we remember that the Holy Spirit is always the Spirit "of" Yahweh, the Spirit "of" Christ, we are reminded that as we may not deify objects, neither may we deify our own subjectivity, our feelings. The popular tendency to reduce all myths, all enchanted stories, of God to psychology is a sophisticated example of the tendency to deify our feelings and subjectivity. God, said Joseph Campbell (most recently famous through his television interviews with Bill Moyers), "is but a convenient means to waken the sleeping princess, the soul."[9]

Campbell is one of the more recent thinkers of modernity, those thinkers since the early eighteenth century who so affirmed the autonomy of human beings that they presumptuously appropriated for themselves the functions of God. What Paul Tillich once labeled critically as "self-sufficient finitude" aptly describes the modern understanding of human beings.[10] William A. Clebsch puts it more

---

[9]Joseph Campbell, *The Hero with a Thousand Faces* (Princeton: Princeton University Press, 1949), 260.

[10]Paul Tillich, *The Religious Situation* (New York: Meridian Books, 1956), chap. 2.

colloquially and directly when he says that "Europeans [meaning the 'quintessentially modern'] singly and collectively became their own do-it-yourself deities."[11] Deifying our subjectivity is one variant on this modern denial of God.

God's Spirit is not just another name for whatever we may think of as "spiritual." God's Spirit is the Spirit that brings well-being and blessing, the Spirit that reconciles the alienated, that gathers the scattered into community, that rescues the fallen, illumines the confused, gives hope to the hopeless. The human spirit, as we have all too many occasions to observe, is frequently enough self-abusing, self-destructive, capable of doing catastrophic damage to the well-being of others.

The time-honored theological way of making this point is to insist that the Spirit and the word of God are identical, that the Spirit is always the Spirit "of" Yahweh, the Spirit "of" Christ. Whatever the Spirit now does, it will not be out of character with what the Spirit did in Christ. If we idolize our subjectivity and separate the Spirit from the word of God, then the spirit (lower-case "s") will attach itself to something else. Perhaps our word-less spirit will suggest that we attach ourselves to the latest charismatic leader, political or ecclesiastical, to come down the street.

The classic New Testament story of the Spirit is the creation of the spiritual community, the church, in Acts 2. Community implies communication. Without communication there is no community, and without community there is no communication. The Holy Spirit is the indwelling, the in-breathed, Spirit. But this Spirit is not dumb, not word-less. The Spirit is everywhere the ruach Yahweh, the Spirit of Christ, acting today in character with what Jesus did on the hills of Galilee, working well-being, creating or redeeming relationships, reconciling, engendering community, bringing blessing, welcoming the nobodies, treating the poor like royalty, receiving strangers kindly.

Pluralism and Other Religions

All religions, Christianity no less than any other and possibly more so, have traditionally claimed to be absolute. Each is the "one true religion." The others have been deemed false or, in somewhat more generous form, true, but not quite as true as our own. If there

---

[11]William A. Clebsch, *Christianity in European History*, 242.

were to be a discussion among representatives of various religions, "our" religion would put each of the others in its place at the table. The superiority of our own religion, its preeminence, is assumed. Various groups of theologians and spokespersons for different religions have sought to overcome these attitudes through dialogue and seminars, and some churches, notably the Roman Catholic Church, have issued statements about the religions of humanity.[12]

Such attitudes of superiority have been considerably, if not widely, supplanted by the practice of conversation between and among the religions. This practice, when engaged in by Christians, is a faithful effort to live up to the highest insights of our tradition, to begin to make good on our understanding of the promise to Abraham and Sarah that the peoples of the world would find their descendants to be a blessing. As we Christians may slowly be learning that we can receive gift and blessing from the God of Israel and the Israel of God without grasping the blessing for ourselves and denying it to Jews, so we may also be open to give and receive blessing and well-being from other religions.

Conversation requires allowing others to speak in their own voices, granting them the freedom to define themselves, rather than defining them in terms comfortable to us. This can be unnerving, even threatening, although those whose trust in the Spirit of God and Christ is profound may not feel at all disquieted. I have long been involved in the conversation between Christians and Jews and can report from experience that Christians so engaged have always come away from the encounter with an enriched, deepened, and greater appreciation of their own faith. We are better Christians than we were for having come to a more appreciative understanding of Jews and Judaism.

It has become a conviction of mine that the Holy Spirit is present in all attempts to welcome, for example, Jews, Muslims, or Buddhists into friendship and to try to engage in genuine conversation with them. I say "has become a conviction" because I started on this path not because of this conviction, but spurred on by some negative and unwelcome encounters with Christian smugness toward all other

---

[12]For the Roman Catholic Church see the Second Vatican Council's "Declaration on the Relationship of the Church to Non-Christian Religions," in *The Documents of Vatican II*, ed. Walter M. Abbott, S. J. (New York: Guild Press, 1966), 660–68.

religions and particularly toward Judaism. Often in theology we talk about "changing our minds," when the reality is more complex. Sometimes we find that our minds have gotten themselves changed, and we look back in retrospect and try to figure out how it happened. This is how I came to this conviction. It corresponds to the biblical witness to the Spirit as everywhere enlivening everyone and overcoming alienation with reconciliation, breaking down the barriers that we erect to human community.

This is not to say that interreligious conversation is nice and easy. To the extent that dialogue is genuine, we not only face the charm, the attraction of other faiths. At the same time we face our inability to negotiate the differences between and among them, and between us and them. Deep down, the religions of the world are not the same: Buddhists are not Christians with a taste for saffron-colored robes; Jews do not believe in Jesus Christ, although that does not define them as the anti-Jewish tradition thought it did. In dialogue, Jews define themselves. Buddhist "nothingness" as ultimate does not equate to what we mean by God, nor to what the metaphysically stout of heart mean by "Being-Itself": but it does engender a distinctive kind of compassion from which we may learn.

Our understandings of faith get stretched in dialogue, breaches and holes appear where all had been solid ground. One's inner fundamentalist gets nervous, one's inner liberal feels all warm and fuzzy, but these are not helpful reactions. In these voids that show up in our understanding, God may reveal Godself in ways that strain and buckle our self-assured certainties.

Like the man who said he could tell that a train had passed by because he saw its tracks, we can tell that the Holy Spirit is present in occasions of dialogue and conversation when people are genuinely concerned to overcome a troubling, shameful past and open the way for new opportunities for communities of faith. We can tell that the Spirit has been present because we get a whiff of the wind of God, we see the vestiges of the Spirit. The nuances hinting at the Spirit's presence are friendship, mutual respect, broader and deeper community, and a more capacious, more generous view of things. The greatest gift of the Spirit is love.

Liberating the Spirit

"Now the Lord is the Spirit, and where the Spirit of the Lord is, there is freedom" (2 Cor. 3:17). The grand sweep of the biblical witness to the Holy Spirit declares that the Spirit liberates the oppressed from injustice. "Here is my servant, whom I uphold, my chosen, in whom my soul delights; I have put my spirit upon him; he will bring forth justice to the nations" (Isa. 42:1). When in our theology we liberate the Spirit from the captivity of the church, the liberating Spirit frees the church from its addiction to those structural sins that so sorely tempt it. Throughout its history, the church has struggled inconsistently with the tension between the liberating Spirit and attempts to stifle the Spirit.

In the fourth and fifth centuries, Christianity became established and bureaucratized. Earlier, Christians had risked their lives by identifying with the church. Now joining it was the thing to do, the way to move up the social and economic ladder. The monastic movement arose as people fled not so much from the world as from the world in the church. Movements of the Spirit became increasingly suspect. The church got its organizational house in order, formed a canon, fixed a creed, and established the authority of the bishop as the final arbiter of matters of interpretation. There was no longer any room for the Holy Spirit in the ecclesiastical inn. Fewer Christians still prayed "*maran atha*," (our Lord, come) or "*veni, Creator spiritus*" (come, Creator spirit). Some continued to long for the return of Jesus, awaited the liberation of the oppressed, and agreed with Paul that the "agony of this present age is not worth comparing to the glory that is soon to be revealed to us." But they were squeezed out of the bureaucratic church as it learned to live with the Empire that had crucified Jesus and executed the martyrs.

The spirit-movements in the history of the church are easy to caricature. Luther remarked of his contemporaries at Münster that "they had swallowed the Holy Spirit, feathers and all." Yet it was these spirit-movements, the Montanists, the radical Franciscans, the utopian and chiliastic movements, that remembered that this present world, in its misery, poverty, oppression, and apparent godforsakenness, is not the kingdom of God. They remembered that the Spirit groans with suffering humanity and the suffering creation.

Such Christians as Joachim de Fiore, Pierre Teilhard de Chardin, Bernard Lonergan, Johann Baptist Metz, and Juan Segundo argue that the self-transcendence of humanity, in the form of consciousness, culture, and politics, is a genuine experience of the Spirit's liberative power. Christians judge the validity of an experience of the Spirit not by how much people whoop and holler, but by whether it leads people to find themselves in the only way that Christians can–by understanding themselves in the light of the word articulated by Jesus Christ, that we serve him only as we meet the needs of "the least of these," as we participate in the struggle for truth, justice, and shalom.

The Christian Life

A Grace-ful Life

Coming to the topic of the Christian life, we remind ourselves that the Spirit is always the Spirit *of*—the Spirit of, the power of, our renewed life in Christ. Christians are those who can understand themselves in any ultimate sense in terms of, and only in terms of, God's unmerited love. We know that we are loved by God; we know this definitively from the revelation of God in Jesus Christ. Our life is established in God's gracious love, founded in the fact that nothing can separate us from the love of God in Christ, and guided by the Holy Spirit.

Martin Luther reminds us that every Christian is and remains *simul iustus et peccator*, "at one and the same time justified and a sinner." Christians are those who understand that they are justified by grace through faith. The shortened expression, justification by faith, is sometimes used. It is well intended, but can lead to a misconception. We are justified by God's grace, received through faith. The prepositions are important. Faith is not some work we do, some decision we make, that justifies us. Were we able to justify ourselves, God and Christ would be quite unnecessary to our faith, and we could content ourselves with our own good efforts.

That we are justified by God's grace through our response of faith is the first point to make in understanding the Christian life. Appropriately understood and lived, it is a grace-ful life. Understanding this, appropriating it, and not just acknowledging it, relieves us of several difficulties. We are relieved from having to lie to ourselves and others about our worth and achievements. We are freed to be honest, to admit our sins, failures, and shortcomings. How many families are crippled, how many relationships alienated, how many people deeply hurt because we are unable to admit mistakes, to confess sins, to apologize to and reconcile with those we love? We are free from having to acquire some significant status in the world by piling up about ourselves the trinkets and garbage of a consumerist society. We are freed to accept the fact that we are accepted, clear that that means "warts and all."[13] African American Christians have learned that God's gracious love permits and requires them to say "I am somebody."

At the same time, that we are justified by God's grace and not our own doing reminds us that the Christian life, like so many other matters we have discussed, is never a secure possession. The commitment of faith needs to be renewed time and again, the message of God's forgiving love allowed to penetrate to the heart again and again. The word of grace is a word that bears repeating, because we who hear it find that it never grows stale. As much as it calls us to repent, it reassures us of God's incomprehensible fondness for us.

Growing up in Grace

Paul, in writing to the Corinthians, distinguished between "spiritual people" and "infants in Christ" (1 Cor. 3:1). This is not an invidious distinction, nor one set in stone. Infants can grow up, mature. Paul urges his readers not to be "conformed to this world," but "transformed by the renewing of your minds" (Rom. 12:2). Such transformation is our topic. The knowledge of God is a transformative knowledge; it does not leave us in the same condition in which it found us. Growing up is possible by God's grace, by God's gift. God asks of us nothing that God has not previously made possible for us to do. But growing up is also a task, a project. We are responsible for responding to God's grace with some commitment of our own. Becoming a Christian is not the spiritual version of watching a sitcom. We have to be engaged in our own lives, not spectators of them.

Traditionally, this topic is discussed under the heading of "sanctification," a word that means "to become holy." But "holy" is a word that may easily be misunderstood and brings with it connotations of priggishness, of being holier-than-thou, of being concerned with the peccadilloes of life, or of being separatist (holy things were typically "set apart"). So we choose a word that conveys a sense of growth, of developing beyond infancy. Developing in the Christian life is not an automatic process, like the ripening of a banana. The

---

[13]Paul Tillich coined the helpful expression, "accept that you are accepted" as a way of translating justification by grace. See *The Shaking of the Foundations* (New York: Scribner's, 1948), 153–63.

Christian life has its ups and downs, its abysses of despair as well as its heights of joy. But in the grace of God and the empowerment of the Spirit, development in faith, hope, and love does take place.

Growing up in our understanding of the gospel. The Christian life can be graced by a deepening discernment of what faith involves and a more complete commitment to it. Faith can become illuminating in relation to a wide range of problems. Faith can not only seek, but find understanding. Since this is what theology is all about, it is unseemly for a theologian to deny it. The doctrine of the perseverance of the saints tells us that God's grace does work in a person's life and that maturation in this life, spiritually growing up, is possible. It is not easy; it comes with work and struggle, study, and reflection. Judaism regards study and thinking as among the highest forms of prayer. So let us set it down: Spirituality is about spiritual discipline, the practices of the life of the Spirit. Chief among these are study and thinking theologically. Indeed, the seminary seeks to introduce students to precisely this work and struggle and makes its own demands on one's capacity for perseverance. But there are more difficult struggles (such as facing up to the realities of oppression or grieving the loss of a child) that threaten to break faith. The grace of God is sufficient not only for our sin, but for our weakness and, relying upon it, we may be given the gift of perseverance.

Growing up in Christian freedom. Christian freedom (see Galatians) is freedom *from* law understood as having to meet certain conditions in order to be justified by God and freedom *for* becoming genuinely helpful to one another, freedom for the deeper and appropriate intent of Torah. Christian freedom is freedom to love the neighbor, freedom to meet the needs of the neighbor. This we do when we "live by the Spirit," when the gifts of the Spirit, "love, joy, peace, patience, kindness, generosity, faithfulness, gentleness, and self-control" (Gal. 5:22–23) characterize our life. This is freedom to "fulfill the law of Christ" (6:2). In law the voice of the vulnerable other comes to expression. Genuine Christian freedom is not freedom *from* law understood as *torah* (the "way of life" as revealed by God for us to walk). Are we free from the law that says "you shall not kill"? Christian freedom is freedom in relation *to* law—freely walking the path of faith, the way of life which we are given and called to walk. True freedom keeps God's torah.

Growing up in our awareness of the death-dealing powers that shape so much of life on earth. Awareness includes awareness of the demonic as well as the divine. We can become more aware of our own ambiguity and lack of faith, more aware of our need for God's grace, and more gracious in dealing with others. We can become more aware of all that crushes both human life and the nonhuman life with which we are bound in a covenant of moral obligation. We can come to see and act upon the claim that our faith is to be lived out in this complex set of relationships in which we are set. How are we to understand ourselves and so to act in a pluralistic, post-Holocaust, nuclear/ecological age in which 1,800 children an hour die for lack of a dollar's worth of vaccine apiece and elementary nutrition? That most of these matters are far from the minds of most of those who fill the pews is a major problem for the church. How is the church to enable people to understand what it means to be Christian in the only world in which they live?

Growing up in our solidarity with others. Solidarity means identifying with the nobodies, those whom Jesus gathered about himself, the destitute and neglected, the homeless of our time and place. Solidarity is the social spirituality of love. Growing up in the Christian life means having an increasingly large circle of those with whom we practice communion. Such solidarity is part of the very being of the church. The Spirit creates the church (Acts 2:1–21) by establishing one community from "devout Jews from every nation under heaven"–Parthians, Medes, Elamites, and so forth, each group speaking its distinctive language. A formula for chaos and conflict is transformed into one community hearing and speaking about "God's deeds of power."

One of the greatest challenges and opportunities facing the church today is that of overcoming the fact that the church reflects in its makeup the stratifications and divisions of society. Most typical Protestant churches are composed of people of one economic class, usually middle to upper-middle class. The presence of any of the poor, the hungry, or those audibly mourning would be a source of discomfort. But growing up in the Christian life entails entering into ever larger and more diverse relations that are generated and maintained by the Spirit. Growing in the Christian life means entering into ever larger sets of relationships.

The Spirit of Christ works to break down the "dividing wall, that is, the hostility" (Eph. 2:14) between the insiders and the outsiders of God's house. The reconciling Spirit works on the church still, and on each of us personally, to reconcile all humanity, in all our diversity, with one another, with our fellow creatures, and with God. God is not finished with us.

Increasing communion does not stop with other human beings, not even with those different from us. We are also in a covenant of moral obligation with what Genesis calls all "the living things." Nature itself has become an endangered species. Our consumerist lifestyles and sprawling cities, the paving over of farmland to create new shopping malls to replace old ones left behind, only themselves to be left behind in a generation—all contribute to the oppression of nature. Having the spiritual backbone to deal with this problem will be a struggle. Yet we are given and called by God to be a blessing and to serve the well-being of our fellow creatures. With the guidance and empowerment of the Spirit, we may respond to this challenge faithfully.

Growing up in Christian joy. Given all the challenges just enumerated, to end this discussion talking about joy may seem paradoxical. Yet there are people keenly aware of the problems of the world who nonetheless have about them an exhilaration, a deep sense of being loved into freedom and freed into loving, that testify otherwise. At its heart, the Christian life is one of eucharist, gathered regularly around a table where we give thanks for the love of God and neighbor so graciously given to us. As we began this discussion of the Christian life with a quote from Martin Luther, we round it off with another from him. "Faith," said Luther, "is our life" (*fides vita nostra est*).

Faith is confidence in God's gracious love made known to us in Jesus Christ. Therefore faith is the living, busy, active thing that makes us joyous toward God and all God's creatures. Like a good tree, faith yields good fruit, and puts itself at the service of the concrete needs of the neighbor. Opportunities to do what the rabbis called "deeds of loving-kindness" are God's gracious gifts to us. Faith receives them joyfully. The exercise of faith takes place within the ordinary relations of human life that constitute the public realm.

Being Called

"As all Christians," said William Law, "are by their baptism devoted to God and made professors of holiness, so are they all in their several callings to live as holy and heavenly persons, doing everything in their common life only in such manner as it may be received by God as a service done to him."[14] Every Christian has a

---

[14]William Law, *A Serious Call to a Devout and Holy Life* (New York: Paulist Press, 1978), 76.

call, a vocation, from God. This call is to be lived out, as law indicates, in our public lives. The task of the ordained minister is to "equip the saints." This does not mean to get everybody busily employed within the walls of the church building on its business, but to empower the people of God to live lives of what Bonhoeffer called "holy worldliness."

Talking about Christians as having a calling, a vocation, is not heard as often among churches as it once was. Perhaps this is because such talk got associated almost exclusively with taking upon oneself a vocation to the ordained ministry. When such talk disappears, however, what passes for the Christian life can become oddly curved in upon itself, the epitome of sin, or it can simply take its content and definition from the culture. Yet every Christian is called and claimed by God to live a life that will be one of blessing and well-being to others. There is a teaching in Judaism that to do a deed of loving kindness is to "mend the world" (*tikkun olam*).[15]

Christians are those who understand themselves to be graciously loved by God, and so understand themselves in turn to be those who are to love God with all their selves and their neighbors as themselves. As such, every Christian has a vocation. Every Christian life has a purpose. Each Christian is given and called by God to participate in God's mission to the world, that of contributing to its blessing and well-being. Such election or calling is no more now than it was in Abraham's time an election to some kind of entitlement. It is an election to be of use, to be helpful. We are called to liberate our neighbors from oppression and injustice, to welcome the poor and smelly into community, to recreate human dignity where it has been crushed, to restore joy and love to the brokenhearted. The Christian vocation is to be a light to the world, to let people see by our deeds, as well as hear by our words, that freedom, justice, and love can take root and flower in human life.

---

[15]See Emil Fackenheim, *To Mend the World* (New York: Schocken Books, 1984).

Chapter 9

Companions on the Way:
The Church

The Enigma of the Churches

Thinking about the church is difficult, because we who do the thinking are the church. Thinking about the church is thinking about ourselves. In a peculiar sense, we are both the subjects doing the thinking and the objects about which we are thinking. This presents us with several problems, not the least of which is that we are here, possibly more than anywhere else in theology, tempted by ideology. Joseph Haroutunian made us aware that no theological doctrine had escaped being articulated so "as to function in the rationale of these [ecclesiastical] establishments and their practices."[1]

If anything, Haroutunian understated the point. Doctrines have functioned not only to distort truth in the interest of ecclesiastical establishments, but in the interest of particular groups within the

---

[1]Joseph Haroutunian, *God With Us* (Philadelphia: Westminster Press, 1965), 279.

church. Arguments against the ordination of women on the grounds of their natural inferiority to men serve the ideological interests of a dynastic line of male clergy. Arguments claiming that outside the visible church there is no salvation discount the possibility that God transcends the church or that other communities of faith may have insights worth considering. When thinking about the church, we must also think critically about ourselves, lest our propensity to glorify ourselves rather than God go unnoticed. In this doctrine, perhaps more than any other, we need to remember the old theological rule that all our thinking must be done "to the greater glory of God."

Contemporary Challenges

We turn to some of the more salient issues of our time facing us in the attempt to think seriously about the church today. After articulating these problems, we will turn to the scriptures and tradition in search of the resources to respond to them.

Identity and Inclusivism

No issue bedevils most contemporary American churches more than that of identity and inclusivism. If not an obvious factor in most conflicts that face the churches, it is never far from the surface. Further, depending on one's point of view, being either too concerned with identity or too open to influence from the culture is at the root of much of the numerical decline of major American denominations. What had once been a large denomination or congregation has often become a "little flock." Why is this so?

In an excellent study of this question, Martin Marty argues that the so-called "mainstream" Protestant churches "have themselves to blame for their troubles."[2] The mainstream's problem is its "boundarylessness," its tendency to disperse its energies into the surrounding world. The task facing it is that of "centering."[3] But because both our people and the larger society need churches that can communicate, boundarylessness is not altogether bad. It is preferable to the restrictiveness of the more introverted churches that are out of communication with the pressing issues of the time. The question then is: How can the churches be open without loss of

---

[2]Martin Marty, *The Fire We Can Light* (Garden City: Doubleday & Co., 1973), 120.

[3]Ibid., 141.

identity, or how can they be centered without being closed off? Marty suggests that the answer is found in the concept of the "heart" or "core" (from the French *coeur*, heart) of the church.[4]

The church testifies to God's purpose of bringing blessing and well-being to all of God's creation. Hence, the church is called to overcome in its own life all the obstructions of ethnicity, class, race, and gender that tear at the fabric of human community. The true meaning of "inclusivism" is that the church may not prohibit from its life any of the God-given diversity of the human family. Nor may any of the important servant roles in the church be banned to people on the basis of gender, race, class, or ethnicity. The false meaning of inclusivism is that the church must be equally open to and affirming of whatever values and ideas are floating around in the culture. That is a relativism that overlooks the fact that the gospel of Jesus Christ contradicts some points of view.

The church must find its center and make it known. This core is the "central or universal part, the 'heart' of anything." To paraphrase Paul Tillich, the church needs "the courage to be itself." For the church to find its heart is to find the courage to proclaim and teach what is at its heart and what it is given and called to proclaim and teach. A church that knows its heart—the gospel of Jesus Christ—will neither dissipate into the culture at large nor close itself off from its context. Instead it will have a "magnetic center," a heart that attracts, and openness at the edges.[5]

Indifference to Teaching the Christian Faith

That a large contributor to the lack of a sense of centeredness is inattentiveness to teaching the Christian faith has long been suggested by concerned observers of the contemporary church scene. Jeffrey Hadden's central thesis was that the mainline Protestant churches were embroiled in a deep crisis that had the potential to "seriously disrupt or alter the very nature of the church." The struggle, he contended, was "over the very *purpose* and *meaning* of the church."[6] It is "a crisis of *belief*" because the laity had not been engaged in the theological work of reinterpreting the Christian faith for a new situation.

---

[4]Ibid., 219–33.
[5]Ibid., 220.
[6]Jeffrey Hadden, *The Gathering Storm in the Churches* (Garden City: Doubleday & Co., 1969), 5.

Consequently, it was also a crisis of authority, specifically that of the clergy.[7] Ministers had lost their authority as authentic teachers of the Christian faith, Hadden maintained, largely because they had not exercised it. Personally they had developed a new understanding of the meaning and implications of the Christian faith, but they "have not succeeded in communicating this understanding to the laity."[8] He predicted that this crisis of authority would come to a head over the involvement of the clergy in political and social issues. By "teaching" Hadden means the reinterpretation of the Christian faith in ways that are pertinent to the contemporary context and appropriate to the Christian faith, ways that are arguably relevant and arguably Christian. In other words, teaching means theological education in the church. Once central to the task of every ordained minister, it has fallen into neglect with negative consequences in all aspects of the life of the church. Dean M. Kelley seconded Hadden's point with his own argument that the central function of religion has always been that of "explaining the meaning of life in ultimate terms."[9] Churches are successful to the extent to which they can interpret the meaning of life in ultimate terms in ways that make sense to their members.[10]

William McKinney and Wade Clark Roof suggested in their sociological study that people drop out of church life altogether because the mainline churches became "something of a 'culture-religion,' captive to middle-class values, and somewhat lacking in their ability to sustain a strong transcendent vision."[11] Thomas Luckmann pointed out that the result of this lack of teaching and theological education in the church was a "secularization [of the church] from within...the substitution of secular for religious contents within the mainline Protestant churches."[12] Langdon Gilkey made it clear that when a church does not educate its members

---

[7]Ibid., 6.

[8]Ibid., 230.

[9]Dean M. Kelley, *Why Conservative Churches Are Growing* (New York: Harper & Row, 1972), 37.

[10]Ibid., 45.

[11]William McKinney and Wade Clark Roof, *American Mainline Religion* (New Brunswick: Rutgers University Press, 1987), 22.

[12]Quoted by Peter Berger in "American Religion: Conservative Upsurge, Liberal Prospects," in *Liberal Protestantism: Realities and Possibilities*, ed. Robert S. Michaelsen and Wade Clark Roof (New York: Pilgrim Press, 1986), 24.

theologically, the lay voice simply reflects the voice of the culture.[13] In a church governed by the laity, this is not good news. Edward Farley asked why the church is content to rest in the medieval pattern of an educated clergy and an uneducated laity.[14]

The churches will not inherit the promise to them of being founts of blessing and well-being, either to themselves or their neighbors, unless serious steps are taken to reverse this situation. Nor will the remedy be a quick fix. Yet we cannot continue to fail to communicate the excitement of Christianity to the next generation.

Too Little or Too Much?

A frequent temptation facing the church, throughout its history, has been that of believing either too much or too little about the church, that is, about itself. Either way, we miss the church's particular identity, what it is given and called by God to be and do. Among Protestants, evangelicals and charismatics frequently assert too much about the church. Unrestrained claims about the Spirit and such phenomena as glossolalia (speaking in tongues) or about the scope and character of biblical inerrancy strain all credulity. Or, related to another topic soon to be dealt with, it is claimed that "outside the church there is no salvation," as if we had nothing to learn from the history of the church and theology as to the destructive impact of such teaching both on the church and members of other religions.

Believing too little about the church is found in those typically mainline congregations where the assumption often seems to be that the church is there only to meet the needs of people for private religious experience, for therapy, or for the warm social environment of the country club (except with lower dues). To so regard the church is to lose sight of its distinctive mission of taking part in God's purpose of bringing blessing and well-being to the world. Interest in matters of truth, justice, a transformed community life, witness to the larger world, care for the poor and the widows whom the economy grinds underfoot, all take a backseat to the needs of the middle and upper middle-class to adjust successfully to the demands of life.

---

[13]Langdon Gilkey, *How The Church Can Minister to the World Without Losing Itself* (New York: Harper & Row, 1964), 84.

[14]Edward Farley, *The Fragility of Knowledge* (Philadelphia: Fortress Press, 1988), 85.

This temptation to think too little of the church goes hand in hand with typical American individualism and privatism. Sometimes it is individualism with a twist, the twist being the self-image that some people have of themselves. That image seems to be a shelf of wine glasses each only partially full, each representing a "need" to be filled. Such folk participate in churches to get their "needs" met. The church should meet our needs, of course, but one of its responsibilities is to educate us as to what our ultimate needs really are and then set about meeting them. One of those needs is that the church is a community with a purpose, and that participating in such a community is being a member of the body of Christ.

Whichever tendency prevails, believing too much or too little about the church, what is lost is the heart of the church; what gets called "church" turns out, in either case, to be less than a redeemed community of blessing and well-being.

Sheer Discrepancy

The church's self-description, encountered in scripture, tradition, and preaching, is remarkable for its high-flown language. The church is "the people of God," we are the very "body of Christ," a "communion of saints," the "fellowship of the Holy Spirit." When the traditional marks or identifiers of the church are listed, we hear that the church is one, that it is catholic or universal, that it is holy, and apostolic. The Reformers added to these two others: The church is where the Word is rightly preached and the sacraments rightly administered. More informally, a local congregation may bill itself as "a caring community." All of these things are said with a straight face, perhaps a smile, but seldom tongue-in-cheek, hinting that the truth might be more complex.

While such self-descriptions have their point, they are terribly misleading if taken as descriptive of the life of the churches. Sometimes the church seems to be anything but the "people of God," and barely distinguishable from any other people, more a communion of sinners than saints. Not only holy, churches are often the scene of conflict, inflicting pain on people. Sometimes, as in Northern Ireland or the former Yugoslavia, different churches are deeply entangled in ethnic conflict and warfare. Sometimes, as at Jonestown and Waco, they seem to be all curse and no blessing. The churches are at best ambivalent mixtures of what God gives and calls them to be and what they actually are. The churches are at least as divided as they are one, as biased and partisan as they are catholic (universal), as care-less as caring. Enough people have experienced the churches at their worst that it is surprising that therapy groups for those suffering from "church-a-phobia" have not thrived.

The church is both/and, both holy and less-than-holy, both united and divided, both caring and care-less, both the people of God and the people who really know how to have a fight, both blessing and curse. Our first recorded awareness of this point is given to us by Paul the apostle, who said that we have the "treasure" of the knowledge of the glory of God "in clay jars" (2 Cor. 4:7). The older translation, "in earthen vessels," better conveys Paul's intent. "We have this treasure in garbage bags" is a way to say it that makes clear that the grace of God is always, as Luther said, "hidden beneath its opposite," as the glory of God was hidden beneath the crucifixion of Jesus.[15]

To begin to get clear about these matters, we stipulate a normative definition of the church.

The Purpose of the Church

The church is that community of people called into existence by God, through the Holy Spirit, to live from and by the gospel of God, witnessing to the grace and command of the gospel as the call and claim of the God of Israel offered in Jesus Christ to the church on behalf of all the world, and doing so both to remind itself of what it is about and on behalf of the world that it might, one day, reflect the glory of God.

This definition does not describe actual churches. It is one attempt to state what God gives and calls the church to be, what the church essentially (in its very being, its *esse*) is and ought to be. God does not commission the church to be or do anything that God does not graciously empower it to be and do. The character or identity of the church is a matter of faith. Helpful as various attempts to describe and analyze churches empirically, sociologically, psychologically, culturally, and so forth might be, such efforts cannot define what God gives and calls the church to be.

---

[15]Martin Luther, *Luther's Works,* ed. Harold J. Grimm and Helmut T. Lehmann (Philadelphia: Muhlenberg Press, 1957), vol. 31, "Explanations of the Ninety-five Theses," rubric 58.

The churches manifest their true identity, as Paul Tillich argued, only fragmentarily and ambiguously.[16] Yet the churches are, in spite of themselves, faithful. The churches are one, holy, catholic, and apostolic "in spite of" all the ways in which they are not so. They take the risk of teaching, proclaiming, and studying the word of God. They take the risk of raising up their own critics. Taking this risk is a sign of faithfulness. The churches pray "forgive us our sins," recognizing at least tacitly that there are some sins for which the church needs forgiveness.

What prevents the church from losing its identity entirely is that it keeps reminding itself that it is not what it ought to be. The church reminds us (we are the church, after all) that nothing about the church is perfect; it also remembers that God has not given up on it, that God is faithful to the church as God was to Israel when Israel sinned. The Reformation understanding of the church as *ecclesia reformata et semper reformanda* ("the church reformed and always reforming"), of which the church also reminds us, requires that we continue to bring the church under the scrutiny of its own gospel, calling it to self-criticism and self-understanding. We do this on the assumption that the church lives by grace, a grace that both allows and demands criticism.

The Classic Marks of the Church

In the year 381 at Constantinople, in what came to be known as the Nicene Creed, the church confessed: "We believe in one, holy, catholic, and apostolic church."[17] These four adjectives–one, holy, catholic, and apostolic–have ever since been known as the four "marks" of the church. They are the distinguishing, identifying marks of the church. The bishops at Constantinople did not invent these four marks out of thin air. They drew them from statements and stories about the church in the New Testament, chiefly from the account of the creation of the church at Pentecost.

The church is one, united, because the Spirit of God creates the church as one out of a miscellany of peoples, cultures, ethnicities, and languages, referred to in Acts as "devout Jews from every nation under heaven" (2:5). Oneness does not mean sameness or

---

[16]Paul Tillich, *Systematic Theology*, vol. 3 (Chicago: The University of Chicago Press, 1963), 165–72.

[17]John H. Leith, ed., *Creeds of the Churches*, 33.

homogeneity. The unity of the church is supposed to be exciting, not boring. Unity is a koinonia of the diverse. Unity means that what God has joined together, we should not tear into pieces. To affirm that the church is one is to deny that any part of the church can say to any other part that it is not a member of the one body of Christ. The members of the church are inseparable from God, Christ, and one another. This kind of unity rejoices in all the human diversity of which it is composed. Unity is not supposed to describe some invisible, spiritual church. Unity is to be made visible ("let your light shine so that all may see by your deeds") in our deeds of loving kindness, in our attempts to mend the world, in our efforts to meet the needs of the "least of these," in our attention to one another, in our proclamation, and in the sacraments of baptism and the Lord's supper.

Unity is a way of specifying well-being. Consequently, the unity of the church means that the church is given and called to deny and reject all forces, all powers and principalities, that would tear asunder the body of Christ. We deny that the church should be divided along lines of class, race, gender, nationalism, economic systems, and ideologies, or for that matter that the church should be apart from and against the people Israel, when we affirm that the church is one.

Therefore, in reflecting critically on its life, the church is responsible for discerning the difference between divisions that issue from sin or failure and legitimate diversity. Which differences are creative, and which issue only in animosity and estrangement?

What unity has to do with growing up in the Christian faith, being increasingly transformed by the revelation of God in Christ, is this: The communion into which we are welcomed by the church is one of learning ever anew what it means to love others, some of whom we may find "unworthy," even as we have been so unworthily loved.

The church is holy because it is created by the Holy Spirit. The church is not holy in itself, nor because its members are distinguished either by their comparatively higher standards of moral behavior or their no-longer-fashionable styles of dress. The "saints" of the church are those justified sinners who are its members. We never cease being *simul iustus et peccator,* a point that the greatest saints of the church never forgot or forgot to apply to themselves. God graciously gives and calls the church to holiness as part of its justification. God graciously offers us the gift of a new and radically transformed life, a gift had for the asking. The community of saints (*communio sanctorum*) is, therefore, also a community of sinners (*communio peccatorum*). It, too, is *simul iustus et peccator,* at one and the same time justified and a sinner. The church is holy on the condition that it confesses its unholiness. The church is holy insofar as it engages in acts of worship that celebrate and re-present God's gracious redemption of it (as of all humanity).

Affirming that the church is holy says more about God than about the church. Affirming that the church is holy says that the Holy Spirit redeems and reconciles the church, gives it new life in the midst of, and in spite of, its sin and error.

Paul typically addresses his letters "to all God's beloved (in Rome or Corinth) who are called to be saints" (1 Cor 1:2; Rom. 1:7). Christians are not descriptively saints; we are "called to be saints." We are given and called, beckoned, to a life transformed by the love of God made manifest in Christ. We are so called not in order to be accorded some higher status, but in order to put ourselves to the task of being a light to the Gentiles, transforming the world and its death-dealing ways. We are given and called so to immerse ourselves in the world as to be the leaven in the lump, transforming it for the sake of its well-being. We are called to be in the world, not of it.

The church is catholic (ecumenical) in several senses. In the ancient church, the term catholic had three meanings. It referred to the whole inhabited world and so designated the universality of the church among all peoples and cultures. The church is both local (the church in Corinth) and universal. Paul's efforts to unite the churches in the service of the saints in Jerusalem (1 Cor. 16:1; 2 Cor. 9:1) is an early sign that the local church anywhere is genuinely church so long as it is in unity with all others who also have the same one Lord, one faith, one baptism. Catholic had the meaning of "orthodox," as opposed to heretical and meant, primarily, that the church was not gnostic or docetic in its understanding of Christ (that is, the church affirmed that Jesus Christ was truly human, not merely apparently so).

Paul Tillich had a great ecumenical insight into the nature of the church when he said that to be authentic it must manifest in its life both "Catholic substance" and "the Protestant principle." Catholic substance is an incarnational term that refers to concrete embodiment of the holy, of God, in our midst. Without "Catholic substance," the church is empty. Without "the Protestant principle," the church is blind to its own faults. The "Protestant principle" is the prophetic, critical awareness that nothing about the church is fixed for all time, there is nothing that does not require self-criticism, repentance, renewal, and rethinking. Without the critical principle, the church becomes idolatrous and demonic.[18]

The third meaning of "catholic" was that the church included people from all the social and economic strata of society. Widows rich enough to have a large house in which the house-church could meet, the poor, and slaves were all included in the church's catholicity. The church's inclusivism extended across economic lines, an extension that subsequently has given the church difficulties. To profess the catholicity of the church is to contradict the notion that God's love is graciously given only to those in the socioeconomic class with which we are comfortable. The church as participant in God's mission is to be a source of light, blessing, and well-being for all creation.

This catholicity was expressed by the church in its awareness that it had "one Lord, one faith, one baptism, one God and Father of all" (Eph. 4:5–6). The church confesses one faith, shares one baptism, carries out the mission or purpose of God and Christ to the world, and gathers together a diversity of class, race, ethnicity, gender, and culture around one table. Catholicity is one way in which the church continues, when it does it authentically, to put into practice the activity of Jesus in welcoming all into his egalitarian community of blessing and well-being. A church that is not a church of the poor does not have the mark of catholicity. A church that fails to do works of love toward the neighbor does not have the identifying mark of catholicity.

The church is apostolic because it has been given the apostolic message (the gospel) and called to an apostolic function. It is apostolic insofar as it is faithful to this message and responsible to and for the continuity of the Christian tradition. It is apostolic because in no generation, in spite of all its sin and failure, has it been utterly without faithful witnesses to the gospel of Jesus Christ. In this sense we may say that by the grace of God, the church never utterly defects from the gospel. God will raise up some prophet in the midst

---

[18]Paul Tillich, *Systematic Theology*, vol. 3, 245.

of the desertion from faith. In this sense, apostolicity says more about God's faithfulness than about the church's faithfulness.

Some traditions regard "apostolic succession" as the critical issue in apostolicity. The idea of apostolic succession arose in the early church as a way of making clear that there was in every major city a historic line of authentic teachers of the Christian faith, whose successive lines of ordination could be traced back to an original apostle. The point was to emphasize the public and known character of the church's teachings, and thereby to distinguish them from certain "new" heresies. The problem with the idea, as it developed, is that it located apostolicity in the office of bishop.

Certainly the church "sets aside" ministers to announce/teach the apostolic gospel. Yet this gospel can be announced and taught by any member of the *laos theou* (the people of God). Theology may and should be done by any member of the people of God. It is the people of God who are the bearers of apostolicity. The clergy bear it too, as members of the people of God, and because they are ordained to be authentic teachers of the faith. Teaching, preaching, representing, living out the apostolic message is an essential practice of the church. Because the church is the people of God, apostolicity can never properly be understood to legitimate ecclesiastical dictatorships, arrogance with regard to religious truth, or hierarchism.

Hans Küng pointed out that *diakonia* (service) is the word used in the New Testament for ministry.[19] All leadership in the church is that of a servant ministry, service enacted out of love for God and love for one's neighbors in the church and in the world. Every office of leadership in the church is and should be one that extends love and freedom, solidarity and liberation, to all members of the church. Domination and authoritarianism have no place in the life of the church. Genuine authority, authentic teaching of the Christian faith, is carried out by the method of being a servant and results in enhanced freedom. As God loves us into freedom and frees us to love, so we should love one another into freedom and free one another to love.

Being an apostle (*apostolos*) means being sent out on a mission. Paul or one of his students writes: "For this gospel I was appointed a herald and an apostle and a teacher" (2 Tim. 1:11). The synoptic

---

[19]Hans Küng, *The Church* (New York: Image Books, 1976), 495–611.

gospels use the word to tell of Jesus' sending the apostles out to preach (Mk. 3:14). Paul uses "apostle" to mean "apostle of Jesus Christ," whose chief work was to preach Christ (Gal. 1:16) or the gospel (1 Cor. 1:17), primarily to those who had not yet heard it.

God sends the whole people of God to go to those whom Jesus went to in his ministry, to the destitute, the hungry, and those who mourn, to the "least of these." God calls Abraham and Sarah and sends them into the future of God's promise. God calls Israel to be God's people and sends Israel into the world to be "a light to the Gentiles." The mark of apostolicity makes clear the continuity and connection between the church and the people Israel. Both Israel and the church are to impart God's purpose of blessing and well-being to all the peoples of the earth. God's intent to bless all creation means that Israel's vocation is in the context of universal inclusion of all peoples and that the church's calling to be a blessing to the Gentiles cannot invalidate God's calling of Israel to participate in God's offer of life and well-being.

The Church's Identity and Anti-Judaism

Nonetheless, Christians have long argued that a primary way to understand the church is as a "replacement people," the people who replace the people Israel in covenant with God and in God's affection. Anti-Judaism is the dark underside of the church's systematic distortion of its own confessed marks. In the anti-Jewish tracts of the church's history, we see another doctrine of the church: The church is a replacement people, a Gentile and, in this sense, a universal people; a superior people, and most importantly, we.

As the church misinterprets itself as "displacing" (superseding) "the Jews" in God's favor, so the church becomes a replacement people. Tertullian speaks of God's "transferring his favor" from the Jews to the Gentiles. Grace "comes to an end" for Jews when the church "begins."[20] Later, Cyprian, bishop of Carthage in North Africa, claimed that since "the Jews have fallen out of favor because of their conspiring against the Lord, the Savior has built up from among

---

[20]See Tertullian's tract *An Answer to the Jews* in *The Ante-Nicene Fathers*, vol. 3, ed. Alexander Roberts and James Donaldson (Grand Rapids: Eerdmans, 1978), 151–73.

the gentiles a second assembly or church."[21] At the other end of the Mediterranean, Cyril of Jerusalem claimed: "The grace of life will no longer abide in Israel, but among the Gentiles."[22]

The replacement people is therefore a Gentile and universal people, unlike the old, ethnocentric Jews. As Augustine of Hippo put it: The new covenant is with the Gentiles, while the Jews "have remained stationary in useless antiquity…this old Israel is Israel according to the flesh, blind to the signs of the times, the enemies of God."[23] This replacement people is a church of "all peoples which are under heaven," with the obvious exception of one people, that one people whom the scriptures clearly declare to be chosen by God to be the light to the Gentiles.

This replacement, Gentile people is also a superior people, "more honorable, abler," claimed Tertullian, "to give Christ a better acceptance, with a better liturgy, new ceremonies different from old, Jewish and legalistic rites." Christians are able to pray to God, whereas Jews cannot, since the Father is known only through the Son and Jews do not know the Son. Christians are also morally superior to Jews, possessing a spiritual freedom that they do not. One thing at least is clear: The capacity of some Christians for self-congratulation and smugness is unbearable.

The payoff of this anti-Judaism is that the church is we: We receive the benefits of Christ that are bestowed only upon the members of the church who, unlike Jews, are blessed, saved, redeemed, and set upon a superior course of life: "The Gentiles rather than the Jews attain to the kingdom of heaven" (Cyprian).

Such displacement/replacement ideology utterly contradicts the deepest message of scripture that God is steadfastly faithful, storing up grace for thousands of generations, and that God keeps God's promises even or particularly when we do not. Paul the apostle, a Hebrew born of Hebrews of the tribe of Benjamin, whose vocation

---

[21]Cyprian, *Three Books of Testimonies Against the Jews*, in *The Ante-Nicene Fathers*, vol. 5, ed. Alexander Roberts and James Donaldson (Grand Rapids: Eerdmans, 1978), 507–28.

[22]See *The Works of St. Cyril of Jerusalem*, vol. 2, trans. Leo P. McCauley, S. J., and Anthony A. Stephenson (Washington: Catholic University of America Press, 1970), 9, 15.

[23]See Augustine's "In Answer to the Jews" in *Saint Augustine: Treatises on Marriage and Other Subjects*, ed. Roy J. DeFerrari (New York: Fathers of the Church, 1955), 391–414.

it was to bring light, blessing, and well-being to Gentiles, resound-ingly underscored God's faithfulness precisely in relation to the people Israel when he said: "The gifts and the calling of God are irrevocable" (Rom. 11:29).

The Church and the Jewish People

It is time to revisit the quotation from Joseph Haroutunian given at the beginning of this chapter.

> There is no doctrine in orthodox Christian theology that is not in line with the purposes and interests of the ecclesiasti-cal establishments called churches. These establishments have been the "arks of salvation" or places outside of which there is no salvation. Hence, not only the doctrine of salva-tion, but also the other doctrines have been so stated and elaborated as to function in the rationale of these establish-ments and their practices.[24]

The church should frame its doctrines so as to be appropriate to the gospel of Jesus Christ, not so as to justify and reinforce its own power. Theology and the Christian witness are always to be made "to the greater glory of God," not to that of the churches.

Gustavo Gutierrez proposes a decentering of the church, turn-ing it away from its "ecclesiocentrism" toward an existence that is not "for itself," but "for others."[25] The *adversus Judaeos* tradition is the most severe instance of the ecclesiocentrism that Gutierrez criti-cizes. Were the church to understand itself in relation to God, Christ, the gospel, the neighbor, and the "least of these" and place them in the center of its concern, it would discover that it now has to "criti-cize every sacralization of oppressive structures to which it might have contributed."

By transcending and eliminating ecclesiocentrism, what is meant is that Christians are not called to believe "in" the church. Hans Küng makes clear that the ancient creeds talk of believing in God, Christ, and the Holy Spirit, but not of believing "in" the church. Instead, they simply say: "I believe the church" (*credo ecclesiam*). The absence of the preposition "in" signifies that the church can hardly

---

[24]Joseph Haroutunian, *God With Us*, 279.
[25]Gustavo Gutierrez, *A Theology of Liberation* (Maryknoll: Orbis Books, 1983), 256–69.

be said to believe in itself, at least not in the same sense that it believes in Christ. Does the community of sinful people place radical
trust in itself? But "we believe the church" because in it we have
ever and again been laid bare before the promise and command of
the God of Israel, freely given to us by God, and freely received on
our behalf by Jesus Christ through the Holy Spirit. Here we learn of
God's grace toward us, and here we are called to respond with gratitude. Anti-Judaism signals an extreme ecclesiocentrism.

An old metaphor for the church is that of the ark of salvation.
Derived from the story of Noah's ark and from the gospel stories of
Jesus and the Twelve in a boat during a storm, it is a good and powerful metaphor for the church. Yet it is a way of talking that is subject to abuse, especially when, in fits of ecclesiocentrism, we imagine
ourselves to be the only ones whom God loves and redeems, the
only apple of God's eye, the only ark riding out the storm. Not all of
those whom God elects and wills to save participate in the life of the
church. To affirm apostolicity is to deny that God is faithful to God's
promise to bring life and well-being to all God's peoples. Anti-
Judaism in the history of the church shows that the church long
understood itself as the church against the people Israel (with some
exceptions for which we are grateful). Now we face the task of being
the church in a post-Holocaust context, in which the payoff of centuries of anti-Judaism cannot be honestly denied. That task is to
become the church *with and for* the people Israel. It is the task of
guarding and protecting the well-being of the stranger and of welcoming the stranger to become a friend.

Women and the People of God

A glance around any typical church on Sunday morning will
disclose that more women than men are present in it. Familiarity
with all the workings of its life will similarly divulge the fact that
women do by far the greater amount of the church's work in carrying out its mission. Yet, looking further will reveal that women are
still massively underrepresented in its official leadership positions,
in the clergy, in positions of denominational importance, or in some
cases such as the Roman Catholic Church, altogether absent from
the ranks of the clergy. The church has not been a particularly friendly
place for women.

Banned either totally or largely from its ordained ministry and
other decision-making positions, women gather in women's organizations to study the Christian faith, understand the scriptures, come

to grips with the mission of the church to a world in need, and to imagine what the church might look like were it faithful to God's promise to bring blessing and well-being to all people, women included. Some committed women members of the church fear that a split may already have occurred "between the church as community and the church as institution."[26]

Key to reimagining the church in such ways as to make it a genuinely welcoming community for women, a safe place for them to be Christian, is rethinking what it means for the church to be the "people of God." People of God is the earliest and most inclusive image of the church. It is borrowed from the scriptural understanding of the people Israel as the people of God, the *qahal Yahweh*. The image carries political overtones, in the sense of being concerned with the well-being of the people, the body politic, a reminder that we should be concerned with the well-being of all the people of God, not just men. Paul universalized the meaning of the church as the people of God, removing all boundaries that artificially separated peoples from one another, including those of "male and female."

Women who come to understand the church as the people of God quickly see that the church is not centered on a line of ordained males with women at the periphery. They come to the conviction: "We are the church." The church is a community, a communion of persons freely engaged in relationships of mutuality and love. The church is the (but not the only) people of God because God gives and calls the church to be God's people and a sign of blessing and well-being to all people. We are not the people of God because, like any good voluntary association, we decided to so constitute ourselves.

We are the people of God because of what God has done to and for us in Jesus Christ. God has made us, who were no people, who were Gentiles of differing and warring tribes and ethnicities, into God's people. All people in the church, men and women, stand before one another on the same and equal footing: on the basis of God's gracious love for each and all. The only way in which we can appropriately understand ourselves in any ultimate sense is in terms of God's unfathomable love for us. Whether I am male or female is

---

[26]Mary E. Hines, "Community for Liberation," in *Freeing Theology,* ed. Catherine Mowry LaCugna (New York: HarperCollins, 1993), 164.

proximately important, but ultimately unimportant. When we make maleness (or for that matter, femaleness) ultimately important, we absolutize what is relative and commit idolatry. We, who are not only different but alienated from and in conflict with one another, have been graciously reconciled by God into a communion of love and mutuality.

Therefore, to say that the church is the people of God is to say that all forms of sexism and patriarchy amount to heresy and are to be rejected.

An Oasis of Freedom for African Americans

The great insight of liberation theology lies in its central claim that God's salvific activity on behalf of humanity is aimed more toward the predicament of the poor, more toward the human than toward the restricted Christian community. Wherever there are sharp class differences, where many are destitute, weeping, and hungry, the church is given and called to take sides with the oppressed and to work for the redemption of inhuman social relationships. The church is given and called to give evidence of "a new and radical service of people" as well as work for "radically new social forms."[27]

In North America it is African American theologians and African American churches where the radicality of these liberation themes is most visible. It is no secret that the worship hour on Sunday morning remains the most segregated hour in American life. Forced by slavery, segregation, and racism to be a church of African American people, the African American church has provided an oasis of freedom in a barren landscape of oppression. Here a people who are elsewhere scorned and looked down upon can hold up their heads with the dignity befitting the children of God and know that in God's eyes they are "somebody." Here people who otherwise had to shuffle could walk with strong steps. Here people otherwise deprived of hope could find the courage to be themselves and to trust in and pray for the coming of God's reign. Here a people who were forced by myriad social forces to bite their tongues could find their song and sing it.

The African American church has been a safe place for people of color. It has played a constitutive role in the very survival of African

---

[27]Gustavo Gutierrez, *A Theology for Liberation* (Maryknoll: Orbis Books, 1983), 56, 256.

Americans, and as post-Holocaust theologians know, survival is witness to liberation and hope. Created by the opposing forces of racism and racial self-respect, African American churches provide us with a paradigm of what it is to be church: an anti-racist understanding and practice of the Christian faith. These churches testify, argues Peter Paris, to the prophetic principle that before God all human beings are equal.[28] In Christ there is neither black nor white.

African American theologians would be the first to confess that the prophetic principle of black churches stands in relation to those communities as gift and command of God, as that to which they are called and that in relation to which they are to be criticized. Yet the African American church provides for the rest of us both a model and a challenge: a model of what the church might be, were it to affirm the principle that before God all people are equal, and a challenge to recognize the heretical nature of most of our churches in their (usually) unspoken racism and their betrayal of God's purpose to bless all people with well-being. In relation to African Americans, white churches have responded to their plight with a mixture of indifference, sloth, and blindness to the death-dealing ways of racism.

The Church of the Poor

Jesus led a movement that he called the kingdom or rule, the *basileia*, of God. He both proclaimed and practiced a different kind of rule, a kingdom that was a radical alternative to the kingdoms of such other kings as Caesar and Herod. His kingdom was not one of domination, but of service, one of welcome for the destitute and the marginalized, one that included the poor and homeless. This communitarian, egalitarian movement (egalitarian in the sense of "whoever would be greatest of all must be servant of all") of the nobodies of Galilee acted out a new way of being human. That new way repudiated the classism of the Rome-dominated world. This new communion of love, of welcome for the outcast, of free and open eating (incredibly important in a subsistence economy), of mutual service was both the reality of God's reign and a sign of its further actualization.

Yet the church gradually lost this vision and became increasingly allied with the rich and powerful forces of the ancient world. It

---

[28]Peter Paris, "The Social World of the Black Church," *The Drew Gateway* 52/3 (Spring, 1982): 8.

all began with feeding the destitute, the hungry, and the mourners on a Galilean hillside. The poor reclined to eat, being treated like royalty, and the disciples served the meal, doing the work of the nobodies of that world, women and slaves. Mark is the first to tell this story, and he deliberately places it after the story of Herod's banquet. We saw earlier that the two stories are mirror images of each other.

By the time the church is becoming established in the early fourth century, it finds itself embracing Herod's way of doing things. After the Council of Nicea, a lakeside suburb of Constantinople, in 325 C.E., the emperor Constantine invites the bishops to an imperial banquet. Here is a description of that banquet from the church historian Eusebius:

> Detachments of the bodyguard and troops surrounded the entrance of the palace with drawn swords, and through the midst of them the men of God proceeded without fear into the innermost of the Imperial apartments, in which some were the Emperor's companions at table, while others reclined on couches arranged on either side. One might have thought that a picture of Christ's kingdom was thus shadowed forth, and a dream rather than reality.[29]

The function of the bodyguard and troops is to protect the emperor and his guests from the rabble in the streets below. The bishops, no longer serving the poor as the disciples once did, now themselves recline on the king's couches and are treated as royalty. All is as it was before Jesus, much that he was about conveniently, or perhaps agonizingly, forgotten.

The church was attacked and conquered by its surrounding culture. Persecution could not kill the church. Acceptance and establishment could. This attack proved irresistible. To the extent that the church still regards itself as established, culturally if not legally, it identifies with the well-to-do and fails to notice that instead of challenging the social stratifications of its society, it reflects them in its own life.

Classism is prejudice against people who are economically underprivileged. It divides people into categories defined by social status,

---

[29]Eusebius, *Life of Constantine*, 3.15, quoted in Crossan, *Jesus: A Revolutionary Biography*, 201.

wealth, political influence, and lifestyles. Classism is the practice of assigning lower worth and merit to people who are in the lower economic classes. That there are economic differences between people is a fact. What classism adds to this fact is that it sets such inequalities in stone. Such institutionalization of economic differences is seen in India with its caste system. In the United States, where once we had slavery, now we simply have class. Classism is inimical, hostile to the well-being of people caught in the economic lower classes. Many an informal discussion of poor people makes clear the prevailing assumptions that they get what they deserve, they do not merit better treatment, only the shiftless are homeless in such a booming economy.

Classism is most effective when it is invisible, which in North America it largely is. It can come to attention in the church, however, if we become conscious of who is missing when the congregation gathers for worship. In most so-called mainstream churches, the lower classes shine by their absence. Liberation theology may have taught the pastor about the church of the poor, but the chances that the pastor will ever deal with such a church are slim. The chances that the congregation will become conscious of its middle and upper-middle class orientation are slimmer still.

H. Richard Niebuhr, in his influential book *The Social Sources of Denominationalism,* argued that denominationalism "represents the accommodation of Christianity to the caste system of human society." The churches minister to and mirror distinctive class concerns. As such they are symbols of "the victory of the world over the church, of the secularization of Christianity, of the church's sanction of that divisiveness which the church's gospel condemns."[30]

Let us suppose that when we extol the early church, we mean what we say. If that church is in some sense our model, what was it like, and how might it serve to correct and challenge our capitulation to the world? Luke describes one such community: "All who believed were together and had all things in common; they would sell their possessions and goods and distribute the proceeds to all, as any had need" (Acts 2:44–45). Paul does not describe a primitive form of socialism, but he does depict churches that met in the house of a wealthy person (the house would have had to be large enough to

---

[30]H. Richard Niebuhr, *The Social Sources of Denominationalism* (New York: Meridian Books, 1957), 6, 25.

function as a house church), in which property and wealth were put to a Christian use. All members of the community were important, each had a gift from God that was to be exercised on behalf of the community, and the whole community was the bearer of ministry.

Such early churches, not surprisingly, especially attracted the very kinds of people whom Jesus drew into his movement. They were lured by the vision and the reality of a new kind of communal life, a life of communion with God, Christ, and one another, a life liberated from the social stratifications of the Hellenistic world, a life in which there was no Greek, no barbarian, no slave, no free, no male, no female, but all were one in Christ. They were freed into loving one another and loved into being free for one another in ways that transcended the barriers not only of culture and ethnicity, but particularly of class.

The early church brought blessing and well-being to the poor, the dirty, the smelly, the homeless, those whom Jesus called "the least of these." What would the church today look like were it to follow him?

Models of the Church

Among the excellent books on models of the church, three of the best are: H. Richard Niebuhr, *Christ and Culture*; Avery Dulles, *Models of the Church*; and Paul Minear, *Images of the Church in the New Testament*.[31] Niebuhr is famous for having come up with five "ideal types" of the church: Christ against culture, Christ of culture, Christ above culture, Christ in dialectical tension with culture, and Christ transforming culture. Many readers of Niebuhr assume that "Christ transforming culture" is the obvious model to adopt. Niebuhr, to the contrary, emphasized the contextual nature of the decision about which model is most appropriate. In our post-Constantinian time, neither identifying the church with the culture nor seeking to make the culture the foundation of the church, which is then above the culture, is helpful or appropriate. Any preferred model of the church must be critically contextual, and we must take carefully into account the context in which we live. Stanley Hauerwas makes a

---

[31]H. Richard Niebuhr, *Christ and Culture* (New York: Harper, 1951); Avery Dulles, *Models of the Church* (Garden City: Doubleday, 1974); and Paul Sevier Minear, *Images of the Church in the New Testament* (Philadelphia: Westminster, 1960).

powerful argument that the Mennonites have been right all along. The church has a distinctive witness to make, and it can make this witness most authentically by letting its character as a community be defined by its story rather than by the culture.[32]

A Community of Memory, Story, and Connectedness

Walter Brueggemann helps us to see a long-overlooked model of the community of faith in the Hebrew Bible.[33] Prior to the rise of the institution of kingship in Israel, we find the first model. The community of Israel nurtured and shaped its life and faith by reenacting the exodus liturgy that called into question the power structures of the day (pharaoh and the local city-states of Canaan). The Sinai covenant brought with it an ever-new process of interpretation of God's will and way that the Bible calls torah. The hermeneutical process of the people Israel meant that Israel continued to think and rethink its faith and practice in light of its liberation. Such continued interpretation in relation to ever-changing contexts is the church trying to discern the will of God. Ancient Israel had neither stable institutions nor a sympathetic civic leadership; and it had no prophets. It had to improvise. Completely unestablished (it had never been established), and with no security whatsoever, the community relied on telling and retelling its story and teaching it to its children well. This suggests a partial model of the church for our post-Constantinian time—a church that improvises, that is shaped by its liberating liturgy of exodus/Sinai and crucifixion/resurrection, that works hard at interpreting its scripture and its context in relation to one another, and that sees to it that it both hears and tells its story.

A similar model is found at the other end of the Hebrew Bible, one that begins in exile and continues in second-temple Judaism. This model also characterizes the earliest churches. Again, the community exercised no influence on public policy, being ruled over by imperial warlords of successive empires. The big temptation it faced was to meld into the surrounding culture and allow its distinctive identity to disappear. The oppressive Syrian and Persian emperors successively asked: Why not give up circumcision and eat a little

---

[32]Stanley Hauerwas, *A Community of Character* (Notre Dame: University of Notre Dame Press, 1981).

[33]Walter Brueggemann, *A Social Reading of the Old Testament: Prophetic Approaches to Israel's Communal Life*, ed. Patrick D. Miller (Mineapolis: Fortress, 1994), 263–75.

pork? In response the community took as its main task preserving and re-creating the language and practices of its faith in order to secure its own survival.

It worked at recovering memory and rootedness and connect-edness. It developed a learned recovery of its heritage to combat the tendency to forget its identity-conferring story and to sink into the culture at large. It developed the practice of hope, filling its mind and heart with the promises of God. Its eschatological/apocalyptic talk were subversive of the status quo of the death-dealing powers who lorded it over them and all others. It became an intensely tex-tual community. It formulated its scriptures; it began to canonize its scripture; it interpreted its scriptures. It created the early forms of the synagogue, the place of the text, the "house of study" (*Beth Midrash*), and developed a new type of religious leader—the rabbi—who was a teacher of the tradition.

This presents part of a good model for the church in a post-establishment time when it cannot rely upon the culture to tell its story for it, or when that culture peddles so many stories, and stories that are so inadequate to the human beings to whom they are told, as to be an essentially "story-less" culture. The church has to learn how to tell its own story, teach its own faith, sing its own song, de-velop the skills to use its own language if it is going to survive as church.

A Communion of Blessing and Well-being

All Christian life, and every Christian life, has its origin and context in the *koinonia*, the church created by the Holy Spirit, the giver of life and well-being. Both the beginning of the faithful Chris-tian life and its continued existence are possible only in the koinonia created by the triune God whose life in itself and in our invitation into it is a life of mutual love in freedom and freedom to love. The church envelops the individual Christian in an interrelationship of communion and blessing. Christians are dependent on the church and on Christ who is active in the church. We find Christ in this interrelationship of communion and blessing; here we are loved into freedom and freed to love. There is no such thing as being Christian on one's own, apart from the communion of well-being created by the Holy Spirit.

Paul expressed this by calling the church the body of Christ. He was not merely using a metaphor when he talked of the community, united through word and sacrament, as the body of Christ. He meant what he said: The community of believers is the body of Christ, the earthly body of the risen Lord.[34] Paul did not think that each of us, as individuals, possesses some kind of essential human nature. Rather, he saw the "being" of each of us as constituted by the actual relationships in which we participate. Who we are as human beings is given shape and form in our relations with others. Our being is a being-in-communion with one another and with Christ. It is in, through, and by means of this set of relationships that God seeks to bring about salvation among human beings.

Further, this communion of love and blessing is not static; it is a communion on the move. The church is a movement of "companions on the way." To say this is to emphasize, first, that the church is a communion. It is not a building, although it may erect buildings to carry out its purposes. It is a peculiar kind of communion, one composed of those with (*cum*) whom one breaks bread (*panis*), companions, in the presence of Jesus Christ. We are friends of Christ and one another because Christ first befriended us: "I have called you friends" (Jn. 15:15). Being friends of the One who is the Friend of all means that we too are to befriend and be a blessing to all. It means being a people who keep company with God, who graciously keeps company with it. It is being a community of companions on the way to a goal. That goal in its proximate form is clear in its purpose of spreading in the world the love of God and the love of neighbor, of bearing witness to the world of an alternative to its death-dealing ways: the way of life and well-being. The ultimate goal is eschatological and two-fold: the transformation of this world and ultimate redemption in God's life.

The church had its origins in a small band of Galileans gathered around an itinerant teacher who talked and put into practice what he called "the rule of God," God's kingdom. Never, without losing all sense of what it is given and called to be, can the church forget that it is an eschatological communion. *Eschaton*, the Greek word from which we get "eschatology," has to do with the end, in the sense of "aim" or "purpose," of God's dealings with the world. This aim is to bring life, blessing, well-being, redemption, and reconciliation to a world torn apart by the sin-laden, death-dealing powers of

---

[34]See Ernst Käsemann, "The Theological Problem Presented by the Motif of the Body of Christ," in *Perspectives on Paul*, trans. Margaret Kohl (Philadelphia: Fortress Press, 1971), 102–21.

destruction and brokenness. As an eschatological community the church witnesses to God's purposes for the world. As a community that seeks to live out the Christian faith the church enables the world to see, to witness, the alternative of life and well-being. The church does this when, even while confessing its sins and failures, in its own life it welcomes all sorts and conditions of people into a communion of mutual love and blessing. Mindful both of the brokenness of the world and the church's own need of mending, the church will never confuse itself with the kingdom of God.

Companions on the Way

The concern that the church survive as church, instead of blending into the surrounding culture and losing its distinctive identity, has to do with the mission, the purpose of the church. The church is given and called by Jesus to be "the light of the world" (Mt. 5:14), as Israel was and is called to be a "light to the Gentiles." That too many mainstream Protestants continue to assume, perhaps unwittingly, that they are culturally established militates against their taking seriously the call to be a light to the world. It is precisely their failure to constitute an alternative to what it means to be a good American that is the major reason they are found to be insipid. It is why so many "good Americans" find no need for the "middle man" between themselves and American culture.

Mainstream Protestants need to rediscover the excitement of being a community on the way, a pilgrim people, "whose citizenship is in heaven" (Phil. 3:20). Where there's an exciting mission, supportive companions are important. Where one's companions are excited, things move. Jesus is, as usual, out ahead of us, "the pioneer and perfecter of our faith" (Heb. 12:2).

Chapter 10

Help for the Way:
Preaching, Sacraments, and Ministry

Means of Grace

The church is the community of God's people, "called out" of various ethnic identities to become the people of God and set on the way of life toward the goal of God's reign. Along this way and in this company the community studies and wrestles with the strange God who has set them on this course, converses with those who have studied the things concerning Jesus Christ longer than they have, celebrates together out of grateful response to the exuberant gift to them of God's gracious love, and invites others to participate in the well-being with which God intends to bless them. Here we pause to consider some of the ways in which the community talks about some of the things it does together.

Preaching, baptism, the breaking of bread (the eucharist or communion), and prayer are means of grace. In these customary activities of the church, the good news of Jesus Christ, that we are unconditionally loved by God and given and called by God to a new and transformed life to be lived out in love and service to the neighbor, is again and again re-presented. Preaching, baptism, and the eucharist re-present the good news of God's gracious love and total claim upon us. They express our yes-saying to God's grace and our intention in return to love God with all ourselves and our neighbors as ourselves. They are means of grace because they make us again and again aware of a word that bears repeating, that God's love comes to us freely from God and not because of any merit on our part, and that we are to respond to this word in faith.

Through these means of grace, by the activity of the Holy Spirit, the church is constituted. They are what Tillich calls the "constitutive factors" of the church, its "sacraments," ordinances or rites. The best way to make clear what we mean by these expressions is to use the traditional term "means of grace."[1] The sacraments are means of grace because through them God's grace is presented anew to us.

The availability of God's grace is not limited to the sacraments, nor available only to those who participate in the sacraments. The purpose of every aspect of the church's life is to proclaim, teach, and extend the way of God, the way of life and well-being, in and over the lives of God's people, on behalf of God's beloved world. God gives and calls God's servants to witness to that love, in words acted out in deeds and deeds interpreted by words, in the world. The constitutive factors in the koinonia of the apostolic church were "the apostles' teaching…, the breaking of bread and the prayers" (Acts 2:42), preaching/teaching the gospel, the sacraments, and prayer. Prayer is as much a means of grace as baptism or the breaking of bread, because it is not only our turning to God, but God's approach to us and a mode through which God accomplishes God's purposes.

The term "means of grace" rejects two alternative interpretations of the habitual practices of the church. The means of grace are not legalistic requirements that we must meet in order to cajole God into loving us. That is a "works-righteous" interpretation. Our ultimate salvation does not hinge on whether or not, or in what way, we participate in the means of grace. Nor is salvation limited only to members of the church. To refer to these practices as means of grace also repudiates the overly spiritualized notion that such things as bread, wine, and water intrude into our relation to God. God is immediately active and present in the means of grace, because God, who acts in the present, is the ground and end of all being and therefore present to us "in, with and under," as Luther said, any and all actualities.

---

[1]Paul Tillich, *Systematic Theology,* vol. 3, 188–92.

How Many?

There is no reason to limit the means of grace. "The world is charged with the grandeur of God."[2] Anything or anyone may be a means of grace (even a book in systematic theology!) provided we receive it as such. God created and continues to create the world. "And God said," says Genesis, and John continues: "All things came into being through" the Word. Because the world is word of, is worded by, the word of God, anything or anyone may be a means of grace. The church selects some to be means of grace in a stricter sense because they re-present the good news of Jesus Christ. So the word, written and oral (preaching, teaching, conversing), is a means of grace, as are baptism in the name of the Trinity, the breaking of bread, and prayer in the name of Christ. The Holy Spirit, God's Spirit, is active in the means of grace (as the Spirit is active everywhere) through which we experience the Holy Spirit.

For centuries particular sacraments were defended on the grounds that they had been "instituted" by Jesus of Nazareth. Roman Catholics argued that when Jesus told his disciples to feed his sheep, he instituted ordination to the priesthood as a sacrament. Disciples of Christ referred baptism to the great commission (Mt. 28:18–20), which is understood as Jesus' institution of it. It is not likely, given the present state of New Testament scholarship, that Jesus instituted any sacrament. As Alfred Loisy put it: "Jesus foretold the Kingdom, and it was the Church that came."[3]

The churches have also determined the number of means of grace somewhat arbitrarily. The Roman Catholic church counts seven sacraments. The Reformers reduced the number to two. They did this by arguing that only those acts of the church could be called sacraments that had been (a) clearly instituted by Christ and that (b) entailed both a promise of Christ (the good news) and a material element (bread, wine, water). Only baptism and the breaking of bread met these criteria. Most Protestant churches officially observe two means of grace.

---

[2]Gerard Manley Hopkins, *The Poems of Gerard Manley Hopkins,* ed. W. H. Gardner and N. H. MacKenzie (New York: Oxford University Press, 1967), 66.

[3]Alfred Loisy, *The Gospel and the Church,* trans. C. Home (New York: Charles Scribner's Sons, 1909), 4.

There are difficulties with this decision. First, in reducing the means of grace from seven to two, Protestantism lost what the church in 1,500 years of experience had gained: a way to bless every crisis point in the life cycle of a person. Whatever their "official" positions, in the life of the churches many things function as means of grace. Second, as Loisy indicates, biblical scholarship questions the idea that Jesus "instituted" any sacraments. It is equally clear that Jesus instructed his disciples to do many things other than practice baptism and the Lord's supper: to teach, to pray, to love the neighbor, to go into all the world, all of which are means of grace. So are things that he apparently did not command, such as hymn-singing and conversation or building a house for the poor. Perhaps we should say that there is no definite limit to the church's means of grace, but that some, particularly baptism and the eucharist, must always be practiced. So also, however, must others: preaching, teaching, and meeting the needs of "the least of these."

What makes the breaking of bread and baptism constitutive factors in the life of the church is their meaning, not our ability to determine with precision when and where they originated. From early on they have been part of the life of the church, but observance of them (as well as the form of that observance) developed at different speeds in different times and places. Baptism and the breaking of bread are means of grace because they express, in the form of action, the central content of the gospel, and because they are connected to the church's witness to the significance of Jesus Christ. God's love is concretely re-presented in the breaking of bread and baptism, which are actions of continuing divine grace.

The Word as Means of Grace

Preaching and teaching the gospel are means of grace. Preaching is the self-disclosure of God's love graciously offered to each and all and, therefore, commanding that justice be done to each and all in the form of an announcement. This announcement can only be appropriated in faith; it confronts us with the necessity of deciding whether we will understand ourselves in any ultimate sense in terms of, and only in terms of, God's love freely offered to us. The announcement of the word of God in preaching is its objective character; its appropriation in faith is its subjective side. An excessively objective view of the means of grace downplays the necessity that they be received in faith. An exclusively subjective view conceals the objective reality of God's grace. Because we all are both justified and yet sinners, *simul iustus et peccator,* this word bears repeating. We can take it to heart as a new and fresh word every time we hear it. Good preaching always includes both announcement (*kerygma*) and teaching (*didache*).

Lively preaching of the gospel tells us who God is, who Jesus Christ is, who we are, and how through the witness of the church we come to understand ourselves truly in relation to God, Jesus Christ, and the neighbor. It helps us think about what we are given and called to do in the actual context of our lives here and now. When we hear the gospel properly, we hear it as the voice of God speaking to us.

The word as a means of grace is a trustworthy and living word. It is trustworthy because it speaks of the faithfulness of God, who is the God of a singular promise and a singular command, the promise of God's grace lovingly offered and the command to love God with all our selves and our neighbors as ourselves, thus fulfilling all the law. It encapsulates the structure of biblical faith, the structure of promise and command, the indicative (what God has done for us) and the imperative (therefore what we are to do). It is a living and lively word. It lives in preaching and teaching, in oral tradition and conversation.

The task of preaching is to make the word of God pertinent to each generation–to interpret the new events, problems, insights, the context of that generation–in the light of the word and to reinterpret the Christian tradition in the light of the contemporary context. Lively preaching contributes to blessing and well-being by helping Christians deal with the questions and challenges of life in this time and place. To preach well is to do practical theology well. The good news for the preacher is that the Holy Spirit is at work on the minds and hearts of the congregation to help them receive the word of preaching. This is no reason not to do the job well, but it explains why God can work with preaching that is not perfect. Since no preaching is perfect, this is good news.

Christian preaching is rooted in scripture as witness to God's self-disclosure in the history of Israel, the Torah, the prophets, and, definitively, in Jesus Christ. Preaching has a three-fold responsibility to scripture, of which the first is exegesis. Preaching should enable listeners to understand the biblical text by grasping the question to which the text is an answer. What did this text mean to those who first wrote and first heard or read it? Second is that of interpretation. How do we so understand the text as to enable us to address some critical question we face in our context? The meaning of the text has to be translated into an appropriate and understandable message to the contemporary congregation. Third is application. What are we to do? Lively preaching relates the meaning of the text to the contemporary situations, personal and social, with which the hearers are confronted.

Both the promise of God's love (gospel) and the command that justice be done (law) must be interpreted anew—as to what they entail—in each generation. For example, the church is now coming to realize that God's gracious love for each and all includes women among the "all," and that doing justice to women includes affirming their right to be liberated, to be regarded and treated as self-determining, self-constituting persons, not defined and determined by males as objects of male perception and action. Preaching helps the community figure out what steps it needs to take next as it walks the way of life through the thickets of the complex present.

A discussion on the word of God as means of grace is incomplete without reference to the Hebrew Bible. The "scriptures," which is the New Testament word for the canonical writings of Israel (which the New Testament regarded as authoritative), are every bit as much word of God as are the apostolic writings. Wherever in the history of the church the connection between the two was severed, as in Gnosticism and Marcionism, the relation of redemption to creation and to history was also dissolved, resulting in radical misinterpretations of both.

The task of preaching is one of the most important responsibilities facing a parish pastor. Here we do our most basic job of caring for the congregation. Preaching gives the church an opportunity to look at life from a Christian perspective, rather than through the lens provided by television talk-shows, hate radio, or consumerism. It furnishes the preacher with an opportunity to reframe all the contemporary issues in the light of the Christian witness. It is a chance to tell the truth, to invite people into that "sane asylum" that the church ought to be, a community where we can talk sense with each other about who God is, who we are, who the neighbor is, how we ought to live, and to do so in clear distinction from the prevailing pablum that passes for standard fare in the culture.

Baptism as Means of Grace

Preaching "announces" the gospel of Jesus Christ. Baptism and the eucharist dramatically "act out" the same meaning to which preaching gives expression. The Protestant tradition gives us a useful set of terms with which to articulate the similarity and difference between preaching, on the one hand, and baptism and the eucharist on the other. Preaching is an "invisible word" (*verbum invisibile*). Baptism and the eucharist are "visible words." We hear the gospel preached. In baptism and the eucharist, we see it reenacted. Each is a visible word (*verbum visibile*).

To say that baptism and the eucharist are means of grace is to deny the claim that without them God's grace cannot be communicated nor God's love apprehended. As with everything else connected with God's grace, the means of grace are a gift. We may not turn the free gift of God's unconditional love into a condition apart from which God is not free to love. Their significance lies in the fact that in them the central core of the gospel meets us in a concentrated way in the form of an act. In baptism and the eucharist the word is seen, felt in the waters of baptism, tasted on the tongue, smelled, and dramatized, acted out with verbal accompaniment.

Traditionally, baptism has been the initiating sacrament, the breaking of bread the renewing sacrament. Baptism introduces us into the covenant that God renews with us in the supper. Paul interprets baptism as incorporation. He identifies the baptism of believers with that of Jesus at his crucifixion:

> Do you not know that all of us who have been baptized into Christ Jesus were baptized into his death? Therefore we have been buried with him by baptism into death, so that, just as Christ was raised from the dead by the glory of the Father, so we too might walk in newness of life. (Rom. 6:3–4)

The gift of baptism confers on a person a new identity and a new community. The baptized, by being baptized into Christ (1 Cor. 1:13; Gal. 3:27), receive a new identity.

Baptism is self-involving; it entails the individual's yes-saying to God's grace. But it is not individualistic. It does not leave the individual isolated, but welcomed and placed in a new community. It is not accidental that Paul refers to baptism when addressing believers at Corinth about their quarrels and dissensions (1 Cor. 1:10–17). Believers constitute one body, because they are baptized into one body. Paul rejects the notion that individual gifts or behaviors influence only the life of an individual.

Baptism is no mere rite of initiation. Rather, it marks a radical break in the life of the believer. Growth and maturity occur after baptism, which is an incorporation into the body of Christ, those actual relationships of mutual love and well-being that we call the church. Since a person is always a person-in-relation-to-other-persons, this incorporation has profound implications for who we are.

Traditionally, various churches have appealed to the New Testament for confirmation of their baptismal practices. Whatever the New Testament actually says, it has been made both to affirm and deny every controverted point about baptism. The true picture is more complex. Both believing adults and children seem to have been baptized in the early church (Acts 2:39; 10:23–48, etc.). Whole households are said to have been baptized, and households included people of all ages. Nor is the mode of baptism utterly clear in the New Testament. The verb *baptizein* has connotations of immersing, but we cannot conclude from this what the actual practice was. In a number of matters, we find references to a variety of practices (Acts 10:44–48; 11:15–18; 8:14–17). Some disciples of Jesus practiced the baptism of John (Acts 19:1–7) and some practiced proxy baptism on behalf of the dead (1 Cor. 15:29). On one thing, matters are clear: The New Testament is far more interested in what baptism means about new life than it is in the age of the candidate or the manner of baptism.

Baptism, said Alexander Campbell, is a "pardon-certifying," not a "pardon-procuring" ordinance.[4] In baptism, the good news of God's gracious love, spoken in the word, is here acted out, a verbum visibile. The point of baptism has everything to do with God's grace and our faith as the appropriate response to that grace. Baptism stresses both poles of the gospel: the gift of God's gracious love and our yes-saying to it by way of response.

Infant or Believers' Baptism? Twin Dangers

The Reformers agreed that because baptism symbolizes death and resurrection, immersion is the preferable form for baptism. Immersion of a repentant believer is important, because faith (saying yes to God's grace) is also symbolized by baptism. Yet, neither Luther nor Calvin required believers' baptism and both allowed and practiced infant baptism, because the presence of faith in the candidate does not "make" the baptism, but "receives" it. Baptism

---

[4]Quoted in Williamson, *Baptism: Embodiment of the Gospel* (St. Louis: Christian Board of Publication, 1987), 36.

depends on God's gracious promise. To withhold baptism from children on the basis of their lack of faith would imply that the good news of God in Jesus Christ depends on our ability to receive it, which would be justification by works all over again. Infant baptism evinces the unmerited grace of God.

The strengths of Calvin and Luther are obvious, particularly in the ways in which they interpret baptism in relation to the gospel. Their weaknesses are two. First, it is unclear how an infant receives a means of grace in faith or witnesses to its faith before the congregation. Second, neither Luther nor Calvin really challenged Christendom and its union of church and state. Infant baptism in the context of a state-supported church meant that everybody born in a country was automatically baptized. The church tended to lose its distinction from and capacity to witness to the surrounding culture. The twentieth-century discussion of baptism arose in this context.

Theologically, the danger of believers' baptism is works-righteousness. By stressing the importance of faith or the necessity of being baptized in the correct form, advocates of believers' baptism can fall headlong into works-righteousness. As a member of a denomination that practices believers' baptism, I know whereof I speak. The corresponding danger of infant baptism is cheap grace. When infants are indiscriminately baptized and teaching and Christian nurture are neglected, we have the problem presented to us by the Nazis and the Holocaust: All the Nazi leaders were baptized Christians and died in good standing in their churches. All the killers in Auschwitz were baptized Christians. Karl Barth began his lectures on baptism during the Holocaust by stating: "The present distress of the church–often enough bemoaned–may well be connected with the fact that up to now she has devoted to this question of order all too little attention..."[5] The misfortune of infant baptism has been that throughout much of Christian history it has been compromised by the establishment of the church and by the fact of virtually indiscriminate baptism of a whole citizenry. When this happens, something else also develops: the theological inability of the church to be a light to the Gentiles. A United Methodist minister and theologian comments:

---

[5]Karl Barth, *The Teaching of the Church Regarding Baptism* (London: SCM, 1948), 36–37.

The meaning of the Holocaust for Christians is at least this: when the baptized betray their baptism, when those who have been grafted into history flee back out of history, when the "new men" and "new women" in Christ cast off the new life and become part of the dying age again, the "old Israel" is left alone as the sign that the God who is God yet rules.[6]

However, there is no necessary connection between infant baptism and the state church of Christendom. Nor is it the case that the mere practice of believers' baptism guarantees that those practicing it will avoid falling into their own form of culture religion. This has been the fate of many such churches in North America. The lesson is that practitioners of either infant or believers' baptism must pay careful attention to the further growth and development of baptized Christians in their understanding and living of the Christian life in the community of the church. If we do not, baptism will be nothing more than a familial, cultural ritual that marks either the birth or adolescence of a person. Perhaps they will return to church later in life to be married and subsequently to be buried.

Yet, being part of the body of Christ means more than showing up only when one needs to be "hatched, matched, or dispatched." All churches, and particularly those that baptize infants, must "guard themselves against the practice of apparently indiscriminate baptism and take more seriously their responsibility for the nurture of baptized children to mature commitment to Christ."[7] Believers' baptism churches are challenged to "express more visibly the fact that children are placed under the protection of God's grace."

Ethically, baptism is the ritual of inclusion or solidarity. In baptism, people are publicly declared to be loved by God regardless of race, class, or gender. Baptism holds up to view the fact that all human beings are created in God's image, loved by God, and are the neighbors whom God has given us to love. Here, the category of "neighbor" includes the stranger, who comes in her differentness and with the questions that strangers in their differences always raise. In baptism, we enter into covenant with God and one another and begin to grow in acceptance of the claim that the covenant makes upon us. We become morally responsible to and for one another.

---

[6]Franklin H. Littell, *The Crucifixion of the Jews* (New York: Harper & Row, 1975), 79.

[7]*Baptism, Eucharist and Ministry* (Geneva: World Council of Churches, 1982), Faith and Order Paper No. 111, 6.

Contemporary congregations face several problems with regard to baptism. Panic over declining numbers and concern for "church growth" raises the temptation of engaging in indiscriminate absorption of large segments of society with too little attention to Christian nurture and education. Among many believers' baptism traditions, the liturgy for baptism is in atrocious condition. Often baptism is perfunctorily stuck into a service of worship that otherwise ignores it. If baptism is as important as such churches say it is, they should make that importance clear in their celebration of it. Again, in believers' baptism churches, our provision for Christian education prior to baptism is markedly uneven, often consisting of nothing more than a handful of pastors' classes or a weekend "lock-in" event, a good sign that things are not being taken seriously.

In baptism, the church constitutes itself. If the church is so to constitute itself as to be able to make a witness to the world, it will attend to the discipline of baptism. Like the people Israel, the church is given and called to be a light to the nations. Its life of blessing and well-being is not to be hoarded, but shared with the world. This, however, is not possible if the church does not constitute itself as such a witnessing community. Herein is found the importance of paying attention to the practice of either baptizing repentant believers and nurturing them into a mature life of faith or seeing to the Christian nurture and maturation of those baptized as infants.

The Breaking of Bread as a Means of Grace

The breaking of bread as a means of grace conveys the self-bestowal of God's love—the identical love met with in the word as announcement—in the form of action. The function of the sacraments is the same as that of preaching. They confirm and proclaim the promise of God to be gracious. They are not means of grace in the sense that the grace of God is exclusively channeled through them. They make visible and confirm what is given to us by the grace of God.

Grace is what God is. It is God's free and unfailing resolve to be for and with all God's creatures, even us, despite our failures to be for God and for the neighbor. Grace is not one attribute of God among others (such as wrath) with which it alternates. It is God acting out of God's deepest being. This grace is the cause of faith, and we encounter grace (or God) in the word of God and in the other means of grace. The sacraments are God's gracious gift to us of God's presence.

"Realistic" and "symbolic" interpretations of the sacraments are misconceptions that live in a parasitic symbiosis with each other. Realism interprets God's grace as a substance that works in a physical way below personal relationships and appropriation by faith. Calling the eucharist a "medicine" is an example of this. The gift received in the sacrament is something other and less than God's personal self-disclosure. The "symbolic" (simple memorial) view arose chiefly to deny the realistic view. By saying that in the eucharist all that happens is that we "remember" Christ, we deny his living presence. The symbolic view rightly reminds us that the bread and wine are bread and wine, not something else. But it errs in placing all the emphasis on our remembering. The breaking of bread loses its character as divine gift and grace. The realistic and symbolic views unite in obscuring the presence of the living Christ.

Christians affirm that Jesus Christ is present at the Lord's supper because they trust his promise to be with them. "Where two or three are gathered in my name, I am there among them" (Mt. 18:20). An old rule for understanding scripture reminds us to pay attention to prepositions, personal pronouns, and the tenses of verbs. The words of institution indicate the speaker: "my," as in "This is my body." The tense is the present: "is." When we hear the words of institution appropriately, we hear them as said to us now by the living Christ. Jesus Christ now says to us what he said to the disciples long ago. He invites all the needy, including us, to his table. Christ is actively present in the breaking of bread as the One who gives us the grace of God. Christ is truly present at the supper as its host, wherever two or three are gathered in his name.

Some interpreters reduce the breaking of bread to a memorial of what once happened, a commemoration of Christ's death on the cross. This understanding contradicts the idea of *anamnesis* in the early church, according to which "remembrance" moves what happened in the past into the present as a living actuality. As Christ was present at the Last Supper and at the meals he shared with his disciples, so Christ in the Supper is present with his disciples "always, to the end of the age" (Mt. 28:20).

The many churches interpret the meaning of the breaking of bread in many different ways. These diverse interpretations are important only if they help us to clarify what is genuinely Christian. If they do so, they cease to be peculiar to separate churches and contribute to the richness of meaning available to all Christians.

How We Observe the Breaking of Bread

The form of the eucharist should reflect its meaning. Breaking the bread and pouring the wine act out what is intended.

As the form of baptism ideally should be that of immersion, expressing that the candidate is buried with Christ in death and raised with him to newness of life, so the form of the Lord's supper should express its meaning.

As to what kind of bread is used for the breaking of bread, we should not forget the strong link between it and the Passover meal celebrating God's liberation of Israel from bondage in Egypt. The bread of the supper represents also the bread that the Hebrew people ate in the exodus, the unleavened bread that had to be baked in haste. This is the bread of freedom, of liberation from every form of subjugation. Using unleavened bread and recalling the connection between the breaking of bread and liberation from all forms of enslavement would greatly enrich the meaning of the eucharist. When the bread of the eucharist loses its deeply biblical connotations, it is evacuated of its liberative meaning. The "bread of heaven" theme of the eucharistic discourse in John 6 recalls the manna given by God to the people in the wilderness, real bread that prevented real starvation. This bread is food and those who partake of it are commanded by God to respond to the needs of the hungry.

Ethics and the Breaking of Bread

There are many ethical implications of participating in the breaking of bread. Here we mention only two. The first is that people may not be barred from participating in the Lord's supper because they are members of the wrong race, age, class, ethnic group, or denomination, or have the wrong sexual orientation. In the Lord's supper we share in God's gracious gift to us and practice the open hospitality of Jesus, welcoming the stranger. It is self-contradictory to allow such forms of discrimination to rule our social, political, and economic arrangements in "the world" or in the church. The second is that we cannot be content with "spiritually" feeding the hunger of the soul, while allowing people to suffer from physical hunger, as though such hunger were not itself deeply spiritual. We must not forget that a major feature of Jesus' ministry was feeding the hungry, and that our earliest testimony to the eucharist shows that it was not a symbolic supper but the "full meal deal." We who celebrate the breaking of bread must see to feeding the hungry.

Another issue has to do with the question of children participating in the eucharist. In churches that baptize believers, not-yet-baptized children are typically excluded from participating in the breaking of bread. Postponing communion until after baptism was a defensible action in the early church. Then many people came in to the church from various surrounding cults. Lest these people think that Christianity was simply another version of something they already knew, considerable education had to take place prior to their being admitted to the eucharist. A reading of Paul's first letter to the Corinthians illustrates the point.

But when children participate in worship, Sunday school, and youth groups and are being responsibly educated in the Christian faith, such a restriction hardly seems necessary. The breaking of bread is a testimony to the welcome that Jesus unconditionally extends to all. It is where Christians most conspicuously practice the kind of open hospitality that characterized the praxis of Jesus. The open hospitality of the table should also include children.

Prayer as a Means of Grace

The gospel of Jesus Christ is announced and explicated in the preaching and teaching of the Word. The heart of the gospel is acted out in the visible words of baptism and the eucharist. The same gospel is re-presented to us in prayer, which is therefore a means of grace. Prayer calls our attention to God, to Jesus Christ, to the needs of the neighbor, and to our own needs. In prayer we praise God for God's great grace, give thanks to God for doing for us and for the world the things that only God can do, articulate our understanding of the neighbor and the neighbor's needs in prayers of intercession, and petition God for our own needs in petitionary prayer. Prayer, in short, represents to us the Christian understanding of God, the neighbor, and ourselves.

Prayer is addressed to the God to whom Jesus prayed, the God of Israel.[8] Christian prayer is always appropriately addressed to the One to whom Jesus prayed, in keeping with the old theological rule, "always pray directly to God" (*oratio semper dirigatur ad Patrem*).

---

[8]The best study of the relationship between the Lord's Prayer and Jewish prayer is *The Lord's Prayer and Jewish Prayer*, ed. Jacob J. Petuchowski and Michael Brooke (New York: The Seabury Press, 1978).

Christian prayer is offered to God "in the name of" Jesus Christ who presents Christians with the gracious call and total claim of the God of Israel.

The God of Israel is the covenantally related God of the Bible who "hears" the prayers of the people and responds to them (Ex. 2:24). Yahweh is not to be understood on the model of Aristotle's "unmoved mover" or on that of the utterly immutable and impassible God of too much of the Christian tradition. Nothing is as destructive of our desire to pray, to be in conversation with God, as the assumption that God neither is nor can be affected by anything that we say or perform or contemplate. "Prayer has no sense," comments Schubert Ogden, "unless God...is genuinely affected by all that we say and do."[9] If prayer is in any sense meaningful and neither an exercise in futility nor reducible to a form of autosuggestion, its "minimal condition" is that God can "hear" our prayer. God's love for us is not only outgoing and creative, but also receptive and responsive. "Our simplest actions, our most private thoughts, can matter to us because they matter to God. They make an everlasting contribution to the world preserved in God...This includes our prayers."[10]

God is our ultimate companion upon whom we may utterly rely and in whom we may place unconditional trust. We may rely on God to do for us everything that it is possible and appropriate for God to do for us, and we may trust God to enfold our lives into God's life where we will be everlastingly cherished and saved from being lost, forgotten, and condemned to transience and meaninglessness. Hence, we may pray to God confident that our prayers will be heard, that they will affect God, and that God will respond to them. This does not mean that God will give us the answer we want to receive. God responds to prayer in a manner appropriate to God's purposes for God's creatures and to the power of love that God exercises in the world. It does mean that God will give us the answer we need, if we are open to receiving it.

Why Pray?

We do not pray, as Luther said, to instruct God, but to instruct ourselves. Our "praying teaches us to recognize who we are and

---

[9]Schubert M. Ogden, *The Reality of God*, 67.

[10]Martha Graybeal Rowlett, *In Spirit and In Truth* (Nashville: The Upper Room, 1982), 139.

who God is, and to learn what we need and where we are to look for it and find it."[11] A wise pastor used to say that we do not pray to get God on our side, but to get ourselves on God's side. John Calvin pointed out that we need to "observe to what end the Lord instructed his people to pray, for he ordained it not so much for his own sake as for ours."[12] The Lord's Prayer begins with this petition: "Your kingdom come, your will be done on earth as it is in heaven" (Mt. 6:9–13). Norman Pittenger says this of prayer:

> Prayer is the intentional opening of human life to, the align-ment of human will with, and the direction of human desir-ing toward the cosmic Love that is deepest and highest in the world because it is the main thrust or drive through the world toward sharing and participation in genuine good– and hence toward the truest possible fulfillment of human personality as God wishes it to become.[13]

The problem that besets many of us with regard to prayer is that when we pray, the only thing we open is our mouths. The point of prayer is that we shall open our minds and hearts to God. Prayer is opening oneself to the leading of God's Spirit.

Prayer in Services of Worship

God as definitively revealed in Jesus Christ is the covenant-making Yahweh of the Bible, not the unmoved mover, but the most moved mover of the prophets and the rabbis. This God is the God of an extraordinary promise and an extraordinary command. The promise is that God's all-embracing love is freely offered to each and all and therefore also to us. The command is that in response to such radical and unfathomable love we are to love God with all our selves and our neighbors as ourselves.

The public function of prayer in public worship is to bear wit-ness before and to the congregation as to who God is, who Jesus Christ is, who the neighbor is, and who we are. Prayers of thanks-giving and doxology give voice to our understanding of God. We offer prayers of adoration or praise to God in thanksgiving for a radical love that gives purpose and meaning to our lives.

---

[11]Martin Luther, *Luther's Works*, vol. 21, ed. Jaroslav Pelikan (St. Louis: Concordia Publishing House, 1956), 143.

[12]John Calvin, *Institutes of the Christian Religion*, 852.

[13]Norman Pittenger, *Praying Today* (Grand Rapids: Eerdmans, 1974), 27.

Prayers of intercession express our understanding of the neighbor. To pray for the neighbor in need is to remind ourselves that the neighbor is someone given to us by God to love. It is one explicit way of loving the neighbor. Prayers of petition articulate our understanding of ourselves. They remind us of who we are in relation to God and what our needs are.[14]

We do not pray in order to call to God's attention something that might have escaped God's notice. Nor do we seek to persuade God to do something that God might otherwise have forgotten to undertake. God is always doing for us everything that it is possible and appropriate for God to do for us. God leaves up to us, God's covenant partners, to do for each other and ourselves all those things that are within our power to do for each other. Hence, the point of prayer in the church is to remind us of what the Christian faith teaches us about who God is, who the neighbor is, who we are, and what we ought to do. Prayer is another way of making the Christian witness, recalling to us that we are people who do not know how to pray as we ought. Prayer is a means of grace offered to us and for our benefit, through which we are redeemed from the unbelief that absentmindedly neglects to attend to the Christian understanding of God, the neighbor, and the person or community praying.

Public prayer is one of the clearest manifestations of the priesthood of all believers. The priesthood of all believers does not mean that we are all ordained clergy. It means that all of us are to be priests to one another, counselors of one another, those who can engage each other in conversation about matters of faith and life. So we pray in church to be reminded about what it means to be radically loved by God and claimed by God as those who are to love God with all our hearts and our neighbors as ourselves.

Praying and Doing Justice

"We do not know how to pray as we ought," said Paul, which is why "the Spirit aids us in our weakness" (Rom. 8:26). Asking God to do things that we are readily capable of doing is a good example of "not knowing how to pray as we ought." God is always doing for us everything that it is possible for God to do for us, such as love us. Praying for God's love, then, makes perfect sense, as long as we understand that asking for it is a condition of our receiving it, not of

---

[14]An excellent book on prayer is Marjorie Suchocki's *In God's Presence: Theological Reflections on Prayer* (St. Louis: Chalice Press, 1996).

God's offering it. Love is a strange kind of gift—it has to be wanted to be received.

Another way to not know how to pray is to fail to see the connection between praying and doing justice. A life of prayer divorced from a life committed to working for justice for the neighbor, a life spent in doing what the rabbis called "deeds of loving-kindness," is inauthentic. One major purpose of prayer is to make us more open to God's intent to convey blessing and well-being to God's creatures. A life of prayer requires accompaniment by a life of usefulness to the neighbor. A life of usefulness to the neighbor is a life of prayer, some moments of which we spend on our knees.

Consider the parable of the nagging widow and the unjust judge. Luke says that Jesus told this parable "about their need to pray always and not to lose heart" (Lk. 18:1–5). We cannot pray "always" if what that means is that we are to spend one hundred percent of our time in the posture of prayer. The only way to pray "always," "without ceasing," is if the larger pattern of our life is one in which we seek justice (as the widow did for herself). Paul makes the same point Jesus does when he says that how we present our living bodies, how we throw ourselves into the life of the world, is our "spiritual worship" (Rom. 12:1). We can only "persevere in prayer," as Romans 12 makes clear, if we do it in all those physical, mundane acts of loving-kindness that the needs of our neighbors so graciously afford us.

The Ministry as Means of Grace

The Holy Spirit calls the whole people of God to participate in the ministry of the church. God both entrusts all of us with this ministry and calls us to it. The whole people of God, the *laos*, is the fundamental bearer of ministry. All Christians have the ministry of testifying to the grace of God disclosed in Jesus Christ throughout the whole range of life's involvements. The people of God carry out ministry in deed and word, in work, service, witness, worship, and meeting the needs of "the least of these." Working for God's justice in the world, relieving suffering, struggling for peace, reconciling the estranged are all the heart of the ministry of God's people. Ministry belongs to the church as a whole. It does not trickle down from the clergy to the laity. It wells up from the laity to those whom they choose from among themselves to be clergy. Only in the context of the ministry of the whole people of God, the priesthood of all believers, can we comprehend ordination and the ordained ministry.

The term "re-presentative" is one that we have used quite a lot in this discussion of proclamation, baptism, the breaking of bread, and prayer. Each of these activities of the church re-presents, presents again, the good news of Jesus Christ. So the ministry of the people of God re-presents the ministry of Jesus Christ, in which all Christian ministry is grounded, to the church and to the world.

The ordained ministry re-presents to the people of God their own ministry. This way of defining the significance of the ordained ministry has the dual advantage of distinguishing it from the ministry of the whole people of God from which it derives, but doing so in a way that is nonhierarchical. Its further advantage is that it makes clear the self-contradiction involved in barring any group of laity, such as women, from participating in that ordained ministry that re-presents to them their own ministry.

Ordained ministers serve the church as representative ministers. The care of the churches is placed into their hands as they are entrusted with the role of servant-leadership in many of the activities of the church's witness. While no one would deny the importance some clergy express of experiencing God's calling of them to the ordained ministry, two points are worth noting. First, God calls all God's people to be ministers. Second, the responsibility of the people of God is to seek out and find for its ordained ministers those persons most able to carry out the tasks of ordained ministry.

Limitless as those tasks are, they share three basic features. Ministers are called to conform to God's commandment of love in service on behalf of others both in the church and in the world. They are to witness to the gospel of Jesus Christ through their preaching and teaching, through the habitual activities of the church in baptism and the eucharist, and in deeds of loving-kindness (service and mission). Theirs is the responsibility to oversee the congregation, the koinonia of the church, in pastoral care, education, witness, mission, worship, and the quality of its life together.

Ordained ministers are called to exercise genuine authority (not authoritarianism) in the life of the church. Jesus' rule that whoever would be first in the community must be servant of all applies here. Whoever would be pastor must be servant of all. The pastor serves God, Jesus Christ, and the good news and in so doing serves the well-being of the congregation.

The task of the representative minister is to "equip the saints," so to relate to the laity as to empower and enable them to carry out that fundamental ministry of the people of God that the ordained ministry represents. Ministers do this by preaching in ways that are authentically biblical, appropriate to the gospel, that make sense to the laity, and that address the context in which they have to live out their lives as Christians. Ministers do this by presiding over the worship and sacramental life of the church in ways that penetrate to the heart of the gospel and the heart of the believer.

Ministers equip the saints through their role as educators in the Christian faith. Education in the faith, coming to mature grips with it in relation to the questions, challenges, and issues of the time, is how most laity become adult, mature Christians. Education takes many forms, can be creative and enjoyable, and deals with many topics. When a suburban church youth group participates in building a house with Habitat for Humanity with a pastor who hammers nails along with them while explaining why Christians do this sort of thing, incredibly important and formative Christian education takes place. Never doing such a thing also conveys a powerful message. The rule is this: Everything we do teaches something to somebody. Everything, then, can be an occasion for making the teaching explicit and putting the words into action.

Ministers equip the saints through sound administration of the life of the church. Widely known for being as difficult as "herding cats," church administration requires patience, leadership, creativity, and vision. In his famous discussion of our spiritual worship as how we present our living bodies, how we throw them into the life of the community and the world, Paul listed administration as one major form of spiritual worship. Without creative and compassionate administration, the whole life of the church suffers.

Chapter 11

The Goal of the Way

Eschatology and the Life to Come

Eschatology derives from two Greek words: *eschaton*, meaning the end, and *logos*, meaning word, thought or thinking. Eschatology is thinking about the end, that is, the aim or goal of God's self-involvement with God's creatures. Its first topic is what Judaism calls "the days of the Messiah," that future state of this world when God's intent with God's creatures shall have been realized, when redemption shall have been accomplished. This is not "the end of the world" as so often luridly depicted. It is instead the end of the age dominated by the death-dealing ways of the world. It is the inauguration of the new age characterized by blessing and well-being, by the universal presence of shalom, by the end of all forms of oppression, by freedom from want, from hunger, from oppression, from fear, and from ignorance.

Its second topic is what Judaism calls "the world to come," our ultimate resurrected life in God beyond history. The point of eschatology in this sense is not to discourage engagement with the challenges and problems of this incompletely redeemed world, but

to provide reassurance that such engagement is ultimately important and inescapable. Any proper Christian understanding of
eschatology contradicts the claim that our ultimate salvation in God's
life undercuts our obligation to work for the redemption of the world
from all forms of subjugation.

Apocalyptic Language

Apocalyptic is a form of eschatology, a subcategory of it. It is
the Jewish or Christian hope for God's promised future expressed
in highly metaphorical and symbolic language. The four horsemen
of the Apocalypse (Rev. 6:1–8), drawn so powerfully by Albrecht
Dürer in a 1498 woodcut, illustrate the point. They are God's agents
of destruction. They come to bring conquest, war, famine, death,
and pestilence. As an end to Egypt's oppression of slaves could not
be accomplished because of Pharaoh's hardness of heart without
plague and destruction, neither can Rome be expected to go
peacefully.

The way to interpret such apparently fanciful language is not to
literalize it and take it either as an accurate picture of how the world
will end or to take it as a key with which to interpret the entire world
scene at the present. The interpretive insight is to note that the author of Revelation used metaphorical language to deal with the harsh
political realities of his time. God will bring an end to Roman oppression, but do not expect Caesar to go gently from the scene. He
will leave destruction in his wake. Yet the oppression will end.

We owe one of the more effective uses of which I am aware of
apocalyptic language in the twentieth century to Paul Tillich. In his
August, 1942, radio broadcast into Nazi Germany, Tillich dealt with
the recent air raids on the German cities of Cologne, Lübeck, Bremen,
Hamburg, and Mainz.[1] His topic was "the fire that rains from
heaven." He said:

> ...when we read of the four horsemen, who, according to
> the book of Revelation, would ride along over the world–
> war, hunger, fire, pestilence–we took that for poetry, and a
> worthy object of a great picture; but we were too far re-
> moved from that to take it for reality. Now it has become
> a reality! The four horsemen of destruction are raging

---

[1]See Paul Tillich, *Against the Third Reich,* ed. Ronald H. Stone and Matthew
Lon Weaver (Louisville: Westminster John Knox Press, 1998), 146–50.

throughout Europe and the entire world, and fire is raining from heaven in ever-fresh streams. The conception of the end will not be realized in human memory until Europe, and particularly Germany, is reduced to a heap of ruins.[2]

As we saw in our discussion of Jesus in the context of the Roman Empire, we here need to remember: Apocalyptic language is a way of seriously engaging real history.

Eschatology in the Practice of Jesus

All the synoptic gospels describe Jesus' ministry in summary statements as "preaching the gospel of God" (Mk. 1:14), "preaching the gospel of the kingdom" (Mt. 4:23; 9:35), "preaching the good news of the kingdom of God" (Lk. 4:43; 8:1; 16:16). The key term is the "rule, reign or *basileia*, kingdom of God." Mark defines Jesus' proclamation of the gospel in terms of "the kingdom of God": "The time is fulfilled, and the kingdom of God has come near; repent, and believe in the good news" (Mk. 1:15). This sentence contains the main features of Jesus' proclamation and practice.

"The kingdom of God has come near" (Mk. 1:15; Mt. 10:7; Lk. 21:31). "The kingdom of God" refers to the obvious rule of God whose government will bring to an end the history of the world *as we know it* and will bring judgment on it (Mt. 10:15//Lk. 10:12; Mt. 24:37–44//Lk. 17:26–36). The basileia is at hand; it will come within the lifetime of Jesus' own generation (Mk. 9:1; 13:28–30; Mt. 10:23). Therefore, "the poor" are blessed, because they belong to this coming realm (Lk. 6:20//Mt. 5:3), when God will put right all injustices (Lk. 16:19–31; 18:7f.; Mt. 23:33). This is the gospel to "the poor" (Mt. 11:5//Lk. 7:22; Lk. 4:18). Jesus teaches his disciples to pray "your kingdom come" (Mt. 6:10//Lk. 11:2).

The soon-to-come rule of God sharpens the challenge of Jesus' preaching to the point of crisis. In the light of God's coming rule, people must decide and decide now, without delay. The note of warning sounds loud and clear in the parables of crisis: the parable(s) of the absent householder, for whose return the servants must be prepared (Mk. 13:34–36; Lk. 12:36–38; Mt. 24:42, 45–51//Lk. 12:42–46); the parable about the thief in the night (Mt. 24:43f.//Lk. 12:39f.),

---

[2]Ibid., 47.

and the parable of the five wise and the five foolish virgins (Mt. 25:1–12).

That Jesus' expectations did not unfold, at least in the way the texts seem clearly to anticipate, has always been a problem for Christian theology. A writer later in the first century asked: "Where is the promise of his coming? For ever since our ancestors died, all things continue as they were from the beginning of creation" (2 Pet. 3:4). It is not an acceptable solution to this problem to ignore or deny the imminent expectation of the kingdom in Jesus' preaching. To do that is to set to one side, as relatively unimportant, the plight of "the poor" and "the least of these" for whom and with whom Jesus exercised his ministry. At the same time, even more extraordinary was Jesus' proclamation that the rule of God was in some way already being realized through his ministry.

"The time is fulfilled." Jesus also proclaimed that the rule of God, with its promise of blessing and well-being, was already manifesting itself through his words and actions. The cherished hope for the "days of the Messiah" or messianic age or reign of God was already coming to pass (Mt. 11:5//Lk. 7:22; Mt. 11:11//Lk. 7:28; Mt. 11:12//Lk. 16:16, etc.). "But blessed are your eyes, for they see, and your ears, for they hear. Truly I tell you, many prophets and righteous people longed to see what you see, but did not see it, and to hear what you hear, but did not hear it" (Mt. 13:16f.//Lk. 10:23f.).

Parables containing the note of fulfillment (instead of future expectation) are those of the wedding feast (Mk. 2:18), new patches on old garments and new wine in old wineskins (Mk. 2:21f.), the treasure hidden in the field and the pearl of great value (Mt. 13:44–46), and the end-time harvest (Mt. 9:37f.//Lk. 10:2).

The tension in Jesus' preaching between hope already fulfilled and the imminence of what-is-not-yet is a problem for theology. It is most simply resolved (perhaps) by recognizing a close link between the two in Jesus' mission. The certainty that the eventual rule of God was already operative in and through his ministry brought with it the conviction that its full revelation could not long be delayed. Yet, it was and still is.

"Repent, and believe in the gospel." The response Jesus sought for can be summed up in two words: repent and believe. Repentance is stressed in several places (Mt. 11:21//Lk. 10:13; Mt. 12:41//Lk. 11:32; Lk. 13:3–5; 15:7–10; 16:30). Here Jesus looks for a radical turn-around of the basic direction of the lives of his hearers and their attitudes (see the parable of the prodigal son [Lk. 15:17] and the story of the rich young man [Mk. 10:17–31] and Zacchaeus [Lk. 19:8]).

The other side of this trust in God is faith. The object of faith here is, the texts often emphasize, not Jesus alone but God working through Jesus to bring God's future.

The offer that Jesus held out to repentance and faith was that of participation in the eschatological rule of God and its blessings: "Blessed are you who are poor, for yours is the kingdom of God" (Lk. 6:20; Mt. 5:3). This contrasted with Caesar's rule, of which no one said to the poor: "Yours is the kingdom of Caesar." This included the blessings of forgiveness and acceptance, an offer presented in several parables, those of the huge debt, the unmerciful debtor, the parable of the two debtors, the Pharisee and the tax collector, and the prodigal son. In the feeding stories, Jesus embodied this acceptance by including all the "lost sheep of the house of Israel" within the scope of his movement and fed them real food. This free and open eating expressed the heart of his message, for these meals were the foretaste of the messianic banquet of the new age (Lk. 14:13, 16–24). See Mark 2:17: "I have come to call not the righteous [to the feast] but sinners."

The ethical corollary of Jesus' message and ministry is both personal and social. Personally, sinners were invited to repent, to return to the God of Israel, whose message and mission were actualized in the life and ministry of Jesus. Communally, this turning entailed becoming involved in an inclusive, egalitarian movement that featured free healing, free hospitality, free and open eating, and a free welcome to the stranger. The great commandment, "You shall love the Lord with all your heart…, You shall love your neighbor as yourself" (Mk. 12:28–31), was the hallmark of the Jesus movement. Anything that hindered the expression of that love was to be set aside.

Israel's Hope

Ever since Abraham and Sarah were called forth from Ur of the Chaldees (Gen. 12:1–3), biblical hope has always been a hope that responded to God's promise of inclusive well-being and a hope of a people on the way. The earliest church understood itself as a people "of the Way" (Acts 9:2). Throughout the Bible, God's will for God's creatures is articulated with the metaphor of the "way" that we are called to walk. Revelation, torah, scripture all provide light for the way and a lamp for the feet of the faithful as they try to walk the way of life and avoid the way of death.

God's way has a goal. Israel used a variety of images for this goal, some referring to a goal that is within history and some to a goal beyond history. Later in its life Israel would name these two goals, respectively, "the days of the Messiah" and "the world to come." The "days of the Messiah" have to do with that future, anticipated time when peace and righteousness reign over all the world. The world to come refers to what we might call a "heavenly condition."

The basic term for the goal of the way is "redemption." Redemption is both this-worldly (these days we call it "liberation") and ultimate, in which case it signifies our conclusive salvation by God not only from oppression but also from sin, finitude, death, ignorance [idolatry], and transience—simply succumbing to the passing of time. "Resurrection" by God into the richness of God's life is the term for this second meaning of redemption. God is the Redeemer who liberated Israel from slavery in Egypt, and this Redeemer God is also the Creator who will ultimately redeem Israel and all the world. Redemption is the completion of creation.

Israel's hope has always been primarily social. It has been for the salvation of the people Israel, of all people, and even that the lion would lie down with the lamb and the desert burst into bloom (Isa. 11). This hope remains stubbornly historical. Concern for ultimate salvation never minimizes hope for the emancipation of people and nature from oppression. Rather, confidence in ultimate salvation reassures us that action directed at accomplishing concrete hopes for peace and justice is ultimately important. It is ultimately important because it is important to the God who is ultimate.

The pillars of Israel's faith are God, the covenant sealed in the Torah, and the people Israel. Israel never forgets the covenant in its hope. God's covenant partners are called upon to do everything appropriate to finite covenant partners. Bringing about concrete historical redemption is tiring work, but God "gives power to the faint, and strengthens the powerless" (Isa. 40:29). God's covenant partners are called upon to do what God gives and empowers them to do. If the nuclear and environmental threats to all life on earth, human and nonhuman, are to be dealt with, it will not be done "over our heads."

Coupled with the hope for Israel has always been a universal hope, that all the world would come to know and serve God and adopt the "way of life" and reject the "way of death." All this historical hope is called "the days of the Messiah." Jewish messianic hope focuses more on the conditions of the messianic age than on the figure of the Messiah.

The resurrection of the dead has been an important part of Israel's hope from Pharisaic times to the present, not as the central form of individualistic hope, as has so often been the case with the church, but as an expression of each faithful Jew's hope of participating in the future redemption of the world. From as early as God's question to Ezekiel about the valley of dry bones, "Mortal, can these bones live?" (Ezek. 37:3), resurrection was a way of talking about the restoration of the people Israel: "Thus says the Lord GOD: I am going to open your graves, and bring you up from your graves, O my people; and I will bring you back to the land of Israel" (Ezek. 37:12). Resurrection is God's answer to the problem of exile and oppression, the reconstruction of the people Israel in the land of Israel. The crisis of exile was no more solved in the time of Jesus, when Jews in Israel lived under the occupation of Caesar, than in the time of Ezekiel and the Babylonian exile. We cannot divorce resurrection from the this-worldly hope of Israel in God's promised redemption.

With the hope of Israel comes understanding oneself as part of a people on the way. Redemption lies out ahead; creation is far from complete. Israel hopes as a people on the move, whose history is going toward the fulfillment of God's promises to God's world that God gave through the torah and the prophets. The story is not over; we are in the middle of it. The persistence of this hope in spite of the actual course of history, and all too often in spite of persecution from the church, (in the form of forced baptism, population expulsion, pogrom, legal, political, and economic sanctions enacted against Jews by councils of the church), presents us with a rugged witness of faith before which we can only stand in wonder. Here is an example of what the doctrine of decisive revelation can do for you: Jewish hope has rested in the confidence that one single historical event, the exodus/Sinai complex, revealed the final truth about reality and about the nature and will of God, in spite of all other historical evidence to the contrary.[3]

This quick overview of Israel's hope is presented with the conviction that it can help us in our conversation about our hope and

---

[3]See Irving Greenberg, "Judaism and History," in *Perspectives in Jewish Learning*, ed. S. Kazan and N. Stampfer (Chicago: The University of Chicago Press, 1977), 43–45.

with the suggestion that we cannot stop praying and working for the peace of Jerusalem and all the world and for the speedy coming of God's redemption.

The Church's Hope

The beginning of the church's hope is grounded in Jewish hope. Jesus' message and ministry as presented in the gospels was of the fulfillment of what every faithful Jew wanted: God's intention that his creatures enjoy life and well-being was being actualized in the midst of Roman oppression. Jesus in his praxis of the rule of God foreshadowed the fuller and future coming of God's kingdom and also gave evidence of what that kingdom was already like in the here and now. The early church's confidence that Jesus was the decisive first act in the drama of God's liberation complicated matters so far as Jewish forms of hope were concerned.

Early on, eschatological hope seems to have claimed that Jesus had come, been crucified and raised, exalted and affirmed by God, and would shortly return to initiate the next era of history. "Truly I tell you, this generation will not pass away until all these things have taken place" (Mk. 13:30). Paul, who had preached this same message to the church in Thessalonica, had to explain to his congregation there "about those who have died" (1 Thess. 4:13), but nonetheless went on to assert that "the day of the Lord will come like a thief in the night" (5:2).

The point forced upon us by these two statements is that we may never properly separate claims about Jesus Christ from talk of that future redemption that remains to be accomplished. To the extent that we neglect eschatology, to that same extent we neglect to notice the absence of shalom, of justice, of equality, of hunger from the world. To neglect eschatology is to fail to notice the massive absence of redemption from the world's experience.

Eschatology and the Heart of the Gospel

There is no way for the Christian witness to be appropriate to the gospel of Jesus Christ unless the church understands and articulates that gospel eschatologically. The gospel of Jesus Christ proclaims the gift of the love of God graciously offered to each and all and the command that we love God with all our selves and our neighbors as ourselves and, therefore, seek to do justice to them. We cannot understand ourselves in relation to the gospel without actively working to liberate the neighbor from oppression. Yet sober experience and prophetic/eschatological awareness remind us that the "way of death" and not the "way of life" is still the rule of human history. Indeed, the Bible ends on this very note in the book of Revelation, written for an oppressed and persecuted community, in an eschatologically climactic vision of the new Jerusalem in which there will be no more death (Rev. 21).

Further, the prophetic/eschatological faith of the Bible and the ministry of Jesus in which this faith eventuates is always critical of contemporary social, political, and economic arrangements. Such faith always envisages larger and more inclusive communities of love (*agape*) and justice. Jesus not only preached the coming and present reign of God; he also practiced it in the movement that he led. A church that neglects eschatology also neglects the widow and the orphan, the least of these, those excluded from the benefits of society by the power arrangements that favor the influential, the very ones to whom Jesus went—the lost sheep of this world.

In the Bible there is a dialectic of love and justice. Too much preaching of love manages to empty it of all significance by neglecting its dialectical relation to justice. We are by God's grace given and empowered to love our neighbors as ourselves and thereby do justice to them, because we have first been loved. Love makes justice or greater justice possible. At the same time, a proactive approach to issues of justice (characteristic of the bulk of the biblical witness) knows that comparatively greater achievements of justice make possible more love. The more barriers between people can be broken down, the more possible it is for them to love each other. The more the powers-that-be want to prevent people from liking each other, the more they find it necessary to erect barriers between them (see, e.g., the church's making of ghettos for Jews mandatory by the Synod of Breslau in 1267 or Pope Paul IV [1555–1559]). Justice, on the Christian understanding, is the social form of love.[4] Love is always social; love is a social term. Justice is the form that love takes. To talk otherwise is self-contradictory or empty.

---

[4]See, e.g., Paul Tillich, *Love, Power, and Justice* (Oxford: Oxford University Press, 1954).

God as understood in scripture is the Triune One who interacts with all others, who effects all others and is affected by all others. God who is creative-responsive love is also the love that calls us forward into God's future. God called Abraham and Sarah out of the security of Ur into the risky insecurity of God's future, onto a way, chasing after a promise. God called the church out of all the peoples of the world and out of the securities of idolatry into the challenge of faith. Faith in the God of the Bible is openness to God's future. The Bible envisages alternative futures: the way of life and well-being or the way of death. We are given and commanded to choose the way of life and well-being.

Hence, eschatology and covenantal responsibility cannot be detached from each other. While it is God's promise and our hope that God will not ultimately be defeated and that the way of life will result in redemption for all, including those "whom we have loved long since and lost awhile," this does not obviate our moral responsibility. Our choices are moral, at least in part, because they make a difference to the future. The church, in its essential nature, is a sign to the world of an alternative possibility, of a way of living in shalom with each other and with God's good world.

God's purpose is the reconciliation of all God's creatures with God, with themselves, with each other. God will never cease from God's quest for universal reconciliation. Jesus in his ministry opposed and overcame the tendency to draw lines between the insiders and the outsiders of God's people. Paul opposed the tendency to draw lines between the insiders and the outsiders of God's house and understood the work of Christ, in part, as reconciliation, as breaking down the walls of division between Jews and Gentiles, Greeks and barbarians, slaves and the free, women and men. It is the saddest observation to have to make that the church, in its history, managed to reinstate all these divisions. Remembering, however, that the reign of God is ahead of us forces us to recognize that God is not done with the church, and that scripture testifies to a New Jerusalem when all will know the Lord, and there will be no more church. There will be no metal folding chairs in the New Jerusalem.

Eschatology and Christology

Eschatology emphasizes that Jews and Christians, in their disagreement about whether Jesus is the Messiah (the anointed one, the Christ), are both right. This statement is not paradoxical, although admittedly it seems to be. For the people Israel, there is no such thing as the coming of the Messiah without the coming of the "days of the Messiah," the era of liberation, shalom, blessing, and well-being for all peoples and creatures. The daily newspaper with its abundance of atrocity stories about famine, war, pestilence, and fire indicates that despite Jesus' having come we still live in what Paul called "the sufferings of this present time" (Rom. 8:18). For the early church and because that church kept alive the authentic hopes of Israel, the only way to affirm that Jesus was the Messiah was in the context of a lively expectation that he would come again in his "second coming" or *parousia* (see Mt. 13:24–30 or the parables of watchfulness). As long as the eager hope for Jesus' return to finish the messianic task of transforming the world was kept alive, Christian hope shared with Jewish hope the expectation that the Messiah was yet to come or yet to come again.

As the eschatological hope for real, this-worldly change slowly faded from importance in the church, Jesus' practice of the kingdom with its orientation to what still lies ahead of us was increasingly forgotten. Instead, all history "before Christ" was interpreted as the period of the fall, and the church's history after Christ itself became the new era hoped for and "predicted" by the history and prophets of Israel. The second coming of Jesus was reinterpreted as happening at the end of history when the judgment is made on all people as to their ultimate destiny in either heaven or hell. Scriptural eschatology faded from the scene (some of the effects of this are described in the following). The idea began to take hold that the biblical story is all about a new religion, ours, and how we, the church and the Christian era, somehow replace the kingdom of God. Instead of worrying about why the swords and nuclear armaments are not yet beaten into plowshares, why the instruments of death have not been turned into tools for well-being, Israel ought to "get religion" by converting to Christianity. The end, the goal, of God's dealings with the world has already happened, and Jews missed it.

An appropriate understanding of biblical eschatology rejects this point of view. Jesus' entire praxis was lived out in spirited anticipation of the coming of God's basileia, God's rule of blessing and well-being, into this world of death-dealing oppression, into "the sufferings of this present time." "To reaffirm Jesus' hope in his name," says Rosemary Ruether,

> is not to be able to claim that in Jesus this hope has already happened, albeit in invisible form. Nor does it mean that it is only in his name that this hope can be proclaimed. It is

simply to say that, for those who were caught up with him in that lively expectation, it is now in his memory that they reaffirm his hope.[5]

Setting christology in an eschatological framework reminds us that God's self-disclosure in Jesus Christ's practice and life was neither the last nor the next-to-last act in the divine-human drama. Everything that God was up to in blessing God's creatures with life and well-being was not wrapped up and exhausted in Jesus Christ. He is not the concluding event in the eschatological story. In him we encounter in an anticipatory way that future that God still holds out ahead of all God's creatures, including Jews and Christians. The meaning of Jesus' life and praxis is ahead of us, not yet fully disclosed.

The gospels of Mark and Matthew acutely maintain this eschatological context for understanding the life and praxis of Jesus. At the Last Supper, Jesus says: "I will never again drink of the fruit of the vine until that day when I drink it new in the kingdom of God" (Mk. 14:25; Mt. 26:29). The event of Jesus Christ stands to us parallel to the event of the exodus. The exodus hopes for liberation remain ahead of us; all people are not yet free from being ground underfoot by the pharaohs of the world. In Christ we have a foretaste of God's reign. We have some ideas for what it will be like, enough to know that to whatever extent it was actualized in the life of Jesus, nonetheless, by his own testimony it awaits us in the future.

The Fading of Eschatology in the Church

Early church attitudes toward the eschaton went through several stages. The stages, roughly, are these: First, a this-worldly eschatology that remained keenly aware that the job of redemption was not finished and awaited Jesus' imminent return, his parousia, so that he could finish it. Second, chiliastic literalism (the soon-anticipated return of Jesus and his 1,000-year reign, with alternatives on this scenario in terms of pre- and post-millenarian versions; the final conflict of Armageddon will occur before or after the reign of Jesus). Third, a decided cooling-off of apocalyptic fervor; this can be seen in Luke/Acts and the gospel of John (3:36, "Whoever believes in the Son *has* [present tense] eternal life").

---

[5]Rosemary Ruether, *Faith and Fratricide* (New York: The Seabury Press, 1974), 249.

Similarly, in Judaism in the late first century the Pharisee who is credited with reestablishing Judaism without the temple, Johanan ben Zakkai, is quoted as saying: "When you are planting a sapling and someone comes and tells you 'the Messiah has arrived,' first finish planting your tree and then go and greet the Messiah." In the church, eschatological-apocalyptic fervor waned and/or was discouraged but was never officially disavowed. For the early church, the non-occurrence of the parousia gave rise to alternative interpretations. For the eschaton, Luke/Acts substitutes the spread of the church around the Roman Empire; for John, being faithful *is* to have eternal life now.

By the fifth century, the church is established and its situation is that referred to as "Christendom." Augustine's *City of God* is a non-apocalyptic book with an apocalyptic title (see Rev. 21). The "kingdom" of God increasingly becomes identified with the spread of the Catholic church over the face of the earth.

The eschatological tension in the faith of the early church faded and disappeared. It became privatized and was reduced to the ultimate salvation of individuals in heaven. Even the afterlife was brought under the church's bureaucratic control. Limbo and purgatory were added to heaven and hell. Limbo was ostensibly the place to which the souls of unbaptized children went. Purgatory was the spot for those neither bad enough for hell nor good enough for heaven; there they were "purged" of their venial sins. By the sixteenth century, the indulgence-peddler Tetzel, whose excesses jump-started the Reformation, typified those who sold "indulgences," which allowed persons to move the souls of those in limbo or purgatory into heaven.

As the Holy Spirit was squeezed out of the tightly bureaucratic church, so the expected reign of God was forced to live outside mainstream church life. The "spirit" movements in the church kept alive the vision of an alternative future that would be God's future and that criticized the church's growing complicity in the power-arrangements of this world. The lively expectation of the kingdom of God was kept alive among the radical monastic groups who fled from the world in the church, such as the medieval Franciscans and Joachim de Fiore with his three ages of the Father, Son, and Spirit; and later in the Reformation era with the Münsterites, whom Luther accused of "swallowing the Holy Spirit feathers and all."

In the modern world, hope (an indispensable character of all movements that seek to liberate people from oppression) was kept alive by secular forces: August Comte with his three ages (like

Joachim de Fiore) of religion, metaphysics, and science, or Karl Marx with his secularized version of biblical eschatology that held out for the "classless society" as a this-worldly future and secular substitute for the kingdom of God.

Modern criticisms of Christian hope are chiefly focused in the writings of Karl Marx, which have been taken seriously by theologians such as Paul Tillich, Reinhold Niebuhr, and more recently the political theologians, Latin American liberation theologians, and African American theologians. When Christians allow their hope to be interpreted in ways that are easily falsified (all those predictions of the end of the world by next Thursday at noon, after which there is the usual recalculation), and when this is combined with the privatization of religion (Jesus is my individual passport to heaven and nothing more), this-worldly hopes leave the church and become revolutionary or utopian.

Marx's "classless society" is a this-worldly kingdom of God without God. That Marx and his doctrine could arise and flourish is a trenchant judgment on the failures of the church to keep alive the hope that Jesus offered to the destitute, the hungry, and those who mourn. Marx rightly regarded the bourgeois form of Christian hope, the promise to the poor and oppressed that the justice that should be theirs on earth would be given to them in heaven, as "the opium of the people." We should note that when he called religion the opiate of the people, he did so in a context not usually quoted: "Religious suffering is at the same time an *expression* of real suffering and a *protest* against real suffering. Religion is the sigh of the oppressed creature, the sentiment of a heartless world, and the soul of soulless conditions. It is the *opium* of the people."[6] To say this is not to agree with Karl Marx. Far from it, it is to say that, had the church remained faithful to its eschatological vision, Karl Marx could never have gained an audience.

The Days of the Messiah

We talk of one pole of eschatology, the ultimate or everlasting pole, as "heaven" or "eternal life." The other pole has to do with the future of and in this world. This pole is what Jews call "the days of the Messiah" or what Christians refer to as "the kingdom of God" or

---

[6]Karl Marx, "The Critique of Hegel's Philosophy of Right," in *Karl Marx: Early Writings*, ed. T. B. Bottomore (New York: McGraw-Hill, 1963), 43–44.

the "New Jerusalem" come down from heaven to earth. These terms refer to the future of this world when the world will be different from what it is now, not "another world," but "this world, other" than it is, a future time when there will be no more oppression, manipulation, war, economic deprivation, racism, sexism, or religious narrow-mindedness. An adequate eschatology must include both emphases.

It would be a catastrophic mistake were the future of this world the only way in which eschatological matters were discussed. Just as any proper theology must affirm that trust in ultimate salvation reinforces commitment to work for the "mending of the world" and thereby deny what is meant by other-worldliness, so it must also deny that salvation is limited to liberation from oppression in this world. What seems to be going on when this limitation is put into effect, whether consciously or unconsciously, is that the doctrine of ultimate salvation is dismissed because certain authors do not or cannot figure out how to make sense of it. That is not a question to be avoided. Let us suggest that we make sense of it by understanding all such statements as statements about God and God's love for us.

What is wrong with reducing or limiting salvation to liberation from this-worldly oppression? There are at least three answers to that question. First, if salvation is totally this-worldly, arriving only in some future state of emancipation from oppression, then all those who die without being liberated are not saved, but damned. Visiting a cemetery in which slaves are buried in unmarked graves brings some sobriety into our theology. So does a trip to the Children's Memorial at Yad Vashem, where the one and a half million Jewish children slaughtered by the Nazis are memorialized. Experiencing bereavement at the death of one's own young child does the same. In such moments the words "salvation is exclusively this-worldly" turn to ashes in one's mouth. That salvation or liberation is solely this-worldly is a bad joke chanted over the graves of those who died oppressed.

Second, on any realistic assessment of human history, we will never arrive at a utopian state of total liberation. The liberated will never be any more than liberated sinners, who will find new groups to oppress. History is terribly instructive in this regard. After the church exited from its period of oppression at the hands of the Roman Empire, it took all of three years to request the emperor to use force to put down the Donatists. In so short a time, the oppressed become the oppressors. Our projections of future ideals are the projections of finite, ignorant, and sinful people and, if they come to pass, will generate new groups seeking liberation from this new oppression. For example, the enthusiastic supporters of Jacksonian democracy in the nineteenth-century United States were quite heedless of the rights of native Americans, whom they promptly set off on the Trail of Tears.

Third, utterly this-worldly movements for change, unsupported by any understanding of how God acts not only to emancipate but ultimately to redeem, will either fail to understand how their energy for change is renewed in the face of repeated failure or will run out of gas. For these reasons and for the coherence of Christian theology, therefore, while affirming the necessity of our engaging in the this-worldly effort to liberate our neighbors from oppression, we simultaneously deny that such efforts can be coherently detached from the divine promise and Christian hope of eternal, ultimate salvation.

Deprivatized, Political Eschatology

We best understand the this-worldly pole of eschatology by de-privatizing eschatology and interpreting it politically. Deprivatizing means exactly what it says: Eschatology reminds us that salvation is both ultimate, because this world is not our final home (rather, the loving grace of God is our final home), and proximate; this world, other than it is now, is one goal of the way of life that is committed to work and witness on behalf of God's intent that all God's creatures be blessed with well-being. While salvation is deeply personal, it is never merely private; persons are profoundly social. No one is finally saved until all are saved.

Interpreting eschatology politically means several things. First, we should accept the fact that we will not bring in utopia and try instead to make incremental gains in justice, reconciliation, equal-ity, liberty, and sustainability. What Jewish theology calls the task of "mending the world" (*tikkun olam*) is an infinite task which we are given and empowered to take up by God. We may neither fail to take it up nor expect to complete it. Proximate, realizable images of hope are critically important. Can we farm in such a way as to avoid losing two bushels of topsoil for every bushel of grain harvested? Can we eat more simply (sufficiently lower on the food chain) to ease the stress on the land and allow the poor to simply eat? Could we revive the biblical ethic of eating? Could we live more simply so that others could simply live? Could we organize adequate public transportation and thus reduce some of the air pollution and global warming for which we are responsible? Could we North Americans develop an ethic of making do with less so that others might make do at all? Need it be so difficult to arrange our employment procedures as to open them to all, equally, without regard to race or gender? Must interreligious relations be governed, at worst, by hostility, at best by benign neglect, and always by a smug sense of our superiority? Can we see the significance to God's good creation of planting trees and tending the garden in which we have been placed? Could a rural church concern itself with the situation of migrant workers, with the education of their children, and with their living conditions?

"Our problem" in these regards, said John Cobb, "is not that we believe too much but that we do not believe enough. We must cease to be afraid to be thought fools for Christ's sake."[7]

All Christians need to recognize that how we use our language and talk about our world largely conditions how we see it. A major pastoral task is to teach the congregation how to talk, as Christians, about the urgent issues facing the church and the world in the only context in which we live. Or will we concede to the powers-that-be, the corporations, the advertisers, and the false needs of a consumerist society the prerogative of setting the terms of the discussion?

Deprivatizing and political interpretation mean that we practice the hermeneutics of both suspicion and trust on social, economic, and political systems and practice it consistently. That is, we cannot just subject other people to suspicion and invest total trust in ourselves. There are two names for that: "self-deception" and "false consciousness." The lesson of the hermeneutics of suspicion is that all forms of systemic oppression are interlinked. No progress on issues of oppression according to race, gender, economic class, ideology, religion, or ethnicity will be made as long as these issues and those advocating them are alienated from one another.

Ultimate Salvation

The other pole of eschatology has to do with ultimate or everlasting salvation. Typically, it is discussed with the use of such images

---

[7]John B. Cobb, Jr., *Christ in a Pluralistic Age* (Philadelphia: Westminster Press, 1975), 181.

as the last judgment, eternal life, heaven and hell, and the resurrection of the dead. Against the temptation to literalize any or all of these images, a temptation to which the church has too often succumbed in its history, we need to remember the cautions Jesus uttered against pretending to know more than is given us to know. In his reported dispute with some Sadducees, their literalism about marital relations is denied (Mk. 12:18–28//Mt. 22:23–33; and Lk. 30:27–40). And he reminds his followers that of "that day or hour no one knows, neither the angels in heaven, nor the Son, but only the Father" (Mk. 13:32 //Mt. 24:36).

The question that eschatology, with regard to this "ultimate" pole of eschatology, asks and answers is a limit or existential question (what a limit question is was discussed in the beginning of the chapter on the doctrine of creation). Eschatological statements are not scientific or pseudoscientific predictions about how the world will end. An existential question is a question that arises in one field of endeavor or discourse but cannot but answered within the terms of that field of endeavor or discourse. For example, "Why be moral?" is a question that cannot be answered by moral reflection except by begging the question and saying something like, "Because you ought to!"

The eschatological question is such a limit question. It arises within a realization of the ambivalence of history, looks into the depths of the historical situation (what Paul called "the agony of this present age"), and asks: Why be moral? Why love my neighbor as myself? What difference does it make, or will it make, when or if we will all be blown away in a nuclear blast or slowly killed off by environmental collapse or when the earth is burnt to a crisp when the sun goes nova? A limit or existential question is a request for reassurance, for an answer that says "Yes, you, your life, and how you live it, ultimately matter."

Answers to such questions are theological; the questions that theology answers are limit or existential questions. Theological statements are statements of the Christian faith about the ultimate significance of life. By way of reminder, in referring to theological statements as existential, I do not mean that they are reducible to statements about human beings. I mean that theological statements are statements about how we understand ourselves in relation to God, to the neighbor, to ourselves, to the world in which we live, and that therefore they are also statements about how we should live in a world that we so understand. Existential statements are theological (they are about God), ethical, and self-involving.

The triune God is the One to whom you and what you do and what happens to you matters. This is so because the God of the Bible is no impassible absolute (an increasingly quaint-looking nineteenth-century way of speaking of God), but the One who not only effects all others but is affected by all others. God is always God "for us" and God "with us" (*Immanuel*). One of the more typical promises that the God of the Bible in "steadfast love" (*hesed*) for us makes is that God will always be "with us," no matter what–even in the valley of the shadow of death (Ps. 23) and to the end of the age ("And remember, I am with you always, to the end of the age"–Mt. 28:20). God is the One who has the final word on the meaning and significance of our lives and who raises us into God's life.

Here, we face one of those options where, according to William James, we have a "right to believe," a right to choose what to believe. What our ultimate end (destiny) will be is not a matter that can be empirically confirmed or disconfirmed or logically validated or denied. Whatever we believe is a matter of choice, and we are forced to choose, to decide. Which decision we make is a matter of momentous importance, because we either choose to wear about ourselves a mantle of doom or one of ultimate confidence that allows us to dismiss some kinds of fear ("perfect love casts out fear"– 1 Jn. 4:18). There is an ethical consequence of our choice, because to decide to believe in the ultimate victory of God's love over death, transience, and nihilism undergirds and makes sense of our moral life, whereas the alternative denies that how we live our lives makes any ultimate difference. So the option is between believing that God's loving grace will triumph, or believing quite the opposite, that it will not. If we take our clues about ultimate reality and what is ultimately real from the decisive revelation of God in Jesus Christ, we will choose one way.

Symbols, Images, and Metaphors

Symbols, images, and metaphors of heaven, life after death, and the resurrected life are best understood as ways of talking about God rather than as knowledgeable statements about what we have not experienced. The point of an existential/ontological interpretation of eschatology is that God, who is perfectly related to all of

God's creatures, "presides over the world with a tender care that nothing be lost."[8] In the world of finite reality, we are all too much acquainted with both perishing and loss, but in God there is no perishing and no loss, and the passage of our present life into God's life "is not its death."[9] Eternal life is the gift of the God who is eternal, and hence the only One who can bestow such a gift on mortal creatures. Believing in this gift is fundamentally a matter of radical trust in God, not some spurious theory about our own purported "immortality" of which scripture knows nothing. Christians may confidently entrust our lives to God's care and keeping. There, in the bosom of Abraham as the old saying has it, God will continue to work transformatively with all of us justified sinners.[10]

We are taken into God's life, cherished by God, judged by the love of God that is a "consuming fire" (Heb. 12:28–29), and transformed into the image of God in which we are made. The good news about the judgment of God upon us, in traditional Christian symbolism, is that we are to be judged by Christ, who sits at the right hand of God. The one who judges us is the one who came that we might have life and, to that end, even died for us. According to the parable of the last judgment (Mt. 25:31–46), the one question that will be put to us is not whether we can adequately articulate the doctrine of the Trinity, but whether we fed the hungry, gave drink to the thirsty, clothed the naked, welcomed the stranger, visited the sick and those in prison. All our answers will be confessions of inadequacy at best, sin and failure at worst. But by God's astonishing grace, we will all be saved. The God of Jesus and of Israel does not turn away the needy.

All Will Be Well

We end where we began, with a quote from Julian of Norwich: All will be well. Dame Julian affirmed that all will be well and that for a good theological reason. "Although an earthly mother may possibly allow her child to perish, our heavenly Mother Jesus can never allow us who are his children to perish."[11] The Christian tradition has had difficulty concluding that, indeed, all will be well.

---

[8]Alfred North Whitehead, *Process and Reality: Corrected Edition,* 1978, 346.
[9]Ibid., 349.
[10]Marjorie Suchocki has made some striking proposals in this regard in her *The End of Evil* (Albany: SUNY Press, 1988).
[11]Julian of Norwich, *The Revelations of Divine Love,* anthologized in *Women and Religion,* ed. Elizabeth Clark and Herbert Richardson (New York: Harper & Row, 1977), 111.

The greater bulk of the tradition asserted that only some will be well. An unambiguous affirmation that God's loving grace will ultimately triumph has come from only a few thinkers in Christian history. Most have affirmed that human beings face a dual destiny and will be consigned either to heaven (life with God) or hell (life in alienation from God). Some give the power of ultimate decision-making to us in our good works or in their absence. We, they say, have the power to make the ultimate decision concerning our destiny. We have the last word in this matter. God does not.

For example, Chrysostom asserted that "the fires of hell have no end," that punishment is eternal, that justice requires that we all burn eternally, but that grace saves some from this fate. He confesses that this "burdensome message" disturbs him, but that nonetheless "*each man's work will become manifest.*"[12] Similarly, Augustine of Hippo, speaking of heaven, argued that "only the worthy will gain acceptance there," but that part of the joy of heaven would consist in our being aware "also of the eternal wretchedness of the damned."[13] Part of the well-being of the "worthy" will consist in their consciousness of the ill-being of their friends and neighbors. In this case, one wonders whether the "worthy" have attained to maturity in the Christian life.

To the contrary, Gregory of Nyssa argued:

> In due course evil will pass over into nonexistence; it will disappear utterly from the realm of existence. Divine and uncompounded goodness will encompass within itself every rational nature; no single being created by God will fail to achieve the kingdom of God.[14]

Origen, who defined the highest good as becoming "as far as possible like God," argued that humanity was initially created in God's image but that "the perfection of God's likeness was reserved for him at the consummation." In the end God will truly be "all in all" and there will "no longer be any contrast of good and evil, since evil nowhere exists."[15] "For to the Almighty," says Origen, "nothing is impossible."

---

[12]See Chrysostom's *Homilies on 1 Corinthians 9–13,* in *Documents in Early Christian Thought,* ed. Maurice Wiles and Mark Santer (Cambridge: Cambridge University Press, 1973), 251–56.

[13]Augustine, *City of God,* trans. Marcus Dodds (New York: The Modern Library, 1950), 864–67.

[14]Gregory of Nyssa, *Sermon on 1 Corinthians 15:28,* in Wiles and Santer, eds., *Documents in Early Christian Thought,* 257–59.

[15]Origen, *On First Principles,* book 3, chap. 6, secs. 1, 3–5 (London: 1936).

Augustine and Chrysostom operate with two different and mutually contradictory assumptions. One is a works/reward scheme according to which we get what we deserve. The other claims that no one deserves eternal life, yet that God arbitrarily selects some out of the mass of perdition (*massa perditionis*). Each assumption is theologically incoherent. The works-righteous assumption denies the heart of the gospel, that God graciously justifies the ungodly. The assumption that God's grace is arbitrary renders it capricious and denies that God is trustworthy. Faith, radical trust in God's constant, steadfast love, *hesed*, denies both assumptions.

Neither Chrysostom nor Augustine explains why God's love is to be understood as either powerless to overcome our sinfulness or capricious and not to be trusted. Nor does either account for how it is that Christ "suffered for sins once for all [not only for some], the righteous for the unrighteous, in order to bring you to God" (1 Pet. 3:18). The theological error is to deny what Paul "surely" affirms, namely that "the grace of God and the free gift in the grace of the one man, Jesus Christ, [have] abounded for the many" (Rom. 5:15). "So one man's act of righteousness leads to justification and life for all" (Rom. 5:18). Here is the theological choice: The revelation of God's grace in Christ either is or is not sufficient "once for all" to bring us to God. If we choose to say that it is not sufficient, then we should cease talking about grace. Should we wish to affirm God's grace, we shall have to let it be sufficient.

Our hope is in the love of God graciously made known to us in Jesus Christ. It is a hope for the whole person, and therefore for society and the earth. It is a hope in the all-inclusive love of God who embraces all in the scope of God's grace. It is hope for life with God, not merely individual life, but the social/communal life of God's realm, the great banquet with Jesus and all the saints. It is a radical confidence that all will be well because underneath are the everlasting arms.

The triune God who will ultimately redeem our lives from insignificance and transience is the same God who commands us to do works of love, to liberate the neighbor from oppression. God has self-disclosed God's self to us as a God of life, communal love, welcome, and well-being. God gives and empowers us to accept the option of life and well-being, to be a blessing to our neighbors and ourselves.

Bibliography

Abbott, Walter M., ed. *The Documents of Vatican II.* New York: Guild Press, 1966.

Achtemeier, Paul J. "*Omne verbum sonat:* The New Testament and the Oral Environment of Late Western Antiquity." *Journal of Biblical Literature* 109, no. 1 (1990): 3–27.

Adams, James Luther. "Tillich's Concept of the Protestant Era." In Paul Tillich, *The Protestant Era*, ed. James Luther Adams, 273–316. Chicago: The University of Chicago Press, 1948.

Aquinas, Thomas. *Summa Theologiae.* Ed. Fathers of the English Dominican Province. London: Oates and Washbourne, Ltd., 1914.

Athanasius. *On the Incarnation of the Word.* In *Christology of the Later Fathers*, vol. 3 of the Library of Christian Classics, ed. Edward Rochie Hardy, 55–110. Philadelphia: The Westminster Press, 1964.

Augustine of Hippo. *City of God.* Trans. Marcus Dodds. New York: The Modern Library, 1950.

———. *On Christian Doctrine.* Trans. D. W. Robertson, Jr. Indianapolis: Bobbs-Merrill, 1958.

———. *Saint Augustine: Treatises on Marriage and Other Subjects.* Ed. Roy J. DeFerrari. New York: Fathers of the Church, 1955.

Aulen, Gustaf. *The Faith of the Christian Church.* Philadelphia: Fortress Press, 1960.

Austin, Richard C. *Hope for the Land: Nature in the Bible.* Atlanta: John Knox Press, 1988.

Bammel, Ernst, and Moule, C. F. D., eds. *Jesus and the Politics of His Day.* Cambridge: Cambridge University Press, 1984.

Barnabas. *The Letter of Barnabas.* In *The Ante-Nicene Fathers*, vol. 1, 137–49. Grand Rapids: Eerdmans, 1979.

Barr, James. *The Scope and Authority of the Bible.* Philadelphia: The Westminster Press, 1980.

Barth, Karl. *Church Dogmatics.* Edinburgh: T. & T. Clark, 1956.

———. *The Teaching of the Church Regarding Baptism.* London: SCM Press, 1948.

Baum, Gregory. *Essays in Critical Theology.* Kansas City: Sheed & Ward, 1994.

Beardslee, William A. "Recent Hermeneutics and Process Thought." *Process Studies* 12, no. 2 (1982): 65–76.

Beck, Norman A. *Anti-Roman Cryptograms in the New Testament.* New York: Peter Lang, 1997.

Berquist, Jon L. Correspondence via e-mail, April 14, 1998.

Birch, Charles, and Cobb, John B., Jr. *The Liberation of Life.* Cambridge: Cambridge University Press, 1981.

Boers, Hendrikus. *Who Was Jesus?* San Francisco: Harper & Row, 1989.

Borg, Marcus. *Jesus, A New Vision: Spirit, Culture, and the Life of Discipleship.* San Francisco: Harper & Row, 1987.

————. *Meeting Jesus Again for the First Time.* San Francisco: Harper-SanFrancisco, 1994.

Brawley, Robert, ed. *Biblical Ethics and Homosexuality: Listening to Scripture.* Louisville: Westminster John Knox Press, 1996.

Brock, Rita Nakashima. *Journeys by Heart.* New York: Crossroad, 1988.

Brown, Delwin. *Boundaries of Our Habitations: Tradition and Theological Construction.* Albany, N.Y.: SUNY Press, 1994.

Brueggemann, Walter. *The Land: Place as Gift, Promise, and Challenge to Biblical Faith.* Overtures to Biblical Theology. Philadelphia: Fortress Press, 1977.

————. *A Social Reading of the Old Testament.* Ed. Patrick D. Miller. Minneapolis: Fortress Press, 1994.

Buber, Martin. *On Zion.* Trans. Stanley Godman. New York: Schocken Books, 1973.

Buechner, Frederick. *Now & Then.* San Francisco: HarperCollins, 1983.

Burnham, Frederic B., ed. *Postmodern Theology.* San Francisco: Harper & Row, 1989.

Calvin, John. *Institutes of the Christian Religion.* Ed. John T. McNeill. Trans. Ford Lewis Battles. Philadelphia: The Westminster Press, 1960.

Campbell, Joseph. *The Hero with a Thousand Faces.* Princeton: Princeton University Press, 1949.

Carr, Anne. *Transforming Grace.* San Francisco: Harper & Row, 1988.

Cassidy, Richard J. *Jesus, Politics, and Society: A Study of Luke's Gospel.* Maryknoll: Orbis Press, 1978.

Chrysostom, John. "Homily I Against the Jews." In *Jews and Christians in Antioch,* ed. Wayne A. Meeks and Robert L. Wilken. Missoula: Society of Biblical Literature, 1978.

Clark, Elizabeth A. *Women in the Early Church.* Collegeville, Minn.: The Liturgical Press, 1983.

————, and Richardson, Herbert, eds. *Women and Religion.* New York: Harper & Row, 1977.

Clebsch, William A. *Christianity in European History.* New York: Oxford University Press, 1979.

Cobb, John B., Jr. *Christ in a Pluralistic Age.* Philadelphia: The Westminster Press, 1975.

————. "Economism or Planetism: The Coming Choice." *Earth Ethics* 3 (Fall, 1991).

————. *Process Theology as Political Theology.* Philadelphia: Westminster Press, 1982.

————. *Sustainability.* Maryknoll, N.Y.: Orbis Books, 1992.

————. *Talking about God.* New York: Seabury Press, 1983.

Craddock, Fred. "How Does the New Testament Deal with the Issue of Homosexuality?" *Encounter* 40, no. 3 (1979): 197–208.

Cross, Theodore. *The Black Power Imperative.* New York: Faulkner Books, 1984.

Crossan, John Dominic. *Jesus: A Revolutionary Biography.* San Francisco: HarperCollins, 1993.

Cyril. *The Works of St. Cyril of Jerusalem.* Trans. Leo P. McCauley, S.J., and Stephenson, Anthony A. Washington: Catholic University of America Press, 1970.

Danby, Herbert, trans. *The Mishnah.* London: Oxford University Press, 1933.

Davis, Stephen T., ed. *Encountering Evil.* Atlanta: John Knox Press, 1981.

Dewey, John. "Time and Individuality." In *Philosophers of Process*, ed. Douglas Browning, 208–44. New York: Random House, 1965.

Dillenberger, John, ed. *Martin Luther: Selections from His Writings.* Garden City, N.Y.: Anchor Books, 1961.

Dulles, Avery. *Models of the Church.* Garden City, N.Y.: Doubleday & Co., 1974.

Dunn, James D. G. *Jesus, Paul and the Law.* Louisville: Westminster/John Knox Press, 1990.

————. *Unity and Diversity in the New Testament.* Philadelphia: Westminster Press, 1977.

Ebeling, Gerhard. *The Word of God and Tradition.* Philadelphia: Fortress Press, 1968.

Eckardt, A. Roy. *Reclaiming the Jesus of History: Christology Today.* Minneapolis: Fortress Press, 1992.

Edwards, Jonathan. *The Works of President Edwards.* 4 volumes. New York: Leavitt and Trow, 1843.

Erlich, Paul R., Sagan, Carl, et al. *The Cold and the Dark.* New York: W. W. Norton & Co., 1984.

Fackenheim, Emil. *To Mend the World.* New York: Schocken Books, 1984.

Farley, Edward. *Deep Symbols: Their Postmodern Effacement and Reclamation.* Valley Forge, Pa.: Trinity Press International, 1996.

————. *The Fragility of Knowledge.* Philadelphia: Fortress Press, 1988.

————, and Hodgson, Peter C. "Scripture and Tradition." In *Christian Theology: An Introduction to Its Traditions and Tasks*, ed. Peter C. Hodgson and Robert H. King, 61–87. Philadelphia: Fortress Press, 1985.

Fasching, Darrell J. *Narrative Theology after Auschwitz.* Minneapolis: Fortress Press, 1992.

Felix, Minucius. *The Octavius.* In *The Ante-Nicene Fathers*, vol. 4, 173–98. Grand Rapids: Eerdmans, 1979.

Flew, Antony, and MacIntyre, Alasdair. *New Essays in Philosophical Theology.* London: SCM Press, 1955.

Flusser, David. "A New Sensitivity in Judaism and the Christian Message." *Encounter Today* 5, no. 1 (Winter, 1970).

_____. "Jesus, His Ancestry, and the Commandment of Love." In *Jesus' Jewishness,* ed. James H. Charlesworth. New York: Crossroad, 1991.

Foucault, Michel. *The Archaeology of Knowledge.* Trans. A. M. Sheridan Smith. London: Tavistock, 1972.

Fredriksen, Paula. *From Jesus to Christ.* New Haven, Conn.: Yale University Press, 1988.

Gager, John. *The Origins of Anti-Semitism.* New York: Oxford University Press, 1983.

Gaventa, Beverly Roberts. "Romans." In *The Women's Bible Commentary,* ed. Carol A. Newsom and Sharon H. Ringe, 313–20. Louisville: Westminster/John Knox Press, 1992.

Geertz, Clifford. *The Interpretation of Cultures.* New York: Basic Books, 1973.

Gilkey, Langdon. "God." In *Christian Theology: An Introduction to Its Traditions and Tasks,* ed. Peter C. Hodgson and Robert H. King. Philadelphia: Fortress Press, 1985, 88–113.

_____. *How the Church Can Minister to the World Without Losing Itself.* New York: Harper & Row, 1964.

_____. *Message and Existence.* New York: Seabury Press, 1979.

_____. *Reaping the Whirlwind.* New York: Seabury Press, 1976.

Ginzberg, Louis. *The Legends of the Jews.* Vol. 1: *From the Creation to Jacob.* Philadelphia: Jewish Publication Society, 1909.

Grant, Robert M. *Gods and the One God.* Philadelphia: Westminster Press, 1986.

Greenberg, Irving. "Cloud of Smoke, Pillar of Fire: Judaism, Christianity, and Modernity after the Holocaust." In *Auschwitz: Beginning of a New Era?* ed. Eva Fleischner. New York: KTAV, 1977.

Gregory of Nyssa. *Catechetical Oration 37.* In *Documents in Early Christian Thought,* ed. Maurice Wiles and Mark Santer. Cambridge: Cambridge University Press, 1975, 194–96.

Gutierrez, Gustavo. *A Theology of Liberation.* Maryknoll: Orbis Books, 1983.

Hadden, Jeffrey. *The Gathering Storm in the Churches.* Garden City: Doubleday & Co., 1969.

Harnack, Adolf. *What Is Christianity?* Trans. Thomas Bailey Saunders. New York: Harper & Brothers, 1957.

Haroutunian, Joseph. *God With Us.* Philadelphia: Westminster Press, 1965.

Hartshorne, Charles. *The Divine Relativity.* New Haven: Yale University Press, 1948.

Hauerwas, Stanley. *A Community of Character.* Notre Dame: University of Notre Dame Press, 1981.

Hegel, Friedrich. *On Christianity: Early Theological Writings.* Trans. T. M. Knox. New York: Harper & Brothers, 1961.

Heschel, Susannah. "Anti-Judaism in Christian Feminist Theology." *Tikkun* 5, no. 3 (1990): 25–28.

_____. "The Denigration of Judaism as a Form of Christian Mission." In *A Mutual Witness,* ed. Clark M. Williamson. St. Louis: Chalice Press, 1992, 33–47.

Hick, John, and Hebblethwaite, Brian, eds. *Christianity and Other Religions.* Philadelphia: Fortress Press, 1980.

Hilberg, Raul. *The Destruction of the European Jews.* New York: Harper & Row, 1979.

Hopkins, Gerard Manley. *The Poems of Gerard Manley Hopkins.* Ed. W. H. Gardner and N. H. MacKenzie. New York: Oxford University Press, 1967.

Horsley, Richard A. *Jesus and the Spiral of Violence.* San Francisco: Harper, 1987.

Horsley, Richard A., and Hanson, John S. *Bandits, Prophets and Messiahs.* Minneapolis: Winston, 1985.

Hosinski, Thomas E. *Stubborn Fact and Creative Advance.* Lanham, Md.: Rowman & Littlefield, 1993.

Irigaray, Luce. *Sexes and Genealogies.* Trans. Gillian C. Gill. New York: Columbia University Press, 1933.

James, William. *Pragmatism.* Cleveland: World Publishing Co., 1955.

_____. *The Will To Believe.* New York: Dover Publications, 1956.

Janzen, J. Gerald. *Abraham and all the Families of the Earth: Genesis 12–50.* Grand Rapids: Eerdmans, 1993.

_____. *Exodus.* Westminster Bible Companion. Louisville: Westminster John Knox Press, 1997.

Jenson, Robert W. "The Triune God." In *Christian Dogmatics,* vol. 1, ed. Robert W. Jenson and Carl E. Braaten. Philadelphia: Fortress Press, 1984.

Johnson, Elizabeth A. *She Who Is: The Mystery of God in Feminist Theological Discourse.* New York: Crossroad, 1994.

Johnston, Carol. *And the Leaves of the Tree Are for the Healing of the Nations.* Louisville: Presbyterian Church (USA), Office of Environmental Justice, 1997.

Kant, Immanuel. *Religion Within The Limits of Reason Alone.* Trans. Theodore M. Greene and Hoyt H. Hudson. New York: Harper & Brothers, 1960.

_____. *"What Is Enlightenment?"* Trans. and ed. L. W. Beck. Chicago: University of Chicago Press, 1955.

Käsemann, Ernst. *Perspectives on Paul.* Trans. Margaret Kohl. Philadelphia: Fortress Press, 1971.

Kazan, S. and Stampfer, N., eds. *Perspectives in Jewish Learning.* Chicago: The University of Chicago Press, 1977.

Keck, Leander. *A Future for the Historical Jesus.* Nashville: Abingdon Press, 1971.

Kellenbach, Katharina von. *Anti-Judaism in Feminist Religious Writings.* Atlanta: Scholars Press, 1994.

Kelley, Dean M. *Why Conservative Churches Are Growing.* New York: Harper & Row, 1972.

Kelsey, David H. "The Theological Use of Scripture in Process Hermeneutics." *Process Studies* 13, no. 3 (1983): 181–88.

Knowles, Louis L., and Prewitt, Kenneth, eds. *Institutional Racism in America.* Englewood Cliffs, N. J.: Prentice-Hall, 1969.

Küng, Hans. *The Church.* New York: Image Books, 1976.

LaCugna, Catherine Mowry, ed. *Freeing Theology.* New York: HarperCollins, 1993.

————. *God For Us: The Trinity and Christian Life.* New York: HarperCollins, 1991.

————. "God in Communion with Us." In *Freeing Theology,* ed. Catherine Mowry LaCugna, 83–114. New York: HarperCollins, 1992.

Lamb, Matthew L. "Liberation Theology and Social Justice." In *Process Studies,* vol. 14, 1985.

Law, William. *A Serious Call to a Devout and Holy Life.* New York: Paulist Press, 1978.

Lee, Bernard J., ed. *The Becoming of the Church.* New York: Paulist Press, 1974.

————. *The Galilean Jewishness of Jesus.* New York: Paulist Press, 1988.

Leith, John, ed. *Creeds of the Churches.* Richmond: John Knox Press, 1973.

Levenson, Jon. *Creation and the Persistence of Evil.* San Francisco: Harper & Row, 1988.

————. *Sinai and Zion.* San Francisco: Harper & Row, 1985.

Lifton, Robert. *Boundaries: Psychological Man in Revolution.* New York: Vintage Books, 1970.

Littell, Franklin H. *The Crucifixion of the Jews.* New York: Harper & Row, 1975.

Lodahl, Michael. *Shekhinah/Spirit.* New York: Paulist Press, 1992.

Lohfink, Norbert F. *Option for the Poor.* Berkeley, Calif.: Bibal, 1986.

Loisy, Alfred. *The Gospel and the Church.* Trans. C. Home. New York: Charles Scribner's Son, 1909.

Lucas, George R. *Two Views of Freedom in Process Thought.* Missoula, Mont.: Scholars Press, 1979.

Lull, David J. "What Is 'Process Hermeneutics'?" *Process Studies* 13, no. 3 (1983): 189–201.

Luther, Martin. "On The Jews and Their Lies." In *Disputation and Dialogue,* ed. Frank E. Talmage, 34–36. New York: KTAV, 1975.

_____. *Martin Luther: Selections from His Writings.* Ed. John Dillenberger. Garden City, N.Y.: Anchor Books, 1961.

_____. *Luther's Works.* Ed. Harold J. Grimm and Helmut T. Lehmann. Philadelphia: Muhlenberg Press, 1957. Vols. 21, 31.

McDaniel, Jay B. *Earth, Sky, God and Mortals.* Mystic, Conn.: Twenty-Third Publications, 1990.

_____. *Of God and Pelicans.* Louisville: Westminster/John Knox Press, 1989.

McFague, Sallie. *Models of God.* Philadelphia: Fortress Press, 1987.

_____. *Super, Natural Christians.* Minneapolis: Fortress Press, 1997.

Macmurray, John. *Persons in Relation.* London: Faber and Faber, 1961.

Marty, Martin. *The Fire We Can Light.* Garden City: Doubleday & Co., 1973.

Marx, Karl. *Karl Marx: Early Writings.* Trans. T. B. Bottomore. New York: McGraw-Hill, 1963.

Meier, John P. "Reflections on Jesus-of-History Research Today." In *Jesus' Jewishness,* ed. James H. Charlesworth. New York: Crossroad, 1991.

Meland, Bernard. *Fallible Forms and Symbols.* Philadelphia: Fortress Press, 1976.

Merchant, Carolyn. *The Death of Nature: Women, Ecology, and the Scientific Revolution.* San Francisco: Harper & Row, 1980.

Michaelsen, Robert, and Roof, Wade Clark, eds. *Liberal Protestantism: Realities and Possibilities.* New York: Pilgrim Press, 1986.

Migliore, Daniel L. *Faith Seeking Understanding.* Grand Rapids: Eerdmans, 1991.

Montefiore, C. G., and Loewe, H., eds. *A Rabbinic Anthology.* New York: Schocken Books, 1974.

Moore, George Foot. *Judaism in the First Centuries of the Christian Era.* 3 vols. Cambridge: Harvard University Press, 1927–1930.

Morse, Christopher. *Not Every Spirit: A Dogmatics of Christian Disbelief.* Valley Forge: Trinity Press International, 1994.

Myrdal, Gunnar. *An American Dilemma.* New York: Harper & Row, 1964.

Neusner, Jacob. *A Rabbi Talks with Jesus.* New York: Doubleday, 1992.

_____. *From Politics to Piety.* Englewood Cliffs, N.J.: Prentice-Hall, 1973.

_____, trans. *Torah from Our Sages: Pirke Avot.* Dallas: Rossell Books, 1984.

Neville, Robert C. *The High Road around Modernism.* Albany, N.Y.: SUNY Press, 1992.

_____. *A Theology Primer.* Albany, N.Y.: SUNY Press, 1991.

Niebuhr, H. Richard. *Christ and Culture.* New York: Harper & Brothers, 1951.

_____. *The Meaning of Revelation.* New York: Macmillan, 1941.

_____. *The Social Sources of Denominationalism.* New York: Meridian Books, 1957.

Oakman, Douglas E. *Jesus and the Economic Questions of His Day.* Lewiston, N.Y.: Mellen, 1986.

Ogden, Schubert M. *Faith and Freedom.* Nashville: Abingdon Press, 1989.

_____. *Is There Only One True Religion Or Are There Many?* Dallas: Southern Methodist University Press, 1992.

_____. "The Metaphysics of Faith and Justice." *Process Studies* 14 (1985): 87–101.

_____. *On Theology.* San Francisco: Harper & Row, 1986.

_____. *The Reality of God.* New York: Harper & Row, 1966.

_____. "Toward a New Theism." In *Process Philosophy and Christian Thought,* ed. Delwin Brown, Ralph E. James, Jr., and Gene Reeves, 173–87. Indianapolis: Bobbs-Merrill, 1971.

Pagels, Elaine. *The Origin of Satan.* New York: Vintage Books, 1995.

Paris, Peter J. "The Social World of the Black Church." *The Drew Gateway* 52, no. 3 (Spring, 1982).

Pelikan, Jaroslav. *The Emergence of the Christian Tradition (100–600).* Chicago: The University of Chicago Press, 1971.

_____. *Jesus Through the Centuries.* New Haven: Yale University Press, 1985.

_____. *The Vindication of Tradition.* New Haven: Yale University Press, 1984.

Perdue, Leo. *Wisdom and Creation.* Nashville: Abingdon Press, 1994.

Perrin, Norman. *Rediscovering the Teaching of Jesus.* New York: Harper & Row, 1976.

Petuchowski, Jacob J., ed. and Brooke, Michael. *The Lord's Prayer and Jewish Prayer.* New York: The Seabury Press, 1978.

Pittenger, Norman. *Praying Today.* Grand Rapids: Eerdmans, 1974.

Placher, William. *Narratives of a Vulnerable God.* Louisville: Westminster/ John Knox Press, 1994.

Plaskow, Judith. "Christian Feminism and Anti-Judaism." *Cross Currents* 28 (1978): 306–9.

_____. *Standing Again at Sinai.* San Francisco: Harper & Row, 1989.

Rad, Gerhard von. *Moses.* New York: Association Press, 1959.

Ramsay, Ian T. *Religious Language.* London: SCM Press Ltd., 1957.

Rivkin, Ellis. *What Crucified Jesus?* Nashville: Abingdon Press, 1984.

Roetzel, Calvin J. *The World That Shaped the New Testament.* Atlanta: John Knox, 1985.

Roof, Wade Clark, and McKinney, William. *American Mainline Religion: Its Changing Shape and Future.* New Brunswick, N.J.: Rutgers University Press, 1987.

Rowlett, Martha Graybeal. *In Spirit and In Truth.* Nashville: The Upper Room, 1982.

Ruether, Rosemary Radford. *Faith and Fratricide.* New York: The Seabury Press, 1974.

_____. *Sexism and God-Talk.* Boston: Beacon Press, 1983.

Runciman, Steven. *A History of the Crusades,* vol. 1. Cambridge: Cambridge University Press, 1951.

Russell, Letty M. *Human Liberation in a Feminist Perspective: A Theology.* Philadelphia: Westminster Press, 1974.

Sanders, E. P. *Paul, the Law, and the Jewish People.* Philadelphia: Fortress Press, 1983.

Sanders, James A. *Canon and Community.* Philadelphia: Fortress Press, 1984.

Sanhedrin, Babylonian Talmud.

Santer, Mark, and Wiles, Maurice, eds. *Documents in Early Christian Thought.* Cambridge: Cambridge University Press, 1973.

Schiffman, Lawrence H. *Texts and Traditions: A Source Reader for the Study of Second Temple and Rabbinic Judaism.* New York: KTAV, 1998.

Schiller, Gertrude. *Iconography of Christian Art.* Vol. 2. Trans. Janet Seligman, Greenwich: New York Graphic Society, 1972.

Schleiermacher, Friedrich. *The Christian Faith.* Ed. H. R. Mackintosh and J. S. Stewart. Edinburgh: T. & T. Clark, 1928.

Segundo, Juan Luis. *Our Idea of God.* Maryknoll: Orbis Books, 1974.

Seiferth, Wolfgang S. *Synagogue and Church in the Middle Ages: Two Symbols in Art and Architecture.* Trans. L. Chadeayne and P. Gottwald. New York: Frederic Ungar, 1970.

Shelley, Bruce L. *Church History in Plain Language.* Waco, Tex.: Word Books, 1982.

Sloyan, Gerard S. *Jesus in Focus: A Life in Its Setting.* Mystic, Conn.: Twenty-Third Publications, 1983.

Soulen, R. Kendall. *The God of Israel and Christian Theology.* Minneapolis: Fortress Press, 1996.

Stambaugh, John E., and Balch, David L. *The New Testament in its Social Environment.* Library of Early Christianity. Philadelphia: Westminster, 1986.

Steussy, Marti. "Judaisms in the Time of the Second Temple." In *The Church and the Jewish People,* ed. Clark M. Williamson. St. Louis: Chalice Press, 1991, 7–14.

_____. "Sex and the Bible." Unpublished classroom lecture, Oct. 23, 1997.

Suchocki, Marjorie Hewitt. *The End of Evil.* Albany, N.Y.: SUNY Press, 1988.

_____. *The Fall to Violence: Original Sin in Relational Theology.* New York: Continuum, 1995.

_____. *In God's Presence: Theological Reflections on Prayer.* St. Louis: Chalice Press, 1996.

Tanner, Kathryn. "Creation, Environmental Crisis, and Ecological Justice." In *Reconstructing Christian Theology,* ed. Rebecca S. Chopp and Mark L. Taylor. Minneapolis: Fortress Press, 1994.

Tertullian. *An Answer to the Jews.* In *The Ante-Nicene Fathers,* ed. Alexander Roberts and James Donaldson. Grand Rapids: Eerdmans: 1978, 507–28.

Tillich, Paul. *Against the Third Reich: Paul Tillich's Wartime Radio Broadcasts into Nazi Germany.* Ed. Ronald H. Stone and Matthew Lon Weaver. Louisville: Westminster John Knox Press, 1998.

_____. *The Courage To Be.* New Haven: Yale University Press, 1952.

_____. *The Dynamics of Faith.* New York: Harper & Brothers, 1957.

_____. *Love, Power, and Justice.* New York: Oxford University Press, 1954.

_____. *The Protestant Era.* Ed. James Luther Adams. Chicago: The University of Chicago Press, 1948.

_____. *The Religious Situation.* New York: Meridian Books, 1956.

_____. *Systematic Theology.* Vol. 1. Chicago: The University of Chicago Press, 1951.

_____. *Systematic Theology.* Vol. 2. Chicago: The University of Chicago Press, 1957.

_____. *Systematic Theology.* Vol. 3. Chicago: The University of Chicago Press, 1963.

_____. *Theology of Culture.* New York: Oxford University Press, 1959.

_____. *Theology of Peace.* Ed. Ronald H. Stone. Louisville: Westminster/ John Knox Press, 1990.

Torrance, Thomas F. *Theology in Reconstruction.* Grand Rapids: Eerdmans, 1975.

Toulmin, Stephen. *Reason in Ethics.* Cambridge: Cambridge University Press, 1964.

Tracy, David. *On Naming the Present: God, Hermeneutics, and Church.* Maryknoll: Orbis Books, 1994.

van Buren, Paul M. *Discerning the Way.* New York: Seabury Press, 1980.

_____. *The Edges of Language.* London: SCM Press, 1972.

Vermes, Geza. *Jesus the Jew.* New York: Macmillan, 1973.

Walsh, Michael. *The Triumph of the Meek.* San Francisco: Harper, 1986.

Weeden, Theodore J. "The Potential and Promise of a Process Hermeneutic." *Encounter* 36, no. 4 (1975).

Wegner, Judith Romney. "Leviticus." In *The Women's Bible Commentary.* Ed. Carol A. Newsom and Sharon H. Ringe, 36–44. Louisville: Westminster/ John Knox Press, 1992.

Wengst, Klaus. *Pax Romana and the Peace of Jesus Christ.* Trans. John Bowden. Philadelphia: Fortress Press, 1987.

Whitehead, Alfred North *Adventures of Ideas.* New York: The Free Press, 1933 (republished 1967).

_____. *Modes of Thought.* New York: The Free Press, 1938.

_____. *Process and Reality: Corrected Edition.* Ed. David Ray Griffin and Donald W. Sherburne. New York: The Free Press, 1978.

_____. *Religion in the Making.* New York: Meridian Books, 1960.

_____. *Science and the Modern World.* New York: New American Library, 1925.

Wilken, Robert L. "*Insignissima Religio, Certe Licita?* Christianity and Judaism in the Fourth and Fifth Centuries." In *The Impact of the Church Upon Its Culture,* ed. Jerald C. Brauer. Chicago: The University of Chicago Press, 1968.

Williams, A. Lukyn. *Adversus Judaeos.* Cambridge: Cambridge University Press, 1935.

Williamson, Clark M. *Baptism: Embodiment of the Gospel.* St. Louis: Christian Board of Publication, 1987.

_____. "Doing Christian Theology with Jews: The Other, Boundaries, Questions." In *Introduction to Christian Theology,* ed. Roger A. Badham, 37–49. Louisville: Westminster John Knox Press, 1998.

_____. *A Guest in the House of Israel: Post-Holocaust Church Theology.* Louisville: Westminster/John Knox Press, 1993.

_____. *Has God Rejected His People?* Nashville: Abingdon Press, 1982.

_____. "Process Hermeneutics and Christianity's Post-Holocaust Reinterpretation of Itself." *Process Studies* 12, no. 2 (1982): 77–93.

_____. *When Jews and Christians Meet.* St. Louis: CBP Press, 1989.

_____, ed. *The Church and the Jewish People.* St. Louis: Christian Board of Publication, 1994.

_____, and Allen, Ronald J. *A Credible and Timely Word.* St. Louis: Chalice Press, 1991.

_____, and Allen, Ronald J. *The Teaching Minister.* Louisville: Westminster/John Knox Press, 1991.

Wilson-Kastner, Patricia, ed. *A Lost Tradition.* Lanham, Md.: University Press of America, 1981.

Woodbridge, Barry A. "An Assessment and Prospectus for a Process Hermeneutic." *Journal of the American Academy of Religion* 47, no. 1 (1979): 126.

Wright, G. Ernest. *The Biblical Doctrine of Man in Society.* London: SCM Press, 1954.

Wright, N. T. *Jesus and the Victory of God.* Minneapolis: Fortress Press, 1996.

_____. *The New Testament and the People of God.* Minneapolis: Fortress Press, 1992.

_____. *Who Was Jesus?* Grand Rapids: Eerdmans, 1992.

Wyschogrod, Michael. *The Body of Faith: God in the People Israel.* San Francisco: Harper & Row, 1989.

_____. "Christology, the Immovable Object." *Religion and Intellectual Life* 3 (1986).

Yoder, John Howard. *The Politics of Jesus.* Grand Rapids: Eerdmans, 1972.

Young, Pamela Dickey. *Christ in a Post-Christian World.* Minneapolis: Fortress Press, 1995.

Index